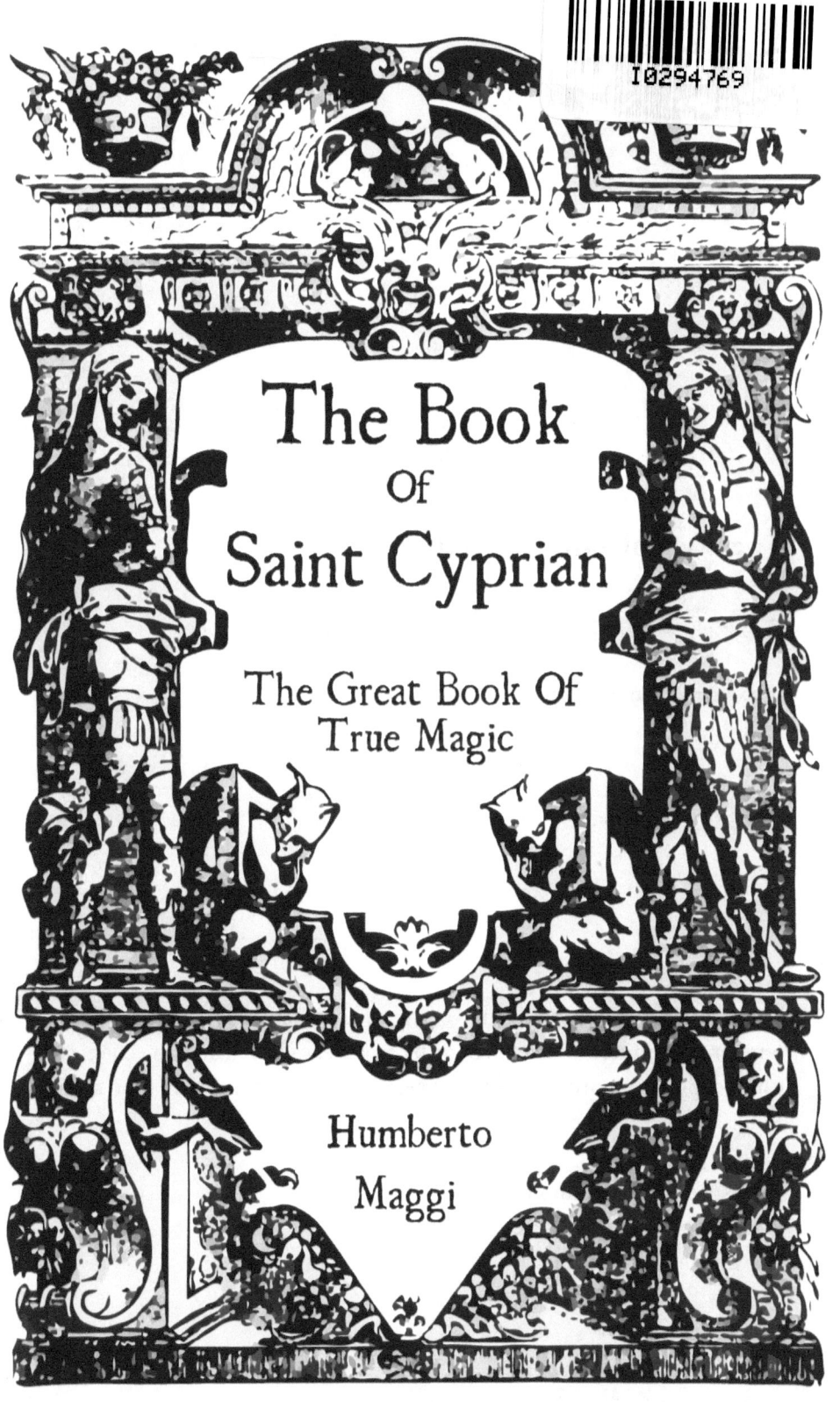

The Book Of Saint Cyprian

The Great Book Of True Magic

Humberto Maggi

The Book of Saint Cyprian

Copyright © 2018 by Nephilim Press and Humberto Maggi

ISBN: 978-0-9987081-3-3

No part of this publication may be reproduced, stored in a retrieval system, or transmitted in any form or by any means, electronic, mechanical, photocopying, recording or otherwise, without the prior permission of the Publisher.

Published by Nephilim Press
A division of Nephilim Press LLC
www.nephilimpress.com

The author would like to thank Kim Huggens for her help with the first revision of the material, giving many important suggestions and advice, and Robert Cook for his incredible artwork that conveys the spirit of this work in a manner that St. Cyprian himself would have been proud of.

Acknowledgments

It is impossible to do any serious research on the Books of Saint Cyprian without resorting to the studies by Don Felix Castro Vicente, the famous scholar and grimoire collector from Spain.

Felix contributed generously with information and images, which allowed this volume to be completed.

We once again express our gratitude to Joseph H. Peterson, especially for having provided us with his file of the *Véritable Magie Noir* for comparisons.

Asterion Mage very kindly recreated the Cyprian Magical Circle after the instructions in one of the source texts.

Some ideas and lots of information used in this book were gathered during conversations with Jake Stratton-Kent, whom I consider a true master. His edition of *The Testament of Cyprian the Mage* is landmark in the research on the Cyprianic tradition.

Nicholaj Frisvold helped with precious insights on the Kimbanda traditions associated with Saint Cyprian and kindly allowed me to publish one of the most important Magical Secrets related to the Sorcerous Saint from his own book.

Docteur Caeli D'Anto very kindly allowed me to use his translation of a traditional Kimbanda prayer, together with instructions for offerings and the photograph of his Saint Cyprian altar.

Contents

Saint Cyprian, the Devil's Scribe 1
Prologue 7
About This Edition 11
The Books of Cyprian 17

The Origins of The Book

Admonition 69
The Ancient and True Manuscript of this
Book was Found in the Tower of Tombo 71
To the Faithful Readers 75
To the Entire World 77
Introduction 79
Spells of Saint Cyprian or the Marvels of the Devil ... 83

Vita Cypriani

Conversio 109
Confessio Sancti Cypriani 123
Passio 145
The Life of Saint Justina 153
Life of the Saints 159
Sts. Cyprian and Justina 163
St. Cyprian of Antioch 165
Life of Saint Cyprian 173
Repentance and Virtues of Saint Cyprian 181

Great Requisition	185
Life of Saint Cyprian	191
The Legends	193
One Episode in the Life of Cyprian	197
History of Saint Cyprian and Clotilde	199
Story of Cyprian and Adelaide	205
One Episode in the Life of Cyprian	209
Story of Cyprian and Elvira	213
Encounter between Cyprian and Saint Gregory	221
Encounter of Cyprian with a Witch	225
Encounter of Cyprian with a Poor Woman Full with Children	229
How Saint Cyprian Invented the Cards	231
The Witch of Évora	233

The Magical Art

Instructions of Cyprian	241
Necessary Knowledge to Exercise the Magical Arts	243
Essential Qualities to Profess the Magical Arts	245
On the Necessary Qualities	247
Elemental Knowledge for the Magical Art	249
Ceremony of Magic	253
On the Instruments that are Necessary to the Magical Arts	257
Preparation of the Instruments	265
Magical Rod	271
The Magical Vestment and the Way to Prepare It	273
The Preparation of the Vestments	275
Magical Perfumes	277
Magical Ink	281
The Virgin Parchment	283
Great Circle of Protection	285
The Magical Circle	289
Magical Ceremony	293
Ecstasy and Abstraction	297
Ritual of Invocation	299

The Art of Invoking the Dead 303
Hours and Virtues of the Planets 305
Inauspicious Days 307

Talismans and Amulets

The Secret of the Secrets................................. 311
On Talismans.. 313
Magnetic Talismans 317
The Great Talisman 319
On Talismans.. 321
On Mixed Talismans 325
Medal... 337
The Red Dragon and the Infernal She-Goat................. 339
Ring Of Solomon... 345
Magical and Portentous Ring 347
History of the Wonderful Ring............................. 349
Great Talisman of the Constelations 353
Celestial Talisman 355
Talisman Exterminator..................................... 357
Talisman of Isis.. 359
Ordinary Talismans 363
Useful Explanations about the Talismans 373
Magical Amulets... 375
On the Way of Making the Amulets and
Talismans Possess Virtues and Efficacy 381

The Book of Spirits

Invocations Pacts and Exorcisms........................... 387
Invocation of the Gnomes 407
Invocation of the Superior Celestial Spirits 409
The Chiefs of the Six Legions............................. 413
Influences of the Stars 419
Hour, Month, Season 423
Celestial Spirits and Infernal Spirits.................... 425

The Prayers of Saint Cyprian

PRAYER OF SAINT CIPRYAN 433
ORISON. 441
NEW ORISONS FOR THE OPEN HOURS. 445
MAGICAL ORISON OF SAINT CIPRYAN. 447
ORISON TO THE CUSTODIAN ANGEL 449
ORISON TO ASSIST THE SICK AT THE TIME OF DEATH 453
USEFUL ORISON TO HEAL ALL DISEASES. 457
ORISON OF THE JUST JUDGE 461
ORISON WHICH PRESERVES FROM LIGHTNING 463
PRAYER TO SAINT EXPEDITE 465
ORISON TO SAINT EXPEDITE. 467
ANOTHER PRAYER TO SAINT EXPEDITE 469
ORISON. 471
CYPRIANI CITATIO ANGELORVM 473
DIMISSIO CYPRIANI 475
ORISON OF THE MIRACULOUS BLACK SHE-GOAT 477

Exorcisms

VADE RETRO SATANA. 481
INSTRUCTION TO THE RELIGIOUS THAT WILL TREAT ANY MALADY. . . 483
SIGNS THAT THERE IS MALEFACTION IN A CREATURE 487
FIRST CONJURATION 491
SECOND CONJURATION 493
THIRD CONJURATION. 495
THE WAY TO CLOSE A DWELLING 499
EXORCISM TO EXPEL THE DEVIL FROM THE BODY 501
WHY GOD ALLOWS THE DEMON TO TORMENT CREATURES 503
WHY GOD ALLOWS THE DEMON TO TORMENTS CREATURES 505
NAMES OF THE DEMONS 507
ON GHOSTS 509
ORISON TO ASK GOD FOR THE GOOD SPIRITS .511
VISIONS AND APPARITIONS. 515
EXORCISMS. 517
HOW TO PREPARE THE BLASTING ROD TO PUNISH THE DEVIL 523

ORISON TO PLACE RULES UPON DEMONS..........................525
TRUE ORISON TO EXPEL THE DEMON FROM THE BODY 527
DIABOLIC SPIRITS... 529
PRAYER OF SAINT MICHAEL AGAINST
SATAN AND THE REBEL ANGELS..................................537
ANOTHER PRAYER OF SAINT MICHAEL 539
EXORCISM 543

Magical Treasures

WAY OF USING THE ROD 547
HIDDEN TREASURES IN ENCHANTED PLACES 555
WAY TO DISENCHANT TREASURES................................559
DISENCHANTMENT OF TREASURES 561

Magical Secrets

SPELLS OF CYPRIAN 589
TRUE TREASURE OF BLACK AND WHITE MAGIC 593
MYSTERIES OF SORCERY 611
OCCULT POWERS OF HATE AND OF LOVE.........................637
SECRETS OF SORCERY TAKEN FROM ONE
MANUSCRIPT OF GREAT ANTIQUITY 657
THE SECRET MIRROR OF SOLOMON.............................. 667
GREAT SECRETS OF SORCERY FROM THE MAGE ARTHAPHERNES..... 669
THE EXECUTION OF THE EXPERIMENTS 677
EROTIC SPELL OF CYPRIAN OF ANTIOCH 687
A RITUAL FOR MAKING SAINT CYPRIAN YOUR PATRON 691
SAINT CYPRIAN OIL.. 693
HOW TO HONOR, SERVE, AND WORK WITH SAINT CYPRIAN 694

PREFACE
Saint Cyprian, the Devil's Scribe

By Nicholaj de Mattos Frisvold

The Black Books of Saint Cyprian are remarkable in the way they break down the distinction between the ideas of high and low magic as developed and popularized by Eliphas Levi. Saint Cyprian is the saint who, with one foot in Hell and the other in Heaven, paid reverence with both hands. This is evident in the Grimoire ascribed to Saint Cyprian called *Clavis Inferni sive magia alba et nigra approbata Metatrona* (Golden Hoard, 2009), which means "*The Key to hell as mediated by white and black magic as affirmed by Metatron.*" That *Metatron* is called upon as the angelic intelligence of intersection in this mystery is interesting in its own right. It speaks of the transmission of the timeless tradition that does not judge the worship of both hands in a dualist dichotomy. Not only this, *Metatron* is also the prophetic voice of *Raziel* and the gatekeeper of the Enochian mysteries which count the fall of the angelic host.

Saint Cyprian's legacy is a curious one, serpentine I would say, in how he slithers through the Solomonic Tradition, the lesser key, and sorcerous formulas. We find a radical open-mindedness in the books ascribed to him where Peter of Abano's *Heptameron* is fused with various forms of *mantike*, astrology, and spells detailing how to take occult power and destroy enemies. Most famous is perhaps the workings involving toads and black cats in manners not befitting a pious priest.

But Saint Cyprian was not a pious priest. His tale and story, as told in *The Golden Legend*, speaks of a lovesick magician, hell bent on gaining the sexual favors of the saintly Justina. His magic was found powerless, and, consequently, he submitted to the higher power represented by the True Cross. The legend tells that Justina became the head sister of a convent, while Cyprian became the Bishop of Antioch, because he demonstrated such divine gifts being possessed by him... In *The Golden Legend*, we learn that Cyprian made three attempts to seduce Justina by magical means before he surrendered. The number three being associated with the three crows of the cock related to Saint Peter's denial of Jesus Christ. The triple denial is the mystery of acceptance. Most likely, Saint Cyprian did accept the power of the Cross, but if we look at his legacy, he was clearly a saint who served with both hands, the prototype of the Haitian *bokor* and of Goethe's Faust. He was the dark mirror of Saint Peter, sharing the keys to Heaven and Hell as a consequence of a triple denial...

The triple denial is important in relation to *Kimbanda*, especially *Kimbanda de Raiz*. In several strands of *Kimbanda*, we have a few saints of importance, and one of them is Saint Cyprian. This legacy is evident seeing that several *Kimbanda* workings apparently had some interaction with Cyprian's books in a direct or alternated form. And in the *mythosophia* of *Kimbanda*, he has his place. Oral lore tells that Saint Cyprian was the student of *Exu Meia Noite* (Midnight Exu), and it is said that it was *Exu Meia Noite* that was given the powers of Jesus Christ taken by *Exu Mor* as he exhaled his last breath. The triple denial of Saint Peter is replicated in the motive of the three crosses at Calvary where the supreme and True Cross is flanked by the two thieves also crucified. Together they make of the triple cross of threefold denial which is the zodiacal circle of completion.

This mystery is also replicated in an infernal code in Marlyse Meyer's research wherein she discovers a witches' rune in the annals of the tribunal of Inquisition—as also replicated in one of the many Iberian "Cyprians"—speaking of a conjuration of infernal powers that reads as follows:

Saint Cyprian, the Devil's Scribe

By Barrabás, by Satanás and Lucifer
By Maria Padilla and all her legions

The triple denial cast an infernal shadow where Maria Padilla is given all power, just like Cyprian gave Justina all power and succumbed to her faith in an act of love and submission. I believe it is from this legend—amongst others—we find the root of *Pomba Gira Maria Padilha* having seven husbands. Maria Padilha became the inspiration for the crownless Queen, the fire that bends cross and denial to her favor.

I believe it is important to take notice of the motive of love in the serpentine web of Saint Cyprian's legacy, because this ties so well into how the many Exus ultimately protect their Queen; it is like we see here a nefarious chivalric order grooming and blooming.

In contemporary Kimbanda, Saint Cyprian is rarely placated, but his legacy still lives on in his many books, as the bishopric twin of *Exu Meia Noite*, both with a foot in Hell and the other in Heaven. It is a beautiful imagery for Saint Cyprian, the bishop of letters with one cloven hoof…

If we look at the many books ascribed to Saint Cyprian in Iberia, we find a general base in *Heptameron* fused with diabolism and various forms of divination, and these books started to surface in the late 17th century. Curiously, we also find "Cyprians" in Scandinavia, and the earliest I have found is a text in Norway dated 1491 and another one in Denmark, Siprianus Kunstebok, dating to 1345. But a host of others followed, finding a peak in the eighteenth and nineteenth centuries. These books are for the most part written on a basis of folk magic mediated by need. They contain spells and advice for keeping cattle healthy and crops abundant—but here and there we find Solomonic or Ecclesiastical remnants. Passages of the Bible or barbarous names were used to effectuate simple folk magic. For instance, we find in one text from 1790 (NB Ms 8° 10, Trolldomsarkivet, UiO) an exorcism that aims to expel all unclean spirits in the name of the Father, the Son, and the Holy Spirit. But this appeal is in the end given to Saint Cyprian to effectuate as the trusted one of the conjurer—and the saint who holds the keys to Heaven and Hell. I find this beautiful and in the spirit of Saint Cyprian.

It is told that Saint Cyprian ventured to Evora in Portugal where he was said to enter into a joint tutorship with a conclave of witches. They imparted their knowledge to him, and he imparted his to them. This legacy was passed down in bits and pieces through the conclave of witches and explains not only the great amount of Cyprians we have but also why there are so many. They were all books received in part and mediated by need and spirit to seek completion. What Cyprian gave as his legacy was a daimon of ink and inspiration.

There is a good bounty of Cyprians in Iberia and Brazil, but we find triple this amount in Scandinavia. We can ask why, and the answer is simple: reformation. Scandinavia and the British Isles went through a hard period of Christianization around the year 1000 and then again with the reformation in the 16th century. The first Christianization was a hard battle in which Scandinavia was sort of Catholic—and this was fine—because the magical theosophy of Catholicism was, after all, not so disturbing to the customs of the few people who cared. For the learned ones, *The Golden Legend* came and with much Catholic material that was deemed magical and proper by, for instance, Snorri Sturlasson who penned the Eddas. When the reformation came and Protestantism took over, a desire for the "Old Faith" overcame those of learning, and one element in this Old Faith was Saint Cyprian and his sorcerous legacy.

I believe this explains why the Cyprians became so widespread in Scandinavia—it was a way of preserving the legacy of the Old Faith. In countries Catholicized and that remained so, this crossroad was less evident, but yet a legacy worthy of preserving was noticed—and continued. In Iberia and Brazil, it was about continuing a legacy that spoke about serving with both hands—it was about holding hands with the Devil and God—in the conviction that all were divine, and because of this, sin and everlasting life were always dancing around in a field of angels of possibility and maidens of desire. The upright stature, the magician-bishop, became an ideal laid down as a blueprint for any "Cyprian" speaking of the truth that power known is not necessarily power exercised, but the wisdom and knowledge of Heaven and Hell is indeed a necessity.

Because of this, the Cyprians are many—and they show complete disregard for any limit between white and black magic. There is no left hand or right hand in the spells and conjurations carrying the ink trail of Cyprian. There is only knowledge raging up and down on the ladder of wisdom. To heal a child from spiritual sickness or take diabolic power by virtue of a black cat's bone was not subject for discrimination—but for knowledge and the wise discernment of wisdom. Hence, Saint Cyprian was given the keys to Heaven and Hell. He was a beloved of the Church as much as he was loved by the Dragon. In Saint Cyprian, we find the power that makes angels cry and ghosts bleed.

Saint Cyprian is, as we read in Meyers and Smith's *Ancient Christian Magic* (Princeton. 1999):

> *I am Cyprian, the great magician, who was the friend of the dragon of the abyss. He called me his son, and I called him father. He placed his crown and his diadem on my head. I suckled milk at his right breast. He made my place at his right hand. He subjected to me every power of his. I ascended up to the Pleiades, and they glided under me like a ship. I learned the whispers of the stars; I took possession of the treasures of the winds. I mastered the whole astronomy.*
> ~ Nicholaj de Mattos Frisvold

Prologue

By Felix Castro Vincente

Perhaps there has never been a book more coveted and sought after than the one we are going to talk about now, or which has awakened more passions and desires to be possessed, to the point that many people fell into madness, got gravely ill, or ruined themselves economically just trying to get one exemplar of it, or trying to put into practice the rituals it contained.

We are talking about the Book of Saint Cyprian, attributed to Saint Cyprian of Antioch. It is a grimoire, that is, a book that gathers magical formulas, linked in the Iberian Peninsula to the disenchantment of treasures, as it had one of its parts specifically dedicated to that affair, including in some versions a list of Treasures of the Kingdom of Galicia and Portugal. It has detailed indications where the treasures can be found. That was one of the main reasons why it was so searched for by the people of the northwestern region of the peninsula as a way to flee from poverty.

The Book of Saint Cyprian has been a book so much revered, feared, and respected as it was searched for, both in Portugal (especially in its northern area) as in Spain (especially in Galicia). It's simple possession supposed a grave sin or a grave problem with the secular and religious justice. Many times in the possession of priests, other times in the hands of healers, no one who crossed with it was left unharmed or indifferent.

Used to treasure hunt as much for remedies and magical recipes by healers and sorcerers, and in every parish, it was said that some family possessed an exemplar of the enigmatic book.

As Mr. Maggi so well exposes, we cannot properly speak of a book of Saint Cyprian, but instead of the Books of Saint Cyprian, since the amount of texts and prayers attributed to this saint is sundry and variable. Perhaps we could talk about a Cyprianic Cicle of magical books, in the same way that the Solomonic Cicle that encompasses all the magical books attributed to Solomon, the magician par excellence of the Jewish religion. And the Cicle of Saint Cyprian owes much to this Solomonic tradition.

We want to propose from the start a verifiable fact, that was overlooked many times by the researchers, especially the ones from the areas of History and Bibliography: that the Book of Saint Cyprian has a great sociological and anthropological value, being a very powerful element in the folk Iberian imaginary, especially Galician and from the north of Portugal. There is not much relevancy in the often repeated discussion about whether the book existed or not, if it was or not written by the Saint Sorcerer, if it is efficient or not, if it is authentic or if it is some crude copy concocted by some author-editor with the intention of easily profiting from the unwary, or if there is only one authentic book, bound with human skin, only seen by some elected people (as I was asked about once). The Book of Saint Cyprian has been a central and frequently used argument in every kind of (real or not) event, tale, account, story of our peoples, and not just as a mythical reference, but as a resource that explains part of the everyday reality, what helps to outline and organize the human experience. As an example of this, we have the case we heard about several times: In every village, it was said that a neighbor had a copy of the famous book, but that was not all to it; the neighbor that supposedly had the book was the one that thrived in the village. He was the one who acquired more land, buying property with his in increasing patrimony. He was the one who had more cows, or the one with the cows giving more milk, or the cows that did not get sick. In other words, the neighbor accused of possessing the book was generally the one who was doing better economically. On the other hand, he could also be the one to whom a succession of disgraces befell over his family. The possession of the book is generally used as an "emic" explanation (an explanation from the viewpoint of the native) for the economic and personal evolution of some member of the small village community.

We must also call attention to the fact that the figure of Saint Cyprian, and his cultural and spiritual relevancy as a protector against evil spells in many countries around the world, is well above the magical texts traditionally ascribed to him. That relevancy is attested by the fundamental role filled by the orisons of Saint Cyprian, which, in our opinion, are foundational and vertebral nucleus of the Iberian Books of Saint Cyprian. The orisons are the prime bibliographical element, to which a posteriori were added layers of magical elements, recipes, lists of magical instruments, mantic procedures, treasure hunting, and even pacts with infernal powers, certainly from other grimoires.

These orisons, which had their origins in the Eastern European and parts of Africa and Arabia, the cradle of early Christianity, were originally written in Greek and Latin and had an autonomous and distinctive development in the Iberian Peninsula. There they were joined to an entire magical corpus, reminding us of the force and endurance of all these material and its uses, which continued to evolve and change, especially in Latin America.

The fame of Saint Cyprian as a magician, prototype of the figure of Faust, spread for all Christianity and later became part of the folk memory, where he is placed at the same level as other famous magicians of Antiquity, like Simon Magus and Solomon. His popularity was and still is great, spreading through all the European geography, principally in the south, with a great number of chapels and churches dedicated to this saint. In Eastern Europe, from Greece, Bulgaria, and even further, until Ethiopia, Syria, and Armenia, he is still a very popular saint. As proof of the antiquity of his cult, we have the many variations of his name, depending on each language: Cyprianus, Cyprien, Cipriano, Ciprián, Cibrán, Cibrao, Civrian, Girpaharan, Kibrian, Kiprian, Kiprianos, Gibrianos, Qoprayanos, etc.

Further evidence of the popularity of the figure of Saint Cyprian is the "Cueva of San Cyprian," located in the sacristy under the Church of San Cebrian, built in 1126. It was famous throughout Europe as a place where the Devil taught necromancy and the occult arts to the students of the University of Salamanca. Such was its fame that Queen Isabella the Catholic ordered it to be closed in early XVI century.

The popular legend of Saint Cyprian also served as inspiration to many literary works, "El Mágico Prodigioso" by Calderón de la Barca (1637), "The martyr of Antiochi" by Henry Hart Milman (1821), "La Cueva de Salamanca" by Miguel de Cervantes Saavedra (1615), "Lo que quería ver el Marqués de Villena" by Francisco Rojas Zorrilla (1645), "Historia de las Cuevas de Salamanca" by Francisco Botelho e Moraes (1731). Other writers, like Walter Scott, Washington Irving, etc., also worked upon these legends. In the ambulant genre of cordel literature, there is an abundance of examples of pamphlets dedicated to the saint, from orisons to poetic compositions and religious hymns, or lives of the saint, sometimes referred to Saint Cyprian and Saint Justina, sometimes just to Saint Cyprian.

Almanacs with the name of the Saint were published at the end of the XIX century in Lisbon.

About This Edition

It is with a great pleasure that I write the prologue for this book by the friend, bibliophile companion, and cyprianophile Humberto Maggi. I must confess that when he first contacted me, I thought he was one of the many who through the Internet asked me for help, magical advice, etc. That began to happen since my first article about the Book of Saint Cyprian was published in 2005 in the Revista Hibris of bibliophilie, of my friend Don Pepe Grau de Alcoi, from Alicante in Spain. The article was uploaded in the Internet and had a viral diffusion all over the net, without any order and without citing the authorship.

One day, I received an email from Humberto, and, in face of his perseverant insistency and his interesting questions, I realized that his interests in the subject had nothing to do with the other persons who contacted me before. I began to provide him with information, during an epistolary relationship which lasted some years, to help him with his purpose of writing a book about the Book of Saint Cyprian, something I myself have being working with during more than ten years without coming to an end. Because the figure of Saint Cyprian of Antioch, the saint with whom we are busy here, is a multifaceted figure with multiples aspects, and the books, prayers, and magical recipes attributed to him are like the Book of Sand from the works of J. L. Borges, formless, without end and boundless, as was indicated by Jerusa Pires Ferreira in one of the most important books written to date on the subject, "O Livro de Sao Cipriano: Uma

Legenda de Massas." In this work of research, the literary critic qualifies the attributes to the Saint as belonging to the "fringe culture," or the "liminality" or marginalization of the culture. The Book of Saint Cyprian is such a liminal work, shifting without a fixed form, ambivalent and which evoke all kinds of emotions at once, fear and respect on one side, and the eagerness to possess and unravel their power on the other.

To try to cover all aspects of the Book of Saint Cyprian, after all that was said, would be something like to stem the tide; my interests are fundamentally ethnographic, anthropological, and bibliographic, being the description and comparison of the books aiming at their repercussion in the historical, social, and cultural contexts of the Iberian Peninsula. My own research covers the many publications of the magical texts of the grimoires and its evil uses or the bad destinies it had, research that over the time began to cover more and more aspects of its publications, from the magical to the historical, anthropological, bibliographical, etc.

But Humberto proposed something different, more limited, concrete, and complementary in reference to my research and more in line with the publication of the contents of the more known grimoires. He decided to gather in one volume the "fixed" content of the grimoires attributes to Saint Cyprian, taken from the first "canonical" Books of Saint Cyprian published in the Iberian Peninsula in Portuguese and Spanish, following more or less the typological classification we used in our first articles. His work unites the Portuguese version from the middle of the XIX century divided in three books which contain the story of Victor Siderol, the Spanish versions of Jonas Sufurino that we dated from the end of the XIX century, and the one published by Enediel Shaiah in 1906. To these, he adds other more outside the proposed canon, like the Heptameron o Elementos Mágicos de Gran Cipriano, also from the XIX century. He also cites other versions, like the one published by the historian Bernardo Barreiro in 1885 and the one recently discovered by myself entitled "Cipriano el Temeroso" of 1874. But, instead of just gathering them one after the other, he realizes a work of thematic and systematic organization, dividing by sections

About This Edition

the different subjects (prayers, magical instruments, ceremonial, pacts, invocations, treasure hunt, magical recipes), which give to the work an enhanced value and an evident utility to whoever wishes to comparatively study the concrete aspects of this works.

The figure of Saint Cyprian and the practices associated with him in other magical and religious cultures are also contextualized, including references to the hagiographic traditions attributed to the Saint. Prayers of Saint Cyprian from the different latitudes, references to other European and Scandinavian grimoires attributes to Cyprian, and the classical grimoires have also being studied.

When we mention the "canonical" versions of the Book that are gathered here, they should not be understood as being the most "authentic" and neither the ones written by the Saint himself, but the oldest printed that we found and known until now, published in the XIX century. Manuscript versions had to be circulating before, as there is constancy on the material, as they are mentioned in the processes of the Inquisition since the XVII and especially in the XVIII. Unfortunately, no copy from a Cyprian book has reached us or we still did not find it. We are not sure if this is due to the "good" efforts of the Inquisition or because the proverbial humidity and rainy weather of the peninsular northwest that does not favor the conservation of books or of any other kind of paper. To that, we must add that the majority of the Galician and Portuguese population, the real public of these works, were rural and inhabited very modest houses lacking the ideal conditions to safeguard these books.

The lack of love this kind of magical literature always faced in Spain (and possibly in Portugal) also must be blamed. It was despised and censored by the public, politic, and religious powers. As it was illegal, the publication was scarce in the peninsula in the XVI, XVII, and XVIII centuries, only making a timid appearance in the XIX century due to the disappearance of the Inquisition, but soon after they were censored again in 1936.[1] The university and academic institutions considered these works

---

1 During the XIX century, a progressive decline of the hegemony of the Catholic Church could be noted. For centuries, it caused the civil and ecclesiastic censure of every kind of publication considered to not be orthodox. After half of that century, other alternative religious and spiritualistic movements began to flourish, like masonry, spiritism,

not much more than pamphlets, a minor genre not deserving to be preserved or studied, and the lack of works of the magical and occultist literature in the Spanish libraries, including the material published after the XIX century, is notorious.

So, with this book and others that, certainly, will follow in the future, in the same way that happened in the fields of the svarteboka, the Scandinavian Cyprianus, with the researches of Dr. Thomas Johnsson, a very important labor is done to put on the map the magical studies and the historiography of the Books of Saint Cyprian. These books have an evident interest to the bibliographer, the social scientists, and the scholars and historians of magic practiced in the Iberian Peninsula and Latin America until the beginnings of the XX century. This is a work with the same kind of value of the rest of the classical European grimoires, with which it is related, with the benefit of possibly being the most popular grimoire today when it comes to the practical point of view. It is one of the few that had their genesis (at least in a great part) and development in the Iberian Peninsula, having the special characteristic of including in some of its versions a list of the places with treasures waiting to be disenchanted. There are 174 in the Kingdom of Galicia and 147 in Portugal, the list being certainly based upon the historical evidence of the abundance of archeological remains in the northwest.

---

theosophy, martinism, rosacrucianism, occultism in general with an explosion of publications related to this subject, including works specifically dedicated to magic, like the grimoires. The politic-religious censure of esoteric and magical books was reinstated during the Spanish Civil War (1936–1939) when the rebellious troops took on the flag of the reactionary and uncompromising defense of Catholicism, inclusively enacting public burnings of "heterodox" books in the areas they occupied. After that, during the Dictatorship of Franco (1939–1975), and with the strong and mutual support of the Catholic hierarchy, was introduced again a fierce political-religious censure and the control of the means of communication and of every kind of artistic and literary work. The result of this was the disappearance of this kind of literature in Spain, due to the censorship that was only a little relaxed in the final years of the dictatorship. Francoist censorship was linked to destruction of books in public and private libraries throughout the Spanish geography. Only Latin American publishers continued with the publication of these works in Spanish language during this period, being remarkable for its volume and quality of the ones published in Argentina and Mexico.

About This Edition

I congratulate again Humberto for taking to a good end this initiative, expecting that his book be translated to many different languages, opening a door to the systematic and rigorous study of the Iberian magical books.

Félix F. Castro Vicente
Ourense, Galiza—Northwest of Spain / North of Portugal, 12 de Octubre de 2013.

INTRODUCTION
THE BOOKS OF CYPRIAN

My first grimoire was a *Book of Saint Cyprian*. It was a very beautiful edition, in black hardcover and superior in quality to the ones usually found in Brazil today. It had, printed at the beginning of the book, the Baphomet image of Eliphas Levi.

The content, however, was disappointing. I was in active service in the Army at this time, and among the soldiers it was easy to listen to extraordinary stories about the book, stories which were always about power and fear. However, the book I had in my hands did not contain anything to justify the legend.

First, it had the story of Victor Siderol, a French peasant who by accident found a copy of a grimoire named *Engrimanços de Cipriano*, with which he started a lucrative association with the Devil, making a series of pacts from which he later escaped through repenting and confessing his sins. Prayers and popular magical formulas, like the following one, followed this very large introductory story:

Recipe to be happy in the things that are undertaken

Take a living toad and cut off its head and its feet on a Friday, soon after the Full Moon of the month of September. Put these pieces in the sap of the elder tree for twenty-one days, retrieving them after this time as the church bells begin to toll at midnight. Then, exposing them to the beams of the moon for three consecutive nights, calcinate them in a clay pot that has never been used before. Mix it later with an equal amount of soil from a cemetery, but specifically from the grave belonging to someone related to the person for whom the recipe is made. The person that possesses this can be assured that the spirit of the deceased will watch over them and over all things they undertake, because the toad will not lose sight of the interests of the person.

The presence of this kind of practice is not far from what we usually find in the best-known grimoires, principally in the later examples like the *Grimorium Verum* and the *Grand Grimoire*. In fact, some of the practices found in the *Books of Saint Cyprian* seem to be derived directly from its French predecessors, or from some common source, as we can see:

Grimorium Verum

To Make oneself Invisible.

Collect seven black beans. Start the rite on a Wednesday, before sunrise. Then take the head of a dead man, and put one of the black beans in his mouth, two in his eyes and two in his ears. Then make upon his head the character of Morail. When you have done this, bury the head, with the face upwards, and for nine days, before sunrise, water it each morning with excellent brandy. On the eighth day you will find the spirit mentioned, who will say to you: "What wilt thou?" You will reply: "I am watering my plant." Then the spirit will say: "Give me the bottle; I desire to water it myself." In answer, refuse him this, even though he will ask you again. Then he will reach out with his hand and will display to you that same figure which you have drawn upon the head. Now you can be sure that it is the right spirit, the spirit of the head. There is a danger that another one might try to trick you, which would have evil consequences—and in that case your operation would not succeed. Then you may give him the bottle, and he will water the head and leave. On the next day, which is the ninth, when you return, you will find the beans that are germinating. Take them and put them in your mouth, and look at yourself in the mirror. If you can see nothing, it is well. Test the others in the same way, either in your own mouth or in that of a child. Those which do not confer invisibility are to be reburied with the head.

Grande Livro de São Cipriano

[GLT]
Great magic of the fava beans

Kill a black cat, bury it in your backyard, put one fava bean in each eye, another under the tail and another in each ear hole. After all this is done, cover it with soil, and go to water it every night, at midnight, with a little water until the fava beans sprout, being ripe; and when you see that they are, harvest them at the base. After the harvest, take them to your house and put them one by one in your mouth. When, however, it looks to you that you are invisible, it is because that fava bean has the force of the magic needed, and so, if it please you to enter into any place without anyone seeing, first put the aforesaid fava bean in your mouth. This works through one occult virtue, without it being necessary to make a pact with the devil, like the witches do…

Warning to whoever makes use of this magic

When you go to water the fava beans, there will appear to you many ghosts, with the intent of scaring you, so you do not achieve your intent. The reason is simple. It is because the demon is envious of whosoever will use this magic, without delivering himself to him body and soul, as the witches do, the ones who are called women of virtue. However, do not get scared because they will not do you any harm, and to this you must first of all make the sign of the Cross and at the same time say the Creed.

Years later, I found the pioneer study by Jerusa Pires Ferreira, *O Livro de São Cipriano — Uma Legenda de Massas*, a meticulous research on the phenomenon of mass production of the Books of Saint Cyprian, which included an interview with one of the ghost-writers responsible for some of the different versions of the book. All this was enough to make me consider for some decades the Book of Saint Cyprian to be just a folkloric register of popular superstitions. Not that at that time I was completely free from the popular fear, however. The myth surrounding the book was sufficiently strong then to inspire me to take the book to a secluded place where I tried to call the Devil, and sometime after to rip out and burn the page with the Baphomet image where I had signed my name, throwing the ashes into running water…

After 2008, I started to develop a great and renewed interest in the grimoire literature. Everything started when a friend, with whom I also had fraternal initiatory ties, came to me asking for advice after she began to fear the late effects of a magical operation performed with the first book of the *Lemegeton*. This incident served as the catalyst for a renewal of my interest in the magic of the grimoires, interest that was immediately focused with the reading of the anthology *Howlings* and the edition of the *True Grimoire* by Jake Stratton-Kent, both published by Scarlet Imprint. This renewed interest made me meet, once again, the *Book of Saint Cyprian*.

The Books of Cyprian

As it goes, the *Book of Saint Cyprian* has a much richer and more interesting story than I initially supposed, which I came to find out with the help of the extensive research of the anthropologist and collector of magical books Felix Castro Vicente—certainly the greatest authority on the *Books of Saint Cyprian*.

First, I discovered that there are two parallel traditions of *Books of Saint Cyprian*. There is the Portuguese tradition, whose key exemplar is the *Thesouro do Feiticeiro*, from which there is an available edition from the end of the XIX century in the *Bilbioteca Nacional de Portugal*, and there is the Spanish tradition, which evolved after the edition entitled *Cipriano el Temeroso*, dated from 1874, which in its turn derives from the late French grimoire literature, especially from the *Veritable Magie Noir*. The Portuguese tradition is the source of all other versions subsequently published in Brazil, and it is basically a collection of magical secrets whose roots are to be found in the Late Antique period of the Mediterranean cultures. Many of these secrets have very close parallels with ancient practices like the use of dolls (*kollosoi*) to enchant people, several magical uses for animals like the frog, formulae of popular necromancy, etc. We can compare, for instance, the invisibility spells seen above with a practice to be found in the *Magical Greek Papyri*, and all the three with an intermediary version, to be found in one of the exemplars of the *Magical Treatise of Solomon* or *Hygromanteia*, from the 15th century (MSS Harleianus 5596).

Invisibility[2]

Take the dry skull of a man that did not die a natural death. Go to a secret, inaccessible place and recite these names over the skull.

Grant invisibility, Lord, in the names Theophael, Diokaides, Peridon, Enarkale, Esboiel, Apelout, Gakarkentos, so that this work will be effective.

---

2 *The Magical Treatise of Solomon or Hygromanteia*. Trans. & Ed. Ioannis Marathakis, Golden Hoard Press.

Then, take the seeds of the herb *korakia*. The Romans call *it phabenbesia*, that is to say broad bean. Plant one seed in each of the eyes, and put another one in the mouth. Cover with earth and recite the following.

As the eyes of the dead do not see the living, so these beans may have the power of invisibility, wherever I may go.

And when the beans yield seeds, be careful not to lose any of them, but take them out of their husks and keep them all together. Then, bring a mirror and take each bean in your hand, one by one. If you do not see yourself in the mirror, this particular bean has power. Carry it upon you and go wherever you wish. Nobody will see you.

Cat ritual for many purposes[3]

Take a cat, and make it into an *Esies* by submerging its body in water. While you are drowning it, speak the formula to its back. Take the cat and make three lamellae, one for its anus, one for [its ear holes], and one for its throat, and write the formula concerning the deed in a clean sheet of papyrus, and wind this around the body of the cat and bury it. Light seven lamps upon unbaked bricks, and make an offering. Take its body and preserve it by immuring it either in a tomb or in a burial place.

The four different spells share common features, the most preeminent being the insertion of some magical material (lamellae, beans) inside the holes of a necromantic remain (skull, sacrificed cat).

The way in which this great collection of magical secrets was compiled and gathered until, at some point, it was published by the editors of the *Thesouro do Feiticeiro* is a major enigma, but this volume is an

---

[3] *The Greek Magical Papyri in Translation, Including the Demotic Spells, Volume 1.* Hans Dieter Betz, University of Chicago Press

excellent ethnographic and historical source which has been sadly neglected until today.

The Holy Sorcerer

> He was pre-eminent among young men for skill in perverse arts, would violate modesty by a trick, count nothing holy, and often practise a magic spell amid the tombs to raise passion in a wife and break the law of wedlock.[4]
> ~ PRUDENTIUS

The magical literature developed under the inspiration of the name of Saint Cyprian is an eloquent testimony of the powers of adaptation and survival of magic, even when faced with the censorship and condemnation imposed with religious violence through the centuries. Beginning in the 4th century *era vulgaris* in a polemicist Christian text against pagan freedom and magic, the myth of Saint Cyprian, after some time, came to represent exactly the opposite of what was aimed at by his creator: the supernatural power of the grimoires, accessible to everyone with the courage and capacity to use them.

In first place, it is important to note that there is no indication of the historical existence of Saint Cyprian of Antioch; the Catholic Encyclopedia itself denies his existence:

> The story, however, must have arisen as early as the fourth century, for it is mentioned both by Saint Gregory Nazianzen and Prudentius; both, nevertheless, have confounded our Cyprian with Saint Cyprian of Carthage,

---

4   *Per. 13.21-24*, Prudentius

a mistake often repeated. It is certain that no Bishop of Antioch bore the name of Cyprian.[5]

Although still enjoying the saintly status in the Orthodox Church, the Catholic position towards Saint Cyprian of Antioch became perfectly clear with the removal of their feast day from the calendar of the Roman Rite in 1969, thereby breaking a tradition started in the 13th century. In the revision of the Roman Martyrology from 2001, the name of Saint Cyprian was also removed.[6]

There are three original sources for the legend of Cyprian: the *Conversio*, the *Confessio*, and the *Passio Cypriani* (Conversion, Confession and Martyrdom of Saint Cyprian). Researchers tend to credit both the *Conversio* and the *Passio* to the same writer, with the *Confessio* being written as a late supplement to be put between these texts to try to create a coherent whole. Ryan Bailey, in his introduction to the translation of the *Confessio*,[7] presents a resume of the three works:

Conversio

> The Conversion begins by recounting the conversion of the virgin Justina, who, after hearing the sermons of the deacon Praylius from her window, goes together with her parents to the bishop Optatus and receives baptism. A wealthy man named Aglaidas notices her during her frequent trips to and from the church, and after his advances fail, he approaches Cyprian the magician and pays him two talents to win her over by magical means. Cyprian conjures three demons—the second more powerful than the first, the third being the father of all demons—and sends them to Justina's apartment. Each attempt is unsuccessful as a result of Justina's prayers and

---

5   http://www.newadvent.org/cathen/04583a.htm
6   http://en.wikipedia.org/wiki/Cyprian_and_Justina
7   *The Confession of Cyprian of Antioch: Introduction, Text, and Translation*. Ryan Bailey :Faculty of Religious Estudies McGill University.

her use of the sign of the cross. Convinced of the power of Christ, Cyprian converts and eventually works his way up through the ecclesiastical hierarchy becoming bishop of Antioch.

Confessio

The story concerns a pagan magician who, after numerous failed attempts to seduce the Christian virgin Justina through magic, realizes the power of Christ and converts to Christianity.

Passio

Continuing where the Conversion left off, the Martyrdom tells of Eutolmius, Count of the region of the East, who after hearing of the miraculous deeds of Cyprian and Justina has them arrested and brought to Damascus where they are tortured and thrown into boiling pitch. Since the saints survive the torments of Eutolmius unscathed, they are then sent to Nicomedia where Diocletian condemns them to death by decapitation. After six days their bodies, along with a man named Theoctistus who was decapitated along with them for saluting Cyprian, are then brought to Rome and given an honorable burial.

The Confession

There is an agreement that the text of the *Confession* was written after the *Conversion* and the *Martyrdom*. The aim of the author is clear: It is a polemic written to the pagan public, *"all you who take offense at the mysteries of Christ."* His method is simple: He created the figure of an archmage, initiated in many of the main pagan mysteries of the time, holding vast magical powers, and then denounces him as an unscrupulous servant of the Devil, moved by the most base instincts. What we have here is, again, the imposition of the diabolical Christian dualism over the pagan culture and magical thinking: any kind of knowledge different from the preaching of the Christianity professed by the author is the work of the Devil.

> Cyprian's Confession thus represents magic as a very elaborate art, requiring long study and a thorough knowledge of natural objects and processes. The magician has his books, and he must also be able to read the book of nature. Astrology and other arts of divination are integral parts of magic. But magic is also represented as the work of evil spirits. This involves not merely a Neo-Platonic sort of association of demons with natural forces and regions of earth or sky, but also the specific association of the devil for evil purposes with objects in nature, a doctrine which we shall find again in the works of a medieval saint, Hildegard of Bingen. Furthermore, magic aids in the commission of crime and is dangerous even to the magician against whom the devil may turn. While magic involves study of nature and use of natural forces and associations, and we also hear of "many experiments of magic," it is scarcely represented as operating scientifically in the Confession. It is mystic, confused, shadowy, imitative, imaginary, lacking in solidity and reality, fraudulent and deceptive. Finally, this complex art, this universal system of knowledge, is easily balked and overthrown by the far simpler counter-magic of Christianity, by such methods as a prayer to the Virgin, calling on the name of God, or merely making the sign of the cross.[8]

---

8   *A History of Magic and Experimental Science, Volume I.* Lynn Thorndike.

The text of the *Confession* has historical interest because of its presentation of the popular view of magic and the mysteries at the time, but it does not work as a trustworthy source for the study of them; as Ryan Bailey noted, the author makes several serious mistakes in his descriptions:

1. *Cyprian joined the Mysteries of Mythra when he was seven years old.*

   The Mysteries of Mythra were reserved for adults; the only known exception being the initiation granted by a Pater Patrum (high priest of the cult) to his own son in the 4th century.

2. *Cyprian was dadouxos in the Mysteries of Eleusis.*

   The post of dadouxos could only by filled by a member of the Kerykes family.

3. *Cyprian "carried the torch for Demeter" and submitted to the "white sorrow of Kore".*

   These symbolic references to the Mysteries of Eleusis must also be considered as untruthful: The boy Cyprian could not have taken part in this procession.

The *Confessio* also errs for lack of originality. As Ryan Bailey again testifies:

> In addition to the fact that no bishop named Cyprian appears in the well-known lists of bishops of Antioch, source-criticism of the legend has shown conclusively that neither the plot nor even the majority of the names of the

characters in the legend are original, but were borrowed from other literary works.[9]

Bailey indicates the following sources as having possibly inspired the writer of the *Confessio*:

1. Apocryphal Literature.

    Acts of Paul and Thecla – the portrait of the conversion of the virgin Justina seems a lot like the conversion of the virgin Thecla in the *Acts of Paul and Thecla*, in such a way that there are few doubts that the writer of the *Confession* used it as a source.

    Acts of Andrew – contains many parallels with the legend of Cyprian: a reference to the long period of training of the magician; the magician, after seeing a virgin, goes to her roof to pray and send demons against her; the demons seem to be disguised ("they acted like her brother") just as was the demon in the *Conversion* who disguised as a maiden, and knocked at the door of the virgin; the virgin prays and the demon flees.

2. Literary portraits of the typical magicians from the Greek-Roman novels of the time.

    According to Bailey, the *"graphic representation of the magician Cyprian closely parallels the literary portrayals of magicians typical of the era."* Examples of the genre that Bailey indicates are the *Life of Apollonius* by Philostratus and the *Philopseudes* by

---

[9] *The Confession of Cyprian of Antioch: Introduction, Text, and Translation*, Ryan Bailey.

Lucian. The adventures of the magicians and pagan holy men of the age very often present the theme of great travels in search of initiations, principally to lands strongly connected with magic, like Egypt and Chaldea. In addition, stories about magicians paid to bring the desired woman to their clients are common: In the *Philopseudes,* Lucian tells the story of Glaucias, who appeals to a magician arrived from the Hyperborea to win over his beloved Chrysis. In the *Confessio,* Cyprian describes necromantic deeds very similar to Erichtho's, the dreadful witch describe by Lucan in the *Pharsalia*.[10]

After the *Conversion*, the *Confession*, and the *Martyrdom*, the three most important mentions made of the magician converted to saint are as follows: the panegyric Gregory Nazianzus uttered in 379 CE.; the poem about the life and martyrdom of Cyprian written by Prudentius at the end of the 4th century; and the epic poem in hexameters by the Byzantine empress Eudocia in the 5th century. Felix Castro, in a private correspondence, also mentions:

> The Martyrology of Nokerio (830–912) mentions his condition as a magician and the episode of his conversion after failing to make Justina fall in love with Aglaide. The Martyrology of the venerable Beda only mentions his condition as a sorcerer. It appears also in the Roman Martyrology.

Gregory confuses the Cyprian from Antioch and the real Cyprian, who was bishop at Carthage. Cyprian from Antioch would have been martyred under Dioclecian in 304 CE, but the Cyprian from Carthage

---

10 *The Confession of Cyprian of Antioch: Introduction, Text, and Translation,* Ryan Bailey.

preceded him, have being martyred under Valerian in 258 CE. The panegyric mix both, and according to Bailey:

> [...] the story Gregory tells, however, is the story of a pagan sorcerer who employs demonic magic in his attempts to seduce a Christian virgin. Gregory's obvious confusion of the two Cyprians is of crucial importance for dating the Confession since a number of elements in Gregory's discourse point specifically to the Confession as his source. In addition to the references to public confession, worship of demons, sorcery as the trademark of Cyprian's nefarious activities, and Cyprian's appetite for carnal pleasure (24.8), Gregory refers to Cyprian's personal infatuation with an unnamed virgin, a theme which is found only in the Confession.[11]

Prudentius also made confusion between the two Cyprians, and the empress Eudocia united the contents of the *Conversio*, the *Confessio*, and the *Passio* in her poem.

The *Books of Saint Cyprian* published at the end of the 19th century usually present as an introduction a simpler version of the life of the saint. The intermediary sources from which these popular narratives were based, which drew from the texts cited above, were probably the Menologion by Symeon Metaphrastes (who amalgamated the *Conversio* and the *Passio* into a single text in the 10th century), the *Golden Legend* by Jacobus de Voragine in the 13th century, and the *Flos Sanctorum* by Pedro de Ribadeneira from the 16th century.

---

11 *The Confession of Cyprian of Antioch: Introduction, Text, and Translation*, Ryan Bailey.

The Magic of Cyprian

The legend of Cyprian gave birth to two distinct magical currents. First, as a magician converted to martyr and saint, prayers and exorcisms attributed to him were (and still are today) considered particularly powerful against spells, demonic possession, the evil eye, etc. Secondly, magic and conjurations attributed to Cyprian, dating from the period of time prior to his conversion, would have an exceptional efficacy, as the legend puts him at a level of power which rivals that of Solomon and Simon Magus. When we come to the *Book of Saint Cyprian* from the modern age, we see that the different versions present a juxtaposition of both currents.

A chronology of the magic directly associated to Saint Cyprian includes erotic spells, apotropaic prayers, talismans, and, of course, books. To describe a complete chronology of references to the name of Saint Cyprian in the magical literature is practically impossible, but we tried to present here all the significant references we know. A complete study of the presence of Cyprian in magical texts should mention many prayers and amulets of Arabic, Coptic, Ethiopic, Armenian, and Greek origin, which are outside the context of this edition.

Erotic Spell of Cyprian of Antioch

This spell from the 11th century starts in a similar way to the prayers of Cyprian, with a short biographic confession, apparently inspired in the original *Confessio*. Curiously, however, to the confession and acknowledgment of the Christian God, the presumed Cyprian of the spell follows with a long adjuration asking for the intercession of the "father of the aeons" to force the "great minister of the blazing flame," the archangel Gabriel, to conquer the virgin Justina for himself. The adjuration of Cyprian to the archangel by the power of God becomes then the model for the enchantment.[12]

Secreta Cypriani

A magical treatise from the Lower Middle Ages, identified in the manuscript Oxford Bodleian Digby 30 (olim A224), from the second half of the 15th century.

The Art of Cyprian

A copy of this grimoire was part of the collection of the British occultist Frederick Hockley (1809–1885) and was presented for the first time in an article by Adam McLean in the Hermetic Journal - Volume 11. McLean describes the material: *"The Art of Cyprian is a work of white magic, and in particular unfolds a 'Christianised' system of magic. From purely internal evidence and comparing it with similar works, one might suggest that it was written in the mid-sixteenth century, during the period of the Christian Kabbalism of Pico della Mirandola, Reuchlin, Francesco Giorgi, and John Dee. The 'Art' of Cyprian is the raising of spirits through a series of what amounts to extended prayers, all of a Christian-Kabbalistic orientation."*

Trithemius and Agrippa

"Trithemius apparently owned a demonological treatise bearing his name"[13]; Agrippa in the Book III of the *Occult Philosophy* ("Of Goetia and Necromancy") writes that *"and now in these days there are carried about books with feigned titles, under the names of Adam, Abel, Enoch,*

---

12   *Ancient Christian Magic, Coptic Texts of Ritual Power*, edited by Marvin Meyer & Richard Smith.
13   Grimoires: A History of Magic Books, Owen Davies.

Abraham, Solomon, also Paul, Honorius, Cyprianus, Albertus, Thomas, Hierome and a certain man of York."[14]

Verus Jesuitarum Libellus

Grimoire falsely attributed to the Jesuits, it contains one *Citatio Angelorum* and one *Dimissio* attributed to Cyprian. It is included in the second volume of the *Das Kloster*, a collection of magical texts published in 12 volumes in the 19th century by Johann Scheible.

De Nigromancia

Falsely attributed to Roger Bacon, it says in its instructions that *"when you begin working in all operations of this Art, you must during the time of preparation for the conjurations have a Mass of Saint Cyprian said and any other Mass which is required, to be said by the Priest by custom."*

Scrolls of Cyprian

According to Owen Davies' "Grimoires," *"'Scrolls of Cyprian' were worn as talismans in Armenia into the modern period, with an account of his life and times appearing in a popular Armenian book of protective 'prayers for all occasions' printed in Constantinople in 1712."*

Cyprien Mago ante Conversionem

According to Owen Davies, this is a book printed in French and Latin, mentioned in a French trial of 1841. With the spurious date of "Salamanca 1460," it is

---

14   Three Books of Occult Philosophy, Henry Cornelius Agrippa (edited by Donald Tyson).

described as containing "magic, cabbalist and diabolical images, and instructions on how to obtain a treasure of eighteen million with the help of the Devil."

Instructions of Cyprian

Sloane MS 3851, a manuscript from the 17th century published by David Rankine[15] has a list of six magical instructions attributed to Saint Cyprian.

The Scandinavian Black Books from the 17th and 18th centuries

The tradition of books of magic in the North of Europe had the name of Cyprian as the author of diverse titles, although a certain confusion had arisen after some time about the character. Owen Davies mentions that Cyprian is presented by some as an evil Dane expelled from Hell in Denmark and by others as "a tender and decent student" in Norway. A summary by Bard Sundsfjord, mentioned by Skinner and Rankine, says that *"according to one early nineteenth century source, the Cyprianus was a horrifying, nefarious tome known to everyone in the countryside as 'Cyprianus,' whereby one can conjure up and put down the devil and get him to do just as one commands, and whose pages teach how to recover lost goods, cure all kind of diseases, remove curses, find buried treasure, turn back the attacks of snakes and dogs, and more…"*[16]

Arde'et or The Disciples

Early-modern Ethiopian Christian magical book, includes a prayer of Saint Cyprian.

---

15   *The Grimoire of Arthur Gauntlet*, edited and published by David Rankine.
16   *Clavis Infernii — The Grimoire of Cyprian*.

The Books of Cyprian

Clavis Infernii – The Grimoire of Cyprian

Published by Skinner and Rankine, from the MS Wellcome 2000, it is a text probably from the 18th century, belonging to the European Solomonic tradition, with influences from the *Heptameron*.

The Book

Bernardo Barreiro (1850–1904), Galician historian, journalist, and poet, in his study about the Inquisition in Spain mentions that, according to the records from the autos-de-fé during the 16th and 17th centuries, neither the people nor the inquisitors in the region seemed to know the work,[17] but we still find our oldest references about a *Book of Saint Cyprian* in the Iberian peninsula in the annals of the Inquisition headquartered in another Spanish area:

> There were very few books of Saint Cyprian quoted in the Spanish Inquisition Tribunals processes. One of the earliest references probably found is from 1610, about a process against Juan de Toledo who had the Book of Saint Cyprian for finding treasures (it appears in the book "Procesos en la Inquisición de Toledo (1575-1610)" (ed. Julio Sierra, Trotta, 2005)), also in the papers known as the Manuscript de Halle, information facilitated recently by M. Rey Bueno and Carlos Gilly.[18]

---

17 Brujos y astrólogos de la Inquisición de Galicia y el libro de San Cipriano, Bernardo Barreiro de Vázquez Varela (1885).
18 Felix Castro Vicente, *The Books of Saint Cyprian*. At http://danharms.wordpress.com/the-books-of-saint-cyprian/

According to Felix Castro, this Juan de Toledo was a Moorish doctor, and the Inquisitorial process said that he "had the book of Saint Cyprian and gave de one from Picatrix to a certain person to find treasures."[19]

From another Inquisition process in the year of 1778, in the declarations of a presbyter named Juan Francisco García and a deacon named Manuel Bázquez Noya, we know that the *Book of Saint Cyprian* (we ignore in what version) was already nicknamed *"the Ciprianillo."* The book was used by a blind and poor confidence trickster named Andrés Congil and his partner Isabel Rodrigues Maceda, la Fanchona.[20]

Again in a reference from the annals of the Spanish Inquisition, we know that in 1802, a presbyter named Ferrol D. Juan Rodríguez was prosecuted for having a *Book of Saint Cyprian*.

Copies of the *Ciprianillo*, as the book became later popularly known in Spain, were certainly circulating around 1885, as it is mentioned again by Bernardo Barreiro. The book appears in the popular narratives as being directly related to treasure hunting, a traditional magical activity, largely spread in Europe and with predecessors recorded even in Antiquity. The hunt for treasure was a magical activity *par excellence* and often subjected to the control of the state. David Rankine gives us a vivid portrait of this activity in 16th century England:

> For example, in 1521, King Henry VIII granted a license to Sir Edward Belknap, John Hertford and John Jonys (a goldsmith) to dig in Cornwall and Devon for treasure. As well as magicians and cunning-folk, priests were frequently called upon by treasure-seekers to raise spirits, as it was believed that such treasures were rarely unguarded. However records do also show that the fairy king Oberion refused to talk to them!
>
> Licenses may have been granted in some instances to control the actions of enterprising individuals who

---

19   *Le magicien-guérisseur du carnet de voyage de 1835 d'Antoine d'Abbadie*. Yvette Cardaillac-Hermosilla. Revista de Estudios Vascos Lapurdum.
20   *El Idioma de la razón: Ilustración e Inquisición en Galicia (1707-1808)"*, Martín González Fernández, Editorial Nigratrea.

sought to make their fortunes illicitly through such quests for buried treasure. In a time before the stability of the banking system, people often buried their money, and had done for centuries since before the Romans. As a result of this the quest for treasure was a common one.

Another instance from the reign of King Henry VIII was recorded by the monk William Stapleton in 1528, where in the pursuit of treasure one Denys of Hofton did bring me a book called Thesaurus Spirituum and, after that, another called Secreta Secretorum, a little ring, a plate, a circle, and also a sword for the art of digging.[21]

Spain and Portugal were places where the treasure fever had deep roots, as their lands were successively invaded through the centuries by the Romans, the Goths, and the Moors, who were believed to have left fortunes behind awaiting the return of their rightful owners. As the fugitives were believed to have protected the treasures with magic, so magic was needed by anyone who looked after them. We can see the importance of the treasure hunt in the statistics of the Spanish Inquisition, which registered 202 accusations of the kind between 1700 and 1820. In the tribunal of Córdoba, for instance, magical treasure hunting corresponded to 15% of the charges and 38% of the convictions of the period.[22]

Apparently, copies of the book were hard to find and were sold at exorbitant prices, which moved Bernardo Barreiro to publish as an addendum to his work *Bruxos e Astrólogos da Inquisición de Galícia* excerpts from the "*famous book of Saint Cyprian.*" Barreiro's aim was to demystify the book that, apparently, brought to ruin people greedily obsessed with treasure. As Felix Castro very well defined:

> Maybe there was never a book so coveted and searched for, neither one which arose more passions and desires to be possessed, to the point many people fell into madness,

---

21 *The Book of Treasure Spirits,* edited and published by David Rankine.
22 *Magie et sorcellerie en Espagne au siècle des lumières 1700-1820,* Valérie Molero.

got sick or ruined themselves economically, just trying to find a copy of the book or attempting to put into practice the rituals it contains. We are talking about the Book of Saint Cyprian, popularly known as Ciprianillo.[23]

This publication by Barreiro is the oldest identification of the contents of a modern Iberian book attributed to Saint Cyprian. Curiously, when reading its pages, the well-informed reader recognizes that the text in question is nothing more than a Spanish version, with many errors, of the French *Grand Grimoire*.

After Barreiro's publication, we find the first Spanish book of the period in which the name of Saint Cyprian is not simply put on the cover of some other grimoire: the *Heptameron o Elementos Magicos, compuesto por el gran Cipriano famoso majico*. Although the title was possibly inspired by the text about ceremonial magic attributed to Pietro d'Abano, the version assigned to Saint Cyprian presents largely different contents. However, it is possible that certain details of the instruction about the magical circle to disenchant treasures are derived from the original *Heptameron*, in the same way the instructions for the use of the magical wand probably owe to the *Grand Grimoire*. As is usual, the *Prologue* tells us about the origin of the book:

> Dear reader, the book I present to you called *Heptameron ou elementos mágicos,* composed by the great Cyprian, which after being lost through an infinity of years, I found by one of these rare accidents, in a library at Amsterdam translated into French, and believing it to be the sole existing edition, I thought excited with the indulgency and that you would receive it with benevolence, translated to your Castilian tongue, for your greater knowledge. One of the causes that moved me to this was its ability to prophesy the forthcoming, and discover occult things,

---

23 *El Libro de San Cipriano*, by Felix Castro Vicente. In Hibris, Revista de Bibliofilia Ano V Número 27 (2005).

its infinity of secrets and talismans to preserve from evil sorceries, and at last other things you will find in it. If my good intention deserves something from you, I ask indulgency to the faults you come to find. Vale.[24]

The assumed date of this edition is 1810, and apparently it was reprinted many times at the end of the 19th century, *"at supposed places and falsifying the date."* Felix Castro continues:

It is a curious edition, as it is very different from the others we will soon comment about, because it does not have evident similarities with the other European grimoires we have commented on (Grand Grimoire, Grimorium Verum, etc.). In fact, we must say that the reference to Saint Cyprian is almost an anecdote as the saint is mentioned, maybe to make the book more attractive, only in the title and in the prologue of the work. At first sight, between the most remarkable characteristics of this version is the apparent antiquity of the same, as we can see by the typography, layout, engravings, and inclusively its archaic language and orthography. In fact, it does not bring sections that are essential to the other editions, such as a resume of the life of the saint, the prayer of Saint Cyprian, list of treasure, etc. Half of the work deals with divinations, astromancy, quiromancy, physiognomy etc., dedicating itself after that to the elaboration of talismans, amulets (some coincide with ones from the *Grand Grimoire* and the *Poule Noir*), the confection of the mysterious wand and its utilization to disenchant treasures, including the making of the magical circle, themes which appear in the other versions (as the one of Jonas Sufurino) as central to them. After that the book talks about philtres and recipes,

---

24 *Heptameron o elementos mágicos,* facsimile of the original edition kindly provided by Felix Castro Vicente.

with just a few for love (what is atypical), but above all to cure infirmities, and to protect the animals from wolves and beasts, what can make evident its antiquity and its interest, to be useful to peasants and not to the settled people who live in the cities.[25]

The next register of the Spanish versions is the edition entitled *Cipriano el Temeroso*, identified by Felix Castro Vicente in a publication dated in the frontispiece from 1874. It is simply a Spanish version of the *Veritable Magie Noir*, translated by a certain Balbino Perez, who for some reason added the name Cyprian to the title. Although almost forgotten, this version is most certainly the origin of the *Book of Saint Cyprian* attributed to the mysterious monk Jonas Sufurino. The Sufurino version, from which the most ancient exemplar examined by Felix Castro apparently belong to the end of the 19th century, has been supposedly printed by the "Imprensa Cabalística de Milano": *Complete book of the true magic or Treasure of the Sorcerer, written in Ancient Hebrew Parchments delivered by the spirits to the German Monk Jonás Sufurino.*

The first part of the Sufurino's uses largely the contents of the French grimoire *La Veritàble Magie Noir*, which, in its turn, owes to the *Keys of Solomon*. The contents of the *Veritable Magie Noir* almost certainly came to the Sufurino's through the edition of the *Cipriano el Temeroso*. However, we find in many portions of the book what can be interpreted as the personal magical and literary contribution of the translator or copyist, giving to the work a greater interest. The presence of the anonymous writer is also felt in the addenda, copied from many other grimoires, as we can see in the description of its contents:

> Contains: The Book of Cyprian or the Treasure of the Sorcerer, the Key of Solomon, Invocations, Pacts, Exorcisms, the Red Dragon and the Infernal She-goat, the Black Hen, School of Sortileges, the Gran Grimoire or

---

25 *El Libro de San Cipriano*, by Felix Castro Vicente. In Hibris, Revista de Bibliofilia Ano V Número 27 (2005).

Pact of Blood, magical Candle to find out enchantments. Recompilation of the Chaldaic and Egyptian magic. Philtres, enchantments, sorceries and sortileges.[26]

We must also add to the description contents from the *Arbatel*. Comparing the illustration of the magical instruments (pp. 202) of the edition of Jonas Sufurino with the ones from one of the editions of the *Veritàble Magie Noir*, and both with the illustration of the same grimoire published in the compendium by Waite,[27] it becomes clear how extensively this material was used.

Mysterious Wand, according to the *Black Hen*
Illustration of *Book of Black Magic and Pacts* by Waite

The illustration of the magical instruments in the Jonas Sufurino's version includes two more instruments, but here we again will not find originality. The *Mysterious Wand* curiously seems to unite the two drawings of the *Magical Rod* that we will find in the grimoire called *The Black Hen*, which originally showed the flexibility of the wand (which was supposed to bend to the point of making a circle), and the *Magical Wand* which seems to copy the *Grand Grimoire*.

---

26 *El Libro de San Cipriano, Tesoro de Hechicero*; facsimile from one of the original editions gently provided by Felix Castro Vicente.
27 *Book of Black Magic and Pacts*, A.E. Waite.

Cover from the Heptameron o Elementos Magicos, *composed by the great magician Cyprian. Image kindly provided by Felix Castro Vicente.*

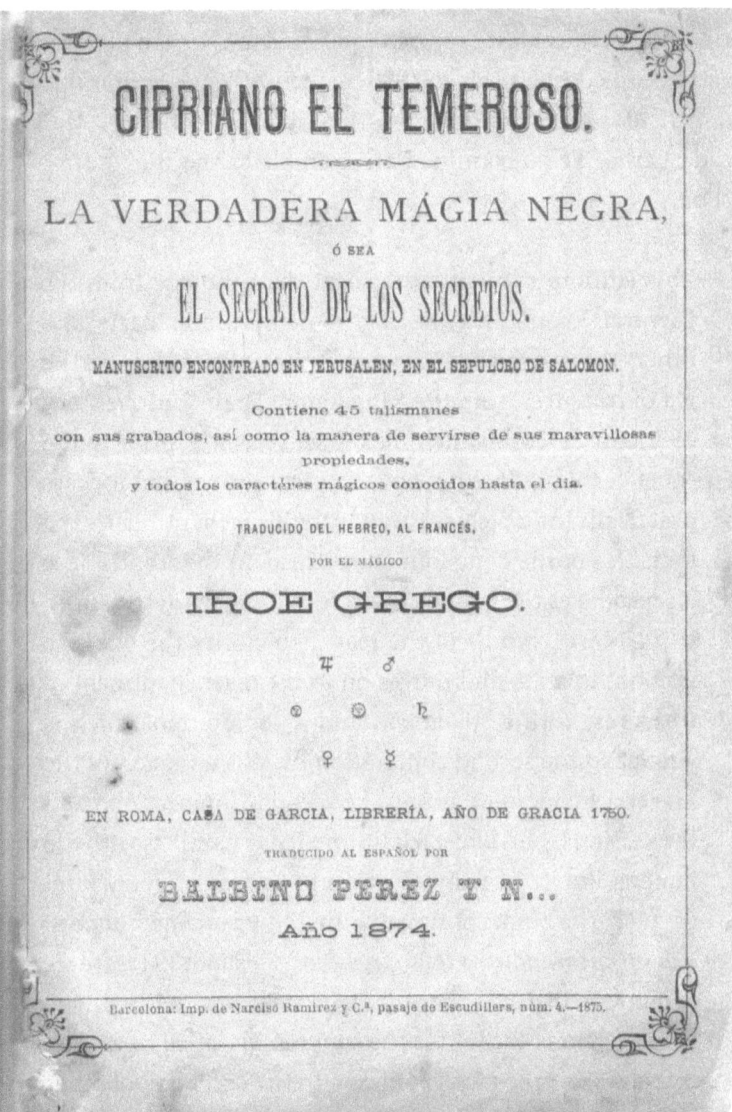

Frontispiece of the edition of Cipriano el Temeroso.
Image kindly provided by Felix Castro Vicente.

In Portugal, the oldest example attributed to Cyprian identified by Felix Castro is an edition prior to 1886, named *Livro de S. Cipriano ou Thesouro Particular do Feiticeiro,* from the Livraria Portuguesa de Joaquim María da Costa. Felix examined an example at the Biblioteca Nacional de Lisboa:

> This edition is much more short than the one from the Livraria Económica, having some common parts and others that we did not see in any other edition. It lacks the list of treasures from the Kingdom of Spain and the story of Victor Siderol (which makes sense as it is prior to the other version), does not have magical recipes, but focuses practically in an exclusive way on the disenchantment of the treasures of the Kingdom of Portugal, in the frontispiece it reproduces the famous triangle to disenchant treasures. It starts with words to the reader to clarify the work he is about to read, and moves on to the disenchantment of treasures, with a statement, and a conjuration which is similar to the second conjuration from the version of the Livraria Económica and to the second Conjuration from the version by Enediel Shaiah, and it has parallels with the famous Prayer of Saint Cyprian to be free of every kind of spell. The book continues with *Tombo ou lugar onde se acham encantados os thesouros*, with a list of 139 treasures to be found in part at the Port D. Gazua, coincident with the other versions except for the suppression of 10 treasures. It follows with sections common in the first book of other works (reasons why god allows the Devil to torment the creatures, cartomancy, the story of Cyprian and Justine, prayer to assist the sick, etc.). Here it includes sections that do not appear at any other version, the story of the *The Devil and his diableries*, about an old woman who tricked death and the devil who goes after her every year, and *The disenchantment of the moura*, which is a magical formula

to disenchant treasures, apparently coming from an oral tradition of great antiquity. The work finishes with the usual formulas, the spell to make a woman say everything she had done or has the intention of doing and with the art of reading the sediments of coffee.[28]

The other version of book, published by the Livraria Económica de Lisboa prior to 1839, the *Grande Livro de S. Cipriano ou Thesouro do Feiticeiro*, is composed in three volumes. The third part presents the story of Victor Siderol and the list of 174 treasures from the Kingdom of Spain. Bibliographical information included in the book itself affirm a Spanish origin for this part of the material, whose rights would have originally been bought from a publisher from Barcelona. This can or cannot be true. In the version published by the Livraria Económica, the First Book coincides with the later Spanish edition published by Enediel Shaiah, the Spanish occultist, and it is basically a manual for exorcisms. Felix Castro compared both texts:

> Until the sixth chapter both books go exactly the same, here the version at hand includes the *Desencanto dos Tesouros, oración e esconxuro para desencantarse dos tesouros, lugares onde existem os encantos, e soma dos haberes de Porto de D. Gazua, rios e águas vertentes*, which is a list of treasures (148 in total) existing in the Kingdom of Portugal in the Port of D. Gazua. Soon follows the same as the version by Enediel Shaiah, with the new system to spread cards, cartomancy, episodes from the life of Saint Cyprian, under the name of *Poderes ocultos, cartomancia, oraciones y esconjuro*. The Second Book is also equivalent to Enediel Shaiah's version, beginning *True Treasure of the Black and White Magic, or Secrets of Witchcraft*, with the same magical formulae

---

28 *El Libro de San Cipriano*, by Felix Castro Vicente. In Hibris, Revista de Bibliofilia Ano V Número 27 (2005).

(except for a few more added here), and follows with the story of Cipriano and Clotilde which is absent from the other versions. Here this version does not include, as in the edition by Enediel Shaiah, the *Ceremonial of Magic* (clothes and instruments of the magician, creation of the magical circle and ritual for invocation), which puts it apart from the idea of an integral grimoire and makes it closer to the idea of a prescription book. It then resumes the same chapter *Mysteries of witchcraft extracted from a manuscript of black magic believed to be from the time of the Moors* including some sections that do not appear in the version by Enediel Shaiah (e.g. Prayer to expel the devil from the body, and stories of Saint Cyprian and Adelaide and Cyprian and Elvira, argument between Saint Cyprian and Saint Gregory about the Catholic Faith, etc.). Many of these conjurations also appear in the section of Chaldaic and Egyptian Magic in the Jonas Sufurino's version and in the one of Saint Cyprian and Saint Justina. The book finishes with a section on physiognomy and another about crossed cartomancy, and an explanation about dreams and nocturnal apparitions with an alphabetical index to interpret them that does not appear in the version by Enediel Shaiah.[29]

The third book tells the story of Victor Siderol, which works the same as the one about Jonas Sufurino to introduce an origin for the book. The German monk and the French peasant betray the image held then in Spain about the magical centers of the age; what is ironic if we remember that, in the past, Salamanca and Toledo were considered the most important places for magical learning in Europe. This edition also contains the *Story of the Evora Witch or Story of the Forever Bride*, which introduces a character that would become very popular. The witch of Evora is a gruesome

---

29 *El Libro de San Cipriano*, by Felix Castro Vicente. In Hibris, Revista de Bibliofilia Ano V Número 27 (2005).

character who owes nothing to the witches of the Latin tradition, like Meroe, Panthia, Erichtho, and Canidia. Although the story happens in Portugal during the Moorish occupation, later Brazilian ghost-writers did not hesitate in making the Witch of Evora a contemporary of Saint Cyprian, and even his master.

This work was the foundation of the Brazilian editions, which therefore lack the sections on Ceremonial Magic we find in the Spanish books.

Enediel Shaiah, pseudonym of Alfredo Rodríguez Aldao, according to Felix Castro, was *"a Galician hypnotist and occultist, born in Pontevedra, who lived in Madrid between the end of the 19th century and the beginning of the 20th, where he had a consulting room for hypnotism. He wrote books on occultism and hypnotism, and translated numerous French works, especially from Papus (Dr. Encausse), to whom he was a disciple, and from Eliphas Levi. He directed the Biblioteca Teosófica of the Editorial Pueyo and was a friend to Mario Roso de Luna."*[30] He edited a collection with three books attributed to Saint Cyprian, with the title "El Libro Magno de San Cipriano, Tesoro del Hechicero." Felix Castro indicated that the many editions of this work are all dated after 1905.

The First Book from the anthology of Enediel Shaiah, as we have seen, coincides with the first book from the Portuguese edition from the Livraria Económica de Lisboa, being mostly composed of instructions and prayers for exorcisms. The Second Book brings important contents of ceremonial magic, because, although it has topics very similar to the Jonas Sufurino's book, it contrasts with it for its markedly more Christianized approach. Jonas Sufurino presents a ceremony of a clearly diabolical nature, with the recommendation, for instance, of not allowing crosses or Christian religious relics in the place where the ceremonies are performed.

---

30 Felix Castro Vicente, in private communication.

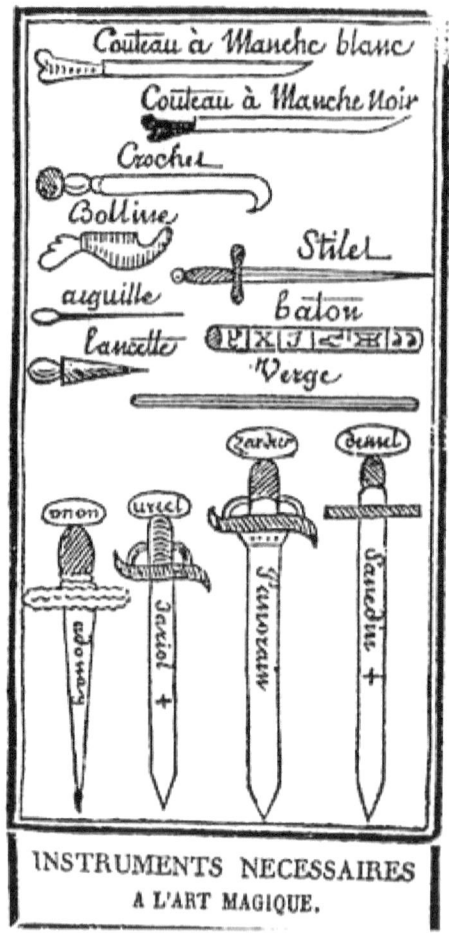

Illustration of the Instruments necessary to the Magical Art from the *Véritable Magie Noir*. Compare with the illustration of the magical instruments from the version of the Book of Saint Cyprian attributed to Jonas Sufurino.

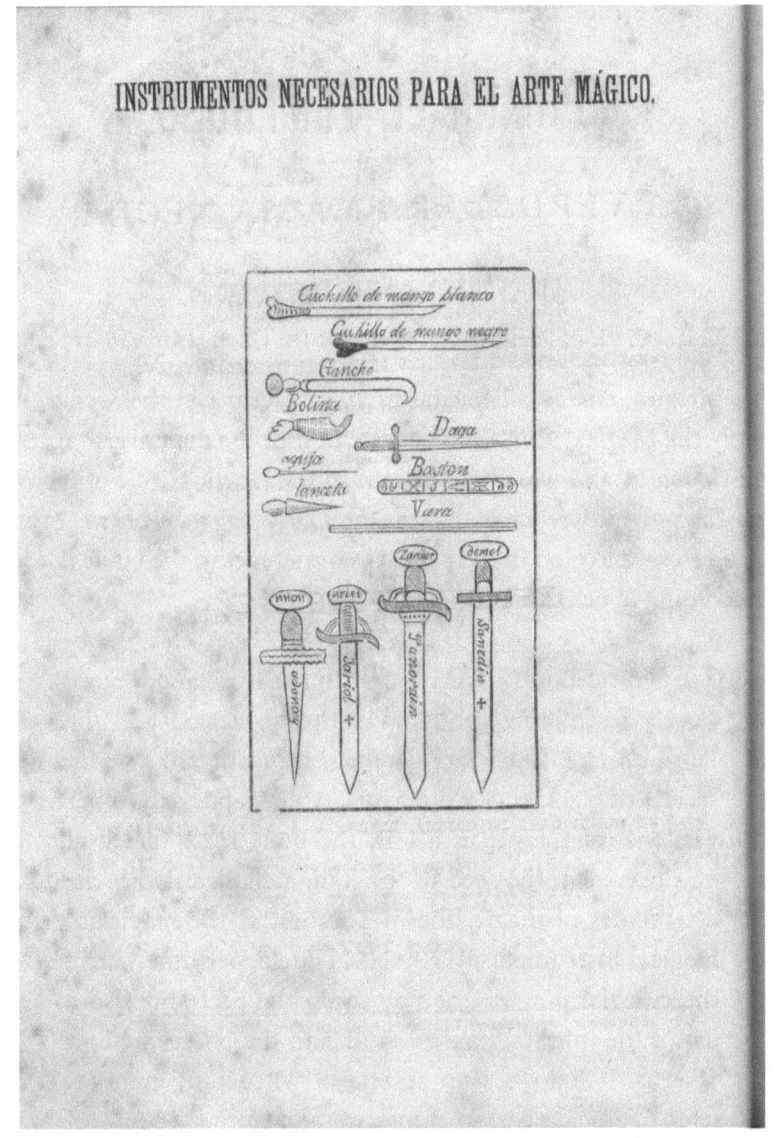

Plate with the magical instruments from the intermediary edition entitled *"Cipriano el Temeroso."* Image kindly provided by Felix Castro Vicente.

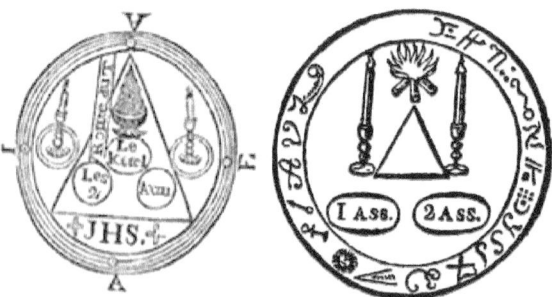

The Magical Circle of Pacts, *Grand Grimoire* The Goetic Circle, *Black Pullet*

The magical circle that Enediel Shaiah describes in the Second Book is simply the Magical Circle of Pacts we find in the many versions of the *Grand Grimoire*, and which is repeated in the Goetic Circle of the *Black Pullet*. The only difference is that, in the *Libro Magno,* a phrase of invocation addressed to God in the outer circumference of the circle is added.

According to Felix Castro:

> The Second Book is the one which has the content more closely resembling the Jonas Sufurino version and the *Libro de San Cipriano y Santa Justina;* it talks about secrets of black and white magic, which appear in other versions (of the broad beans, the bone from the head of a black cat, the seed of the fern, etc.), deals with the ceremonies of magic (the preparation of the magician, magical instruments, the magical circle, perfumes, etc.), the celestial powers, the way to do the pact and also a list of the infernal powers similar to the one in Johann Wierus. It follows with secrets of witchcraft, many of which coincide with the ones we find in the versions of Jonas Sufurino and of Saint Cyprian and Saint Justine although in a different order; others coincide with recipes from the *El Heptamerón,* the following (the ring of Giges, the magical mirror of Solomon, the Secret of the Black Hen, etc.) also appear in the *Grand Grimoire* and the *Dragon Rouge,* the rest (magic of the do acerbic, of the

glass pot, of the black pigeon, the potatoes with sprouts, etc.) appear in the Portuguese editions.

Front page from the exemplar examined by Felix Castro in the National Library of Lisbon.

The Third Book has a part dedicated to the treasures, which it also shares in common with the Portuguese editions, and Felix Castro considers that it may in fact be a translation or adaptation from them, as it presents words in Portuguese in some parts. It also presents the great magical secrets of the magician Artaphernes, a character perhaps inspired by the magician Artéphius from the *Grand Grimoire*, and who here appears as a master to Cyprian.

It remains to comment on the Mexican version, which is basically a re-edition of the *El libro de San Cipriano y Santa Justina, milagros y oraciones de la S.S. Cruz de Caravaca*, published in Barcelona by the Livraria das Ciências Secretas between 1895 and 1920. It contains on the frontispiece the name already famous of Jonas Sufurino, but there is not a mention of the same in the rest of the book. The Mexican edition contains important parts of the Grand Grimoire and, very curiously, some of the most recent editions come with an image created after the Atu V ("The Hierophant") from Aleister Crowley's Thoth Tarot on the front cover—offering, maybe inadvertently, a reinterpretation of the images of Cyprian and Justine more to the taste of modern magicians.

The Present Edition

The central parts of this edition come from the Portuguese version published by the Livraria Economica and from the Spanish versions of the Heptameron, Sufurino and the original sections of the Enediel Shaiah book. To these, many texts, excerpts, chapters, spells, invocations, etc., associated in the magical tradition with the name of Saint Cyprian were added. The intention is to provide the reader with a vast and significant collection of diverse materials directly related to the Cyprianic Magic.

I organized the material according to the subject contained in each text. That means, instead of just copying the entire original books, I divided their contents in separated sections. The source of each text is indicated just below the title in the page, by a three- or two-letter abbreviation. The list of the sources with their corresponding abbreviations is in the end of this Introduction. That allows to a better search of the contents and an interesting comparison between the different sources. If the reader wishes to follow the instructions of one of the books, they can be easily identified by the initial abbreviation.

I considered for long about the use of footnotes in the sections, and in the end I decided to keep it to a minimum. The objective of doing this is to keep the original flavor of the books, which I feel would be mischaracterized by an unnecessary display of scholarship. In the end, any specific doubt about some term or another can be easily researched on the net.

I will now provide a short description of each section.

The Origin of the Book

A common feature of the different Books of Saint Cyprian is an introductory tale about how it was found or rescued, before coming into print. This is a necessary explanation aiming at giving the book credence in the eyes of the reader. Some are very short, others more elaborated.

Vita Cypriani

This section presents a collection of legends and tales about the life of Saint Cyprian. The presence of such narratives is also a repeated feature of almost all editions. All the different stories found in these books are inherited from the originals *Conversio*, *Confessio*, and *Passio*, so I included these three in the beginning of the section.

Our original intention was to use Ryan Bailey translation of the *Confessio*, but after two years trying to contact him in Montreal and Rome, we were forced to produce our own text. To support this, we used the Italian translation edited by Stefano Fumagallim,[31] and the French by Pierre Grimal.[32]

---

31 *Cipriano de Antiochia Confessione, a cura de Stefano Fumagalli*. Mimesis e Meledoro. 1994.
32 In *Romans grecs et latins*, Bibliothèque de la Pléiade. Editions Gallimard.

Of great interest to the development of the modern tales are the medieval text from *The Golden Legend* of Jacobus de Voragine (1230–1298)[33] and the version from the *Flos Sactorum* of Father Pedro of Ribadeira (1526–1611).

Many other tales and anecdotes from the four main sources and other works are included in this section. The reader will see that often curious confusions are made by the anonymous writers of these later stories, between the lives of Cyprian as a saint and as a sorcerer.

The Magical Art

The section that I love most, were we can find different versions of rituals, some more inclined to a Christianized view of magic, others of a declared diabolical inspiration.

The reader can compare the different contents or follow the instructions of the same source after the identification under the title.

Talismans and Amulets

Here we find some interesting explanations about talismans, pentacles, and amulets and some original material (like the intriguing story about the Red Dragon). Some parts of the originals, however, show very clearly to be unskilled appropriation of previous grimoires.

The Book of the Spirits

Here we find almost philosophical descriptions of the spiritual hierarchies, coupled with lists of demons and spirits, almost all of them clearly derived from other grimoires.

I had to make editorial decisions here, leaving outside sections and chapters from the originals that merely repeated other known grimoires, especially the *Grand Grimoire*.

---

[33] From *Witchcraft in Europe, 400-1700: A Documentary History*. University of Pennsylvania Press

The Books of Cyprian

The Prayers of Saint Cyprian

The prototype of the Prayer of Saint Cyprian probably appeared soon after the *Confessio* was written, as all the subsequent prayers attributed to him follow the same pattern:

> *A General Confession*: Cyprian list all the sins and misdeeds he did when he was a magician.
>
> *A General Invocation:* Usually containing names and examples taken from the Bible.
>
> *A General Exorcism:* Here the prayer tries to address every kind of offensive magic that could be the origin of the present difficulties the prayer aims to resolve. It is a catalogue of the offensive spells known to the writer and had varied according to time and circumstances.

The section contains the oldest version I could find, an Arabian prayer supposedly "translated from the Greek." In a private correspondence, Felix Castro provided some additional information about the subject:

> The prayer of Saint Cyprian was prohibited by the Catholic Church and condemned as being superstitious by the Inquisition. It was included in the Index Librorum Prohibitorum (according to Javier Itúrbide Díaz in the Indexes of 1559, 1583, 1612, 1632, 1640, 1707, until the edition of 1844). The oldest prayer we know in Castellan is dated (Itúrbide Díaz 2010) of 1631. It appears in the Expediente de Censura de la Inquisición with the title of "Oración devotissima de San Cipriano, traduzida de Latin en Castellano," translated by Cristobal Lasterra y Santisteban, the author of the work *Liber exorcismorum*

cum adversus tempestates et demones, published in 1631 at Pamplona.

Another kind of prayer to be found in the Brazilian editions of the *Book of Saint Cyprian* seems to be derived from folk conceptions of diabolical magic, inherited from the colonization times when the Portuguese Inquisition exiled witches to Brazil. Those are the "Prayers of the Black She-Goat," a genre with many regional variations. I show here three examples, taken from the research work *Música de feitiçaria no Brasil* ("Witchcraft Music from Brazil"), gathered by the Brazilian poet, novelist, musicologist, art historian and critic, photographer Mario de Andrade.

> ***Prayer of the Black She-Goat*** (Pagelança, Pará): My Saint Catherine, I will go under that hanged man to take a piece of rope to tie the Black She-goat, to take three liters of milk, to make three cheeses, to divide in four pieces, one piece for Satanaz, one piece for Caifas, one piece for Ferrabraz, one piece for his/her infancy. (His/her infancy indicates the desired person.) It is said at Fridays at midnight.
>
> ***Prayer of the Black She-Goat*** (Catimbós, Pará): False Izaura, who wandered through the world, you passed by the feet of the gallows, three black she-goats you found and the milk from them you took, and with it you made three cheeses: one you gave to Lucifer, other to Ferrabraz, and the other to the Limp dog, by the power of these friends of yours I want you to go now, now, now, to the Federal Capital, and from there brings to me the result of the lottery that will win tomorrow, now, now, now.
>
> ***Prayer of the Black She-Goat*** (Catimbós, Rio Grande do Norte): My Saint Marta Elisa, as you walked, in the way you found one Black She-Goat, from it you suckled and swelled up, with the milk you took from it, you made

three cheese, one for Cain, one for Ferrabraz, and other to Satanaz. I want with the power you have that you find a staff with a very thin edge, and touch with it the heart of So and So. Sooth his heart, he wanting it or not, now, now, now, if he does not do what I want, do not let him sleep at ease, or eat, or drink, as long as he does not do what I want (It is to be prayed at noon or at midnight).[34]

Exorcisms

The main part of this section comes from the First Book of the Portuguese edition. The different nature of this First book, when compared to the other parts of the same edition, suggests that a popular manual of exorcism was added at some point to the more sorcerous contents.

It also provides a non-orthodox description of the souls of the departed.

Magical Treasures

The best study I found during my research about the sections on the disenchantment of magical treasures to be found in the Portuguese *Book of Saint Cyprian* (copied with some variations in the Enediel Shaiah version) is the monograph entitled *Las Hondas Raices del Ciprianillo* ("The Deep Roots of the Ciprianillo"), by the writer and Egyptologist Peter Missler. On it, Missler traces the origins of the lists of treasures to the Arab models known since the IX century as *The Book of the Science of Treasures*.

The reason offered for the existence of these books is the same that we find centuries later in Portugal and Spain: The land of Egypt, have being frequently invaded, was left with many enchanted treasures belonging to the noble and rich people who had to, now and then, flee the country. As these people had the hope of eventually returning to claim their possessions back, they put spells and curses on the treasures and wrote down descriptions to help finding and disenchanting then again.

---

34 *Música de feitiçaria no Brasil,* Mario de Andrade.

The success of this literary genre was guaranteed in the years of 932–933, when a great amount of "gold, jewelry, silver and statues incrusted with precious stones" were found in the mastaba of Gizeh, following the indication of a "book written in ancient characters."[35]

The success was so great that associations of treasure hunters were founded along the North Africa, and in some cases, the government issued official taxes over ever finding made.

Missler's paper mention as one of the oldest known indications of the phenomenon of magical treasure hunt in Spain the case of a seer called Juan de Varela, caught by the Inquisition in 1604 and 1609. Varela was accused of possessing "a book where the place of the treasures can be divined" and a "book of nigromancy with which he knows how to disenchant treasures."

He also mentions the testimony of the Father Benito Jerónimo Feijoo (1676-1764) who once had in his hands two manuscripts, one containing a list of more or less twenty treasures, and the other the lengthy instructions to disenchant them, to which nothing less than three priests were necessary to perform.

Missler identified also many other lists of treasures that preceded the ones published in the Books of Saint Cyprian, many of them lacking the magical instructions. He observes that the dropping out of the magical parts possibly happened over time due to them being too difficult and too expensive to perform. That would make the lists unattractive to the country people supposed to buy them.

Magical Secrets

I already mentioned the ancient origin of the magical secrets to be found in the Books of Saint Cyprian. These procedures endured in Europe, especially in the Mediterranean cultures, and their roots can be traced by comparison to the magical literature of the Antiquity.

---

35   *Las Hondas Raices del Ciprianillo,* Peter Missler.

The Books of Cyprian

Stephen Skinner and David Rankine summarized very well their preservation together with the more complex ceremonial instructions in the grimoires, so I will just quote from them:

> Over the last thousand years there have been several distinct streams of Western magical practice. One of these is the Grimoires, which focus on preparation and complex procedures to produce effective communication and interaction with spiritual beings. To this category belong such major works as the *Key of Solomon*, the *Lemegeton* and the *Sworn Book of Honorius*, which have influenced many modern magical traditions and practices. Another stream includes rather simple rule of thumb procedures, which do not involve much preparation, and which might have been used by local village witches or cunning men. From the sixteenth century onwards these latter procedures were often to be found on simple techniques that could be practiced by anybody rather than long and complex rites. Effectively such works made magic available to anybody who could read a book and gather simple ingredients, rather than the moneyed classes with their elaborate paraphernalia and expensive hand-copied grimoires.[36]
>
> These two streams of practice, Grimoires and Books of Secrets, are sometimes found together in the same manuscripts. It is common for the pages of a working grimoire to have been supplemented by its owner with other formulae that he had successfully used or picked up in his course of reading. These snippets are often drawn from books like Agrippa's *De occulta Philosophia*, and the works ascribed to Albertus Magnus, and may be in a different handwriting. In the course of time these notes

---

36 *A Collection of Magical Secrets & A Treatise of Mixed Cabalah*, edited by Stephen Skinner and David Rankine.

in the back of a grimoire were copied along with the grimoire as if they were part of it. Indeed the nineteenth century French pseudo-grimoires of black magic, such as the *Grimoire of Pope Honorius III*, the *Red Dragon* and *Grimorium Verum* are often full of such procedures.[37]

What was left out

The four main sources utilized to bring together this edition offered to their readers chapters on popular Astrology, Chiromancy, Cartomancy, etc. The content of these chapters are very poor and do not differ from the contents of any popular esoteric magazine from today.

These chapters I left out.

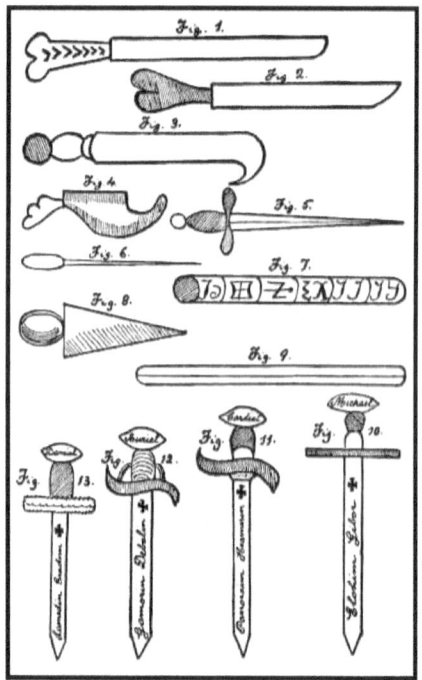

The instruments of Black Magic, from the Grimoire entitled *True Black Magic*, according to Waite.

---

37   *A Collection of Magical Secrets & A Treatise of Mixed Cabalah*, edited by Stephen Skinner and David Rankine.

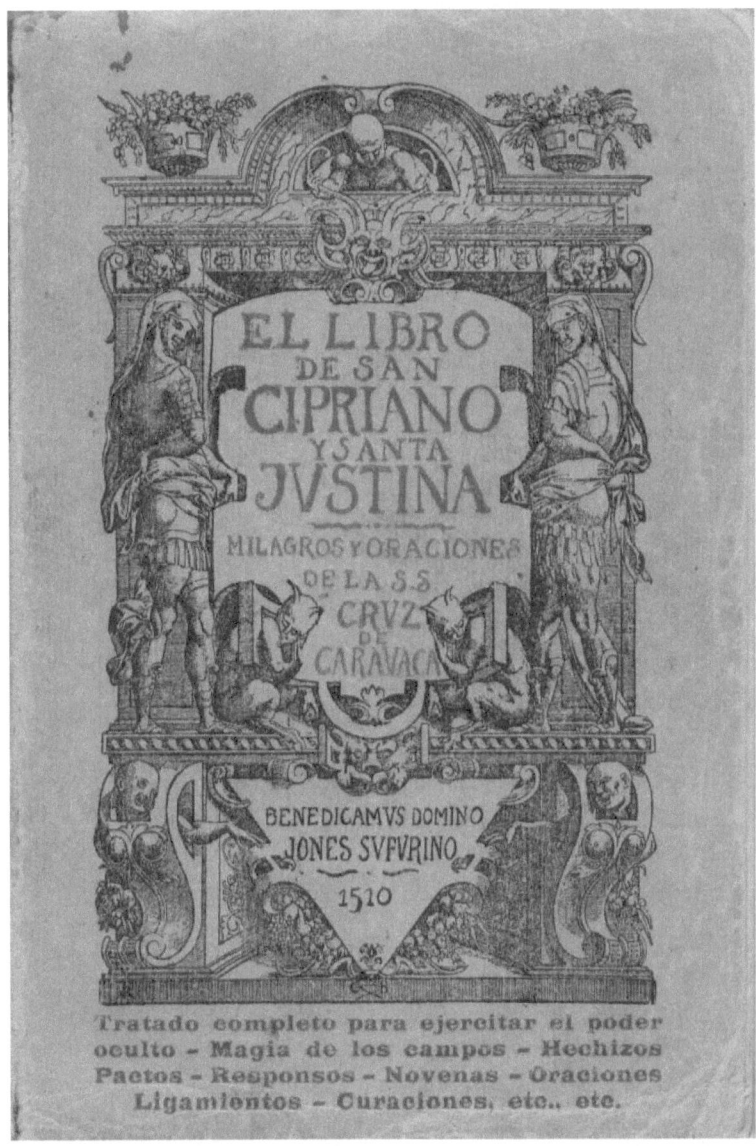

Frontispiece of *El libro de San Cipriano y Santa Justina, milagros y oraciones de la S.S. Cruz de Caravaca.* Courtesy of Felix Castro Vicente.

List of Abbreviations

GLT	O Grande Livro de São Cypriano	Livraria Econômica
VJL	Verus Jesuitarum Libellus	Tradução de Joseph H. Peterson
FLS	Flos Sanctorum	Padre Pedro de Ribadeneira
TDH	El Libro de San Cipriano – Tesoro del Hechicero	Biblioteca Ciencias Ocultas
LSC	El Libro de San Cipriano	EDAF
LM1	El Libro Magno de San Cipriano [Livro I]	Enediel Shaiah
LM2	El Libro Magno de San Cipriano [Livro II]	Enediel Shaiah
LM3	El Libro Magno de San Cipriano [Livro III]	Enediel Shaiah
HEM	Heptameron ó Elementos Magicos	Original in the collection of Felix Castro
HM	Histoire de la Magie	Eliphas Levi
TLN	O Tradicional Livro Negro de São Cipriano.	Pallas
GLC	O Grande Livro de São Cipriano	Lello Editores
GLS	Grande Livro de São Cipriano ou Tesouros do Feiticeiro	Edições Afrodite
ALC	Antigo Livro de São Cipriano o Gigante e Verdadeiro Capa de Aço	Editora Espiritualista
LAE	Les Apocryphes Éthiopiens	Archè Milano
ACM	Ancient Christian Magic	Harper and Collins
MCJ	The Martyrdom of Cyprian and Justa	The University of Chicago Press
SFT	The Sources of the Faust Tradition	Octagon Books Inc
EXU	Exu and the Kimbanda of Night and Fire	Nicholaj Frisvold / Scarlet Imprint
GAG	The Grimoire of Arthur Gauntlet	Edited by David Rankine
WIE	Witchcraft in Europe, 400-1700: A Documentary History	University of Pennsylvania Press
BCW	Blavatsky Collected Writings	H. P. Blavatsky
LTS	Lives of the Saints with Reflections for Every Day in the Year	Rev. Alban Butler.

Frontispiece of the edition published by Enediel Shadiah.
Courtesy of Felix Castro Vicente.

Cover of the Edition published by the Biblioteca Ciencias Ocultas, in Mexico. The illustration is the same from the Spanish editions.

The Origins of The Book

Hurrah! We have managed, after much effort, to bring to the light of the people the true miracles of science. This arduous task required the consent of the cardinals to allow us to translate from Hebrew the manuscripts of the great martyr S. Cyprian, which are in the Library of the Vatican.[38]

---

38 Text of introduction from an old Brazilian edition, referred to in the study by de Jerusa Ferreira, but without identification of title, publisher, or date.

Admonition

[LM1]

With the titles of *de Livro de São Cipriano, Tesouro do Feiticeiro, Hectameron, Cruz de São Bartolomeu e São Cipriano, Verdadeiro Tesouro de Magia Blanca e Negra*, and others of similar fashion circulated a great variety of grimoires printed in many different idioms supposed to be, in each case, a close copy of the book which, according to legend, Satanas himself delivered to the famous magician (soon converted to the doctrines of the true God), after yielding to his powerful conjurations and formulae.

We do not need to strain ourselves too much to see that none of the magical works that are supposed to be heirs to the occult wisdom of this Christian martyr have higher value of authenticity than the ones of similar fashion supposedly written by the Popes Leo and Honorius, and even Solomon himself, to whom is given the paternity of the *Clavicule*. It is enough to open for a moment any of these grimoires to clearly see the many contradictions, falsities, and anachronisms contained in them which show that they would not resist attacks from the most elementary historical and literary criticism.

In fact, there is a big difference between the *authentic* books of Saint Cyprian and the many apocryphal editions that are circulated. The former represent an ancient grimoire, written by someone who displayed undeniable expertise in the magical arts; the latter are nothing more, in the majority of the cases, than bastardized copies of the former, and ill-drafted collections of goetic recipes, taken without discernment from any place, often referring to the recollections of popular tradition. In a number of these poor copies, the lack of original elements is compensated for with the fantasies of the anonymous and callous compilers, in which many mistaken teachings are founded, creating purely superstitious and ineffectual accounts.

Our edition, which reunites in a single tome the three books that are considered to be *authentic,* is for this reason the most complete and unique Spanish edition that reproduces the texts that exclusively make reference to the legend of the magical powers of Saint Cyprian. Its authenticity therefore gives it all the value that it traditionally enjoyed and allows the lovers of these kinds of studies to judge for themselves the content of the work, without the intervention of narrators who, under the shadow of the reputed title, offer a hundred modern and giddy fantasies mixed with dubious formulae of equally dubious provenance.

Enediel Shaiah
S.:/I:.

The Ancient and True Manuscript of this Book was Found in the Tower of Tombo[39]

[ALC]

The first reference made to the existence of the manuscript of this book is found in a parchment from the Tower of Tombo, in which the following is read:

> And there was in that village a man of very bad instincts, who seemed to be in allegiance with the devil; and he was denounced by his closer neighbors as a witch and a sorcerer, and the Holy Office soon arrested him. And he had with him a book of witchcraft and magic and other demonic things, the aforementioned book was completely written on parchment with black and red ink and it was sewed on the spine with thin stripes made from the same parchment. And the man did not want to tell where he had hidden the manuscript so the Holy Office could not go search and burn it. And so obdurate was that man in his mistake, that even when threatened with death at the stake he remained obstinate and did not confess in which place he had hidden it. And he was consumed by fire, but

---

39 The Tower of Tombo belongs to the Castle of São Jorge, a fortification of Moorish origin in the city of Lisbon.

the manuscript remained in a unknown place. And it was said to contain magical formulas and enchantments from the Arabs, Assyrians, Chaldeans, Hebrews, Moors and Phoenicians. And although it was translated in more than half to the Portuguese language, it had parts in runes, and others in Hebrew letters, and also in the letters of the Greek and Arabic alphabet. And that was so the people who saw it could not know what was written. And in the first page of the book which was used as the cover, was its name, which was: The Ancient Book of Saint Cyprian the Giant and True Cover of Steel.

This document belongs to the thirteenth century and, until now, constituted the oldest reference in Portuguese lands. However, further documents mention similar books found in diverse places in Portugal and Italy. In one of these documents, dating to the 14th century, there is the following narrative about some excavations made in a village located in the south of that country:

When digging into the soil to build the foundation of a temple, suddenly the spade of one of the men hit a hard object which seemed to be made of iron. And digging around it, he managed to take from the earth a vase, entirely made of glassy clay which was closed on the top to avoid humidity getting inside, and because it looked to him to be some serious stuff, that man took the vase and carried it to the Bailiff of that region, the Bailiff being a man of great study and knowledge. Having opened the vase, he found inside it a book made of parchment, inside which were written many conjurations, exconjurations, exorcisms, prayers and spells. And the words were written in black ink with the initial letters of each chapter written in red ink; and although the majority were written in Portuguese or Italian languages, there were also parts written in Hebrew and

Arabic, and others in runes. And soon the Bailiff saw that it was a thing of witchcraft and magic, and he thought that if he kept that manuscript he would have difficulty with the Holy Office; because of this he told the man who brought it that he could go back to work and that it was nothing. And the Bailiff broke the vase right there for the man see. but kept the manuscript to hide it later. And so he did, but it is not known if he took profit from the manuscript, keeping it as he promised to do.

And it seems that was the same manuscript that the sorcerer had buried centuries before to avoid the Holy Office destroying it.

There are many references in the great manuscript which would be frowned upon by the Holy Office because of its magical form and the great many parts which could be considered anti-Christian. In effect, the book is a true mixture of Christian prayers with Pagan conjurations: There are petitions addressed to God and to the saints of the Church as much as there are conjurations and invocations to the forces of good and evil, and it is precisely with these forces that magicians work, because generally they do not appeal to God or to the devil, but instead to metaphysical power.

However, the manuscript never came to be printed: initially because the press was not invented, and later because magical manuscripts could not be printed, in reason of their extraordinary characteristics. The manuscript was always copied by hand, as is fitting for books of its kind, as it was believed that, if such a text were composed and printed in typed letters, it would lose part of the force it had.

TO THE FAITHFUL READERS

[TDH]

Here I present to you a book of inestimable value, *The Complete Treatise of True Magic*, written by the German monk Jonás Sufurino. My love for this genre of work always brought me to search in piles of old books, eager to find something that would be little known on the subject. After many years of tiring investigations, my efforts were rewarded. The finding of *The Complete Treatise of True Magic* filled me with great satisfaction.

I found it between others of the same kind, in a small library of a curate in a small village. It was written in German, a language unintelligible to me. But, because of some images throughout the text, and because of some proper names scattered here and there, I deduced that the strange text was about magic. I gave it to an erudite, who carried out his work with great care. When I read the translation, I saw that the small book was in fact inestimable. Composed by the aforementioned German monk Jonás Sufurino, librarian of the monastery of Brocken, the mountain where, according to old legends, the devils and the witches celebrate their covens and macabre dances, the book turned out to be a rich treasure of the true magic.

Said book contains, in effect, the most essential information that can be found in the genre, like the o *Libro de San Cipriano, La Clavícula de Salomón, Innovaciones Pactos y Exorcismos, La Gallina Negra o Escuela de Sortilegios, El Gran Grimorio* or *El Pacto de la Sangre, Candela Mágica para Descubrir Encantamientos, Recopilación de la Magia Caldea o Egipcia*, philtres, enchantments, sorceries, and sortileges.

What was exposed above is enough to make it clear that this is a book of exceptional importance and that, if it is studied with true interest, many useful and profitable things can be learned.

It rests only to recommend that great care be taken in the way and time in which the experiments are done, so they can give the desired result: We must not forget that a small detail is often enough to destroy the best-prepared magical operation.

The Translator

TO THE ENTIRE WORLD

I, Jonás Sufurino, monk from the monastery of Brocken, solemnly declare, prostrated on my knees before the starry firmament, that I had dealings with higher spirits from the infernal court, in Hebrew characters.

I vow that what is contained in this book is the truth. I was an unbeliever, but the evidence took me away from that error. Since I was a child, I was enthusiastic about the study of sciences, and when I became of age, there was no area of knowledge into which I did not delve deeply. But, at the bottom of all of them, there was emptiness to be found. My soul was bewildered, thirsting to find the supreme hidden truth. When I pledged myself as monk in the monastery of Brocken, in keeping with my passion, I asked for the place of librarian, and there, in its vast and very ancient library, I isolated myself completely, passing through the years into the most deep and mysterious studies.

There were countless volumes discussing the Magical Arts. A simple reading from a few of them convinced me that this was what I was looking for. I made the following conclusions: There is no doubt that good and bad spirits exist and that they form relationships with men; there is no doubt that said spirits are endowed with a sovereign intelligence, as religion itself allows them the power to tempt us, to induce us towards good or evil; so, if through magic a man can develop a relationship with these spirits, this man will reach the supreme wisdom.

I was making all these conclusions in my lonely cell and between the dusty books in my library, but I had not yet dared to put into practice the means that would take me to such an end. I decided I must, in order to continue my project.

It was a stormy winter night. The sky looked very dark, covered with huge clouds that, for moments, were illuminated in the reddish flash of lightning. The wind howled horribly between the peaks of the mountain. The rain lashed against the glass in the windows of the monastery. I was not afraid. I waited for midnight. When all the monks had retired to their cells, and perhaps were sleeping, I silently left the monastery and marched to the highest peak of the mountain. When I reached the most high, I stopped. The lightning clashed incessantly over my head. I persisted in my purpose of invoking the King of Hell. The storm lashed against my body and furiously twisted my monastic frock.

But I, firm as the rocks beneath my feet, did not get scared, and I did not hesitate. I judged then it was the right time to call the Devil.

"If it is true that you exist," I screamed with a loud voice, *"oh, powerful Genius of Hell, present yourself to my sight!"*

And at this very moment, during a formidable lightning, there appeared the Infernal Spirit I had invoked.

"What do you want from me?"

"I want," I answered, *"to develop a relationship with you."*

"Granted," he replied. *"Return to your cell. There you shall have me whenever you want; I will reveal to you all the secrets of this and other worlds. I will give to you a book that will be as a catechism of the secret sciences, a catechism that only the initiated can understand."*

And he disappeared. I returned to the monastery. I came to see again my great and mysterious friend whenever it was necessary to me. He, finally, revealed to me the book I leave to posterity, as the golden key which opens and deciphers the supreme secrets of life and nature, completely ignored by the unbeliever or vulgar beings. So mote it be.

Monastery of Brocken. Year of the Grace, 1001.
Jonas Sufurino

Introduction

Where shall be seen the origin and foundation of this book

Having asked Lucifer about fulfilling the promise he made to me in the storm above the mountain, he delivered to me a book written in Hebrew characters on virgin parchment, saying to me,

"This book, written in Hebrew, is the same possessed by the great Cyprian, given to him by me when he forced me by the virtue of a powerful talisman he possessed. It served him to acquire knowledge of the True Magic, with which he acquired dominion over spirits and people. With it he became all-powerful, as you shall also become, if you meditate and execute everything this book contains. I must warn you to never depart from it, and if you wish to burn or throw it into a river, you will find it always in the room you use as a dormitory."

I became very astonished hearing these words, and I asked him to satisfy my curiosity, explaining to me the cause of such a marvel.

"It is very simple," he told me. "This book is washed in the great lake of the Red Dragons that exist in my domains, and because of this none of the elements of the universe can destroy it. Its pages cannot be cut or pierced. Fire is extinguished when it touches it, and water does not wet it."

"And how do you explain that if I throw it far away it returns to my bedroom?" I asked.

"You are very curious, but today I want to please you in everything. This book carries on its pages the cabalistic signs of the Red Dragon and the

Infernal She-goat, or She-goat of the Art, and by the magical virtues of these it will be transported to your room and follow you everywhere, being invisible to everyone but you and the ones who make a pact with you. Do with it as many tests as you want, and you will behold great wonders."

That said, he vanished.

I was struck by these revelations, so that a lot of time passed without myself being aware of what happened, until at last I focused on the book that was within reach and looked like it was inciting me to read it.

I was torn between dread and a curiosity to open it when I remembered that Lucifer told me it was written in Hebrew, a language not known by me. Because of this I felt more at ease, and I turned the first page, expecting to find signs I could not understand.

It was not like that, however, because with great admiration I could read perfectly what was written in many pages, and I found on one of them beautifully drawn a Dragon and a She-goat in a peaceful attitude. The She-goat had traced on her knees some hieroglyphs saying "Art." Everything seemed to be very strange, but in fact everything became familiar as I proceeded reading; but the greater of the surprises was yet to come.

The Dragon and the She-goat started to become animated, to move their eyes, and to grow in size and, finally, stepping out of the book, they prostrated before me, saying with a human voice:

"I am your servant; command and you will be obeyed."

The voice of the She-goat had a tone resembling the bleat of a lamb, and the Dragon had a voice as hoarse and deep as the lowing of a bull.

I was impressed with what I was seeing, but beholding the humble attitude of these animals, I gathered strength and told them:

"I desire nothing now, but if you wish, tell me how I will call you when I need you and what kind of services you can provide to me."

The She-goat, speaking for both, told me:

"I am called Barbatos and this is Pruselas: We are under the jurisdiction of Satanachia, our chief, who is helper to the great Emperor Lucifer and great general of his armies. He sent us to be at your side and obey you in everything, whenever what you command is in agreement with the pact

The Origins of The Book

made with our sovereign Lord. We shall always be at your side, and it will be enough to name one of us to have both at your service."

"That is good," I said to them. *"You can depart."*

As soon as I had spoken these words, without knowing how, they had disappeared from my sight.

Trying to distract myself from so many emotions, I went for a walk, and as understanding grew in my soul, the wonderful happenings came to look more natural.

After that, whilst it was necessary for me to resort to my servants or to their superior chiefs, we could treat each other as true friends, without surprises or fear of any kind. With the objective of being cautious with the possibilities the future held, I proposed to myself to make one copy of the book, with the following written on the title page:

Complete Treatise of the True Magic

or

Treasure of the Sorcerer

There is a dedication, in the following way:

We dedicate this book to the new adept of the unknown sciences.
~ LUCIFER

Under this dedication, the following note is found:

I declare that this book showed me the true wisdom, achieving with its study complete dominion over all creation.
~ CYPRIAN, THE MAGE

Spells *of* Saint Cyprian or the Marvels *of the* Devil

[GLT]

TRUE STORY
THAT HAPPENED IN THE KINGDOM OF GALICIA

Chapter I

From a book lauded in France, entitled The Occult Sciences, *by Mr. Zalotte, we extracted the story that follows:*

Victor Siderol was a ploughman in the village of Court, five leagues away from Paris. This man had great intelligence, and, understanding that the lands of his village were not worthy of such a skilled husbandman, he began to leave part of them uncultivated, resulting in a diminished harvest.

The neighboring farmers, who did collect a great harvest at Saint Michael's day, called him a nickname that offended him and, day by day, made him more miserable.

One afternoon after sowing seeds, he felt a great sadness and released his oxen, leaving the yoke over the plough, and said:

"There I leave you forever, my old plough; may the Devil take you, as with all the rest of the farming utensils I have at home."

When Siderol finished this utterance, he heard resounding in the air these words, which seemed as though they were coming from the bowels of the earth:

"*Take the yoke from it, because I do not want anything that forms a cross.*"

The ploughman, trembling with fright, put the yoke over the back of the oxen, hurried them along, and ran away to the house with his hair standing on end, and almost speechless.

In the next day at dawn, he rose, and, going to the porch of his house, he saw that the farming utensils had vanished, as if by enchantment.

He went then to the place where he left the plough, and it was also nowhere to be seen.

A few days later, he sold his house and all his lands. When this was done he went to Paris, rented a room in the Saint-Honore street, and when he pulled up a wooden slat from the floor to hide the little money he carried, he found a small book of spells, of which he had heard about in his village, but that he completely ignored.

It was the *Spells of Saint Cyprian*.

Chapter II

Inside this surprising book, Siderol saw that he could put himself in close and magical relationship with the unclean spirit.

"*This occult commerce,*" said Victor, "*can have nothing satisfactory for a good man, but it also does not tarnish his nobility, and maybe for that reason I will make my fortune through a pact with Lucifer. The king of Hell must be my friend, as I so freely gave him my plough and collection of tools.*"

After thoroughly studying the magical book, he went down to the courtyard of his residence, where an old lady raised chickens that gave her excellent fresh eggs, cautiously opened the door of the poultry yard, caught a black hen appropriate to the diabolical conjurations, and marched without delay to the crossroads between Revolta and Nevilly; because the devil singularly infects the crosses formed by the meeting of four ways.

He stopped at that place, drew a circle around himself with a wand of hazelnut, put the hen inside, and at midnight he spoke three words that I will not teach you here, because there are too many tempting spirits amongst us and I do not want to promote now, in the beginning of the story, the fantasy of increasing their numbers.

Just after the words were pronounced, the hen began to squawk and died harmoniously singing praises to God.

At this moment, the earth shook, and soon after this convulsion, the moon, entirely stained with specks of blood, descended quickly over the crossroads of Nevilly, and as soon as it rose again to its place, a great lord appeared outside the circle, though he could not enter through the virtue of the magical words.

He was a corpulent man, taller than Siderol, and with much grandeur, who had the large horns of a ram on his head, a long monkey tail which moved graciously between his legs, goat feet, and above all that a pocket wig and a scarlet raiment with gold embroidery, because it is usually in this attire that the devil appears to humans. If at any time you call for him, you will see, full of horror, the figure I just described.

As soon as the peasant saw this great lord, he felt afflicted by an extraordinary cold, and certainly no man, no matter how fearless he judges himself to be, would have enough courage to face the king of the ghosts. When the great lord spoke, his fright increased, because the devil has the power to terrify with the metal of his voice.

When the great lord stopped speaking, the peasant was stunned and felt too embarrassed to answer, because in truth he was not ready in spirit to talk with such a strange apparition.

The question addressed to Siderol was as simple as it was short:

"What do you want from me?"

This is what the devil usually asks of whoever forces him to appear.

Siderol hesitated for a while before deciding to ask, because he had many things on his mind that he wanted to possess, and in such circumstances, he wanted to choose the object that would make him lucky and prosperous, as it is a rule that the demon will only grant one thing each time he is called by somebody.

This illustration, originally published in editions of the Dragon Rouge in the chapter about the "Secret de la Poule Noir," was reprinted in many different grimoires, including the Spanish version renamed "Los Secretos del Inferno." It may have inspired the crossroads scene where Victor Siderol calls the Devil. The text of the Poule Noir, instead of mentioning three words, says that the following words must be said three times: "Eloim, Essaim, frugativi et appellavi." Waite, who reproduced the image, used instead "Euphas, Metahîm, frugativi et appellavi." The illustration was kindly supplied by Felix Castro Vicente.

The Origins of The Book

Chapter III

The French man kept changing his mind as to what he wanted so often and so quickly, and did not make a decision. But the great lord awaited with a submissive and reverent look, and he finally decided, and told him want he intended.

The peasant remembered, finally, that the promise of a rich, beautiful, and seductive future had abused his good faith, and now he wished to be able to read it as easily as he could the textbook of religious doctrine that he learned by heart as a child at school.

He thought that the gift of predicting the future had its advantages, which extended to everything, and that by this system he could guide his conduct and acts, and thus would achieve the possession of every good he could imagine. It is through this method that, after reflections and titanic combats, men could definitively understand their predilections.

When offered a wish, a farmer would ask for snow to fall over his neighbor's fields; a poor priest would ask for the dissolution of the properties of the clergy; a despot, the restoration of the old regime; a wrinkled lady, the return of her lost beauty; a spoiled libertine, the returning of his old vigour; a supplier to the army, one eternity of war; and a visionary, immortality, something no demon could give him.

But Victor asked that the great lord reveal to him the future by speaking in his ear, every time he demanded it, to which the demon agreed, with very good will and very good manners.

Then the devil took from his pouch a quart of marked paper, over which was written a formal pledge of the soul of the donor. He pierced with his staff Victor's little finger, who signed the writ with his own blood, and the devil vanished from his sight after bowing deeply to him.

But the peasant, before deciding to put into practice the art he just bought in exchange for his soul, realized that he had no food, and he did not remember to bring any money with him.

So he asked his familiar demon where he could find at that hour a meal that belonged to no one, because although he was willing to give himself to the devil, he lacked the strength to steal anything.

The spirit answered him:

"*At this hour that is veiled to mankind it is not convenient that you fill your stomach. At four o'clock in the morning leave your house, march at sunrise, and you will find a pile of stones. One of them is carved like a pillar. Raise it and take what you will find there.*"

Chapter IV

The ex-peasant could not allow himself to believe that under a pile of stones he could find a prepared meal that did not belong to anyone. However, as he was sure that the devil could never break the promises he makes to those who pledge him their soul, and an empty stomach demands faith, he did exactly what was ordered by his oracle.

When the time came, he went to the place and walked for a long time without finding the pile of stones. He became desperate and once again called his devil.

The evil spirit confided in his ear:

"*You still have very little faith in my power, and this is the reason you cannot find the stones I spoke about. Do you see that palace far away and those stones piled in a corner?*"

"I see."

"*So, it is right there; go and eat at your will.*"

In fact, the peasant found there what his stomach needed. After walking around, he found the pillar-stone, which had a lever in its base. He turned it around and found under it three planks of wood. He raised them and found a hole where he saw a large dish with a turkey inside, two chickens, and six roasted quails. By the side of the door, there were two big cheese wheels, a loaf of bread and two cakes from Saboya, neatly packed in a towel, and two bottles of wine from the Canary Islands.

The starving peasant, ecstatic at the sight of these things, took from his pouch a handkerchief, and into it he packed, the best way he could, part of the contents which were inside the happy hole, and with hurried steps he took his leave.

The Origins of The Book

Arriving at home, he ate with great appetite the quails, part of the chicken and part of the turkey, and drank with it the two delicious bottles of wine.

But, although his stomach did not complain for food, Siderol did not want to limit himself to only that enjoyment. To acquire the rest, he called his demon and asked if he knew the whereabouts of some hidden treasure that did not belong to anyone.

"*In the bowels of the mountain Carballo is an unknown mine of gold.*"

"*And how can I find it?*"

"*With the cabalistics of the Moors.*"

"*And where is it?*"

"*I will tell that to you soon. But, tell me, do you like to give alms to the poor?*"

"*I do.*"

"*So give to them all the money you have, because as long as you possess even one cent, the earth will not open to give to you the riches it hides within.*"

"Well," said the peasant, "tomorrow I will get rid of everything I own. But, my friend Belzebuth, tell me where else there is any other treasure?"

"*In the village of Meirol there is a cut of diamonds which will open with two of my cabalistic words.*"

"Oh, my lord, tell me. . ."

"Wait!" said the devil, "*First you will know where the treasures lie; afterwards, I will deliver the key to open them.*"

"Come on, friend Lucifer, tell me now where there is a treasure I can find today, and I promise to be faithful all my life and even after death."

"*Did I not tell you, sold soul, that first you have to give everything to the poor?*"

"Ah! Yes, yes; forgive me, my good friend, my benevolent Satanaz."

"*Very well; one proprietor from Bayonne, who is the owner of everything that is there, some three leagues from here, buries every year many hundreds of gold coins inside a purse he has at Biarritz. So you can see that a very rich treasure will be there that you can take, without the need to use words of mine.*"

"But this money is owned by somebody, and I do not want it for me. I only want money that is no longer owned by anyone."

"What do my plans matter to you? You are now entirely my property, and I command you to do whatever I want!"

And with this, Lucifer started to whisper some unintelligible words, before which the peasant fell on his knees, asking forgiveness.

"Calm down," said Lucifer to him. "*I know what I can do to help you. This old usurer will die suddenly tomorrow night, and because he hides from his relatives who did not treat him well, they know not—and never will—of this treasure, that on this same night will be under my power, as will the soul of the old man from Bayonne.*"

"But where is this land which holds such riches?"

"It is near the road of Santiago, far to the North, near the sea."

"My friend Satanaz, what is this country called?"

"It is in the Hispanic plain, in furthest North. . ."

"Then I will never arrive there, because I will die of hunger halfway."

"Don't be a fool. Arriving at the Pyrenees, sit on the road and wait for the pilgrims who come from Rome, those vile dogs who will not sell their souls in exchange for my gifts. You can then go with them, and you will find the treasure of the soon-to-be dead man. Go; march without delay."

"No. You go first to find it," said the ex-peasant humbly.

"Not me," answered the devil. "We did not agree that I would do the work. You asked me for the gift of prediction, and I gave it to you; here ends my commitment."

"Devil, devil! I will do what you command me; but don't you know of any other treasure?"

"I do; in that far away kingdom, there is more gold buried than any other land where the language of the Arabs and Moors is spoken."

"Name the places for me, my kind Belzebuth."

"If you arrive there alive, ask for the villages I will name to you: Rubióz, Outeirello, Taborjo, Lañas, Infiesta, Hyga Buena, Guilbade, Sobroso, Pojeros, Budinhedo, Aranza, Guinza, Caritel, Mondim, Fraguedo, Celeiros, Foçára, Borbem, Mondariz, and—"

"So many, my lord!" interrupted Victor Sideol, amazed with such list of findings.

"Many more! In that country, there are more than a hundred enchanted treasures. You will find there the wealth of more than six kingdoms. Go, then, to your destiny and call me when you need help. As you gave your soul to me, I will make you happy."

"But how will I make the land open so I can extract all that gold?"

"Take this lamp. Transport yourself to the places I mentioned, kindle it whenever you wish for something, and you will be immediately served."

The ex-peasant bid farewell to Lucifer and went to distribute to the poor all the money he had. When he did not have anything left, he left and crossed a large town square. Although he was distracted by thinking about the devil, he noticed a store upon which hung a sign: *"Tomorrow the Gauleza lottery will be drawn."*

Victor realized that he could find fortune through a lottery ticket, but he did not have money to buy one.

Lost in this thought, he began to wander the streets randomly, and as on that day his rent finished, at night he took shelter in the ruins of an old house near Saint Martin.

As the night was dark, he lit his lamp. Suddenly, he saw by door, worn out by time, a gold coin from the age of Clovis.

Siderol was greatly surprised, because he had already forgotten about the virtues the demon told him were contained in the lamp.

He kept the money, and in the morning, he quickly called the demon and asked him, with a certain expression of humility:

"My friend, which numbers will be most rewarded in the game tonight?"

"The biggest five," answered the demon to him, "will be paid today in the numbers 7, 32, 49, 65, and 81."

"And the other prizes? Don't you know on which numbers they will be paid?"

"I know; but these you must leave for the poor. Do not be ambitious; do not desire everything for yourself."

The peasant resigned himself with the answer from Lucifer and went to buy the ticket. They gave to him the number 7. The shopkeeper laughed at him when Victor paid, with an expression of great knavery on his face.

"*Why are you laughing like that?*" Victor asked.

"*It is because this number comes blank!*" answered the broker, laughing even more.

"*Yes?!... Soon you shall see!*"

And Victor Siderol left the shop greeting the broker with all politeness.

In fact, at noon the prizes were drawn, and the goddess Fortune fulfilled her decrees because the devil was completely truthful in the fulfilling of his duties.

Chapter V

That lucky ticket gained him seventy-five thousand gold coins, which were equivalent to two hundred and forty million réis[40]. When Siderol later went back to the broker, the man was not laughing anymore; he offered him a chair to sit upon and paid him the prize.

The first thing Victor did with the money was eat in one of the best restaurants in the city. After feasting like a prince, he went to the tailor, dressed himself in the best suit he could find, shaved, and, taking residence in a good hotel, called his protector Lucifer.

"*What more do you wish?*" asked the demon.

"*My friend, where will I find a young, pretty maiden to be my lover?*"

"*In the Greek theater, where a tragedy by Aeschylus is being performed today,*" came the reply.

This beloved son of fortune then filled his pouch with gold and went to the theatre right away. Amongst the great number of people there, the majority being nobles, he found two women, one already old and the other in the splendor of youth, whose figure fascinated the man: What in the world could be more seductive than this woman?

He moved closer to them with the lack of embarrassment and fear inspired by his wealth. The young lady received him timidly; she pretended a naïve face and with some effort she managed to blush.

Victor was very satisfied to see her with such an innocent look.

---

40   Réis, plural of reais; old monetary unit of Portugal from 1430 to 1911.

The Origins of The Book

He declared his intentions to her, and she answered with honest innocence. The old lady, who called herself mother, came closer to them and said to Siderol that she was greatly satisfied with the union of the girl with such a distinct gentleman.

The presentation being finished, and Siderol being so well received by the two women, he offered his arm to the maiden, which she accepted without any hesitation.

A rich litter waited for them in the entrance hall of the theater. As soon as they got home, the ladies invited him to have supper and served him with all courtesy and civility.

During the supper, Siderol learned that these ladies were provincial and they were at Paris undergoing the legal proceedings of an inheritance, and they explained that the judge would accept two thousand gold coins to settle the lawsuit in their favor. Victor gallantly offered that sum.

They, however, refused with certain reserve, which made him suspect that they did not truly believe he had that much money to spend. So, as he had his money pouch full, he untied it and presented the money to them. They finally accepted but with the clause that they would make a formal declaration. He agreed.

The mother then went to the cabinet to write the declaration and left our man with the charming Rosa.

Siderol thought that after a loan of two thousand coins he could take some liberties, and so he did.

The maiden resisted him firmly, but at the same time without sourness. Virtue is strong enough to withstand the growth of vice. However, love and wine made him cunning and daring.

Rosa fought against the active hands of this man, full of such temerity, and while defending herself from his insistence, she drew back, stepping, without noticing it, on her dress and stumbling. Siderol took advantage of this and pushed her gently. With that impulse, she fell on the couch, and then... only they can confess what happened.

Certainly the reader should guess. I, on my side, have some idea...

Afterwards, the poor thing cried. He ran to dry her tears and, promising to marry her, asked her to not tell her mother. Rosa shrugged her shoulders in a sign of consent. The lady returned a while after and did not suspect anything, she had such good faith...

They started a new conversation, and Siderol invited them to have dinner the next day in his company, in the saloon they had rented in a hotel.

They went.

He had booked with a notary to be there at night, and in the afternoon went to buy a jewel box to offer to his fiancée, the purchase of which was so expensive that when he came back home only a few five hundred gold coins were left.

He gave the jewel box to Rosa and decided to go looking for the notary, who was late, to commit to paper the oath which would tie himself to the one who maddened his senses. The mother and the daughter gave him goodbye with all cordiality and asked him to not take too much time to come back.

Chapter VI

Victor returned after an hour with the notary.

He entered the saloon of the hotel in high spirits and ... not a living soul! He searched the entire building, called the owner of the hotel, asked for the two ladies, and discovered they had left.

Siderol had a foreboding feeling.

He went to the armchair where they had been sitting. The box was gone with the ladies and, in the place of the jewels and the money, he found a note saying: *"When a smart girl finds an ass, a simpleton, she cons him; this is the rule. In the future, before meddling in such affairs, study them first. We wish the lesson to be profitable for you."*

The unhappy Victor began to speak furiously against the devil.

Satanaz appeared and asked him:

"Was it me who caused you to become infatuated with this woman?"

"No," answered Siderol.

"So, you do not have reason to complain about me. For a man to be happy and enjoy my esteem, it is necessary that he do not get involved with

women of this kind. Tell me now: Did you ever hear that I am a great flirt, never committing to one?"

"No," answered Victor.

"This is the reason I achieve everything I want. If I involved women in my business, my works would never get any results."

"But, how will I retrieve the jewels and the money that ingrate took from me?"

"You cannot: Money that has fallen into the hands of adventurous women is the same as if it were enchanted inside the earth without the knowledge of the words to disenchant it."

"But with all your power, could you not get my jewels back?"

"No, because just now I told you I do not want anything that women are involved in. And furthermore, I did not commit myself to work for you, but to give you advice."

"Disappear from my sight, damned one! Disappear right now, as your power is so limited!"

And Victor made a ✠ in the ground.

Suddenly, the demon disappeared.

Victor was left musing, and after a few minutes, he remembered his lamp that would help him win some money again. When he looked for it, however, he could not find it. The demon had taken it with him.

Chapter VII

Siderol was exhausted and with very little money left, but he had learned to foresee the future in the *Spells of Saint Cyprian*, so he decided to write and publish *The Gaul Sorcerer* in Paris, in the place now called Saint Jacques Street.

An astrologer guaranteed him that it would sell many copies for good prices if he filled it with diabolical things.

Siderol managed, then, to write presages of the future, predictions, days in which some high persons of the Church would die, and the bishop decided to have him arrested for being a sorcerer and prepared for him some grates to make him roast for the love of God.

Victor, shivering with fright, called once again to Lucifer, and after asking for forgiveness of his faults, begged to be saved from that danger, which the devil refused.

"*So, what use is the art of prediction to me, infernal spirit, if I cannot escape the persecutions made against me?*"

"*I told you myself where you could find rivers of money, so why involve women? Why write predictions instead of digging up these the treasures? Who told you to bet on the lottery?*"

"*And who invented it, as with all other games?*"

"*It was me,*" answered the devil.

"*Why?*"

"*To bring an end to wicked souls, so that they end their days quicker and the sooner I can take care of them.*"

"*In that case, it is you who drives people towards murder, patricide, and theft?*"

"*What? Do you not yet understand the true and powerful enemy hand which drags humankind toward all excesses?! The game never gave happiness to anyone. Go, go dig the lands I indicated to you and take care of the treasures that are yours. Walk, march! Beyond the old Toletum[41] you will find gold upon gold, and you will say, then, that it was good indeed you made pact with me.*"

And the devil opened the door of the jail for him.

Victor left. He crossed the Pyrenees and took fifty days to cross the Barjacova. In the passage of the province of Valladolid to the kingdom of Galicia, he felt very tired and noticed that the soles of his shoes had completely worn down.

He called his spirit and said:

"*I am barefooted and hungry; give me footwear and food…*"

The devil appeared to him and, pointing forward with his forefinger, asked him:

"*Do you see over there that village between the groves of trees?*"

---

41   Toledo.

"I see."

"It is named Santiguoso; take that road, and you will find food upon a big splint of rock. Fill your stomach and walk to the North, where your fortune is waiting."

"But I cannot walk, my Lucifer; give me some shoes."

"No."

"Why, infernal spirit? Do you not have the power to provide for something so simple?"

"I do."

"So?"

"Listen to me with attention," said the devil. "Did the God you adored before giving yourself to me not say to mankind that he should earn his bread with the sweat of his brow?"

"He did, but I do not want to earn mine that way. I would rather go and disenchant the treasures you indicated to me."

"Very well. Your old God is the king of the heavens, and I am the king of hell. He gives his law to his vassals, and I give mine to mine. To enjoy my protection, it is necessary to make some sacrifices. Go to your destiny, because the reward is well worth the martyrdom of going there barefooted."

"Very well. So give me your blessing."

The devil blessed him, and the peasant left barefooted.

Chapter VIII

Marching always toward North, a few days later he arrived at Bembibre. On the way, he never went hungry, always finding food by invoking the name of the demon that possessed his soul.

In this village, however, no matter how much he called, the devil did not appear, and the hunger tortured Siderol. He went walking toward the river Camba and came upon a high cross ✠ of stone, covered with moss and ivy.

Seeing that symbol of the suffering of Christ, he stopped and trembled. Then, he called again the devil and asked for food. Not receiving an answer, he was about to kneel at the cross, when he felt in his face a gust of fire!

Victor, with the weight of that great pain, fell on the ground, forlorn. He rose after some minutes, looked around, but did not see anyone.

"This is the punishment for wanting to abandon me," said the devil to him. "Damned man! And with this contriteness you want to arrive at the places of treasure and disenchant them!"

"Pardon, pardon, god Lucifer, I have been so hungry!"

"Did I not tell you already, false friend, that my law requires patience? I did not give you food to eat to try your courage. Go, then, to your destiny, and do not betray me again, or else…"

The devil disappeared, and the ex-peasant followed his way, commending himself to his infernal protector.

Close to midnight, he stumbled upon a table by the side of the road, well-supplied with delicacies, and he feasted.

Having finished the meal, he commended himself to the devil again, contritely, and said:

"If I had another soul, I would with sound mind give it to that great lord of Hell…"

The great Lucifer appeared to him dressed as he had been in Nevilly on the occasion he had immolated the black hen and, giving him a hug, told him:

"Because you are such a good friend of mine, I do not want you to tire yourself anymore. Tell me this: Are you ambitious?"

"No, what I want is one treasure that will be enough for me to live without having to work and nothing more."

"Do you see that village in that clearing, which stretches until the base of the small hill?" asked the devil.

"I see, perfectly."

"So, there is no need to go further. That village is named Ababides. Go there; search for lodging and, tomorrow, around this time, go up the hill and light your lamp. At this time, you will pierce your little finger with this needle that I hereby give you."

And Lucifer manifested this needle, delivering it to Siderol.

"And then?" he asked.

"And then you will sign this paper with your own blood..."

"But I already gave my soul; what more exists in me that can be useful to my kind protector?"

"Listen carefully: In this paper is declared the sale of the soul of your children, to be born soon after you get rich. Because you will marry a woman much inclined to procreation."

"But..."

"Do you hesitate? Will you sign it or not?"

"I will sign... but after that...?"

"At midnight, as I said, a crow will perch over the mountain. The place it will scrabble is where the first treasure lies."

"But which words shall I use to open the bosom of the earth?"

"I will not tell you yet, because I fear the earth will open now if I did. Walk, march."

Chapter IX

Victor did everything the devil, his lord, told him to do.

Arriving at Ababides, at midnight on the next day, he waited, and a few minutes later, he saw perching at the crag the black crow. It scrabbled, pecked the ground three times with his beak, but the land remained as it was. There was not even the slightest movement.

Victor lit the lamp, and everything remained in the same state. Desperate, he marched, slowly, towards the bird. Seeing him coming closer, the bird simply flew away and disappeared.

Our man began to rant against the devil, demanding that he either give him the gift of opening the land or give him his souls back.

The devil appeared to him in the guise of a crow and told him:

"What did we agree to? Was it not settled that you would sign at this hour the souls of your future sons to me, with your own blood?"

"Forgive me, great lord," begged Siderol. "Forgive me; I had forgotten this."

And, immediately, he pierced his little finger and signed the writ with blood.

The devil, full with satisfaction, told him:

"Here I leave you; take all the gold you wish."

And taking flight, he disappeared.

Victor remained still, without knowing what to do, looking at the place where the bird had disappeared into the tenebrous darkness of the night.

Suddenly, he heard echoing in that solitude the words:

"*Aurea Hispania! Hiscere Gallaecos Romano!*"

In this moment, the mountain trembled, and an enormous mouth in the earth opened and allowed Siderol to see a large lattice containing golden Roman coins.

Taken by an instantaneous resolve, he went down through that crag which closed after him.

He took off his coat to fill it with money, but suddenly, he saw a big chest of brass, opened it, and found it full of the same metal. He took it over his shoulders, and then he saw the mountain had closed. He had been trapped.

Victor began to cry out about his bad luck with loud screams and put the box down atop the pile of gold.

"My Saint Devil, my powerful king, owner of my soul and of the souls of my unborn children, free me from this prison!" he said, between tears.

Suddenly, he felt the land trembling again in big convulsions and heard resounding in the hole the following words:

"*Hispania! Regicitur in publicum janua!*"

The great cavity opened again immediately, and Siderol found himself above the mountain with his chest of gold coins.

He walked for the rest of the night, and when the day broke, he found himself in the small village of Damil which was in the North.

He stayed in a poor inn, and for eight days, he kept himself barefooted and badly dressed, so as not to arouse suspicions and avoid being robbed of his treasure.

At the end of eight days, he found out there was a house for sale in the suburbs of that village.

He called the devil and consulted with him:

"What do you think of this land? I like these neighbors and could stay here."

"It is very nice," answered the devil. "Neither myself nor the enchanted spirits would allow you to take all this gold to a foreign country..."

"Why?" asked Siderol.

"From Spain you received it; in Spain you will enjoy it. There are beautiful and virtuous women in this region, very capable of giving moral lessons to the French with the passion of that Rosina you found at the Greek theater. So, stay here."

"So I will stay," answered Siderol.

"So, I bless you and you will be happy."

Lucifer, after blessing him, immediately disappeared.

Siderol, taking some coins of gold, soon left for the village of Allariz, searching for a priest who changed old money, returning in the next day to buy the house that was for sale, and there he took his residence.

Chapter X

Victor Siderol started, then, to understand what happiness gained through the means of money was, because he began to enjoy everything he liked; and because the fame of his wealth soon spread in that area, he found himself the target of much attention both from men and women.

As women had always been his delight, he started to look at all of them with great attention, and after a few months, he was married to a beautiful maiden from Podentes.

This interesting peasant girl was named Manuela.

One year passed, and she had given birth to a girl, whose soul the devil soon counted as his.

The parents saw themselves in that little angel and loved each other more and more. But, because fortune is not always truly complete in life, the Frenchman found himself severely ill one day.

He had a violent fever followed by derangement, and it affected him so badly that he did not have time to even consult with the devil.

His father-in-law asked for two doctors and put by his bed the best nurse in the area.

Maybe because of all this expert care, the fever diminished quickly, and Victor soon regained all his senses.

He, then, took the opportunity to know his luck and consulted with his devil.

He called him and asked:

"My Lucifer, where did the doctors see my illness?"

"On the opposite side."

"Is it deadly and fatal?"

"No."

"What must I do to heal it?"

"Send the doctors away and leave nature to its work. It is the only thing in control of the life of all mankind."

So he did, and nature healed him, but his convalescence was long. During it, however, Siderol had the chance of knowing the excellent heart of his beautiful Manuela, whose care never ceased at the head of his bed.

Chapter XI

Manuela was a very well-educated maiden, and was as merry as the Graces. She was also a very sensible girl, candid and cheerful, a woman that he needed, because an honored and rich man goes very well with a sensible and modest wife.

Siderol, after being completely recovered from his sickness, asked his devil how he could repay the wife for her care and kindness.

"Did you not give your hand in marriage?" asked the demon.

"I did."

"Don't you love her greatly?"

"I do."

"So, you pay her very well."

Ten years passed in uninterrupted harmony, and Manuela gave birth to eight children.

Victor, well off from the commodities of his wealth and by the seductive charms of his three girls and five boys, was enchanted by his luck and came to forget the offerings he had made to the devil.

But, one day, hearing a thunderstorm overhead, several bad memories passed through his mind between the clashes of lightning. They filled his imagination and poisoned all of his pleasures.

He thought he had bought such sweet joys with his condemnation, but he had to repay the venture on earth at the highest price!

After that, he began to walk sadly and in deep thought. Manuela felt the sorrow of her husband, even more because she did not know the reason for it. The most tender caresses, the most fervent pleading from her could not reveal the secret of that sadness.

Siderol wished to know if the eternal stakes would be lighter for him in the extremes of old age or if death was near. He was going to ask the devil when he was destined to die, because although he had lost his soul, he wanted, at least, to enjoy the satisfaction of going to disenchant more of the treasures the demon had appointed to him.

Chapter XII

Siderol was deep in his thoughts when without warning Manuela presented herself, accusing him of not loving, because he did not trust his secrets to her.

Would he keep quiet if the secret was of a different nature? Would he not confide his secrets to the bosom of his wife, who would sweeten their bitterness?

Certainly not.

Manuela could not resign herself with that silence and continued to press him with such insistence that Siderol saw himself faced with the need to confess to her, full of sorrow, that he had made a pact with the devil.

Manuela, who had been educated in the Christian way, trembled and ran away, saying that she did not want to live with a condemned man. She feared that the punishment for it was a contagious evil which could be caught with cohabitation.

Young and naïve as she was, inexperienced with the ways of the world, she went straight to tell her mother, in whom her confessor had recommended she place unlimited trust.

The mother, who was not afraid of anything, exclaimed that it was not possible that such a kindhearted man was damned and that she could not believe he was.

The good Manuela insisted in her purpose, and the old Galician lady said that, if what her daughter was telling her was the truth, she would undo everything.

That said, she decided that the holy parish priest of Campo de Moura, which was far from there, should come and put his stole over Victor's head and recite the Gospel of Saint John, because the tip of a stole has prodigious power. She said that three or four exorcisms should be added to this and that, willingly or not, the demon would deliver, without fail, the writs Victor had signed.

The old lady quickly sent a servant, on horseback, to call the old parish priest from Cobello, who came in the following day to perform the exorcisms of Siderol.

But the devil, who is always alert, does not allow the souls that belong to him to escape easily. Seeing the preparations to dispossess him of what belonged to him, he threatened Siderol that if he returned to the church, he would throw him into the depths of Hell!

At this threat, Victor started to scream loudly, to which the mother-in-law ran to help, and she put into the pouch of his trousers a small vial of holy water, with the express order to not remove it.

Manuela observed that it would be good to read the Gospel at this moment, as the feverish state Victor was in would be very uncomfortable for him.

Chapter XIII

They left for the church. The devil, furious at being in danger of losing that soul, was spinning around Siderol, but the magical virtue of the holy water kept him away, and the mother-in-law laughed at his impotent rage.

When they arrived at the church, the good priest opposed his enchantments against the devil's, and the condemned Siderol began to foam at the mouth and to twist his arms and legs. He forced his mouth towards his ears, and after this unusual contortion of his muscles, the devil left the signed writs at the altar.

This happened because the Guardian Angel of Victor appeared at that time over the head of the exorcised, with his golden hair, bluish wings, and white robe.

The priest, finally, had Victor fully confess, because now he had license to absolve him, having snatched him from the claws of Satanaz.

After they had finished the ceremony, Siderol, Manuela, and the mother-in-law returned home. Manuela, at night, did not fear the contamination of damnation anymore and wanted to sleep with her husband in the bed where they had always rested.

They continued to live very well, thanks to the treasure Siderol had disenchanted with the power of the devil, whom he deceived in the end with the protection of the Holy Church.

Siderol, after a happy life, gave his soul to the Creator, in a property he had bought at Sabajares, at 109 years old, leaving his wife with seven sons, eleven grandsons, and three great-grandsons.

Chapter XIV

The people of the village, knowing the way through which Siderol became rich and wishing to imitate him, sometimes used to say Manuela:

"*Ai, if I could guess this, or foresee that, how happy I would be!*"

Manuela invariably answered:

"*All this is very easy, doing what my husband did, but take care against the cunning of the devil.*"

"But he has so many treasures under his great power," many people replied with great curiosity.

"He has, certainly," answered Manuela. "*I do not say to you not to make a pact with him, but as soon as you get what you want, arm yourselves with holy water and throw yourselves into the arms of the Most Holy Church to enter the kingdom of Glory.*"

"*But why did your husband not disenchant the other treasures?*" they asked.

"*Because he did not need them. He used to say that in this country there are many poor people who can disenchant them. And so, if someone can take care of those riches, let God forgive them the sin of having making to make a pact with Satanaz.*"

*
* *

Manuela, who could not resist the longing for her husband, passed away three months later, the day after her 94th birthday.

Vita Cypriani

Conversio

Conversion of St. Justina and St. Cyprian

[SFT]

When our Savior Jesus Christ appeared on earth from heaven and the words of the prophets were fulfilled, the whole world was enlightened with the word and, believing in God, the Father Almighty, and in our Lord Jesus Christ, was baptized in the Holy Ghost. Now there was in the city of Antioch near Daphne a maiden named Justina, the daughter of Aidesios and Kledonia. From her nearby window, she heard from Praylios, a deacon, of the mighty works of God, of the incarnation of our Lord Jesus Christ, of the prediction of the prophets, of the birth from Mary, of the adoration of the magi and of the appearance of the stars, of the glory of the angels and of His signs and wonders, of the power of the cross, of the resurrection from the dead and of the testament to the disciples, of the ascension into heaven and of His resting there, of the seat at the right hand and of the unending kingdom. Seeing and hearing these things from the deacon through the window, the holy virgin could no longer withstand the ardent urging of the Holy Ghost but desired to appear before the deacon face to face, and as she could not, she said to her mother: "Mother, hearken to me, thy daughter. The idols that we worship day by day, which are put together of stones and bits of wood, gold and silver and bones of dead animals, are as nothing. One of the Galileans, if he come upon them, will overcome them all with the word through prayer, without raising a hand."

Her mother, engulfed in the subtleties of philosophy, replied: "Let not thy father know of this thought."

Justina answered: "Be it known to thee, Mother, and to my father that I seek the Christ whom I learned to know through Praylios, our neighbor, hearing about Him for many days. There is no other god in whom one shall be saved." And having said these things, she went away to offer her prayers to Christ by herself.

Her mother, in bed, told all these things to Aidesios. And when they had lain awake for a long time and when the host (of angels) had now approached, Aidesios sees more than a hundred torchbearers in the fortress and, in their midst, Christ who said to them: "Come unto me and I will give you the Kingdom of Heaven."

Aidesios, having seen these things and being astounded at what he had seen, arose at dawn and took his wife and the maiden and went with Praylios into the house of the Lord. And they demanded of him that he bring them to the bishop Optatus. The deacon announced them, and having fallen at the feet of the bishop, they demanded to receive the seal of Christ. But he hesitated until Aidesios told him of his vision of Christ and of the yearning of the maiden for Christ. Aidesios, however, cut off the hair of his head and beard, for he was a priest of the idols. And when he had fallen at the feet of the bishop, the three received the seal of Christ. And then Aidesios, after he had been deemed worthy of the office of a presbyter for a year and six months, departed in Christ.

And the holy virgin Justina went without ceasing into the house of the Lord. But a certain learned man, Aglaidas, of noble family and great wealth, an offense in his manner of living and carried away with the error of idolatry, saw the holy maiden going frequently into the house of the Lord and, having fallen in love with her, made advances to her through many women and men, seeking her in marriage. But she dismissed them all in disdain, saying: "I am betrothed to Christ." But the sophist collected a band and lay in wait for her as she went into the house of the Lord, wishing to gain her by force. Her companions cried out, and those of her household heard it and, coming out sword in hand, made them disappear. But Aglaidas grasped the maiden in his arms and held her fast. The maiden, however, made the sign of the cross and threw him violently on his back to the earth. And with her fist she beat his ribs and face black and blue, tore his garments, and sent him away conquered. And having done these things, like unto her model, Thekla, she proceeded into the house of the Lord.

Aglaidas, enraged, went to Cyprian the magician and agreed to pay him two talents of gold as if the latter were able by his magic to capture the holy virgin—not knowing, poor wretch, that the power of Christ is insuperable. But Cyprian with his magic arts summoned a demon. The demon came and said: "Why hast thou summoned me?"

Cyprian replied: "I love a maid of the Galileans. Tell me whether thou art able to procure her for me." The wretched demon gave his promise as though he had what he did not have. Cyprian said: "Tell me of thy deeds that I may have confidence in thee."

The demon said: "I became an apostate from God in obedience to my father; I threw the heavens into confusion; I cast down angels from on high; I deceived Eve; I deprived Adam of the delights of Paradise; I taught Cain to murder his brother; I stained the earth with blood; I caused thorns and thistles to grow; I assembled theatres; I caused adulteries; I brought together processions; I caused idolatry; I taught the people to make a calf; I prompted the crucifixion of Christ; I made cities to tremble; I tore down walls; I divided houses. Having done these things, how can I be powerless against her? Take, therefore, this philtre and besprinkle the house of the maid from without, and I will go and instill in her the spirit of my father and straightway she will give ear unto thee."

The holy virgin rose at the third hour of the night and made her prayers to God. And as she perceived the onset of the demon and the ardent desire of her reins, she aroused herself to her Master, and when she had sealed her whole body with the power of Him who bore the cross, she said with a loud voice: "O almighty God, O Father of Thy beloved son, Jesus Christ, Thou who hast cast into Tartarus the murderous serpent and saved those who were captured by it, Thou who alone hast spread out the heavens and established the earth, Thou who hast lifted up the torch of the sun and given light to the moon, Thou who hast formed man of earth in Thine own image and stamped him with Thine allwise spirit and placed him in the rapture of Paradise in order that he might enjoy the things created by Thee, who hast not abandoned him when he was banished from them through the guile of the serpent, but, O friend of man, didst call him back through Thy crossbearing power and, having healed his wounds, didst bring him into perfect health through Christ by whom the world has been established, the canopy of heaven spread out, the earth established and the waters stored up and all things recognize Thee as the true God over all, may it be Thy will to save Thy servant through Him and let temptation not touch me! For Thee and Thine only begotten son, Jesus Christ, I agreed to remain a maid." And when she had said these things and had sealed her whole body with the seal of Christ, she breathed upon the demon and put him to confusion.

But the demon went away in disgrace and stood before the face of Cyprian. Cyprian said: "Where is she for whom I sent thee? And why did I lie awake and thou hast missed the goal?"

And the demon said: "Ask me not for I cannot tell thee. I saw a sign and I trembled in fear."

But Cyprian mocked at him and, trusting in his magic arts, summoned a stronger demon. And the latter, boasting likewise, says to Cyprian: "I knew of thy command and of the incompetence of that demon. For that reason, my father sent me to put an end to thy plight. Take this philtre, therefore, and besprinkle her house round about, and I will come and prevail over her."

Cyprian took the philtre and did as the demon had told him. But when the demon came into the house of the virgin, the holy maid rose at the sixth hour of the night and said her prayers to God, saying: "At midnight, I arose to give thanks to Thee for the judgments of Thy righteousness. O Lord God of mercy, Thou law of those in the air and protector of those under the heavens and terror of those under the earth, who didst put the devil to shame and exalted the sacrifice of Abraham; who hast overthrown Baal and slain the dragon through Thy faithful Daniel and made known to the Babylonians the power of Thy divinity; who hast ruled over all things through Thine only begotten son, Jesus Christ; who hast enlightened those things which before were dark and given life to the members which were dead; who hast made rich the poor and set free those who were enslaved to death—be not unmindful of me, Thy maidservant, Thou holy and kindly king, but keep my members unspotted in purity and maintain the torch of my virginity unextinguished in order that I may go in with my bridegroom Christ and may give back in purity the flesh which Thou didst commit to me as a pledge in Christ, for Thine is the glory through Him for ever and ever, Amen." And when she had thus prayed she rebuked the demon in Christ and sent him away confounded.

But the demon, defeated in those things of which he had boasted, stood before Cyprian. And Cyprian said: "Where is she for whom I sent thee?"

The demon said: "I have been defeated and cannot say. For I saw a sign and trembled with fear."

Cyprian, at a loss, called a stronger demon, the father of all demons, and said to him: "What is this weakness of you demons that thy whole power has been overcome?"

The demon said: "I will presently deliver her to thee. Be thou ready."

Cyprian said: "What is the token of thy victory?"

The demon said: "I will agitate her with divers fevers, and after six days, I will appear to her at midnight and will make her ready."

So the demon went away and appeared to the holy virgin in the form of a maiden. And when she had seated herself on the couch, she said to the holy maid of God: "I also wish to discipline my body with thee today, for I was sent by Christ to live the life of a virgin. Tell me, what is this struggle for virginity and what is the reward? For I see that thou art much wasted away."

The holy maid said to the demon: "The reward is great; the struggle, small."

But the demon said: "How was it then that Eve was a virgin in Paradise, while she lived with Adam, but was afterward persuaded, bore children, and attained a knowledge of the good and the world was stocked with children?"

But when the demon was urgent that they pass out by the door, she became thoughtful and very much disturbed and recognized who it was who tempted her and she hastened to her prayers and, sealing herself with the sign of Christ, she breathed upon the demon and sent him away confounded. Recovering from her confusion, she put an end to her distress, saying: "I glorify Thee, Christ, Thou who dost preserve those oppressed by the enemy and dost guide Thy servants in the light according to Thy father's will, who drivest away with the rays of justice the spirits that cause trouble in the night. Grant that I be not overcome by the enemy. Nail fast my flesh to the fear of Thee and have mercy on me through Thy law and glorify Thy name, O Lord."

Deeply ashamed, the demon appeared before Cyprian. Cyprian said to him: "Thou wast conquered by one girl. What power is the source of her victory?"

The demon said: "I cannot tell thee, for I saw a sign and I trembled with fear. Wherefore also withdrew. If thou wilt know, swear to me and I will tell thee."

Cyprian said: "How shall I swear to thee?"

The demon said: "By the great powers which abide with me."

Cyprian said: "By thy great powers, I will not depart from thee."

The demon, taking courage, said: "I saw the sign of the crucified One and I trembled with fear."

Then Cyprian said: "Is the crucified One then greater than thou?"

The demon said: "He is greater than all. For whatsoever mistakes we make or whatsoever things we bring to pass here we shall receive our reward in the world to come. For there is a brazen fork and it is heated and placed on the neck of [the sinner, whether angel or] man; and thus with the hissing of fire the angels of the crucified One lead him to the tribunal and render unto each according to his works."

Cyprian said: "Therefore, I will also make haste to become a friend of the crucified One in order that I may not be subjected to such condemnation."

The demon said: "Thou hast sworn to me and breakest thou thine oath?"

Cyprian said: "I despise thee and fear not thy powers. For during [this] night I have been convinced that ye were overcome by the prayers and entreaties of the virgin and by the making of the sign of the crucified One, with which I seal myself and depart from thee." And saying these things he crossed himself and said: "Glory be to Thee, O Christ. Get thee hence, demon. For I seek after Christ." And the demon went away discomfited.

But Cyprian, having piled up his books, put them on youths and, having come into the house of the Lord and fallen at the feet of the blessed Anthimus, said: "O servant of the blessed Christ, I too desire to serve as a soldier of Christ and to be inscribed in the book of the living."

But the holy bishop, believing that he wished to tempt him, said to him: "Be content, O Cyprian, with them that are outside. Spare the church of Christ. For His power is invincible."

Cyprian said: "I also am convinced that it is invincible. For during this night I sent demons to the holy virgin Justina. And I recognized her prayers and that she overcame the demons with the seal of Christ. Take therefore the books with which I did evil and burn them in the fire and have mercy on me."

The bishop was persuaded and burned his books and blessed him and sent him away, saying: "Hasten, my son, into the house of prayer."

And Cyprian went into his house and shattered all his idols and all night long he beat his breast, saying: "How shall I dare to appear before the power of Christ when I have done so many evil things? Or how shall I bless Him with the mouth with which I have cursed holy men, calling on unclean demons. Therefore will I strew ashes on the ground and fall down upon them silently and beg for God's mercy."

And when it was dawn—it was the great Sabbath—he went into the house of the Lord. As he proceeded slowly on his way, he prayed, saying: "O Lord, if I am worthy to be called a perfect servant of Thine, grant me as I enter Thy house to hear a prophetic word from Thy holy scriptures."

And as he entered, the psalmist David said unto him: "Behold, O Lord: keep not silence: be not far from me."

And again from Hosea: "Behold, my servant shall deal prudently."

And again David: "Mine eyes prevented the night watches, that I might meditate in thy word."

And again Isaiah: "Fear not, Jacob my servant and beloved Israel, whom I have chosen."

And again the Apostle Paul: "Christ has redeemed us from the curse of the law, being made a curse for us."

Then the psalmist David: "Who can utter the mighty acts of the Lord? Who can shew forth all his praise?" Then the light of the Gospels. Then the sermon of the bishop. Then the prayers of the catechumens.

The deacon bade the catechumens withdraw. Cyprian remained seated, and Asterius the deacon said to him: "Go outside."

Cyprian said: "I have become a servant of the crucified One and dost thou cast me out?"

The deacon said: "Thou art not yet become perfect."

Cyprian replieth: "My Christ liveth who hath put to shame the demons, saved the virgin, and had mercy on me. Therefore, I will not go out unless I am become perfect." Asterius then brought the matter to the bishop. And the bishop bade him come, and when he had examined him thoroughly according to the law and had prayed with such fervor that creation was shaken, he took him and baptized him. And on the eighth day, he became a reader and expounder of the divine mysteries of Christ, and on the twenty-fifth day, subdeacon and doorkeeper of the divine mysteries of the sacred court, and on the fiftieth day, deacon of Christ. And grace against demons was with him, and he healed all suffering. He turned many away from the mad worship of idols and persuaded them to become Christians. And when the year was passed, he became the bishop's coadjutor, occupying for sixteen years a seat in the presbytery. Then the blessed Anthimus convoked the bishops of the cities round about, consulted with them concerning that which was expedient for the church, and then resigned to him the episcopal see. Within a few days, the sainted Anthimus departed in Christ, commending his flock to him. And when he had put his affairs in order, the sainted Cyprian appointed the holy virgin to the position of deaconess and called her Justina and made her mother of a convent. But Cyprian enlightened many and turned them away from every heresy and added them to the flock of Christ. To whom be glory and power for ever and ever, Amen.

II. Of S. Justina

Justina the virgin was of the city of Antioch, daughter of a priest of the idols. And every day she sat at a window by a priest who read the gospel, of whom at the last she was converted. And when the mother of her had told it unto her father in his bed, Jesus Christ appeared to them with his angels, saying: "Come to me, I shall give to you the kingdom of heaven." And when he awoke, anon they did them to be baptized with their daughter. And this virgin was strongly grieved and vexed of Cyprian, and at the last she converted him to the faith of Jesus Christ. And Cyprian from his childhood had been an enchanter, for from the time that he was seven years old he was consecrated by his parents to the devil. And he used the craft of necromancy and made women to turn into juments and beasts as them seemed and many other things semblable. And he was covetous of the love of Justina and burnt in the concupiscence of her and resorted to his art magic that he might have her for himself, or for a man named Acladius, which also burnt in her love. Then he called a devil to him, to the end that he might by him have Justina, and when the devil came, he said to him: "Why hast thou called me?"

And Cyprian said to him: "I love a virgin; canst thou not so much that I may have my pleasure of her?"

And the devil answered: "I that might cast man out of Paradise and procured that Cain slew his brother and made the Jews to slay Christ and have troubled the men, trowest thou I may not do that thou have a maid with thee, and use her at thy pleasure? Take this ointment and anoint withal her house without forth, and I shall come and kindle her heart in thy love, that I shall compel her to assent to thee."

And the next night following, the devil went and enforced him to move her heart unto unlawful love. And when she felt it, she recommended herself devoutly to God and garnished her with the sign of the cross, and the devil, along with all afraid of the sign of the cross, fled away from her, and came again to Cyprian and stood before him. And Cyprian said to him: "Why hast thou not brought to me this virgin?"

And the devil said: "I see in her a sign which feared me, that all strength is failed in me."

Then Cyprian left him and called another devil stronger than he was. And he said: "I have heard thy commandment and have seen the non-power of him, but I shall amend it and accomplish thy will." Then the devil went to her and enforced to move her heart in love and inflame her courage in things not honest.

And she recommended her to God devoutly and put from her that temptation by the sign of the cross and blew on the devil and threw him anon away from her. And he fled ail confused and came before Cyprian, and Cyprian said to him: "Where is the maid that I sent thee for?" and the devil said: "I acknowledge that I am overcome and am rebutted, and I shall say how, for I saw in her a sign horrible, and lost anon all my virtue."

Then Cyprian left him and blamed him and called the prince of the devils. And when he was come he said: "Wherefore is your strength so little, which is overcome of a maid?"

Then the prince said to him: "I shall go and vex her with great fevers, and I shall inflame more ardently her heart, and I shall arouse and bedew her body with so ardent desire of thee that she shall be all frantic; and I shall offer to her so many things that I shall bring her to thee at midnight." Then the devil transfigured himself in the likeness of a maid and came to this holy virgin and said: "I am come to thee for to live with thee in chastity, and I pray thee that thou say what reward shall we have for to keep us so."

And the virgin answered: "The reward is great, and the labor is small."

And the devil said to her: "What is that then that God commanded when he said, 'Grow and multiply and replenish the earth?' Then, fair sister, I doubt that if we abide in virginity that we shall make the word of God vain, and be also despising and disobedient, by which we shall fall into a grievous judgment, where we shall have no hope of reward, but shall run in great torment and pain."

Vita Cypriani

Then by the enticement of the devil the heart of the virgin was smitten with evil thoughts and was greatly inflamed in desire of the sin of the flesh, so that she would have gone thereto, but then the virgin came to herself and considered who that it was that spake to her. And anon she blessed her with the sign of the cross and blew against the devil, and anon he vanished away and melted like wax, and incontinent she was delivered from all temptation.

A little while after, the devil transfigured him in the likeness of a fair young man, entered into her chamber, and found her alone in her bed, and without shame sprang into her bed and embraced her and would have had a done with her. And when she saw this, she knew well that it was a wicked spirit, and blessed her as she had done before, and he melted away like wax. And then by the sufferance of God she was vexed with axes and fevers. And the devil slew many men and beasts, and made to be said by them that were demoniacs that a right great mortality should be throughout all Antioch, but if Justina would consent wedlock and have Cyprian. Wherefore all they that were sick and languishing in maladies lay at the gate of Justina's father and friends, crying that they should marry her and deliver the city of that right great peril. Justina then would not consent in no wise, and therefore everybody menaced her. And in the sixth year of that mortality she prayed for them and chased and drove thence all that pestilence. And when the devil saw that he profited nothing, he transumed and transfigured him in the form of Justina for to defoul the fame of Justina, and in mocking Cyprian he advanced him that he had brought to him Justina. And came to him in the likeness of her, and would have kissed him as if she had languished for his love. And when Cyprian saw him and supposed that it had been Justina, he was all replenished with joy and said: "Thou art welcome, Justina, the fairest of all women."

And anon as Cyprian named Justina, the devil might not suffer the name, but as soon as he heard it, he vanished away as a fume or smoke. And when Cyprian saw him deceived, he was all heavy and sorrowful, and he was then more burning and desirous in the love of Justina and woke long at the door of the virgin, and as him seemed he changed him sometimes into a bird by his art magic, and sometimes into a woman, but when he came to the door of the virgin, he was neither like woman or bird, but appeared Cyprian as he was. Acladius, by the devil's craft, was anon turned into a sparrow, and when he came to the window of Justina, as soon as the virgin beheld him, he was not a sparrow but showed himself as Acladius and began to have anguish and dread, for he might neither fly ne leap, and Justina, dreading lest he should fall and break himself, did do set a ladder by which he went down, warning him to cease of his woodness, lest he should be punished as a malefactor by the law. Then the devil, being vanquished in all things, returned to Cyprian and held him all confused before him, and Cyprian said to him: "And how art not thou overcome, what unhappy is your virtue that ye may not overcome a maid, have ye no might over her, but she overcometh you and breaketh you all to pieces? Tell me, I pray thee, in whom she hath all this great might and strength."

And the devil said: "If thou wilt swear to me that thou wilt not depart from me ne forsake me, I shall show to thee her strength and her victory."

To whom Cyprian said: "By what oath shall I swear?"

And the devil said: "Swear thou by my great virtues that thou shalt never depart from me."

And Cyprian said: "I swear to thee by thy great virtues that I shall never depart from thee."

Then the devil said to him, weening to be sure of him: "This maid maketh the sign of the cross, and anon then we wax feeble and lose all our might and virtue, and flee from her, like as wax fleeth from the face of the fire."

And Cyprian said then to him: "The crucified God is then greater than thou?"

And the devil said: "Yea, certainly he is greater than all others, and all them that we here deceive, he judgeth them to be tormented with fire inextinguishable."

And Cyprian said: "Then ought I to be made friend of him that was crucified, lest I fall hereafter into such pains."

To whom the devil said: "Thou hast sworn by the might and virtues of my strengths, which no man may forswear, that thou shalt never depart from me."

To whom Cyprian said: "I despise thee and forsake thee and all thy power, and I renounce thee and all thy devils and garnish and mark me with the sign of the cross," and anon the devil departed all confused.

Then Cyprian went to the bishop, and when the bishop saw him, he weened that he were come to put the Christian men in error and said: "Let it suffice unto thee, Cyprian, them that be without forth, for thou mayst nothing prevail against the church of God, for the virtue of Jesus Christ is joined thereto, and is not overcome."

And Cyprian said: "I am certain that the virtue of our Lord Jesus Christ is not overcome," and then he recounted all that was happened and did him to be baptized of him. And after, he profited much, as well in science as in life. And when the bishop was dead, Cyprian was ordained bishop and placed the blessed virgin Justina with many virgins in a monastery and made her abbess over many holy virgins. S. Cyprian sent then epistles to martyrs and comforted them in their martyrdom.

The earl of that country heard of the fame and renomee of Cyprian and Justina, and he made them to be presented before him and demanded them if they would do sacrifice. And when he saw that they abode steadfastly in the faith of Jesus Christ, he commanded that he should be put in a caldron full of wax, pitch, and grease, burning and boiling. And all this gave to them marvelous refreshing and did to them no grief ne pain. And the priest of the idols said to the provost of that place: "Command me, sire, to stand and to be before the caldron, and I shall anon overcome all their virtue." And then he came to fore the caldron and said: "Great is the god Hercules, and Jupiter the father of gods." And anon the great fire issued from under the caldron and anon consumed and burnt him.

Then Cyprian and Justina were taken out of the caldron and sentence was given against them, and they were both beheaded together. And their bodies were thrown to hounds and were there seven days, and after they were taken up and translated to Rome, and as it is said, now they rest at Placentia. And they suffered death in the seventh calends of October, about the year of our Lord two hundred and eighty, under Diocletian.

Confessio Sancti Cypriani

The Confession of Saint Cyprian[42]

All of you who despise the mysteries of Christ, look at my tears and come to know the power of everything these mysteries contain. And you, who take delight in the works and teachings of the demons, I invite to listen to my words and see the shameful and ridicule derision to be found in them.

None of you could be a greater adorer of demons than I was, none of you could be more curious than me about the beliefs in the false gods, and neither will ever be best served by the power granted by them.

My name is Cyprian, and at the end of my first infancy, I was consecrated to Apollo, as a precious gift, and soon I was taking part as a very young initiate in the sacred ceremonies where the Dragon was celebrated.

Before my seventh year, I was introduced to the mystery of Mithras, and although at Athens I was a foreigner, thanks to the care of my parents I received the citizenship of this city. Because of that, when I was ten, I could carry the lightened torch of Demeter and attend dressed in white to the mourning of Kore. I served the serpent of Pallas, honored

---

42 The original Greek title is ΜΕΤΑΝΟΙΑ ΤΟΥ ΑΠΟΥ ΚΥΠΡΙΑΝΟΥ."

at the Acropolis, where I was raised to the honor of being a guardian of the temple.

I climbed Mount Olympus, the dwelling of those believed to be the gods, where I received the teaching on the interpretation of the echo and on the understanding of the murmurs. I knew trees, which can bestow visions, and herbs, believed to receive their powers from the gods. There I saw the succession of the seasons worked by the continuous change of the wind and the variation of the days, caused by the discordance of powers contrary to each other.

I contemplated at that place and I saw the choir of demons raising hymns, others inclined to incite war, others ready to spread discord, deceiving, confusion, and uncertainty.

I also saw the multitude which follows each god and goddess in the forty days of my stay in that place. From that place, like it was a royal palace, they send many spirits, which go to the diverse kingdoms, and I saw how each of them works on the earth and over every people.

I fed on fruits and only after the fall of the night and, even before I made fifteen years of age, I was taught by seven hierophants about the virtues that each one possessed. And my parents wished with all their soul that I knew all that existed over the earth, in the sky, and in the sea—not only what relates to the creation and corruption of herbs, trees, and living bodies according to Nature, but also about the virtues which exist on each of them, which the sovereign of this world impressed, in the tentative of hindering the Creation of the Most High.

I travelled to Argos to take part in the celebrations of the mysteries of Hera, and I was initiated in the knowledge of the willingness of the Air to unite with the Ether, and of the Ether to join the Air, and at the same time of the Water with the Earth, and of Water with the Air.

I went after that to Elis to find the temple of Artemis Tauropolos in Sparta. There I came to know how matter unites and separates, and about the exalted and ambiguous hidden meanings of the terrible tales and obscure stories. I learnt the secrets of the divination practice at Phrygia, which is done with the liver of animals, and with the Barbarians I was trained to divine the future from the flight of the birds and from the contortions of many animals, and to interpret the delirious voice of the seers.

I learnt to interpret the sound made by cracking wood and stone, the voices of the dead, which rise from the sepulchers, and the screak of the doors. There were no secrets for me about the flow of the blood caused by its effects or about the contractions and extensions of the spams of the body. I knew how to change words in the numbers and numbers in words. I learnt to identify the simulated diseases, the fictitious from the natural, and when one is natural although interpreted as fictitious. Moreover, I learnt how to discern which oaths are heard by the gods and which are not heard and acknowledged, and all the tricks to cause discord.

Nothing I ignored about what I saw in the earth, in the water, in the sky, and about the art of commanding the apparitions, and about what is interesting to know. And it was not strange for me the knowledge of the mutable things, or of the mechanic and artificial objects. I dedicated myself to the practice of the spell using the Scriptures, and many other things like that.

After these happenings, I went to Memphis in Egypt when I was twenty years of age, and there I acquired the experience of the most secret mysteries. By penetrating in the temples, I was initiated in the knowledge of what is proper to the contact with the demons of the terrestrial regions. I knew where to conjure and how to banish them, in which star they prefer to abide, their law and action, and what they dislike.

I knew which ones are their chiefs and about the ones that make them flee. I learnt how they abide in the darkness and how they can penetrate the soul and the body. Also about the nature of the communion with them and the things that against them oppose resistance.

I certified about the effects of their powers in the souls and bodies of the ones who have commerce with them, what kind of actions they can realize: cause agitation, give knowledge, enhance memory, bring terror, lead to error, enrage end cause convulsions and screams, amnesia, agoraphobia and other phenomenon of the same kind.

I learned the signs of the rain and of the earthquake, and I was taught about how the earth and the sea can be moved and influenced by the magical power, although all this is done to contradict the Providence of God.

I saw the souls of the giants who are imprisoned in the darkness, looking like they were supporting the earth, like men who must endure a very heavy weight. I did not fail to notice the allegiance of the serpents with the demons and the power of the bitter poison of the serpents to lose the inhabitant of the land. From that place, the spirits of the air bring the effluvia of that poison to afflict men, using matter as the medium to spread the evil power.

I came to a place where the demons through their metamorphosis took different aspects, being prepared by the Devil to oppose the divine creation and provoke the error. The evil spirits use this ability to help the men with whom they are connected by an impious pact.

I testified, also in that place, how the impious devotion is born, and the knowledge devoid of reason, the unrighteous justice and the confusion in the order.

There I saw the image of the untruthfulness, having a multiple form, and the three forms of the fornication, under the aspect of blood, of scum and of gall. The image of wrath I saw, made of stone, solitaire, rugged, and beastly. The image of deception, astute, ready to flatter, its body covered by tongues instead of hair. I saw the demon of hate, blind, with four blazing eyes at the top of the head, and countless feet issuing from the head, but without a belly, because its passion does not have guts. The image of envy, which equaled the other on its malignant attitude, but had a different image, with a tongue like a scythe.

There I saw the image of wickedness, very thin, with many eyes and in them instead of pupils it had darts, always ready to harm by its insidiousness and malice.

The image of avarice stopped in front of me, with a long and thin head, with a mouth in the back and other in the chest, devouring earth and stones, but its body was ever weaker because it vomited everything. I also saw the image of the love of gain, thin of body like a sword and with so long eye pupils they seemed to fall toward the ground. I saw the image of the commerce, with a disgusting appearance, quick and stingy, carrying over his back a pack with all he had.

The image of vanity was well fed and fat, but lacking any bones. I saw the image of idolatry flying high, with large wings promising to shelter everyone but without a limb that the wings could shade. I noticed the image of hypocrisy, full of wickedness, with a large chest, which lapsed without a sound, as its body was whirled in a thousand directions by the spiraling wind.

The image of madness did not escape me, being young, hermaphroditic, naked and without shame, empty and defenseless; I saw at the same time the image of temerity, with an enormous tongue bigger than his body; the image of stupidity, with the head tilted and the heart soft and floppy, dripping and incapable of keeping anything. In short, I witnessed all the appearances of the vices, the appearances the demons use to get into the world.

I knew at that place the three hundred and sixty vices, the vainglory, the false virtue, the wisdom empty of any value, the inane justice, with which they led the Greek philosophers to their and the vain concepts.

All of them were covered in beautiful ornaments, but lacking substance, fast turning to dust and shadow. And the three hundred and sixty-five images of the vices were worn by the demons to the detriment and deceit of man.

To not waste more time with the details of my tale, which could fill a large book, I will narrate only a small part of everything I saw, from which you can perceive the zeal I applied to my impiety.

When I was thirty years old, I left Egypt and travelled to Chaldea to learn about the nature of the motions of the ether, which the Chaldeans affirm to happen when in contact with the fire, although the wisest of the Magi say it occurs when the light shines through it.

From them I learned the differences between the planets, how they affect the plants, and about the choir of the stars, which are arrayed as warriors in an army. They taught me that there is a demon to each star, and about their mansions, their conjunctions, their foods and beverages, and about their spiritual unions with men. I was taught about the way to communicate with them through the light, and how to offer them the food and the drinks, as the initiate do.

They showed me how the ether is divided in three hundred and sixty-five parts, each one participating according to its nature in the power of matter, following the commands of their chief, and prone to be influenced by the magical formulas done with the libations and sacrifices. There are, however, demons who refuse to obey, due to their wicked disposition, but always faithful to the light-bearer.

I saw the spirits who inhabit the region between the sky and the earth, and I was amazed to see how their nature was a mixture of air and darkness. I realized, to my surprise, that they make reciprocal agreements and oaths.

In that place, there are dispositions, instructions, zeal, reflections, established with terrible astuteness by their Lord to establish their community. With air, he endowed their minds with a quick wisdom; with earth, he made their tongue sharp; with the element from the underworld, he strengthened their wicked disposition to commit evil actions. Their own prince makes them busy all the time, so they remain away from the faith and the devotion to the Highest. He so acted by the spirit of deceit, confounding everything, and he founded his reign of injustice drinking from the fount of madness.

Believe in my words, when I say that I saw the Devil himself, after calling him with sacrifices, and I embraced and conversed with him, and I was considered worthy of dignity amongst the ones who held the highest positions in his cohort. He said that I was a new Jambres, well apt to celebrate his rites, and considered worthy of his company.

He promised to make me a prince, after my death, and that I would have power and his support whilst living. To that end, he endowed me with a great authority and gave me the command over an infernal phalanx. "Be courageous," he told me when I left, "great Cyprian!" He stood up and accompanied me for a moment, causing the admiration of everyone there. After that, every dignitary of his cohort submitted to my service, knowing well the great favor I enjoyed with him.

His aspect was like a flower of gold, adorned with precious gems. He had in the head a crown made of precious stones, welded together, and his splendor dazzled the entire place, and his garment was in harmony with the rest. When he turned, he made the entire place to tremble.

Around his throne, there was a large cohort of diverse orders, all of them submissive in their acts to his command, slaves of his power.

I saw how he lit the entire place and filled it with phantoms, inspiring in all of us a violent terror. He had imprinted his image in every star, in every plant, and in every work of the Lord, making them ready to fight the Highest and His angels. And through this, he tries to tempt men and make them to be lost, displaying the power of God as it was his, when in fact his power lacks real substance. His power over things in the end is revealed to be inane, a game of shadows. For this reason, when the demons reveal themselves under their true aspect, they dissolve like air, and that is why they try to impress with their presence taking imaginary forms.

I will tell you now, from where comes the substance of these shadows, and there is no other way than through sacrifice. The demons mingle their natures with the smoke and the smell from the offerings and dress with the emanations that come from the wool, the linen, the fabrics, and the dyes used in the temples, so feigning a material form with these things. They use the shadows of these things to take a form and to appear as if they transform in other beings, and for this reason they require the offerings of earthly things like water and fruits and clothes, so they can dress with these shadows and their appearances.

In the same way, as we have in our souls the memories of the dead, with their images, and we see them in our imagination and talk to them in reverie, so the Devil fashions illusory forms to help his followers. He produces a rain without water, a fire that not burns, and he provides a fish that does not feed, and he gives a gold that is nothing but an illusion.

He uses our imagination to make appear a city, a house and fields, hills and countries, herbs and flowers, wool, delicious fruit, showing everything as made with the substance of dreams: That is why he appears to the souls during the sleep. His power is just the power of the imagination to create illusions, but the impious men conjure him to produce these inane representations.

But to me, who did not wish to come near to God, enshrouded in the darkness, what availed to know the lack of power of the Dragon, and that his words are just to boast? I proved, in fact, his wickedness, aware that he creates false images and does nothing that is true.

It was from the virgin Justina that I learned that demons are just smoke and that they are powerless. I saw the Devil, full of hate, attack the virgin, and he had no more power than a mosquito. The young woman persuaded me that the king of darkness, who offered me such great powers, was just a liar. The virgin Justina trampled him down like a vermin.

He stood at her door with thousands of demons, but they could not enter and could not break the wood. A girl defeated him that believed he ruled everything. He, that boasted of upsetting all that is under the heavens, came down to be at the mercy of a woman. Pretending to bend the understanding of every man, saying that the entire world revolves around him, roaring like a fierce lion to terrify everyone, he was nonetheless reduced to the level of a harmless mosquito, unable to enter in the house of the virgin.

I returned to Antioch from Chaldea, where I became a magician like the ones of old; by performing miracles, I proved my proficiency as a sorcerer. I began to build a reputation as a magician and as a philosopher, because I had a lot of knowledge of the invisible things. I pretended to help the others, and a great number came for my spells, some to learn, some to experiment the impious art, whilst others were motivated by the search for pleasure, or by jealously, envy, and malice. To all of them I provided assistance, facilitating their pursuit of pleasure, bending to their desires the person they cared about, or averting their rivals.

The fathers would come to ask for my advice when they believed their daughters to be oppressed by their husbands, and others asked for help on behalf of their servants, mothers, and sisters. And no one was disappointed, because the demons were at my service.

From all this came my persuasion that the Devil was the only true deity, as everything I saw to be under his rule, and to him everything obeyed.

My friends, I did not imagine that any power could oppose his, and neither that my own power would be ineffective against anyone. In truth, I ignored that a power so vast could exist.

I knew very well that the Devil was the father of the epidemics, of injustice, corruption, and of all torments, the protector and instigator of men inclined to evil and injustice, assassins and kidnappers, but because of his great power, I would silence my conscience and venerate him.

One day a young man, very well dressed and handsome, called Aglaidas, came to me because of the great passion he had for a virgin maid named Justina. That was the occasion when I learned about the weakness of the Devil. The entire phalanx of demons at my service was sent against the girl, but they had to retreat without achieving anything. All the demons raised to help Aglaidas were averted by the prayer of Justina and could do nothing.

After ten nights of vigil made by the young lad, and many attempts made by the demons during seventy days, the Devil came in person with the high dignitaries of his cohort. Such was the situation that not only Aglaidas was consumed by his passion for the girl, but also I myself had fallen in love with her. Nonetheless, we saw all the powers of the Devil be defeated and scorned by a simple maiden, and he was incapable of quenching our desires. I asked him: "If the order of nature obeys you, at least assuage our passions, so we will not look as a reason for jokes, after trying so hard without achieving anything."

He then sent to me very quickly the demon of luxury, putting him under my command, saying to him: "If Aglaidas is not freed from his passion, I will surely punish you."

However, no matter how much he tried, he could not achieve anything, and neither in any way could he help us with his power, proving what the Most High teaches: that the Devil cannot change the course of the Nature, but just use it as a lame and hunchbacked knight, who fare well in the battle thanks only to his horse.

A great dispute arose between me and the demons, and between the demons themselves, which began to lament and menace each other. I turned against the Dragon and threatened to leave, and he did not even flinch, well aware of his impotence. He kept silent and patient, afraid that I separate myself from him.

On the fiftieth day, he decided to fool Aglaidas, making him fall in love with another woman, to whom he tried to give the appearance of Justina, but it did not avail, as he could not even give her a true resemblance of our loved one. When I discovered this, I accused him.

In the end, the Devil bid the spirit of Luxury to take the appearance of Justina, to appease the love of the lad. Aglaidas was very happy when she came near him, but when he pronounced her name, the demon lost her shape, turned into smoke, and flew away, because even the name of the virgin became to the demons burdensome like the name of the Virgin Mary.

My friends, I was there when all this happened, and I witnessed the faith of the maiden, the impotence of the Devil, and his lack of true valor. Full of confusion, I was terrified and could not sleep. I tried to transform myself into the appearance of a woman, to take the form of a bird, but as soon as I came near to the house of the maiden, the sorcery was gone, and I was Cyprian again, obtaining nothing from my art.

I transformed Aglaidas into a sparrow, and he flew to the house of Justina and perched in the front of the building. When Justina saw him, he lost his animal shape and would have died from falling, if her mercy did not save him. She advised him to be calm and pray to God, and made him leave the house.

She did not bend to the diseases, pains, and afflictions the Devil used to torture her. Her parents cried and took her for lost, as the doctors forsaken her. Nevertheless, she said to them: "Do not cry. I will not die, and I do not lose my spirit, and I do not feel pain. I do not feel but a light fever, as if blown over me from the air."

In the end, what did we not do to gain her? She protected herself with the sign of Christ and banished all demonic powers. Therefore, I harmed her parents and killed their cattle.

She exhorted them to not despair and to not become discouraged, and due to her virtue, she achieved it, and her parents recovered much of what was lost and received the divine blessing over their remaining riches.

However, they feared that the wrath of the Devil would fall again over her, and so crying they asked her to marry the young man, instead of becoming his lover. Justina, with the sign of the cross, defeated the fear and calmed the agitation.

The Devil then spread the plague over the people of the city and produced an oracle telling that they would only be free when Justina married Aglaidas. Her prayers calmed the disturbed people and purified the city from the plague. The citizens praised Christ and began to insult me, and I was forced to flee from their hate.

I finally saw that against the sign of Christ, nothing could avail and, being alone, I called the Devil and told him: "My downfall, artifice of every error, why did you betray my soul, knowing so well your own weakness? If just the shadow of Christ can defeat you, what will you do when you see him? If you tremble just at His name, what will you do if He comes against you? If the sign of His passion renders you powerless, what will you do facing His true power? If you do not dare to come close even to the sign of the cross, how will you take away someone from his power? You know nothing, cannot defend yourself, have no power, and cannot take revenge upon anyone. Now I know your deceit, and I do not believe anymore in the unreal phantoms of your imagination. You corrupted my mind and strayed my soul, broke my hope, threw my reason into confusion, and defiled my life with your wickedness. I greatly sinned following you, my iniquity became great, and, as a fool, I threw my life away to your power. I misused my learning and abused my culture for my own harm, being at your service. In addition, I lost my fortune by walking after you. I lost my fortune and my soul. If I had at least given my wealth to the poor, I could have some hope of salvation. What became of me? Am I lost without hope? I am wounded, and there is no cure for me. I believed I was living a great life, but I was acquiring at a high price my own tomb. Now I must plead with the Christians for their mercy; I must throw myself at the feet of Justina and beg her forgiveness. Get away from me, evil one, apostate of God; get away from me, enemy of truth and of faith!"

When the Devil heard my words, he came to me to kill me, falling upon me and strangling me. I was not strong enough to oppose his violence, and all my hope was lost, but then I remembered the sign used by Justina and cried: "God of Justina, come do my aid!" I was immediately fortified and, with my hand, I could make the sign of Christ and protect myself. The Devil stepped back and threatened me with a sword. However, I had already tasted the power of the sign of Christ and again and again used it. He had to flee, and from a distance he menaced me, saying: "Christ will never save you from my hands, because he despises the wicked and only aided you to bring you to your destruction. He will reject you, and then you will see the consequences of despising my force. Christ will never save one of mine, and now that you lost my favor, he will not help you."

A great fear took over me when I heard these words, because he had indeed answered me with great cleverness. Because of this, I asked the people that were present there: "Have mercy in front of my misfortune and pray to Christ to appease His wrath, so I can be accepted as a penitent, if He can save me from my past wickedness."

Everyone kept silent, but one man came forward and said: "Be calm, Cyprian; Christ will accept you, because you did not know the evil you did."

Moreover, I answered to him: "What the Devil said will not pass? Will not Christ deal harshly with me in the end?"

He replied: "You had proof that the Devil is a liar, so why now do you believe his word? Do not doubt Christ, because there is no deceit in Him, because He is the very truth; there is no deception in Him, because from His glory springs justice. To help you to understand that He is the source of all goodness, know that He, the creator of all, became a man to save us, and He faced death to deliver us from the consequences of our sin. He joined us in our suffering and gave us the hope for the eternal life, giving the example through Christ, so we all could live in the hope of the day of the resurrection. So, if Christ died for the impious and the sinners, have hope, Cyprian, because He will not deny you. You are one of the wickedest, but He will forgive you entirely. Know the mercy of Christ and do not fear for what you have done. If He prayed for the ones who nailed Him in the cross, how would He reject you? He said, 'Father forgive them, because they do not know what they are doing.' How would He not release you from your impiety when you did not know what you were doing? Fear not, and do not lose your hope, but go to see the bishop and tell him about your decision of come near to Christ."

After he said all these things, I felt relieved, and becoming again confident, I asked: "My dear Timothy, things are really as you say?" And he reassured me with many more discourses.

I then addressed the others, to make known all the deeds of my impiety, and said: "Will you forgive everything I have done, citizens of Antioch? Many times, I committed horrible deeds; I cannot count all the evil I did. I cut open the belly of the pregnant for the work of demons; disguising their appearances, I took many noble women as prisoners, taking them from their cities, forced them to become pregnant, and then killed them. I assassinated their infants, burying them alive, and others I broke their necks, because in doing this the Devil promised his help to me. Young men I buried in honor of Hades, and to please Hecate I decapitated many foreigners who were my guests. The blood of virgins I offered to Pallas, and to Ares and Kronos I sacrificed adult men."

All these things I did to appease the demons and get near to the Devil himself. When I got close to meet him, I offered the blood of every kind of animal in a vase of gold. The Devil accepted my offer and sprinkled it over his crown and over his dignitaries, and then over me, and said: "Accept the power over every being endowed or not with reason, so you can benefit your friends."

Many more I slaughtered and ruined. The benefic services I provided did not really bring any benefits to the clients, as they produced only imaginary results. The evildoings, however, were true, because the demons cannot create but can surely harm. The gold I distributed lasted for just three days, and whoever received it was wronged. I could not innumerate how much adultery I committed, and how many boys I corrupted, even when they did not wish to do wicked things. Who could write down all the crimes I did, wars, wickedness, and damage of every kind? How could God have mercy on me, who did not have any mercy at all? If I had harmed just one or two souls, I could have some hope, but the evil I did is too much.

What else should I mention or omit? The extermination of an entire family, after a perfidious advice given to a friend, the assassination of guests and other men, the harassment of the pious and the insidious harm to the Christians, the rape of virgins, the destruction of churches and houses of prayer, the abduction of illustrious women, and the profanation of the mysteries, as I forced many to betray the secrets of the rites, after what I would declare and mock them. I despised every sacred writ, tearing them to pieces, throwing in the ground and putting fire. I scorned the good people who attend the mass and espoused hatred of baptism. I made ridicule of the liturgy, blasphemed against Christ and God, and rejected the Gospels. Why should Christ forgive me, or even just one of my sins? My life is full of horrible deeds that could not be atoned in a lifetime. I do not know if I will live twenty more years, and that would not suffice to pay for even one of my crimes. How much time would suffice to amend my innumerable impieties? Friends, please tell me, what should I do? I failed to recognize the divinity of Christ, and I cannot ingratiate His forgiveness.

Even if now I know the holiness of His priests, I do not dare to come before them. I know the grace of the Gospels, but I cannot touch them, tormented by remorse. I know that the faith in Christ is an unending mystery, but I lack the force to move so severe mercy. I recognize the ordinance of the Church, but I fear to come to its vestibules. God I now know, but not how to receive His forgiveness. I have a burning desire for living a pious life, but I am overwhelmed by my impiety. I want to be a servant of Christ, but I do not know if He will have me as His slave; I do not ask any price but only want to be His slave. If He does not forgive me, I am the only one to be blamed. For my own faults I will be condemned to the eternal death; I just ask that it is done by His hand. I deliver myself to His power, even knowing that perhaps my guilt surpasses His mercy. I have proof of His power from Justina, and I brought myself to death. I just want to see how Christ is adored. Friends, can I partake of your celebration, to contemplate His divinity? I am full of dread and my soul is full of despair. I do not believe He will forgive me, for there was none worse than me, who surpassed even Jannes and Jambres. These two admitted to have some help from God when they did their magic, when I was totally convinced that

God did not exist. If God did not forgive them, who recognized His power, how can I expect to be forgiven, who did not believe in Him at all? I am not here to boast of my wickedness, knowing too well I must account for my deeds, but I know that His grace is for the truth.

How much of the amount of my wickedness could be showed to you? I accepted evil and the abyss was opened before me, and many others I sank in the sea of impiety. I did not lose myself only into the abyss, but many others I guided to perdition. What shall I lament more? For whom should I cry? The ones I killed with evil perseverance using sorcery? Or the ones that I taught with untiring wickedness? I had many disciples and many of them had the usufruct of my graces, but when it seemed I was friendly helping them, I was in fact sticking a sword at their backs. I pretended to help relatives but, in truth, I caused their destruction. In addition, many I instructed to become magicians. I taught many young men, bringing them to a premature aging, and the old I led to finish their lives in the follies of magic.

People from every part left their homes and families to come to learn from me and were led astray. Moreover, even when they used what they learned to perform good deeds, the acts of magic prevented them of progressing in the way of the faith. As a priest, I performed the mysteries. As an acolyte of demons at the temple I instructed others, prepared philters of love, and became an example of fraud. As hierophant, I sacrificed the hecatomb, and although I benefited many with my magic, of none I had mercy. I inspired many to imitate me, and whoever opposed me I killed. I acted like a traitor to overcome those who resisted me. Many were brought to their knees because of the fear of me.

I complied when they asked me to fly through the air or to walk on the water. Some at their request I transported from place to place in the wings of the wind. I provided winds for ships to sail fast and, from the bottom of the sea, I raised sunken vessels; but others I sunk myself. To amuse my friends and me, I created many illusions, like cascades in the desert and floods inside a house. I enchanted wives so they would flee with their adulterous lovers. I killed children, rejoiced in the ruin of entire houses, killed friends, punished honest slaves without reason. The demons rejoiced that by leading me on this path they achieved to make me surpass even them in wickedness.

Now, my friends, tell me if there is any chance of being released from these things, or rather it would be better if I hang myself? Because the memory of these evil deeds, although not done anymore, is like a suffering death.

I want to learn about the power of Christ and then die the death that is destined for me. This desire is the only thing that keeps me alive, as I lost every hope of salvation. Nothing more I will say about my deeds, or the very foundation of this house would be shaken. The few things I mentioned were for proof of my wickedness. For example, I would separate my soul from my body and fly to the underworld, where it would instigate wars, and perform things even more nefarious than the ones I told. I advised the demons of the air to cause envy in the world, sowed discord between what is above and what is below, and in all of this considered myself as being prodigious.

It is of no use to say more. After all that was said, you who know me, but not everything I did, how can you say that Christ will save me? You used as example the Jews who killed Christ, but I outdid even them, as I claimed to be superior to him and mocked him considering him a simpleton. By illusion, I made the dead look like they lived and the lame appear as if they could run. I used my rhetoric skills to convince many that Christ is not God, just as the Devil did when he made the Jews crucify Him. I called him an ignorant man, who did not know anything about the visible and the invisible things. How, then, can you say that Christ will receive me, after so many sins I committed against Him? How could I repent and expiate my sins? How could I amend for the people I made forfeit their salvations, the murders I did and the murders I advised? All the deceptions, the ravishments, the injuries, and the souls I turned from the path to the light towards the darkness. What matters now that I came to know the True Divinity?

For this reasons, it is better if I cease asking Christ for forgiveness, because it would be better that I silence myself, than incurring in more impiety, bringing upon me revenge rather than forgiveness.

As I said all that, I cried many tears, and everyone else wailed because my words were wise, and they all lamented, because, although they now saw me as I being fair and of good faith, I was in truth unworthy of the divine help. I ripped my clothes and covered my head with ashes, laying on the ground and shed copious tears, crying: "Woe to me. I am forever lost."

While everyone was feeling deeply embarrassed, my friend Eusebio came and answered me, saying: "Cyprian, do not despair, for there is a medicine for all these sins, because you were ignorant when you committed them. You acted like you did to please the Devil, but after you came to know God, you turned to good deeds. Do not afflict yourself unnecessary, as your repentance is like a prayer of forgiveness. Do not listen to the enemy who wants to sentence your soul, but pay attention to those who love you. I know many, Cyprian, that, even not meriting by virtue of their works, made themselves worthy of forgiveness. There were magicians who received acceptance and forgiveness, and so you, who are a magician, will be accepted and forgiven. Why do you continue to macerate yourself, even when already in a state of great weakness? It is no wonder that the Devil did throw you in such state of despair; he is clever and you, better than anyone else, should know this. Remember how cunningly he answered you before the cock crow and how he kept his distance when threatening you? Did he not say that Christ hates the Devil's followers and would threaten them cunningly?

"Nevertheless, you must know that when Christ is present the Devil cannot do anything; so banish from you the temptation of despair. You must invoke Christ to have proof of His benevolence. He does not ask for gifts, nor does He wait to deliver His mercy, and much less does He delude with fantastic illusions. Christ's follower Paul the Apostle well said: 'Keep the word in your mouth and in your heart.' And what is this word? One of faith, of course, placed in His appeal. If the mouth confesses the faith in salvation, and if the heart believes it, so is the faithful saved. You confessed all your iniquities, the ones you made and the ones you caused to happen, and I accept your regret. I and my brothers, we listened in silence so you could relieve your mind from the influence of the enemy and, throwing out his ideas, achieve piety. Now you must calm down, Cyprian, and accept the fact that the human nature is prone to error, ignorance, and that the dreadful way of the demons is to prey on the folly of the youth. There is no need to further discourse over their practices. Give yourself the good advice and do not insist on lamenting on your own destruction. Hear your conscience when it says that you became the toy of the enemy through your own ignorance, that you became yourself the enemy, without knowing it. Let your mind be persuaded that you did evil under the compulsion of evil itself, as the wood that burns because it is touched by fire, and consumes men, cities, and the entire land. As the wood is not to be blamed, but rather the fire, understand that you are not the creator of evil, but that through the error of your ignorant nature, you were seduced by the impiety of the Devil."

"We know of so many who, becoming mad, acted against themselves, like Ajax, who killed himself out of the envy for Odysseus. Some had without conscience killed their own children and relatives, as did Orestes with his mother, Medea with her children, Theseus with Hippolytus. When Paris took Helen, he could not foresee the destruction of Troy. Agamemnon, when he invited Aegisthus, could not know he was honoring his own traitor. Perdiccas was determined to accomplish his vows, not knowing the result would be the punishment caused by love. Oedipus, who attained the glory he sought for, tasted it bitterly, for the price was the involuntary slaughter of his own father, and he ended in a bloody wedding with his own mother. In the same way, when someone is deluded by the Devil, after a life of strife and misery, most of them confess a recantation and, their human natures being taken into account, they escape the consequences of their errors.

"Cyprian, take heed of your rebellion against God and see how your judgment was involuntarily led to it. Your mind was under the influence of the Devil, he who assails many countries like a flood. Who is to be blamed, the humans that are forced to flee or the water that destroys everything? You were the tool that the Devil used to destroy many. Perhaps you would be beyond hope if, coming to recognize the power of Christ, you had insisted upon the impiety of your former ways. As you now know and confess His power over the enemy, clearly you would have done the same before, if you had the chance, publicly renouncing his impiety. Fortify your mind and your will; cease the weeping now that you are reconciled with Christ. You now can bring to the salvation of Christ many more than those you destroyed, proclaiming the goodness to everyone."

But I said: "I cannot stop grieving, as my conscience now afflicts me, for the things I did not dared to confess; I am still stricken, because in the campaign I made against Justina, I sacrificed a child and opened the entrails of women to divine and also many other crimes I committed performing the unlawful arts. In my despair, in my deep need, I charge you, father Eusebius, to prove with the Scriptures if Christ ever saved someone who came to regret such awful deeds like mine."

Eusebius answered: "The Apostle Paul was the cruelest persecutor of Christ's servants, trying even to get Stephen killed. He was not a magician but conspired with letters to expel the faithful from Damascus. After his conversion, he became an appointed vessel, and he recognized the mercy of Christ in face of his ignorance. The Acts of the Apostles says that many who practiced magic burned their books and were accepted in the faith, receiving the forgiveness from Christ, leaving behind their iniquities and the expected retribution for their sins. We can also mention the Babylonian King Nebuchadnezzar, who repented and received back his strength, after being banished as a beast for many years. And there is also the example of Manasseh, king in Israel, who terribly sinned even after he came to know God, but his repenting was received in favor, even after killing prophets, defiling the sanctuaries, and straying so many peoples in the adoration of the idols. The people of Israel, who so often acted impiously and afterwards repented, until the coming of Christ were used to receive forgiveness and mercy from God. Even in the church today, there are plenty who weaken before sin and then repent, shaving their heads in a sign of contrition. Believe in the power of the Gospels, because they are the manna of Christ's grace, teaching that He has mercy and does not condemn. There it is written, as he said to Peter: 'Do not forgive your brother only seven times seven, but seventy times seven.' How would He so not forgive you? Learn that a man may have mercy for his neighbor, but God has mercy for every living being. Why should you believe then that He would be empty of mercy for you? He decreed the destruction of the Ninevites, who were more impious than you, but seeing their regret He pardoned them. Therefore, you too call upon Him, and you will not be rejected. Because of his faith, the thief was granted heaven at the last moment, and so it will be with you, no matter if you are drowned into an ocean of sin."

"Read what the Prophets said, and you will know His goodness. Hosea said to Israel: 'Would I make you like Admah and Zeboim?' but in the sequence he said: 'My heart recoils and within myself my regret is stirred,' meaning His readiness to receive who repents. To Elijah he said: 'Have you seen how Ahab was moved deeply from my presence? I will certainly not bring evils in his days.' And that, after he had already made Elijah prophesy his death for the killing of Naboth by Jezebel; so, why should you doubt your own salvation? God swore over the salvation of the sinner, saying: 'As I live, I surely do not wish the death of the sinner as much as that he converts and lives.' So, if you repent with your whole heart, He will say, 'Even if you lived one hundred years in impiety and repented on the last day, you would certainly not die, but you will live a life facing me.'"

"God cannot lie, because He is Truth himself. Did he not spare His own son to save all the humans and their descendants, and so will not He be conquered by your sincerity? He left the ninety-nine sheep, which are the blessed in the heavenly abode, to descend after the hundredth that was lost. He was crucified for our sins and freely gives Himself to whoever repents and converts. Be courageous, Cyprian, because God did not come for the just, but to bring the sinners to repentance. Repent, then, and you will see that He will embrace you. As the apostle Paul said, 'God wants all human beings to be saved, and to come to the knowledge of the truth.' These are just the few things I know and that I can tell you, Cyprian. However, when you meet the teachers of the Church, pay attention to what they say about penance and repentance. I will also be amongst the pupils, wondering in the excellence of their teachings."

"They are generous to offer help, without pride or arrogance, and do not entertain vain argumentations, miserly procrastinating in the hope of receiving money. Unlikely the sophists, they know that the base of the teaching must be more than good, so the faithful can build upon this sound base toward the foundation of the wisdom, avoiding the danger to be found in other teachings. There you will see a solemn liturgy, not celebrated with cymbals and other instruments, or with men screaming like girls, nor flutes singing songs inadequate to the divine praise. The chorus is sober and do not indulge in unintelligible sounds, the ceremony does not include sacrifices or the consecration of impure things, and there is no fire set on woods to exorcise spirits. The priest is not adorned in such a way that it seems he is going to an insane battle, and the bishops do not mistreat the bulls. The sermon is modest, there are no dissolute banquets, the behavior is correct. The atmosphere is friendly and quiet, with a solemn discipline. The children have the same behavior as the elders, following the divine order. When the assembly is arranged in a circle, around the holy table, you see a holy city obedient to its ruler. The psalmist sings with a simple language, a hymn that gives courage to the heart and purifies the mouth and ears from the profane songs, preparing everyone to the sacred readings."

"Go to them without fear, in an openly way. When you get up, break your fast that is already in its third day. From here, we go to the evening prayer, and tomorrow, according to our custom, we will join the common prayer to celebrate the first seven days of the memory of the resurrection of Christ. Moreover, after that, we will see the bishop. Recover yourself, believe that with faith you will save more than the ones you got lost, and remember me when you will be forgiven, to explain for the usefulness of the people, the dream from which you had being awaken."

I stood up and hugged the head of Eusebio against my chest, and I called him father and angel. His son, who had the same age as me and who had received the same literary learning and who also was a very fine lad devoted to the true religion, also received me in friendship, and they took me to their home and fed me with good food.

We went to the church, and there I could see the choir, so beautiful it was like a choir of angels, singing songs taken from the verses of the Scripture, in Hebrew. They sounded not like men but like the flow of the waves from the sea, a song issued by harmonious creatures of pure rational existence, fulfilling the prophecies uttered by the Prophets when they lived.

The priests preaching were not inferior to the one made by the Apostles themselves and there was no need for an interpretation, as the speech was very simple and supported by quotations from the Bible. The assembly was greatly astonished when we came inside but received us respectfully as guests. After the cult, we returned silently home.

In the next day, I called my protector and said: "Father Eusebio, why don't we go and burn all the books of the Devil?" We proceeded and that we did, in the presence of the bishop, who, as Eusebio promised me, looked more like an angel than a man.

When Saint Justine learned about these events, she shaved her head and sold all her dowry to the poor, believing that my conversion was a double sign of salvation, because Aglaidas also renounced the Devil's works and took refuge on Christ, who saved both of us through her. I also gave all my fortune to the poor and was every day with father Eusebio, who became a presbyter of the Church when I was baptized. Since then, I started to preach to everyone I could, and many I persuaded to convert to the Lord Jesus Christ, through whom and with whom be glory and honor be given to the Father, forever and ever. Amen.

Passio

The Martyrdom of Cyprian and Justa

[MCJ]

The conflict and martyrdom of the holy Cyprian and of the holy Justa; while the word of the prophets is being fulfilled in these days and the word of our Lord Jesus Christ about the seed of wheat and tares, how they grew, and how Novatus was put to shame and conquered by faith, and how the people were scattered and the wolf.

The holy Cyprian was famous in all lands because he wrote many books, and many who were gone astray he gathered to himself from the wiles of the evil wolf, the serpent of old, envying him his people.

And Eutolmius was count of the region of the East when Cyprian the teacher of the Christians was setting aside the glory of the gods and was healing everyone, with a virgin whose name was Justa, and they were disturbing everyone with the books, and their doings were heard of in the region of the East and in every place. And Eutolmius was wroth and he ordered that they cast them into chains and guard them closely and bring them to the city of Damascis. And when they had brought them, then Eutolmius asked them saying, "Tell me, Cyprian, art thou the teacher of the Christians, who didst aforetime lead many astray by thy sorcery by the might of the gods? But now by the sorcery of him who was crucified thou dost bring error and dost disturb the ears of men, and dost advance and exalt him who was crucified above the living gods."

And the holy Cyprian spoke and said to him. "Most wretched man, why hast thou adorned thyself with insolence, and dost thou speak also with pride in the sorceries of demons? For I also once, when I was, with you, equipped with sorcery and with the wisdom of the pagans, since I was blind, slew many and made many commit fornication, and from all this Christ saved me by the hand of his holy virgin."

"And there was a good scholar, of the house of Claudius, who loved this virgin, and he was not pleasing to her. And then he promised her a marriage that was according to law, and he has been unable until now to persuade her. And he came unto me and besought me to heal him of the madness of his love. But I, since I believed the books of sorceries, sent a demon to her, and she withstood him with the sign of Christ. And a third time I sent the chief of the demons, and he too returned conquered by that sign. And therefore I desired to know the power of this sign, and I adjured that demon, while angels burned him."

The Martyrdom of Cyprian and Justina, Middle Ages.

"And he told it all, that he was the discoverer of evil and of every work of wickedness. And then I came to myself. Then I wrote this to him that was bishop before me, and I brought the books of sorcery unto him while all the honorable men of the city were present, and I burned them with fire. And now I beseech thee to leave the other superstition and to return unto the Lord, and the Lord shall be praised. And then thou shalt know the invincibleness of the power of Christ."

And Eutolmius was exceedingly incensed, and he did not dispute his opinion with him, and he commanded them to hang him up and comb him, and to take turns in beating that blessed virgin also with hard thongs of leather. And the holy virgin said, "Praised art thou, O Lord, because when I was unworthy also and when I was a stranger once thou didst make me thine according to thy will to be beaten for thy name's sake."

And the soldiers tired themselves out in beating her, while that holy virgin also glorified God. And he ordered them to stop. And then the holy Cyprian spoke. While they were combing him exceeding much, he had not even said anything, but then the blessed Cyprian spoke and said to Eutolmius, "Why dost thou exalt thyself, tyrant, against God? And thou art deceitful toward the hope of Christ and alien from the kingdom of heaven, into which I desire to enter, that it may be mine on account of this torture."

And Eutolmius spoke saying, "If thou seekest the kingdom of heaven, thou shalt suffer every kind of torture, even greater than this." And he ordered them to lead him and cast him into prison. And he ordered them to put the holy virgin in the house of Teratina.

And when she came into that house, the whole of the house shone with the grace of Christ.

And after a few days, again he ordered them to bring them, and when they came, he said to the holy Cyprian, "Do not for the sake of a mortal man foolishly consent to die."

And the holy Cyprian said to him, "That death which is for God, for those that love him secure life eternal."

And when he heard this, he took counsel and meditated, and he ordered them to heat a frying pan and to cast into it pitch and fat and wax, and to cast the blessed one into it, with the holy virgin.

And the flame did not touch them. And the blessed Cyprian entered first into the frying pan. And the blessed one entered in her turn, and the evil serpent of old cast fear into her heart. And she came and stood by it.

And the blessed Cyprian said to her, "Come, in the endurance of Christ, thou that hast opened the gate of heaven, and hast made me to see the glory of Christ. And how art thou now conquered, who didst confound the demons and didst hold their chief as nothing, by putting on the sign of Christ? How dost thou now let thyself be deceived by the sting of the adversary?"

And then making the sign of the cross she entered into the frying-pan.

And they were both of them refreshed as with the dew of Hermon. And the blessed Cyprian said, "Glory be to God in heaven, and peace on earth. For when Satan fell from heaven peace was wrought in it all, and from the time when Christ came into the world, darkness was ordained for Satan, and by the power of the sign of his cross he forgives his servants, and he cast Satan down to his abode in Gehenna. And for this I praise thee, O Lord God of the fathers, and by thy mercy I pass through this torture for thy name's sake, that this our offering of sacrifice also may be fragrant with good odor."

And when Eutolmius heard this, he said, "I will overcome the madness of your folly."

And Athenus his friend, who presided with him, said to Eutolmius, "Your excellency bids me ascend into the heat of this frying pan in the name of our gods, and we will conquer this so-called might of Christ." And Eutolmius gave him permission, and Athenus drew near unto the frying pan and said, "Great is the god Herakles and the father of the gods Asklepius who gives life unto men." And when he drew near unto the frying pan, the fire found him, and his belly was rent asunder and his bowels gushed out.

And Cyprian was serene, praising God with the holy virgin. And when Eutolmius saw this, he said, "I fear that the might of Christ is unconquerable, and he has made me sad, for Christ has slain me my excellent friend."

And he called Terentinus his kinsman and said to him, "What shall I do to these robbers?"

And Terentinus said to him, "Beware of these holy ones and contend not with these holy ones, because the might of the Christians is unconquerable; but send them unto the king and tell him about them."

And Eutolmius wrote thus saying: "To Caesar the great, lord of the earth, Diocletian, greeting. In accordance with the statute of thy kingdom, I have arrested Cyprian, the teacher of the Christians, with a virgin whose name is Justa, of the region of the East. And behold in the report of his case thou shalt hear the punishments and torture with which I punished them, and they did not obey. And behold I have sent them unto thine authority."

And when the king read, he wondered at the way the blessed ones had been tortured, and he deliberated with his friends about torturing them again. And they said to him, "Not so, it is well that we let them be and assail not power that is invincible."

And he said, "Inasmuch as Cyprian, teacher of Antioch, and the virgin Justa have chosen for themselves the vain teaching of the Christians and have not desired life, but have preferred death, these shall suffer by the sword and shall die."

And they led away the holy one with the virgin to a river named Galius, in the land of Nicomedia, and he asked that they wait for them two hours for prayer. And he made mention of all the churches that were in the world and of all the servants of Christ. And he set the virgin at his right hand and sealed her with the sign of Christ, and he prayed that they crown her first, and it was done. And he said, "Praise unto Christ." And there was a man whose name was Theoktistus, who had come from the country, and he saluted the holy one. And there was looking on a councilor of King Diocletian, and straightway he ordered them to cut off his head. And after him, they beheaded the holy Cyprian also. And he ordered them to give their bodies to the dogs to eat. And for many days, even for six of them, they guarded their bodies, cast forth without to the wild beasts. And against them faithful and good and righteous men, hearing that the holy ones had been crowned, because he was also a man of their own land, even a Roman, lying in wait for them six days, day and night, [and] deceived all those who were guarding them and took away the bodies of the holy ones which were more precious than gold and gems, and they brought honor to the country of Rome. And when the faithful heard the manner of their conflict, with faithful believers they brought them unto Rufina, a prophetess, of the family of Carolinus, and she took the bones of the holy ones and put them in a good place, the name of which was "Esphoru Qaladaphoru," that all who come unto their bones may glorify God and our Lord Jesus Christ and the Holy Spirit.

This was done in the reign of Diocletian and Maximian, in a city of the region of Nicomedia, on the fourth day before the Kalends of October, on the fifth day of the month Dius, which is in Greek the month Ater and in Ethiopic the month Hedar—but for us, while Christ is our king forever and ever. Amen.

On him who writes it, and on our father John who has it written, and on him who reads it, and on him who interprets it, and on him who hears it, may God have mercy upon us all together in the kingdom of heaven. Amen.

COLOPHON OF MS. C.

The martyrdom of the holy Cyprian and of the holy Justa is finished. May their blessing be with the soul of their lover Iyasu and his son, our king Iyoas, and their mother, our queen Walatta Giyorgis (and with their handmaiden Walatta Shelase add. corr.), forever and ever. Amen.

The Life of Saint Justina

[WIE]

The name Justina is derived from justitia, justice; and Saint Justina showed her justice by giving to every person what was due to the person—to God, obedience; to the prelate her superior, reverence; to her equals, harmonious relations; to her inferiors, instruction; to her enemies, patience; to the poor and afflicted, compassion and help; to herself, holiness; and to her neighbor, love.

The virgin Justina was born in Antioch, the daughter of a pagan priest. Sitting at her window every day, she listened to the deacon Proclus reading the Gospel and in time was converted by him. Her mother told her father about this as they lay in bed, and when they had fallen asleep, Christ, accompanied by angels, appeared to them and said: "Come to me, and I will give you the kingdom of heaven!" As soon as they were awake, they had themselves baptized with their daughter.

This virgin Justina had long been pursued by a certain Cyprian, and in the end, she converted him to the faith. Cyprian had been a magician from childhood: When he was seven years old, his parents consecrated him to the devil. He practiced the arts of magic, often being seen to change women into beasts of burden and performing many other marvels. He became enamored of Justina and put his magic to work in order to have her for himself or for a man named Acladius, who also lusted after her. He therefore invoked the demon to come to him and enable him to win the virgin. The demon came and asked him: "Why did you call me?"

Cyprian answered: "I love a maiden who is of the Galilean sect. Can you make it possible for me to have her and work my will with her?"

The demon: "I was able to throw man out of paradise; I induced Cain to kill his brother; I caused the Jews to put Christ to death; I have brought every kind of disorder among men! How could I not be able to let you have one mere girl and do what you please with her? Take this lotion and sprinkle it around the outside of her house, and I will come and set her heart afire with love for you, and compel her to consent to you."

The following night, the demon came to Justina and tried to awaken an illicit love in her heart. Sensing what was happening, she devoutly commended herself to the Lord and covered her whole body with the sign of the cross. Seeing that sign, the devil fled in terror and went and stood before Cyprian.

"Why haven't you brought that maiden to me?" Cyprian asked.

"I saw a certain sign on her," the demon answered, "and I weakened and all power left me."

Cyprian dismissed that demon and called for a stronger one. This one told Cyprian: "I heard your orders and I saw why that other could do nothing, but I will do better and will carry out your will. I will go to her and wound her heart with lustful love, and you will enjoy her as you wish to." So the devil went to Justina and did his best to win her over and inflame her soul with sinful desire. But Justina again devoutly commended herself to God and dispelled all temptation with the sign of the cross, then blew upon the devil and drove him away. The spirit departed in confusion and fled to Cyprian.

Cyprian: "Where is the virgin I sent you after?"

The demon: "I admit I'm beaten, and I'm afraid to say how! I saw a certain terrible sign on her and at once lost all my strength!"

Cyprian scoffed at him and sent him away. Then he summoned the prince of demons and, when he came, said to him: "What is this power of yours that's so low, that a mere girl can overcome it?"

Said the devil: "I will visit her and disturb her with various fevers. I will inflame her spirit with hotter passion and spread hot spasms throughout her body. I'll get her in a frenzy and put fearful phantasms before her eyes. And in the middle of the night I will bring her to you!"

Then the devil gave himself the appearance of a young woman and went to Justina, saying: "I come to you because I want to live in chastity with you, but tell me, I beg of you, what will be the reward of our effort?"

The holy virgin answered: "The reward is great, the labor light."

"Then," said the devil, "what about God's command to increase and multiply and fill the earth? I fear, my good friend, that if we persist in virginity, we shall nullify God's word. By being disdainful and disobedient we shall bring grievous judgment upon ourselves, and while we expected a reward, we will incur torment!"

The virgin began to have serious doubts, induced by the devil, and she felt more strongly stirred by the heat of concupiscence, so much so that she rose and was on the verge of going out. But then she came to herself and recognized who it was that was speaking to her, so she shielded herself with the sign of the cross, then blew on the devil, causing him to melt like a candle. Thereupon she felt herself freed of all temptation.

Next the devil transfigured himself into a handsome young man and came into the room where Justina was lying in bed. Shamelessly he leapt into her bed and tried to envelop her in his embrace. This made Justina recognize the presence of a malignant spirit, so she quickly made the sign of the cross, and again the devil melted away. Then, God permitting, the demon sapped her strength with fevers and killed many people along with their herds and flocks. He also made possessed persons predict that a great wave of death would sweep through Antioch unless Justina consented to marry. For that reason the entire citizenry, beset as they were with disease, gathered at her parents' door and demanded that Justina be given in marriage so that the city could be delivered of this great peril. But Justina absolutely refused, and all were under the threat of death, but in the seventh year of the plague, she prayed for them and drove out the pestilence.

Now the devil, seeing that he was making no headway, changed himself to look like Justina in order to besmirch her good name, and deceived Cyprian, boasting that he would bring Justina to him. Then, but this time looking like the virgin, he came running to Cyprian as if languishing with love for him and wanting to kiss him. Cyprian, thinking of course that it was Justina, was overwhelmed with joy and said: "Welcome, Justma, loveliest of women!" But the minute he pronounced the name of Justma, the devil could not bear it and vanished in a puff of smoke. Cyprian, aggrieved at having been fooled, yearned the more ardently for Justina and took to watching at her door. Sometimes he changed himself by magic into a woman, sometimes into a bird, but when he came close to that door, he no longer looked like a woman or a bird: He was Cyprian. Acladius, too, was changed by diabolic art into a sparrow and flew to the virgin's windowsill, but as soon as she looked at him, he was no longer a sparrow but Acladius, and he felt trapped and frightened because he could neither fly nor jump from such a height. Justina feared that he might fall and break to pieces, so she had him brought down by a ladder and warned him to give up his mad adventure or be punished for breaking the law against trespass.

All these apparitions, of course, were nothing but devilish artifices, and none of them served the devil's purpose, so, defeated and confused, he went back and stood before Cyprian. Cyprian said to him: "So you too are beaten! What kind of power do you have, you wretch, that you can't overcome a simple girl or have any control over her. To the contrary, she defeats all of you and lays you low! But tell me one thing, I beg of you: Where does her greatest strength come from?"

The demon answered: "If you will swear never to desert me, I will reveal to you the power behind her victory."

Cyprian: "What shall I swear by?"

The demon: "Swear to me by my great powers that you will never desert me!"

Cyprian: "By your great powers, I swear to you that I will never desert you."

Now the devil, being reassured, told Cyprian: "That young woman made the sign of the cross, and at once all my strength ebbed away. I could do nothing, and like wax melting at a fire I melted away."

Cyprian: "Therefore the Crucified is greater than you?"

The demon: "Greater than all! And all of us and all those we deceive he turns over to be tormented in the fire that never dies out!"

Cyprian: "Therefore I too should become a friend of the Crucified, so as not to incur so awful a punishment!"

The devil: "You swore to me by the power of my army, by which no one can swear falsely, that you would never desert me!"

Cyprian answered: "I despise you and all your devils, and I arm myself with the saving sign of the Crucified!" Instantly the devil fled in confusion.

Then Cyprian went to the bishop. When the bishop saw him, he supposed that he had come to lead Christians into error and said to him: "Be satisfied, Cyprian, with misleading those who are not of the faith! You can do nothing against the Church of God, for the power of Christ is unconquerable."

Cyprian: "I am sure that Christ's power cannot be conquered." And he told the bishop all that had happened to him and had the bishop baptize him. Thereafter, Cyprian made great progress both in knowledge and in holiness of life, and when the bishop died, Cyprian was ordained to take his place. He established the holy virgin Justina in a monastery and made her the abbess over many holy virgins. Saint Cyprian often sent letters to the martyrs and strengthened them in their struggles.

The prefect of that region heard of the renown of Cyprian and Justina and had them brought before him. He asked them if they were willing to sacrifice to the idols. When they persisted firmly in the faith of Christ, he ordered them to be put in ¡1 heated caldron filled with pitch and fat. But this only refreshed them and inflicted no pain. Then a priest of the idols said to the prefect: "Command me to stand in front of the caldron, and I will outdo all their power!" He went close to the caldron and said: "Great are you, O Hercides, and you, Jupiter, father of the gods!" And behold, fire poured out and consumed the priest. Cyprian and Justina were taken out of the caldron, sentenced, and beheaded together. Their hodlij* wijtc thruwn to the Joj;s and lay tor seven days, then were transported to Rome; and now, we are told, repose in Fiaecnaa, they suffered under Diocletian, on the twenty-sixth day of September, a.d. iSo.

Saint Cyprian and the demon, 14th century manuscript of the *Golden Legend*.

Life of the Saints

Cyprian and Justina, Martyrs

[FLS]

The ways that God our Lord has to save the souls are many and wonderful: because from our ills, He makes good things; from poison, He makes medicine; and from death, life. We see that to be true in the life and martyrdom of Saint Cyprian, who being Mage and Necromancer, preparing traps with the aid of the Demons and Ministers of Hell to make fall into sin the glorious virgin Saint Justina, he was arrested, tied, and converted to Christ, and, with her, afterward he became a Martyr of the Lord. The martyrdom of these Saints Cyprian and Justina happened this way. Saint Justina was from the city of Antioch: Her father was named Dosio, or (as Methafrastes said) Edesio, and her mother Cledonya. They were Pagans, and also was their daughter Justina; but through the doctrine and by a Saint Deacon named Prasso, or Proelio, she converted to the Faith of the Lord, and through it and by a revelation that they had, also converted and baptized were her parents. Justina was extremely beautiful, of very great natural graces, and even much more beautiful because of her virtues, with which her soul resplended in the eyes of the Lord, whom she took as Spouse, and to whom she consecrated her virginity.

Justina was extremely beautiful, endowed with great natural graces, with which her soul was resplandescent in the eyes of the Lord, whom she took as her Espouse, to whom she consecrated her virginity. The Demon was envious of Justina's holiness and pretended to throw it down and make her fall from that perfection in which she was. To do that, he incited a rich and lascivious lad, who was named Agladio, to put his eyes on Justina and to fall in love with her, and by all means, that the love would be blind and that he looked after to attract her to his will. No means were enough to win over the aim of the holy Virgin; because it was founded over firm rock, and it did not have the avenue of the rivers, nor the impulse or the bravery of the storms and of the winds.

As Agladio saw that his intentions were in vain, he took as a medicine for his needs the favor of the Demons, who were inciting him to achieve through them what he by himself could not. There was in the same city of Antioch a great Sorcerer and Necromancer of the name Cyprian; to him, Agladio revealed what he pretended with Justina and the means that he used to try to smooth her and her obstinate spirit, harder than the diamond, that she had; and that, if not through pure love, he could have the maiden he had in his mind, that he helped him with his powerful arts; because he would pay him liberally and would become his perpetual Slave.

Cyprian took under his care to win Justina and attract her to the will of Agladio. He summoned the Demons and sent them to what they had to do: They went once, twice, and three times to the Saint. They assaulted her, and they fought her, transfiguring themselves in a thousand forms and figures. After using their arts and snares against her, they fell defeated and chased: Because the holy maiden, favored by her Espouse Jesus Christ and armed with prayer, fasting, and especially the sign of the Holy Cross, triumphed over them gloriously. Astounded was Cyprian, seeing that his arts had such little force, that the same Demons confessed their weakness, and that they could not prevail against Justina, because she was Christian and was armed with the virtue and the power of Christ crucified.

From this, Cyprian understood that Jesus Christ our Savior was God and was more powerful than all the Demons, whom he so much revered, and with the light of Heaven's lightning in his heart, he determined himself to become a Christian. He went to Antimo, the Bishop, and told him what was happening; and in fact, burning his Necromantic Books and renouncing the Demon and its evil arts, he received the baptism. After, he was ordained Deacon and shone with great holiness, and through him the Lord worked many miracles. And because he had received such great mercy through the Holy Virgin Justina, he had always taken great care to help her and to take ahead her holy aims, making her Abbess and Mother of a Monastery of maidens, who with great purity served the Lord.

The Saints, then, flourishing in the way that we had mentioned, a Count named Eultomio had them arrested and ordered Cyprian to be tormented, his back ripped with whips, and Justina, after giving her many slaps in the face, to be whipped without mercy. After that, they put Cyprian in prison and Justina in the house of an honorable woman. After some days, seeing the constancy and the perseverance that they had in the Faith, he ordered them to be put into a fiery cauldron, full of pitch, tallow, and resin. The Holy Martyrs entered the cauldron and got out without any lesion, through the virtue of that Lord, to whom all the Creatures obey. One priest of the Pagans, named Athanasio, was burnt by the same fire which had forgiven the Saints. From there, they were taken to Nicomedia, and after having suffered other torments with great spirit and joy, they were beheaded. The bodies were left for six days without burial, so the beasts could eat them, but they remained intact, guarded by God. Certain Christians took them one night, put them in a ship, and translated them to Rome, where they were first buried in propriety of Rufina, Noble Matron, and after translated to the church of Saint John of Lateran, where they are until today, by the side of the Baptistery. The Church celebrates the feast of these Saints in the twenty and six of September, which as the day of their martyrdom, being Emperors Dioclecian and Maximiam. These Saints are written about in the *Roman Martyrology*, the one from Beda, Usuardo, Adén, and Metafrasie. We must note that some Greek Authors confound this Saint Cyprian with Saint Cyprian, who was Bishop of Cartage, an illustrious Martyr, and eloquent Writer, whose feast the Church celebrates on the ten and six of this month of September; but they were two, and not one, and of different country, degree, profession, time, and place of martyrdom.

September 26

Sts. Cyprian and Justina

Martyrs

[LTS]

The detestable superstition of St. Cyprian's idolatrous parents devoted him from his infancy to the devil, and he was brought up in all the impious mysteries of idolatry, astrology, and the black art. When Cyprian had learned all the extravagances of these schools of error and delusion, he hesitated at no crimes, blasphemed Christ, and committed secret murders. There lived at Antioch a young Christian lady called Justina, of high birth and great beauty. A pagan nobleman fell deeply in love with her, and finding her modesty inaccessible and her resolution invincible, he applied to Cyprian for assistance. Cyprian, no less smitten with the lady, tried every secret with which he was acquainted to conquer her resolution. Justina, perceiving herself vigorously attacked, studied to arm herself by prayer, watchfulness, and mortification against all his artifices and the power of his spells. Cyprian, finding himself worsted by a superior power, began to consider the weakness of the infernal spirits and resolved to quit their service and become a Christian. Agladius, who had been the first suitor to the holy virgin, was likewise converted and baptized. The persecution of Diocletian breaking out, Cyprian and Justina were seized and presented to the same judge. She was inhumanly scourged, and Cyprian was torn with iron hooks. After this, they were both sent in chains to Diocletian, who commanded their heads to be struck off, which sentence was executed.

Reflection.

If the errors and disorders of St. Cyprian show the degeneracy of human nature corrupted by sin and enslaved to vice, his conversion displays the power of grace and virtue to repair it. Let us beg of God to send us grace to resist temptation and to do His holy will in all things.

St. Cyprian of Antioch

[BCW]

The Aeôns (Stellar Spirits)—emanated from the Unknown of the Gnostics and identical with the Dhyâni-Chohans of the Esoteric Doctrine—and their Plerôma, having been transformed into Archangels and the "Spirits of the Presence" by the Greek and Latin Churches, the prototypes have lost caste. The Plerôma (1) was now called the "Heavenly Host," and therefore the old name had to become identified with Satan and his "Host." Might is right in every age, and History is full of contrasts. Manes had been called the "Paraclete" (2) by his followers. He was an Occultist but passed to posterity, owing to the kind exertions of the Church, as a Sorcerer, so a match had to be found for him by way of contrast. We recognize this match in St. Cyprianus of Antioch, a self-confessed, if not a real, "Black Magician," it seems, whom the Church--as a reward for his contrition and humility--subsequently raised to the high rank of Saint and Bishop.

What history knows of him is not much, and it is mostly based on his own confession, the truthfulness of which is warranted, we are told, by St. Gregory, the Empress Eudocia, Photius, and the Holy Church. This curious document was ferreted out by the Marquis de Mirville (3) in the Vatican, and by him translated into French for the first time, as he assures the reader. We beg his permission to re-translate a few pages, not for the sake of the penitent Sorcerer, but for that of some students of Occultism, who will thus have an opportunity to compare the methods of ancient Magic (or as the Church calls it, Demonism) with those of modern Theurgy and Occultism.

The scenes described took place at Antioch about the middle of the third century, 252 A.D., says the translator. This Confession was written by the penitent Sorcerer after his conversion; therefore, we are not surprised to find how much room he gives in his lamentations to reviling his Initiator "Satan," or the "Serpent Dragon," as he calls him. There are other and more modern instances of the same trait in human nature. Converted Hindus, Pârsîs, and other "heathen" of India are apt to denounce their forefathers' religions at every opportunity. Thus runs the Confession:

> O all of you who reject the mysteries of Christ, see my tears!... You, who wallow in your demoniacal practices, learn by my sad example all the vanity of their [the demons'] baits... I am that Cyprianus, who, vowed to Apollo from his infancy, was early initiated into all the arts of the dragon. (4) Even before the age of seven I had already been introduced into the temple of Mithra: three years later, my parents taking me to Athens to be received as citizen, I was permitted likewise to penetrate the mysteries of Ceres lamenting her daughter, (5) and I also became the guardian of the Dragon in the Temple of Pallas.
>
> Ascending after that to the summit of Mount Olympus, the Seat of the Gods, as it is called, there too I was initiated into the real meaning of their [the Gods'] speeches and their clamorous manifestations (strepituum). It is there that I was made to see in imagination (phantasia) [or mâyâ] those trees and all those herbs that operate such prodigies with the help of demons;... and I saw their dances, their warfares, their snares, illusions, and promiscuities. I heard their singing. (6) I saw finally, for forty consecutive days, the phalanx

of the Gods and Goddesses, sending from Olympus, as though they were Kings, spirits to represent them on earth and act in their name among all the nations. (7)

At that time I lived entirely on fruit, eaten only after sunset, the virtues of which were explained to me by the seven priests of the sacrifices. (8)

When I was fifteen, my parents desired that I should be made acquainted not only with all the natural laws in connection with the generation and corruption of bodies on earth, in the air, and in the seas, but also with all the other forces grafted (9) (insitas) on these by the Prince of the World, in order to counteract their primal and divine constitution. (10)

At twenty, I went to Memphis, where, penetrating into the Sanctuaries, I was taught to discern all that pertains to the communications of demons [Daimônes or Spirits] with terrestrial matters, their aversion for certain places, their sympathy and attraction for others, their expulsion from certain planets, certain objects, and laws, their persistence in preferring darkness, and their resistance to light. (11) There I learned the number of the fallen Princes, (12) and that which takes place in human souls and bodies they enter into communication with...

I learnt the analogy that exists between earthquakes and rains, between the motion of the earth (13) and the motion of the seas; I saw the spirits of the Giants plunged in subterranean darkness and seemingly supporting the earth like a man carrying a burden on his shoulders. (14) When thirty, I travelled to Chaldaea to study there the true power of the air, placed by some in the fire and by the more learned in light [Âkâúa]. I was taught to see that the planets were in their variety as dissimilar as the plants on earth, and the stars were like armies ranged in battle order. I knew the Chaldaean division of Ether into 365 parts, (15) and I perceived that everyone of the demons who divide it among themselves (16) was endowed with that material force that permitted him to execute the orders of the Prince and guide all the movements therein [in the Ether]. (17) They [the Chaldees] explained to me how those Princes had become participants in the Council of Darkness, ever in opposition to the Council of Light.

I got acquainted with the Mediatores [surely not mediums as de Mirville explains!], (18) and upon seeing the covenants they were mutually bound by, I was struck with wonder upon learning the nature of their oaths to observe them. (19)

Believe me, I saw the Devil; believe me, I have embraced him (20) [like the witches at the Sabbath (?)] and have conversed with him; when I was yet quite young, he saluted me by the title of the new Jambres, declaring me worthy of my ministry [initiation].... He promised me continual help during life and a principality after death. (21) Having become in great honour [an Adept] under his tuition, he placed under my orders a phalanx of demons, and when I bid him good-bye, "Courage, good success, excellent Cyprian," he exclaimed, rising up from his seat to see me to the door, plunging thereby those present into a profound admiration. (22)

Having bid farewell to his Chaldaean Initiator, the future Sorcerer and Saint went to Antioch. His tale of "iniquity" and subsequent repentance is long but we will make it short. He became "an accomplished Magician," surrounded by a host of disciples and "candidates to the perilous and sacrilegious art." He showed himself distributing love-philtres and dealing in deathly charms "to rid young wives of old husbands, and to ruin Christian virgins." Unfortunately Cyprianus was not above love himself. He fell in love with the beautiful Justine, a converted maiden, after having vainly tried to make her share the passion one named Aglaides, a profligate, had for her. His "demons failed" he tells us, and he got disgusted with them. This disgust brings on a quarrel between him and his Hierophant, whom he insists on identifying with the Demon; and the dispute is followed by a tournament between the latter and some Christian converts, in which the "Evil One" is, of course, worsted. The Sorcerer is finally baptized and gets rid of his enemy. Having laid at the feet of Anthimes, Bishop of Antioch, all his books on Magic, he became a Saint in company with the beautiful Justine, who had converted him; both suffered martyrdom under the Emperor Diocletian; and both are buried side by side in Rome in the Basilica of St. John Lateran, near the Baptistery.

(1) The Plerôma constituted the synthesis or entirety of all the spiritual entities. St. Paul still used the name in his Epistles.

(2) The "Comforter," second Messiah, intercessor. "A term applied to the Holy Ghost." Manes was the disciple of Terebinthus, an Egyptian Philosopher, who, according to the Christian Socrates [Scholasticus], while invoking one day the demons of the air, fell from the roof of his house and was killed" (Eccl. History, lib. I, ch. i, cited by Tillemont, t. iv, p. 584).

(3) Des Esprits, Vol. VI, pp. 169–83.

(4) "The great serpent placed to watch the temple," comments de Mirville. "How often have we repeated that it was no symbol, no personification but really a serpent occupied by a god!"--he exclaims; and we answer that at Cairo in a Mussulman, not a heathen temple, we have seen, as thousands of other visitors have also seen, a huge serpent that lived there for centuries, we were told, and was held in great respect. Was it also "occupied by a God," or possessed, in other words?

(5) The Mysteries of Demeter, or the "afflicted mother."

(6) By the satyrs.

(7) This looks rather suspicious and seems interpolated. De Mirville tries to have what he says of Satan and his Court sending their imps on earth to tempt humanity and masquerade at séances corroborated by the exsorcerer.

(8) This does not look like sinful food. It is the diet of Chelas to this day.

(9) "Grafted" is the correct expression. "The seven Builders graft the divine and the beneficent forces on to the gross material nature of the vegetable and mineral kingdoms every Second Round"--says the Catechism of Lanoos.

(10) Only the Prince of the World is not Satan, as the translator would make us believe, but the collective Host of the Planetary. This is a little theological back-biting.

(11) Here the Elemental and Elementary Spirits are evidently meant.

(12) The reader has already learned the truth about them in the course of the present work.

(13) Pity the penitent Saint had not imparted his knowledge of the rotation of the earth and heliocentric system earlier to his Church. That might have saved more than one human life--that of Bruno for one.

(14) Chelas, in their trials of initiation, also see in trances artificially generated for them the vision of the Earth supported by an elephant on the top of a tortoise standing on nothing--and this, to teach them to discern the true from the false.

(15) Relating to the days of the year, also to 7-x-7 divisions of the earth's sublunary sphere, divided into seven upper and seven lower spheres with their respective Planetary Hosts or "armies."

(16) Daimon is not "demon," as translated by de Mirville, but Spirit.

(17) All this is to corroborate his dogmatic assertions that Pater Aether, or Jupiter, is Satan! And that pestilential diseases, cataclysms, and even thunderstorms that prove disastrous come from the Satanic Host dwelling in Ether--a good warning to the men of Science!

(18) The translator replaces the word Mediators by mediums, excusing himself in a footnote by saying that Cyprian must have meant modern mediums!

(19) Cyprianus simply meant to hint at the rites and mysteries of Initiation as well as the pledge of secrecy and oaths that bound the Initiates together. His translator, however, has made a Witches' Sabbath of it instead.

(20) "Twelve centuries later, in full renaissance and reform, the world saw Luther do the same [embrace the Devil, he means?]--according to his own confession and in the same conditions," explains de Mirville in a footnote, showing thereby the brotherly love that binds Christians. Now Cyprianus meant by the Devil (if the word is really in the original text) his Initiator and Hierophant. No Saint--even a penitent Sorcerer--would be so silly as to speak of his (the Devil's) rising from his seat to see him to the door, were it otherwise.

(21) Every Adept has a "principality after his death."

(22) Which shows that it was the Hierophant and his disciples. Cyprianus shows himself as grateful as most of the other converts (the modern included) to his Teachers and Instructors.

LIFE OF SAINT CYPRIAN

extracted from the
FLOS SANCTORUM or LIFE OF ALL SAINTS

[GLT]

Cyprian (named *the Sorcerer,* to be distinguished from the famous Cyprian, bishop of Cartage) was born in Antioch, situated between the Syria and the Arabia, belonging to the government of Phoenicia. His parents, idolaters, and provided with copious riches, seeing that nature gifted him with the proper talents to conciliate the esteem of men destined him to the service of the false deities, instructing him in all the science of the sacrifices that were offered to the idols, in a way that no one, like him, had so deep knowledge of the profane mysteries of the barbarous genteelism.

At the age of thirty years, he made a travel to the country of Babylon to learn Judiciary Astrology and the most hidden mysteries of the superstitious Chaldeans. And to the grave fault of employing in such studies the time that was granted to him to know and to follow the truth, increased Cyprian's malice and his iniquity when he dedicated himself entirely to the study of magic to achieve through this art a close commerce with the demons, practicing at the same time a lie impure and absolutely scandalous.

And, although a true Christian named Eusebio, who had being his companion of studies, made many times vigorous censures about his bad life, trying to take him from the deep abyss in which he saw him precipitated, not only did Cyprian despised his exhortations and censures, but also use his infernal ingenuity to mock the sacrosanct mysteries and the virtuous teachers of the Christian law, in a hate through which he even united himself to the barbarous persecutors to force the Christians to renounce and renegade Jesus Christ.

The life of Cyprian had reach this state when the infinite mercy of God deigned to enlighten and convert this unhappy vessel of outrage and ignominy into a vessel of election and honor, using and serving from his divine grace to work in the heart of Cyprian this prodigious miracle of its omnipotence in the way we are about to narrate.

In Antioch lived a maiden with the name of Justine, nor less rich than beautiful, who her father Edeso and her mother Cledonia educated with great care in the superstitions of Paganism. However, Justine, gifted as she was of a clear ingenuity, as soon as she heard the preaching of Prailo, deacon of Antioch, she abandoned the gentile extravagancies; and embracing the Catholic faith, in a short time she converted her own parents.

Constituted Christian, the fortunate virgin became at the same time one of the most perfect espouses of Jesus Christ, consecrating to him her virginity and looking after every means to keep this delicate virtue, to which effect she carefully kept the modesty, giving herself to the prayers and retirement. Although all this, seeing a poor lad with the name Aglaide, she captivated so much his wits that he soon asked her to be his espouse to his parents, to what they agreed; but no matter how many diligences such a pretendant had made, he could not get the consent from Justine.

And so, Aglaide made use of the skills of Cyprian, which, indeed, used all the most efficient means of his diabolical art to satisfy his enamored friend. He offered to the demons many and abominable sacrifices, and they promised him the desired success, and then assaulted the saint with terrible temptations and horrible ghosts. However, strengthened by the grace of God, which she deserved through continuous prayers, rigorous austerities, above all, with patronage of the Most Holy Virgin (whom she used to call her most loving mother), she was always victorious.

Cyprian, being vexed for not defeating her, raised again the demon, who was present, and he spoke in that way: "Perfidious, I can see your weakness, when you cannot defeat a delicate maiden, you, who boasts so much about your power and of making prodigious marvelous! Tell me now, from where did this change proceed from, and with which weapons did that virgin defend herself to make useless your efforts?"

And so, the demon, forced by a divine virtue, confess him the truth, telling him that the God of the Christians was the supreme Lord of heaven, earth, and hell; and no demon could act against the sign of the Cross with which Justine constantly armed herself. So that, by this same sign, as soon as he appeared to tempt, he was forced to flee.

"So then, if it is like that," Cyprian replied, "I am really mad in not giving myself to the service of a Lord more powerful than you. And thus, if the sign of the Cross in which the God of the Christians died makes you flee, I do not want to serve myself with your prestige; better I renounce completely all your sortilege, waiting in the kindness of the God of Justine to accept me as his servant."

Then, the demon, irritated for losing that one, through whom he made so many conquests, took his body. However, (Saint Gregory says) he soon was forced to leave, by the grace of Jesus Christ, who was now Lord of his heart. Cyprian had to bear vigorous combats against the enemies of his soul; but the God of Justine, whom he always invoked, supported him with his assistance and made him to be victorious.

Soon, Cyprian looked for his friend Eusebius, also helped a lot for this effect, and told him with lots of tears: *"My great friend, have come to me the blessed time to recognize my faults and abominable disorders, and I hope that your God, who I now confess that he is the only and truly one, will admit me in the community of his lowest servants to the great triumph of his benign mercy."*

Greatly satisfied for such a prodigious change, Eusebius hugged his friend affectionately, and he congratulated on his heroic resolution, encouraging him to always trust in the infallible truth of the most pure God, who never abandons those who sincerely search for him. And so fortified, the fortunate Cyprian could resist all diabolical temptations.

For this effect, he made the sign of the Cross ceaseless, and having always in his lips and heart the sacrosanct name of Jesus, he did not stop of invoking the assistance of the Most Holy Virgin. Seeing, then, all their artifices completely frustrated, the demons made their greatest efforts in tempting him with despair, proposing him, with liveliness of spirit, this and other speeches and reflections:

"That the God of the Christians was, without any doubt, the only true God, but that he was a God of purity, a God that punished with extreme severity even a smallest crimes, the best proof being themselves, that for just one sin of pride were condemned to an extreme punishment. After such a precedent, how would forgiveness be to him, that for the number and gravity of their faults, he already had prepared a place in the deepest of hell? And, therefore, having no mercy to wait for, he should take care just to have fun, satisfying at top speed all passions of his life."

Truly, this vehement temptation put in great risk the salvation of Cyprian. But his friend Eusebius, to whom he referred to, encouraged and comforted him, proposing with benign efficiency that the mercy of God receives and generously forgives all the regretful sinners, even if their sins be great. After that, Eusebius himself, led him to the assembly of the faithful, where people who wanted to be instructed in such luminous mysteries were admitted.

As Saint Cyprian himself asserts in the book of his *Confession*, in the sight of the respect and piety that the faithful were penetrated, worshipping the true God, he was touch lively in his heart. He says: *"I saw singing in that chorus the praises to God and at end of each verse of the Psalms with the Hebrew word Alleluia; everything with such a respectful attention and so sweet harmony, that it seemed to me to be between angels or between celestial men."*

By the end of the performance, the people present were admired that a presbytery like Eusebius, who had introduced Cyprian in that sacred congress. And the same bishop that was presiding found it even more strange;

because he did not consider sincere the conversion of Cyprian. However, he soon dissipated those doubts, burning, in presence of all, his books of magic and introducing himself amongst the number of the catechumen after having distributed all his wealth among the poor.

Instructed, then, Cyprian, and with enough disposition, was baptized by the bishop, and Aglaide, the enamored of Justine, who was regretful for his craziness, wanted to emend his life and follow the true faith. Touched by these two examples of divine mercy, Justine cut her hair as a token of the sacrifice that she was doing for God of her virginity, and she also distributed all the wealth that she possessed among the poor.

After that, Cyprian made marvelous progress in the paths of God; his ordinary life was a perennial exercise in the most rigorous penitence. He often was seen in the church, prostrated on the floor, with his head covered with ash, begging to all the faithful to implore for him the divine mercy. And, in order to humiliate even more and suppress his old pride, he obtained through the force many appeals to obtain the job of sweeper of the church.

He dwelt with the presbytery Eusebius, whom he always venerated as his spiritual father. And the divine Lord, who deigns to make ostentation of the treasures of his clemency over the humble souls and over the great sinners as well, truly converted, conceded to him the grace of doing miracles. This, together with his natural eloquence, contributed a lot to convert to the faith a great number of idolaters, making use of his famous writing of his *Confession*, which, making public his crimes and enormous excesses, encouraged the confidence, not only the faithful, but of the great sinners too.

Meanwhile, the name of Saint Cyprian, his zeal and the numerous conquests that he made for the kingdom of Jesus Christ, could not be ignored by the emperors. Diocletian, who was in Nicomedia at this time, informed of the marvels that Saint Cyprian worked, and of the perfect sanctity of the virgin Justine, gave the order to capture them, what was soon executed by the judge Eutolmo, governor of Phoenicia.

Taken to the presence of this judge then, they answered with a great generosity and confessed with such efficiency the faith of Jesus Christ, that they almost converted the impious barbarian. But, in order to not be judged that he was treating the Christians favorably, he ordered Saint Justine be whipped with two cords and the flesh of Saint Cyprian be torn to pieces with an iron comb, everything with such a cruelty that caused horror even in the pagans.

The tyrant, seeing then that neither the promises nor the threats, not even the rigorous torment, abated the firm steadiness of the generous martyrs, ordered that each of them be thrown in a big boiler full of pitch, fat, and boiling wax. But, the pleasure and the satisfaction that could be admired in the faces and words of the martyrs, gave way to knowing that they did not suffer at all with that torment. And it could be perceived that even the fire which was under the boilers had not even a minimum heat.

That was seen by a priest of the idols, a great sorcerer named Athanasio (who for a time was a disciple of Cyprian himself), and judging that all those prodigies preceded from the sortileges of his old master, and wanting to gain a name and a bigger reputation among the people, he invoked the demons with his magical ceremonies and threw himself deliberately in the same boiler from where Cyprian was taken out. However, he lost his life then, and the flesh was detached from his bones.

This fact gave a new splendor to the marvels of our saint, and there was about to be a great revolt in that city in his favor. Intimated, thus, the judge decided to send the martyrs to Diocletian, who was in Nicomedia at this time, and informed him by writing of everything that had happened. Having read the letter of the governor, Diocletian ordered that, without any more formalities of the usual processes, Cyprian and Justine be beheaded, which was executed on the 26 of September at the banks of the River Gallus, which passes through the middle of the referred city.

And arriving on that occasion to talk in secret to Saint Cyprian, a good Christian called Theotisto was soon condemned to be beheaded too. This fortunate man was a sailor, who, coming from the coasts of Tuscany, disembarked near Bythinio. His partners, who were all Christians, having news of that event, came in the night to seize the bodies of the three martyrs and led them to Rome, where they were hidden in the house of a pious lady, until, in times of Constantine the Great, they were transferred to the basilica of Saint John of Lateran.

Doctrinal Reflections

The great father of the Church Saint Gregory Nazianzen, eulogizing in one of his better prayers the two holy martyrs, Cyprian and Justine, invited not only the virgins, but the married as well, to imitate that saint in the glorious effort that she observed in her combats. The holy doctor says: *"Seeing furiously assailed the innocence of her purity, by the impulses of lascivious men and suggestions of impure demons, she had recourse to the weapons of the pray and mortification, macerating her body with fasts, and invoking with fervor and humility the help of her celestial husband, and the powerful patronage of the Most Holy Virgin."*

"Make use, then, of the same weapons when you see yourselves tempted by the power of the darkness. And the Lord, certainly, will defend you, in order that not only it will be defeated, but, with greater merit and with the promised crown to whom behave with courage in the battle." And finally, the holy doctor concludes by proposing the admirable conversion of Saint Cyprian, extracted from the profound abyss of the iniquity, to animate and comfort sinners (for more oppressed that they see themselves and with innumerable and great faults), to trust always on the divine mercy, which infinitely exceeds all the sins of men, and can, by the virtue of his grace, soothe even the most tough hearts and, reducing them to the exercise of a sincere penitence, elevates them, after, to a most eminent grade of the eternal glory.

Repentance and Virtues of Saint Cyprian

[GLT]

Cyprian (the *Sorcerer*, as we have already told, because from a tender age until he was thirty years old, he held a pact with the devil and had intimate relationships with all the infernal spirits) was born in Antioch, between Syria and Arabia, belonging to the government of Phoenicia. His parents were idolaters and owners of great wealth. Seeing that the nature had endowed him with the necessary talents to gain the esteem of men, they destined him to the service of false divinities, sending him to study the science of sacrifices that were offered to idols, in a way that no one knew deeply like him the profane mysteries of the gentiles. After he had completed his thirty years of life, he made a trip to see a religious man called Eusebius, who was his colleague at school and who, during that time, censured him because of his wrong life, to see if he could move him away from the unfathomable abyss in which he saw him. But Cyprian never wanted to attend his entreaties, and he scorned and ridiculed him.

However, on a certain day, Eusebius had prayed so much to God that his prayers were heard in heaven. The divine mercy condescended to illuminate and convert this wretched victim of the astuteness of Satan into a religiously devoted creature, making use of his divine mercy to show in the heart of Cyprian this great prodigy, by the means that we are going to expose.

There was in Antioch a maiden named Justine, very rich in wealth as well as in beauty, whom her father Edesio and her mother Cledonia educated skillfully in the superstitions of paganism. However, Justine, endowed with a clear ingenuity, after she had heard the preaching of Prailo, deacon of Antioch, renounced to the genteelism, and embraced the Catholic faith, she in short time converted her parents.

The blessed Justine, after becoming Christian, turned into one of the most perfect daughters of Jesus, consecrating to him her virtue and virginity, and trying to acquire by all means this delicate virtue, for which effect, she observed with the highest care the modesty and the retirement. But, despite of this, she saw a poor lad named Aglaide, who liked her so much that he asked her parents to have her in marriage, to which they agreed, but he could not bring this to good effect, because Justine denied to give consent herself. Then, he went to look for Cyprian, who employed all the most efficient means of his diabolical art to satisfy the determination of his friend. For nothing, however, served the spells of Cyprian.

Then, Cyprian, full of desperation, offered to the demons many abominable sacrifices, and they promised all that he pretended, assailing Justine with great temptations and ghosts; however, she, strengthened with the assistance of the grace that she had deserved through prayers and rigorous austerities, and with patronage of the very Most Holy Virgin, was always victorious. The upset Cyprian, for the uselessness of his efforts, turned to the demon that was present there and told him in this way: *"Damned and perfidious, I now see your weakness, because you cannot defeat a delicate maiden, you who boast so much of your power. Tell me with which weapons that saint virgin defended herself in order to turn useless your efforts?"*

So, the demon, compelled by a divine virtue, confessed him the truth, saying that the God of the Christians was the supreme Lord of heaven, earth, and hell, and that no demon could operate against the sign of the Holy Cross with which Justine was armed, so that, by this sign, soon as he appeared to tempt, he was immediately forced to flee.

Cyprian said: "*Then, if it is like that, the Lord has more power than you, and if the sign of the Crux makes you flee, I conjure and annoy you in the name of the God of the Christians.*" And Cyprian put his arms in cross, in sign of the Cross of Christ. The demon, irritated, took control of the sorcerer and threw him into hell. But, in a few moments, the devil was intimated by Saint Gregory to present Cyprian in his old state, what the saint achieved by the force of orisons.

After that, it was hard for Cyprian to live, because the devil was always appearing to tempt him; however, Cyprian quickly put his arms in Cross, and he always drove him away.

Saint Gregory said to Cyprian that he would not be saved until he was separated from all that he had been tied to. Cyprian invested himself with the grace of God and rented a modest house, with the purpose of calling there all the prestidigitations of the demon. Sometime later, Cyprian was elevated by the grace of God to the kingdom of the righteous.

Great Requisition

that was done by SAINT CYPRIAN *to punish Lucifer who always tempted in his prayers*

[GLT]

When Saint Cyprian saw the welfare that he was going to enjoy in Heaven and the evil that was going to supervene if he did not left Lucifer, he resolved to go and punish him in a frightful desert.

SAINT CYPRIAN LEFT HIS PALACE TO PUNISH LUCIFER

Here is how Saint Cyprian requested the demon:

> I, Cyprian, servant of God, whom I love with all my heart, for ten years, I regret, my Lord, that I had not loved you since the day I was born. Rise up, Lucifer, from that hell, come here now to my presence, traitor and false god, who I used to love so much for ignorance.

> *But, now I am undeceived that the God I adore is a true God, powerful and full of goodness, by whom I oblige you, Lucifer, to show up, under punishment of disobedience; when you do not want to obey me you will be punished a thousand times more than I pretend. Appear, promptly, Lucifer, I force you from the part of God, the Most Saint Mary and from the Eternal Father, I conjure you by the force of Heaven and by grace of God, who is on high with open arms and ready to receive those sons who stop adoring idols and false gods, whom I, Cyprian, loved already for thirty years; however, now, with the help of Jesus Christ, I have already left those false deities and adore a Powerful God who is in heaven, with whom I have now the pact, and I will have it until death; and by this same pact that I have with Jesus Christ I cite and oblige you, Lucifer, to appear immediately.*
>
> *Open now the doors of hell. Come to my presence Satanaz. Come from the Orient in shape of a human creature.*

Said that, Lucifer appeared, surrounded by all the demons from hell, as Saint Cyprian says in his book, chapter VIII, page 116:

> *I reach to count three thousand demons around me; however, in vain the demons illude me, and seeing them that they could do nothing, they revolted against me, at once of making fall fire from the stars, and so abundantly that it seemed that all the world was burning. All that to see if they could bury me under the flames of fire; however, I invoked the name of Jesus Christ and the fire never was able to reach me or even hurt me.*

Seeing that Cyprian already had great power under God, the demon resolved to disobey him and retire to hell and to not obey God nor Cyprian; however, it would had been better if he had not did it, because a thousand times more was he punished by Saint Cyprian.

Vita Cypriani

At the end of this requisition, we are going to teach how to prepare the rod with which Saint Cyprian punished the demon.

The requisition continues with how Saint Cyprian took the demon out from hell the second time and came to his presence to be castigated with the magical rod.

Saint Cyprian, seeing that the demon had been withdrawn to hell and closed the doors, he thought a moment about what he had to do or the way by which he would begin to requisite Lucifer and punish him as he deserved.

How Saint Cyprian started to requisite the demon.

I Cyprian præcepitur in nomine Jesus

You, who are in the glory of God Father, of God Son, and of God the Holy Spirit, and in the power and virtue of the Most Saint Mary, and of the Divine Verb Incarnated, and by the power of the Angels of heaven and the Cherubim and Michael, surrounded by the work and grace of the Holy Spirit, and by all this holiness, I command, without appeal and neither grievance, the doors of hell to be opened, and that Lucifer comes now to my presence, in order to be fulfilled and executed my order in accordance to what I have ordered.

Appear immediately, Lucifer, in a figure of human person, without uproar and foul smell.

Be opened now the doors of hell, as were opened the doors of the carcer where some Apostles were captive, and the Angel was elevated to heaven, as Jesus Christ had determined to him.

Jesus, Jesus, I ask and command in you, Most Holy Name, the demon to come now to my presence, without offending my person, neither my body, neither my soul.

Appear, immediately, Lucifer, because I request you by the power of the great Adonis [sic], and by the power and virtue of these holy words that Jesus Christ said, when he was giving his last breath on the cross, when elevating his eyes to the sky, exclaiming with anguish: "My God, my God, forgive them who crucify me, because they do not know what they do."

By these holy words, I conjure you, Lucifer, emperor of hell; come to my presence, without appellation or aggravation, because I oblige you in the name of Jesus and Mary and Joseph, and command you by the virtue of Saint Ubald Francis[43], by these holy words, by the virtue of the twelve Apostles, and by all the Saints of the God of Abraham, of Jacob, and of Isaac, and by the virtue of the Angel Saint Raphael, and all other Saints and virtues of the heaven and orders of the blessed: I request you, Lucifer, by the virtue of the blessed Saint John Baptist, Saint Thomas, Saint Philippe, Saint Marc, Saint Matthews, Saint Simon, Saint Jude, Saint Martin, and by all orders of martyrs, Saint Sebastian, Saint Cosmas, Saint Damian, Saint Dionysius with all his companions, confessors of God, and by the adoration of the king David, and by the four Evangelists: John, Luc, Mark, and Matthew.

I request you to appear, Lucifer, without appellation or aggravation, because I oblige you by the four columns of the sky, in order that you do not fault to my obedience.

I, creature of God, oblige you by the seventy and two tongues that are divided across the world and by all these powers and virtues. Appear, immediately, away four steps from me. If you do not appear in this moment, you will be punished with curses.

In this moment Lucifer suddenly appears, and says: "What do you want from me, Cyprian?"

---

43 Although it is uncertain to what saint the reference here is made, there is saint Ubald of Gubbio (Italian: *Ubaldo*; Latin: *Ubaldus*; French: *Ubalde*; ca. 1084–1160), who was the bishop of Gubbio, in Umbria, today venerated as a saint by the Catholic Church.

"I want to punish you as you deserves," answered Saint Cyprian.

"So, Cyprian, don't you remember the good I did to you? Don't you remember all the maidens you profaned the honor, and that all that was arranged by me? Do you forget the good I did to you? I made you to be the owner of an entire kingdom…"

"Disgraceful! The blameworthy on all this is me! If you had been less generous to me…"

"Fall down, now, now, fire over this man, and be reduced to ashes. Here is the scripture of the pact that you made with me; here is the pact we made and you did not fulfill. It is you who are disgraceful! Let fire fall over you!" said Lucifer.

In the moment Lucifer Said these words, there were so many lightning flashings and thunders, which made the earth to shake.

However, Saint Cyprian was afraid of nothing because his power was strong against Lucifer. Cyprian said to Lucifer: "Still and suspend these thunders and these rays that are falling from high."

Lucifer commanded the entire thunderstorm to cease.

"Will be punished with three thousand blows given with the darting rod," said Saint Cyprian to Lucifer.

"Forgive, forgive Cyprian, do not punish me," said Lucifer.

Cyprian did not obey.

Cyprian captured Lucifer with a chain of horns of virgin ram, and after tying him, said: "You are tied, damned traitor! You tried to steal my soul, for which Jesus Christ suffered so many torments for me; however, Jesus, being good, forgave me my sins, and because of this I will punish you with three thousand blows for being guilt of me offending the good Jesus."

Cyprian punished Lucifer and, in the end, put the precept that he would never again make a pact with any person.

This is the precept why the demon cannot appear to us, being only obliged by God or by all the Saints.

Life of Saint Cyprian

[TDH]

The saint who is venerated with this name was before his conversion to Christianity one of the most famous mages ever known.

Born in Antioch, between Syria and Arabia, from rich and powerful parents, he practiced all the magical arts until the age of thirty years, when he converted to the religion of Christ.

He left written infinite books of sorcery, product of his vast knowledge and of the wonders he executed in his time as magician and that will cause admiration to all people.

He exercised a formidable power over the infernal spirits which obeyed him in all his mandates. He came to effect astonishing enchantments.

He had absolute domain over persons and the elements, his conversion to Christianity happening due to the following rare happening:

There was in Antioch a Christian maiden named Justina, as rich as beautiful, daughter of Edeso and Cleonia, who had raised her in the religion of the Pagans. Justina heard one day the deacon Prailo preaching at Antioch, and hearing the ideal beauties of the Christina religion, she converted to it, achieving sometime after her own parents becoming Christians.

A young lad name Aglaide fell in love with Justina and asked her to be his wife, what he could not get because she had offered herself to Jesus Christ.

Desperate, Aglaide resourced to Cyprian, the Magician, to bend that woman who was so rebellious to be against his desires; and he applied the effect of all his sorceries and enchantments invoking the spirits to help him in his enterprise.

All, however, resulted useless. Justina resisted to all kinds of sortileges because she was under the intercession of the Virgin and was helped by the divine grace of Jesus, having beside this in her right hand the sign of the cross of Saint Bartholomew, which just by itself has power against all kinds of malefactions and enchantments.

Cyprian, full of furor by seeing himself defeated by such a delicate creature, raised against Lucifer and said to him: "What is the reason, oh genius of Hell, that all my power is humiliated by such a weak woman? Cannot you with all the domain you possess submit her to my mandates? Tell quickly what talisman or amulet protects her, which gives such force to defeat me and make useless all my sortileges?"

The, Lucifer, obliged by divine order, told him: "The God of the Christians is Lord of all that was created and I, notwithstanding all my domain, am subject to his commandments, and I cannot attempt against someone who makes the sign of the cross. Of this avails Justina to avoid the temptations."

"So being it like that," said Cyprian, "from now on I deny you and make myself a disciple of Christ."

What he did, achieving later to receive the martyrdom and to be counted amongst the saints.

The Legends

[HM]

The strange narratives embodied in the Golden Legend, how fabulous soever they may be, are referable notwithstanding to the highest Christian antiquity. They are parables rather than histories; the style is simple and eastern, like that of the Gospels, and their traditional existence proves that a species of mythology had been devised to conceal the Kabalistic mysteries of Johannite initiation. The Golden Legend is a Christian Talmud expressed in allegories and apologues. Studied from this point of view, the newer in proportion as it is more ancient, the work will become of real importance and highest interest. One of the narratives in this Legend so full of mysteries characterizes the conflict of Magic and dawning Christianity in a manner which is equally dramatic and startling. It is like an outline in advance of Chateaubriand's *Martyrs* and the *Faust* of Goethe combined.

Justina was a young and lovely pagan maiden, daughter of a priest of the idols, after the manner of Cymodoce. Her window opened on a court which gave upon the Christian church, so she heard daily the pure and recollected voice of a deacon reading the holy gospels aloud. The unknown words touched and stirred her heart so deeply indeed that when her mother remarked one evening how grave she seemed and sought to be the confidant of her preoccupations, Justina fell at her feet and said, "Bless me, my mother, or forgive me: I am a Christian." The mother wept and embraced her, after which she returned to her husband and related what she had heard. That night in their sleep the parents were both visited by the same dream. A divine light descended upon them, a sweet voice called them and said, "Come unto me, all ye that are afflicted, and I will comfort you. Come, ye beloved of my father, and I will give unto you the kingdom which has been prepared for you from the beginning of the world."

The morning dawned; father and mother blessed their daughter. All three were enrolled among the catechumens, and after the usual probation, they were admitted to Holy Baptism. Justina returned white and radiant from the church, between her mother and aged father, when two forbidding men, wrapped in their mantles, passed as Faust and Mephistopheles going by Margaret: They were Cyprian the magician and his disciple Acladius. They stopped dazzled by the apparition, but Justina went on without seeing them and reached home with her family.

Image of Baphomet drawn by Eliphas Levi for his book Dogme et Rituel de la Haute Magie, *popularly confounded with the figure of the Devil and used frequently in Brazilian editions of the* Book of Saint Cyprian.

The scene now changes and we are in the laboratory of Cyprian. Circles have been traced; a slaughtered victim still palpitates by a smoking chafing-dish; the genius of darkness stands in the presence of the magician, saying, "Thou hast called me; I come. Speak: What dost thou require?"

"I love a virgin."

"Seduce her."

"She is a Christian."

"Denounce her."

"I would possess and not lose her: Canst thou aid me?"

"I tempted Eve, who was innocent and conversed daily with God Himself. If thy virgin be Christian, know that it is I who caused Jesus Christ to be crucified."

"Thou wilt deliver her into my hands, therefore."

"Take this magical unguent and anoint the threshold of her dwelling: The rest concerns me."

And now Justina is asleep in her small and simple room, but Cyprian is at the door murmuring sacrilegious words and performing horrible rites. The demon creeps to the pillow of the young girl and instils voluptuous dreams full of the image of Cyprian, whom she seems to meet again on issuing from the church. This time, however, she looks at him; she listens, while the things which he whispers fill her heart with trouble. But she moves suddenly, she awakes and signs herself with the cross. The demon vanishes, and the seducer, doing sentinel at the door, waits vainly through the whole night.

On the morrow, he renews his evocations and loads his infernal accomplice with bitter reproaches. The latter confesses his inability, is driven forth in disgrace, and Cyprian invokes a demon of superior class, who transforms himself into a young girl and a beautiful youth, tempting Justina by advice as well as caresses. She is on the pomt of yielding, but her good angel helps her; she joins inspiration to the sign of the cross and expels the evil spirit. Cyprian thereupon invokes the king of hell and Satan arrives in person. He visits Justina with all the woes of Job and spreads a frightful plague through Antioch; the oracles, at his instigation, declare that it will cease only when Justina shall satisfy Venus and love, who are alike outraged. Justina, however, prays in public for the people, and the pest ceases. Satan is baffled in his turn; Cyprian compels him to acknowledge the omnipotence of the sign of the cross and defies him by making it on his own person. He abjures Magic, becomes a Christian, is consecrated bishop and meets with Justina in a convent. They love now with the pure and lasting love of heavenly charity; persecution befalls both; they are arrested together, put to death on the same day, and ratify in the breast of God their mystical and eternal marriage.

One Episode in the Life of Cyprian

[GLT]

Saint Cyprian says, in one chapter of his book, that one Friday, passing by a desert place, he saw so many ghosts around him that he trembled with fear and lost all his forces to be able to resist them, but the ghosts were witches who wanted to be saved. Soon one of them came to Cyprian and said to him, "Save us, if you understand that after this life we have other."

"How will I save you?" asked Cyprian.

"How did you save yourself, disgraceful?"

"Yes... I am a slave of the Lord! I am a slave of the Lor—"

He did not finish the word.

He fell into a deep sleep.

He dreamed with that the orison of the Custodian Angel would release him from that great danger.

He woke up and saw himself in front of an angel, who immediately disappeared... It was the Custodian!

Cyprian remembered the orison and said: "I, Cyprian, require and conjure the ghosts who appeared to me, under the penance of obedience and superior precepts."

A great thunder was heard in the sky.

Suddenly, Cyprian saw in front of him fourteen witches.

"Who are you?" Cyprian asked them.

"Maria and Gilberta, both sisters," two of them answered.

"And the rest of the ghosts?" replied Cyprian.

"They are my daughters, and, like me, all slaves of Lucifer," said Maria.

"What do you want?" asked Cyprian.

"We want to be saved and, like you, to be slaves of the Lord," they answered together.

Cyprian saved all those witches, and with the orison of the Custodian Angel, he tied all demons, so they never again could disturb them.

Saint Cyprian says that this orison did not work just to the good but to do the evil; however to do evil, it must not be finished.

History of Saint Cyprian and Clotilde

[GLT]

On the day of 15 of January of the year 1009, talking with the Prince Satanaz, Saint Cyprian said, "Oh my friend Satanaz, which supper do you give to me today, in payment for me being so faithful?"

Satanaz answered, "I will give you today a supper, or better, an unexpected pleasure that you, Cyprian, will like."

Cyprian showed he very pleased with the answer and said to Satanaz, "My friend and lord, whom I've loved for ten years with such a fidelity and satisfaction that it seems that I am not happy except when I am close to you…"

Satanaz smiled and said, "As you love me and are so faithful, I will love you in the same way; and so put your fava bean into your mouth and follow me."

Soon Satanaz and Cyprian disappeared.

Eight minutes later, they were above the palace of the king of Persia.

Satanaz opened a hole in the right side of the princess Clotilde's room, then turned to Cyprian and said, "Do you see this princess so beautiful?"

Cyprian answered to him, "I do not believe there is any beautiful girl who can be compared to her."

Satanaz Said to him, "So you see, Cyprian, my servant, that I am your friend, and that I love you with all my heart."

Cyprian, hearing these words, prostrated himself at the feet of Satanaz and said, "My friend and lord, whom I love with all my heart, body, soul, and life, if you can make me enjoy that maiden, I swear to you that I will love you even more than I loved you until now."

Satanaz answered, "I leave her to you. Convince her with your astuteness and arts, and I will be ready to whatever you need."

After that, Cyprian tried to use his magical arts to make the princess follow or call him; however, Cyprian, with all his sorceries, could not convince the princess.

Seeing himself desperate, he came to the palace and went to the cabinet of the king but did not find him.

Irritated with this, he thought, for half an hour, about what he should do.

Suddenly, the king entered by the door of the cabinet and cried in a loud voice, "Help me! Help me!"

On this, Cyprian put the hand into the pouch to take the fava bean and flee; however, no matter how he tried, he could not find it. He put his hand into the left pouch and took a small pipe of silver where he had a little devil (one of the ones I already mentioned to you).

"What do you want?" said the little devil to him.

Suddenly, Cyprian said to him, "I want now four castles around me."

"I will execute your orders in a minute."

In the same moment, the cavalry and guard of soldiers came; however, they did nothing. The combat was so fierce that the palace was completely destroyed.

The king prostrated at the feet of Cyprian and supplicated him to forgive him by the love of whomever Cyprian wanted most.

Cyprian said to him, "You must know that I am a bishop, and, beside this, I possess diabolical arts. You see that this palace is reduced to ruins; what will you give to me, that I put it back as it was before, and that in a minute?"

After that, Cyprian said the following words: *"I command now, by the power of the liberal Magic, that does everything, I command now, now, now, that this palace be raised and stay at its own natural and to golão, bring matão, goes from pauto to chião, to molitão, pexelaispera regra retragarão, oniteprontual fines!"*

At the end of these words said by Cyprian, the palace was exactly as it was before; the king, who saw Cyprian doing such wonders, even more scared, threw himself again at the feet of Cyprian, and said to him, "I ask, I beseech, lord, to forgive me if you believe yourself to be offended by my person."

Cyprian Said to him, "Get up, because you are forgiven, but with the condition you will give to me the princess, who is your daughter Clotilde."

The king, hearing these words, trembled and was motionless, not being able to say one single word. Cyprian again said it loud: "I already told you! Do you want or you don't give me your daughter Clotilde? Otherwise, everything will be reduced to ashes."

The king answered nothing.

Cyprian repeated, "So, what do I say?"

The king became silent again.

Cyprian, angry, gave a loud cry and said, "By all force of my black and white magical art, I command that this realm become entirely enchanted, the king and the queen reduced to two blocs of marble."

His order was executed in five minutes. Cyprian, when he saw everything enchanted, except Clotilde, was enraged against Lucifer and cried in a loud voice, "Lucifer! Lucifer! Appear to me, my Lucifer!"

"Here I am at your orders, friend Cyprian," said Lucifer.

"I want you to tell me," replied Cyprian, "the reason why I cannot satisfy my appetites with this beautiful princess."

The princess, who heard those words, said in a low voice, "If you are the demon, I invoke you in the name of the Lord in order that you say only the truth."

Here the demon, obliged by a divine force, said to Cyprian, "My friend, you will know that there is a powerful God who covers the Heaven and the Earth and has power over everything. If he wants, you and I cannot move from here, because he is powerful. The princess invoked His holy name and I could not but confess the truth, and besides this, the princess says everyday an orison, which delivers her of everything that is temptation from me or from my beloved sons."

Cyprian, suddenly, prostrates himself against the earth and said, "Lord of the high skies, who are You that I do not know? And you, Satanaz, malign spirit, damned Demon, damned, damned, who was my perdition? Damned be the hour in which I was conceived; damned be the uterus which generated me; damned be the father and the mother from whom I descend; damned be the hour I was born; damned be the milk I sucked; damned be how many steps I made in this life! My God, my God, my God, make the doors of Hell open now to swallow this damned man; let him disappear forever! Jesus, Jesus, Jesus, if I still have salvation, answer me from the heights of heavens."

Then, Cyprian heard a voice who told him, "Son, follow the life you have, that I will warn you, one year before of your death in order that you can take of your salvation."

Cyprian kissed the earth and thanked God the benefits He made to him.

However, it was a deception for Cyprian, because that voice he heard was the Demon himself, who, to deceive, ascended to the stars to pretend that it was god who answered to the appeals of Cyprian.

Cyprian, innocently, gave credit to the voice he heard. Very innocent he should be to not remember that that voice could not be from god. However, Jesus Christ, being good and just, did not fail to forgive Cyprian from the sins committed by the immoderate ambition, which the illusion by the power of Satanaz had caused to him. Cyprian retired from the palace and, when he was already distant, heard a voice who said, "Cyprian, Cyprian, avail me in this affliction by the love of that great God of the altars!"

Cyprian trembled and fell on earth.

The good princess Clotilde came close to Cyprian and told him, "I command in the name of God! Get up!"

Cyprian got up suddenly and fixed his eyes on the beautiful princess, saying to her, "What do you pretend?"

The princess answered, "I invoke the holy name of Jesus in order that you, man, do not move from here without restituting the life to my father and to my mother and disenchant all that you have enchanted in this realm by an occult and powerful art."

"Aye," said Cyprian, "all this I will do, but I ask you to tell me which is the orison you say every day, because of which I never could take ahead my depraved desires, using all the sorceries and enchantments."

"The orison I say," answered the princess, "is very simple, and with good will I will teach it to you. Listen ... "

Orison

> I deliver myself to Jesus and to the Most Holy Cross, to the Most Holy Sacrament, to the three relics it has inside, to the three Christmas masses, in order that no evil happens to me. Most Holy Mary be always with me, the guardian Angel of my guard me and deliver me from the astuteness of Satanaz. P.N.A.M.

Cyprian went, after that, to the place of the palace, disenchanted everything he had enchanted, and said to the princess, "Ask for me always in your orisons."

So did the princess and obtained from Our Lord Jesus Christ the forgiveness for Cyprian's sins, who did not walk even one more year in that deceitful life.

Cyprian was saved, because God does not reserve hate to His sons, whom many times he allows to follow a wrong path in order that, in an opportune occasion, he can show them His power.

For all that was exposed, you now see, readers, that the Demon cannot damage whoever says an orison like the one the princess said, and about which we just mentioned to you. Take care in imitating that daughter of God in order that you are not persecuted by the Demon, nor by witches and sorcerers.

We ask so that all persons dedicated to this kind of reading who want to avoid the enchantments and dangerous snares keep in mind this miraculous orison.

Story of Cyprian and Adelaide

[GLT]

Cyprian the sorcerer desired to possess the love of a girl named Adelaide and went to ask her to her parents; however, it was in vain, as they denied it.

Desperate with the answer given by the parents of Adelaide, he was angered so much against them that he sent his little devil, which he always carried in his pouch, to destroy, without delay, the houses and all the possessions of Adelaide's parents.

The orders were executed immediately.

As soon as Adelaide saw her belongings destroyed, she went after Cyprian and said to him, "Man, what wrong did my father did to you to work against him with such ingratitude?"

Cyprian answered, "Don't you see, Adelaide, that I love you so much that I see nothing but the place where you live?"

Adelaide answered to Cyprian, "If it is true what you say to me, pretend that from now on I am your slave, but not your wife, because I am not worthy of marrying you."

"For what reason," said Cyprian, "for what reason do you say you are not worthy of being my wife?"

"Because you being a saint," answered Adelaide, "canonized by God, how can I be your wife, if I am the biggest sinner in the world, as another like me I believe to not exist?"

Cyprian turned to Adelaide, and said, "Girl, if you adore God so much, and even doing this say that you are the biggest sinner in the world, what God of revenge do you adore?"

Adelaide, hearing these words, was amazed and, doubting what she heard, said to herself, *"Which God does this man adore? Perhaps there is another God besides mine? It is not possible!"* She armed herself with courage and said to Cyprian, "Man, I oblige you from the part of God, whom I adore, to tell me which strange god is the one you adore and that obliges you to negate mine?"

Cyprian answered, "The god I adore is Lucifer of Hell!"

Adelaide, hearing that, blessed herself three times and said to him, "I oblige and conjure you by the part of God, whom I adore, to restitute my belongings, exactly as they were."

Cyprian, obliged by the force of the Omnipotent God, returned the possessions to the parents of Adelaide and, after all that, retired without satisfying his desires with Adeliade.

Lucifer, appearing to Cyprian, said these words, "My friend Cyprian, do not bother me all the time; I already taught you how to make all the sorceries and all the magical art. You already have all the power I have; however, as the friend I always was, am, and will be, I will give you one advice so you can possess Adelaide..."

Cyprian said to Lucifer, "You, my friend, whom I love with all my heart, body, and souls, tell me then, what I am supposed to do in this case."

"Take your magical bottle," said Lucifer, "put your fava bean in the mouth and become invisible; in that same moment, go to the house of Adelaide and, as soon as you arrive there, put some of the oil from your bottle at one of the lights you will see there, that both Adelaide as her parents will be frightened with the prodigies they will observe, and you, Cyprian, profit from the occasion to take Adelaide into your possession."

Cyprian went, unhappily, to execute the orders of Lucifer, spirit of wickedness.

After five minutes, Cyprian had already enjoyed Adelaide, and his disgraceful desires were satisfied.

After reading this, maidens, what happened to the girl Adelaide, beseech to the Lord and the Most Holy Mary to deliver you from the astuteness of Satanaz, because the demon prepares so many snares for the Christians that they cannot escape them.

And so, gentle readers, why don't you walk always recommended to Jesus and the Most Holy Mary?

One Episode in the Life of Cyprian

The magical herb and its proprieties

[GLT]

Saint Cyprian says in the page 82, chapter XII of his book: "*The magical herb has so much power and virtue that it cannot be mentioned; not even the demon wanted to discover it.*" However, that was not enough, for Cyprian ignores this magic, because a shepherd found it, whose name was Barnabe.

Cyprian, walking one day on a mountain, saw a shepherd playing with a beetle—the kind usually called stag beetle.[44]

The case is that Cyprian, because of his curiosity, was observing what the shepherd did to the stag beetle, and he saw that the lad was killing and resuscitating it.

Cyprian said to himself, with great admiration, "What is this, or what virtue does this lad have to resuscitate an animal after having crushed it with the foot?"

Cyprian came to the shepherd and said, "What are you doing, good shepherd?"

---

44   Stag beetles are a group of about 1,200 species of beetle in the family Lucanidae.

"I am keeping my flock," answered the shepherd. "Who are you?" asked the shepherd to Cyprian.

"I am Cyprian," he answered with a smile.

"Ai, ai!" said the shepherd. "Peradventure is the Bishop of Cartagena, or it is Cyprian, the Sorcerer?"

Cyprian, hearing these words, said to the shepherd, "What would you do to me if I was Cyprian the Sorcerer?"

"Ai, poor sorcerer!" answered the shepherd. "What would be of you today in this mountain?!"

Cyprian trembled and said to the shepherd, "Calm down, calm down, shepherd, because I am not the Sorcerer, but the bishop of Cartagena."

The shepherd suddenly threw himself on his knees over the ground and said, "Good shepherd, father of the Church, hear my sins and absolve me from them, because you have power to do it."

Cyprian thought with himself: *With good manners, I will know the secret of this shepherd.*

The simple shepherd, kneeled over the ground, made his confession in the following way: "I confess to the Bishop of Cartagena, who has power to forgive my sins."

"According to our doctrine," said the false bishop in the end, "forgiven are your sins, good shepherd."

Thus finished the confession, which was made according to the style of that land.

In the end of the confession, Cyprian, pretending to be bishop, said to the shepherd, "What did you do to that beetle who, after being dead, you resuscitate?"

"I cured him with an herb," answered the shepherd, "which grows in the mount, that only the beetles, the wagtails, and the swallows know."

"So, how did you find it?" asked the fake bishop.

"I was walking around playing," answered the shepherd. "I saw one of these beetles and killed it; a few minutes later, I saw another beetle arrive with an herb between the horns and put it over the dead beetle and it soon resuscitated. I, then, took the herb from it, and I have been killing many animals, but as soon as I touch them with this herb, they resuscitate."

"What great virtue this herb has!" said the fake bishop.

"This herb," said the shepherd, "has virtue to do everything you desire in this life; if you desire to possess this herb, I will catch it for you."

"How it can be fetched?" asked the fake bishop.

"Very easily," answered the shepherd.

How the shepherd fetched the herb

He searched for a nest of swallows which already had eggs and was brooding, and after he found it, he cooked the eggs in boiling water and put them back in the nest without the swallows noticing it.

The swallows, when the time came, saw that there creation wasn't hatching, went to fetch said herb, and put it over the eggs to make the creation born.

The shepherd, who was waiting, went to the place where the nest was, took the herb, and went to give it to Cyprian, the false bishop of Cartagena.

In the *Book of Saint Cyprian*, nothing more is found about the virtues of this wonderful herb.

However, we, on our behalf, say that great virtue has this herb which resuscitate the dead and make the eggs hatch after being cooked.

Note well, readers, this wonder, and we expect that someone curious makes all he can to obtain this herb, and he will be the most happy man in the world.

Story of Cyprian and Elvira

[GLT]

The magic of the animals is the magic that the Demon and Cyprian used to convince the only daughter of a marquis, entitled Marquis of Soria, and the most appreciated by the king of Persia. This girl was named Elvira.

Cyprian, seeing her one day with her parents, supposed that there was not a second maiden who could be like her.

He soon put into practice his diabolical art, demonstrating to the marquis that he desired his daughter.

The marquis, looking well the person Cyprian was, saw that he was a vulgar man, and said to him, "You, man, what do you pretend with my daughter?"

"I," answered Cyprian, "pretend to love Elvira, but not to marry her."

The marquis, hearing those words, became enraged against Cyprian; however, everything was in vain for him, because Cyprian quickly said the following words: "I want now, by the diabolical and magical arts, A.M.N.O.P, that the marquis and the marchioness turn into marble stones!"

Soon was his will satisfied.

Cyprian turned to Elvira, and said to her, "Do you see, girl, what I did to your parents? The same I will do to you if you are against me."

Elvira, frightened with what she just heard, said to Cyprian, "What do you want, man?"

Cyprian answered, "I want you to follow me and stop adoring the false God you adore and love only my laws and my mandates."

Elvira, hearing those words, prostrated on the ground and made to Jesus Christ the following orison: "Lord, if it is your will that I follow this man, say it from the heights, because I am ready to follow Your determinations."

Cyprian, hearing the petition of Elvira, was offended and enchanted her with the same words he used to enchant her parents.

Cyprian was satisfied with his revenge; however, it would be better if he wasn't, because he risked losing his life.

The king, as he was a great friend of the marquis, soon noticed his absence and was bewildered of not seeing him, and said to himself, *"What happened to the marquis and his daughter Elvira and all his family?"*

No matter how hard he tried looking for him in his entire realm, all his efforts were in vain.

One month later, a woman very badly dressed appeared in the palace and said she wanted to talk to His Majesty.

They went to tell the king that a poor woman pretended to talk to him. The king said to his vassal, "Tell to the woman to come in."

The woman entered and did not prostrate on the ground, as was the costume.

The king, seeing that the woman was so unsubmissive, said to her, "Perhaps you, woman, do not deserve to be beheaded in this place, because you lack the due respect to the king?"

"What do you say, barbarian king?" answered the woman. "Spill the blood of a woman when she comes to give you good news and assuage passions you carry so deep in your chest?"

The king then remembered that maybe that woman came to bring news about the marquis and his family and said with a supplicant voice, "Woman, forgive me; you see well that it is my passion for the marquis what makes me feel angry!"

"Today," answered the woman, "you will see the marquis and all his family but with the condition of ordering to kill a man named Cyprian for me."

"Cyprian the sorcerer?" said the king.

"Yes, this one," answered the poor, "and I will advise you on how to do it."

"Yes, woman, tell me what do you understand I must do?"

"Call him here and tell him to present the marquis and his family and that, if he does not do it, he will pay with his very life."

The king, believing in the advice from the woman, did what she told.

He ordered Cyprian to his presence.

When Cyprian came to the presence of the king, he told him, "What do you want, royal sir?"

"I want," said the king, "that you present to me here the marquis and his family, under the penance of having your head cut off."

"With whom do you think you are talking to?" said Cyprian.

"I speak with a sorcerer," answered the king, "who has a pact with Lucifer, the Prince of Hell."

When the king said this, Cyprian invoked all the malign spirits and ordained that the entire palace, and the king and his family, be enchanted.

Then, the king threw himself on his knees at the feet of Cyprian, saying, "Pardon, pardon, great and powerful Cyprian! Disenchant me and my family, because I am not guilty of this."

"Who is to blame?" asked Cyprian, angry.

"The guilt of all this," answered the king, "is a woman who is hidden in my palace."

"This woman," said Cyprian, "let her come, without delay, to my presence."

The king ordered the woman to appear immediately.

"So you, woman, with what pleasure did you want the king to shed the blood of a prudent man without crimes?"

"Without crimes?! Who is the man with more crimes than you," answered the woman, "who enchanted a family who was so much appreciated by the king, my lord? And you say you do not have crimes? Ah!

Disgraceful! You are worthy of a thousand deaths if that was possible. Here is who has power over all your powers and all your astuteness."

Cyprian, hearing what the unknown woman just said, trembled and answered, "What power do you have against my astuteness?"

"I have power over everything, because I am a sorcerer of more age. I was one of the firsts to make pact with Lucifer, and because of that, I have power over all sorceries."

"As you belong to my law," said Cyprian, "I do not want to make you feel the forces of my sorceries. What do you pretend from me, woman?"

"I want you to restitute to the king the marquis and all his family and bring them to the presence of the king."

Cyprian thought for a moment and suddenly said, "Yes, all this I will do, with the condition that Elvira be mine, and I will esteem her as I should."

The woman answered, "So, present them, and Elvira will be yours."

Cyprian's simplicity made him believe in the counsel of the woman. He went quickly, very happy, to disenchant the marquis, the marchioness, and their daughter.

Conversation the woman had with the king whilst Cyprian did not return

"Royal sir," said the woman, "we will kill Cyprian this very day."

"Don't you see," said the king, "that Cyprian has the great power of the Magical Art and that he can enchant all of us with one sole word?"

"No, royal sir, because I too have enough power to thwart all his enchantments and diabolical arts."

Saying that, the woman took care of burning incense in the palace; however, it was all in vain, because Cyprian had a great diabolical force.

However, she made something against him.

Arrival of Cyprian

A few moments later, Cyprian arrived with the marquis, the wife, and Elvira, who were disenchanted.

The king was full with the most vivid satisfaction and said to Cyprian, "Get out from here, man without heart, who have over you the weight of the most horrendous crimes, because of your perverse wickedness and infamy."

Cyprian, enraged with what he just heard, arrogantly said to the king, "So this is the payment you give to me for disenchanting the ones you esteemed? I see that you do not know me well. Just wait and I will fix you."

Cyprian suddenly put the hand into his pouch, and, taking out the little devil, said, "I want now ten castles at my command."

Soon were the orders of Cyprian fulfilled, after what he burnt the palace, but all was in vain, in consequence of the sorcery of the woman, when she incensed the palace.

Cyprian recognized soon that the witch had thwarted his intent and, seeing that he could do nothing, got vexed by the falsity the king used with him.

Encounter of Cyprian with Lucifer

Cyprian was sadly thinking about the betrayal of the king and saying to himself he should leave this world, when Lucifer appeared, who, putting the hand on his shoulder, said to him, "Don't worry, Cyprian, friend of mine, because Elvira will be yours."

"It cannot be," answered Cyprian.

"I judged that you trusted more in me, my Cyprian. Calm down, that everything has its remedy."

Cyprian calmed down with the conciliating words of Lucifer, who conducted Cyprian to a desert and said to him, "You now see, dear friend, that the palace was smoked with rosemary and incense, and because of this we cannot enter there with our diabolical arts; however, it will not be enough to avoid Elvira being yours this very day."

"What must I do to possess her?" said Cyprian, who seemed to burst with satisfaction.

"Take by hand," said Lucifer, "all the animals of the world, especially toads, spiders, rats, snakes, lizards,[45] ants, flies, geckos, finally, all the ones you want or can get; put them into a large cauldron, throw at them a quarter and half of virgin olive oil, and quickly make a fire in a way that the animals melt and become oil, with the only condition that they must be thrown into the cauldron alive. After that, bring me the oil inside a very well-closed glass flask, and you must not smell it."

Cyprian made everything that Lucifer ordained and, as soon he saw it was ready, went to tell him.

Cyprian told Lucifer he had concluded his work and how he did it, then he told him, "You know what to do now with this oil."

"I will listen to your advice," answered Cyprian with curiosity.

"Prepare a light with the animals' oil and, after everything is ready, put your fava bean in the mouth, and say to it that you want to enter the palace without being seen by any person."

Cyprian, before doing what Lucifer told him, asked, "I must do when I arrive there?"

"As soon as you have entered the palace, light your magical light that immediately everyone inside the palace will be frightened: You, Cyprian, put a fava bean inside the mouth of the witch, who must still be there, and another in the mouth of Elvira, and say, *'Favas, follow me.'* As soon as you have elevated the witch to great height, let her fall, because it was her who put you into all these works."

Cyprian made as Lucifer indicated. After he threw the witch from an enormous height, he took Elvira to a desert and said to him, "What do you want, maiden Elvira, that I do to you?"

Elvira answered, "Do to me whatever is your will."

It is not necessary to say what Cyprian did, because the readers will forcibly imagine it.

---

45   The original says "sardões," which means the ocellated lizard (*Timon lepidus*).

Cyprian, just with the animals' oil, could convince Elvira and steal her. He prepared a very rich palace such that a beautiful dove like Elvira could enter it.

As you see, readers, the Devil, after he begins to entangle a creature, does not leave her without first achieving what he wants: Because of that, we recommend that all Christians not forget to make the signal of the Holy Cross every day, three or four times.

Encounter between Cyprian and Saint Gregory

[GLT]

Cyprian and Saint Gregory had one encounter, in which they disputed about the Holy Catholic Faith, and Saint Gregory was the winner

In the third century, seeing Saint Gregory preaching in a temple, Cyprian passed outside and said in a loud voice, "What preaching is that impostor doing?"

One of the listeners said to Cyprian, "It is Gregory."

"Ai, ai," said Cyprian, "what God does that Jew adore! Instead of listening to that impostor, it would be better if you were at your homes doing your jobs."

Saint Gregory, who observed the conversation of Cyprian, smiled and continued with his practice.

At the end of said practice, Saint Gregory went after Cyprian and said, "Man who lacks faith and awe of God, will you not end this life of sin?"

"Ai, with the life of sin!" said Cyprian, bursting into laughter.

"Yes, with the life of sin," said Saint Gregory. "You, Cyprian, walk so deluded with this art of the Demon that you do not want to leave it."

"Say to me, friend Gregory, what God is the one of the Christians and yours, from Whom I have being hearing so many wonders?"

"The god you adores is Lucifer, and the one I adore is a Powerful God, who created the Heavens and the Earth and everything else the Sun has dominion over."

Cyprian quickly answered Saint Gregory, with a countenance full of indignation, "So if you, Gregory, adore a God more powerful than mine, defend yourself with him against my astuteness. And, if you be victorious, I will believe in your God; however, if I win, you will be the victim in this very moment."

Saint Gregory trembled and said to himself, *"If God forsake me, what will be of me! Cursed be the hour I came to meet with Cyprian. My God, my God! If you do not avail me now, what will be of me?"*

Cyprian, indignant with the supplication Saint Gregory was making, yelled in a loud voice for all demons of Hell, and in a few moments, there were so many demons that they covered the earth for a distance of a quarter of league in a square; however, Saint Gregory raised eyes to the sky and said in a loud voice, "Jesus! Jesus! Be with me in this moment of affliction."

At the same moment, a strong thunder was heard, the doors of Hell were open, and immediately all the demons precipitated into the deep of the frightful abyss.

Cyprian, seeing the incident, so worthy of amazement, fell on the ground and was prostrated for a quarter of hour.

After some minutes, Saint Gregory felt a great tremor of the earth he felt admirable.

It was Lucifer, coming from the bosom of the Earth with a coffin of fire and four lions carrying it, and at the sight of this spectacle, Saint Gregory was stupefied; however, he was encouraged with the help from the Lord and said to Lucifer, "I conjure you, damned, from the part of God and say what do you want here?"

"I came to take Cyprian," answered Lucifer.

"Peradventure," returned Saint Gregory, "you, damned, has power to take possession of the living creatures?"

"I," answered Lucifer, "take possession of Cyprian already dead, and he is mine, in body and soul; so we are agreed."

Saint Gregory, hearing what Lucifer said, prayed to the Lord and said to Lucifer, "I conjure you to the deeps of Hell, because Cyprian is not dead."

Saint Gregory touched Cyprian in the shoulders and said to him, "Get up, Cyprian."

Cyprian got up, and soon Saint Gregory said to him, "Do you still do not repent, Cyprian, from this life of sin? It is necessary to be a very wicked man, to see the hand of God trying to save him, and always follow the path of perdition!"

"And you, Gregory," answered Cyprian, "don't you know that I belong to Lucifer, because I formed a pact with him, and I cannot enter into Heaven, where only the just enter and not the ones who follow the path of Hell? So, get away from my sight, or I will use my powers and my diabolical arts."

Saint Gregory got angry against Cyprian and told him very severe words: "Unworthy man, get away from my presence, or I will also use of my means."

Cyprian, at those words, was so offended against Saint Gregory that suddenly the sky was covered of clouds, the air got turbulent, the earth shook, and great lightning fell over the ground in such a way that the world seemed to be ablaze; however, Saint Gregory, with the name of Jesus, stepped on and destroyed the astuteness of Cyprian.

Cyprian, seeing that he was doing nothing, got angry against Lucifer, who appeared to Cyprian and said, "My friend, what do you want from me that you are so angry against your lord?"

Cyprian told him, "You, Demon, what power do you have, that we cannot destroy Gregory."

"Don't you know that Gregory told me that if I never got entangled with him, one year from now he would give me his soul? Because of this, friend Cyprian, it doesn't suit me to combat with him this way; retreat, Cyprian, and leave Gregory."

Cyprian put a fava in the mouth and retired to the city where he had his habitation.

About this case, I did not find anything else written.

Reflexions about what you just read

When the Demon said to Cyprian to leave Gregory, that there was nothing that he could do, because of a contract he had made, it was just to trick Cyprian, to stop him from carrying on making war against Saint Gregory, because the Demon was afraid that Saint Gregory converted Cyprian, and that was the reason that the Demon lied to Cyprian.

Encounter of Cyprian with a Witch

[GLT]

Encounter between Saint Cyprian and a witch who was doing wrongly the sorcery of the skin of pregnant snake, and how He taught her

Saint Cyprian was returning from a Christmas party, and he could not cross the fields where he had to cross because of a flood of the river, and he had to take shelter in a tunnel, made by nature, to spend the night.

He wrapped himself in his thick mantle and went to rest in the darkest part of that hole.

Near midnight, he heard the steps and saw a light. Fearing that it was criminals, he hid under a gross stone. Moments later, inside the cave, a cavernous voice sounded, saying, "Oh magician Cyprian, my king or sorcerers, here I came with four fires and I ask you to help me win the prize of my enamored client."

The Saint was going to get up to interrogate whoever was speaking like that, but he had to recede because of these words: "Oh Lucifer, oh powerful governor of the country of fire, rise from the flames, come to me, and enter this cave, where I come every night, and help me in my craft of consoling unhappy wives."

After that, an annoying smoke ran through the subterranean.

The Saint marched in the direction of the voice and found a disheveled old lady, in front, and with the hair shaved in the back.

"What are you doing here, woman, and who is the Cyprian you invoked?!"

"He was a sorcerer that sometime ago converted to the Christian faith, and who had the gift of working everything he wanted with the help of Satanaz."

"But why did you call him now?"

"I wanted to ask him a recommendation to the demon, to help me in my enterprise, of which depends my fortune in the world and the tranquility of a very rich lady."

"Who is that woman?" asked the saint.

"She is the daughter of the count Erverardo of Saboril, married to the Great-Duke of Terrara, who treats her very badly because of a lady from the court, whom he adores with passion. The daughter of the count promised me a *raza*[46] of gold if I release the husband from the arms of the lover."

"What combustible is that, which suffocates with such an annoying smell?" the Saint asked.

"It is skin of snake with the flower of sage and the root of heather, which I am burning in the name of Satanaz, to smoke the clothes of the duke to see if I can unbind him from that woman. This magic was always infallible when my mother practiced under this vault in which the hands of man took to part. My mother unbound with it many concubinages of nobles and monarchs, but I did it already six times, and the Great-Duke, each time, mistreated the wife."

"It is because you did not put in the principal ingredient, what your mother did not reveal to you."

"Tell me what it is, by the God of the idolaters."

"Are you a Pagan? Do you profess the law of the barbarians?"

"Yes."

---

46 An old measure of approximately 13.8 liters.

"In this case, I will not teach you the secret. You can be sure that you will not save that girl from her martyrdom."

The poor witch started to cry and let herself fall abandoned over some branches of tree, which the shepherds had dragged there during the day.

The Saint raised her with great charity and, after brushing her dress, said, "You were capable of doing the same to me if I had fallen at your feet."

"No!" answered the witch, "because I assume you do not belong to my law, and we just love ours and we have the obligation of practicing evil against the sons of other religions."

"It is because your law is evil! Your religion is the waste of all the others!"

The witch began a convulsive trembling and foaming as if taken by hydrophobia.

Saint Cyprian covered her with the mantle and continued, "The proof is here. Let Jesus Christ forgive me, for taking me as an example. I help you, because my religion, which is Christian, says that everyone is son of the same Omnipotent God and that you must not ask the beliefs of a brother who suffers."

"Blessed it is, this religion, but I cannot take it, because mine would deliver me to hunger and abandonment, and I am supported by the heathen priest."

"And what does importance it have? Do you want to convert and guarantee the means of your subsistence?"

"I want! But how will you make my happiness, being so poor, as my rags show?"

"How? But didn't you say that the daughter of the count Erverardo would give to you a *raza* of gold if you restitute the love of the husband?"

"I said, however ... "

"Tomorrow, at the ninth hour, go meet me at the temple of the Christians, and I will introduce you to the presbyter Eugenio to give you the lustral waters and I will soon tell you the secret that makes this magic so infallible."

"But who are you?"

"I am Cyprian, the old sorcerer, but as soon as I felt in the body the water of the baptism I could not use the power of magic anymore; but as it is for good and I will win a soul for Christianity, I will tell you the way to do this one that you have been searching in vain."

"Tell me, lord, tell me!"

"Wait. Only tomorrow, after being inscribed in the book of the Christians, you will know. Be at peace, and I will wait for you there."

And the Saint, no matter the darkness of the night, went to the house of Eugenio, to tell him what happened.

In the morning, being in the church with the presbyter, he saw the witch coming, who ran to kiss the feet of the priest.

He was baptized in sequence, and at the end of the ceremony, Cyprian called her by his side and gave to her a square parchment, where was written the following orison, making three times the sign of the cross:

> *Oh pregnant snake, by the God who created you, I flay you, by the Virgin I bury you, by your beloved son I burn the skin in four stoves of molten clay. With the flower of sage I marry you, with the root of heather I light you, and with the Sabaean resin[47] I bind you, and done six times the white magic, tear away from the arms of the perfidious lover (so and so), and with this Sabaean resin I incense you, taken today from the temple of Christ. Amen.*

As soon as the witch finished praying this orison and executed these instructions, she went to the way to the palace of the Great-Duke, a few leagues away from the village. In the same occasion the Duke dressed the cloth incensed by the witch, he prostrated himself at the feet of the Duchess, asking forgiveness for his levities. On the next day, he took one eye from the lover and despised her.

The daughter of the count quickly ordered a *raza* of minted gold to be given to the witch and took her as her personal chambermaid.

---

47   The original expression "resina sabéa" also appears in the work of Camões, where it indicates incense from Sheba, a kingdom believed to have existed in Yemen and Ethiopia.

Encounter of Cyprian with a Poor Woman Full with Children

[GLT]

One afternoon, when Cyprian was returning home, he saw a poor woman surrounded by five children, carrying one more on the back, inside some kind of bag, and another in the arms.

Cyprian went to her, saying, "Where are you taking these children, woman? You probably stole them!"

"Stole them, my lord—don't I have anything else to do, when every year I have two?! Ai, my lord, poor as I am, because my husband works on the field and win little, calculate the embarrassments I have to sustain these children, not to mention the ones to come!"

Cyprian, pitiful, asked her, "And you do not want to have more?"

"I, my lord, not even that much..." and quickly correcting, concluded, "Now that they are already here, the poor things, let them grow; but, more, I would give some years of life to not have more."

And at this point, they reached a place where the sea could be seen in all its extension.

When they arrived there, Cyprian said, "I will teach you one recipe to not have more children, but keep from divulging it, because it can be fatal."

"I will keep absolute secret," said the woman.

Cyprian smiled, because he remembered what values a secret in the mouth of a woman, and continued, "If you do not keep it, the harm will be yours." And pointing with the fingers to some crags, he asked: Do you see beyond these shells?"

"I see," said the woman.

"And by the side of the shells, what do you see?"

"Sponges, my lord."

"So take one of them, take out the jelly stuff around it, let it dry, then beat it, take out the sand and any grain attached to it, and you want to copulate, wet it on the water, squeeze it, and put it compressed with the fingers into the vagina, keeping it there during the coitus."

The poor woman, at the height of her contentment, was about to leave, without thanking Cyprian, when he called her. "I still did not tell you the size the sponge must have, and it is the most important."

"It is true," said the woman with sadness.

"I could punish you for your lack of gratitude, because you were leaving without thanking me, but I want to be indulgent. The sponge must have this size..."

And he drew in the sand, with a rod he carried in the hand, one circle.

And it had the size of the palm of the hand of the woman.

***

There are many recipes to women avoid having children; the one above is infallible, and it was used by some people to whom the poor woman revealed what Saint Cyprian, pitiful with her luck, taught her under rigorous secret.

Her talkativeness, however, caused her to be accused of being a sorcerer and she was sent to be burnt by Diocletian.

Later, this recipe was abandoned, because such is its efficacy that it was judged to be a work by the devil.

How Saint Cyprian Invented the Cards

[GLT]

It is reported that there are many people who read cards, but what does it avail them if they do not possess the *Great Book of Saint Cyprian* or *The treasure of the sorcerer*, to study and learn by heart the responsory that must be said, as this Saint used to say?

This is how Saint Cyprian invented the cards: This Saint, after repenting from the evil life he had, went away from his homeland, and there he wandered for seven years. As this Saint had great love for his wife and children and did not know what happened to his parents, he decided to create the cards. The Saint said, *"When I was master of the astuteness of Satanaz, I read the cards by the power of my lord who was Lucifer; however, now, I do not know what I will do."*

He was thoughtful and at night he went to bed. An Angel of the lord appeared to him and said, *"Cyprian, what are you thinking? Peradventure that damned you left has more power than your God, who commands over everything the sun covers? Is still your faith not true?"* And the Angel fled.

Saint Cyprian woke up and said, *"This night I had a very pleasant dream, because who has more power than God? I still remember the day I commanded fire to fall from the sky to the earth by the power of Lucifer. And one woman just saying Jesus made the fire stop from falling. Great is the power of Our Lord Jesus Christ!"*

He was thinking about this and he said, "*Then I will read the cards in the name of Our Lord Jesus Christ*"; and so he did.

Saint Cyprian made great virtues to the cards so it could guess everything he wanted; because of that, everyone who does not do it like that, nothing will avail to him to read the cards. If he does, it is by imposture.

Saint Cyprian took the pack of cards and passed it through seven baptismal fonts of holy water, each one inside its church, and after that, he said over them the creed in cross, meaning he made crosses on the cards with the right hand, and then passed them by the waves of the sea, seven times wrapped, and it did not get wet.

After that, he divined what was going on with his family and many other things he desired.

Responsory that must be said when you are about to read the cards:

> *Oh my most beloved Lord, you who are the God of the universe, allow these cards to declare what I want to know, because, Lord, I do not have more to ask; the Lord be with me and help and succor me; Most Holy Mary, my mother, help me by the intervention of your beloved Son, my Lord, whom with a most lively faith, I love with all my heart, body, soul, and life. Cards, you will not fault me to this by the blood shed by Our Lord Jesus Christ. Amen.*

This way is how the cards are read, and whoever does not do like this will not achieve a good result.

The Witch of Évora[48]

[GLT]

The Witch of Evora or Story of the Forever Bride

Taken from a Manuscript of Amador Patricio
dated in Salvaterra[49] aos 23 de Abril de 1614

The Moor of Evora lived happily with their king Praxadopel, and the Christians loved him also because of how he treated everyone.

The king Praxadopel did many things for the good of his city and its outskirts, like in Montemuro,[50] where he built a castle of which today there are only ruins, and it is called castle of Giraldo.[51]

Walking, then, digging, to make that castle, the sepulcher of Montemuro was found, as well as a house under the ground, six *varas*[52] of length and four of width. It was the lair where the Lagarrona witch did her diabolical sorceries.

---

48 The city of Évora has more than 200 years of history, having been a Celt regional capital; it has archeological treasures that includes megaliths and a Roman temple. It was one of the three main centers of the Portuguese Inquisition, together with Lisbon and Coimbra, in the XVI and XVII centuries.
49 Probably *Salvaterra dos Magos,* a municipality in Portugal.
50 There is a mountain ridge named Serra de Montemuro, which is the eighth highest elevation in Portugal at 1382 meters.
51 The Castle of Giraldo belongs to the district of Evora, and its first fortifications date to the Bronze Age. It was used in the XII century by the half legendary warrior Geraldo Geraldes, as a headquarters to take Evora from the Moors.
52 A measure of about 1.10 meters.

In the middle of the house was a pit the size of a man. Inside, it was all painted with lizards, snakes, and geckos. On the outside, on the borders, there were four stone toads, and between each toad some figurines of boys, each one with half cubit, on their feet. They had in their hands some rods with which they threatened the toads. In one of the corners of the house was the figure of a monster which from the head to the waist was a man, and from the waist down a coiled snake. In the other corner, there was a turtle and over it a crow which had in the beak a bat, like it was eating it. In the other two corners, in each one, one figure of woman, one awakened and the other sleeping; the awakened one had in the left hand the head of a man by the hairs, and at her feet a cattle dog with the mouth open, like it was trying to attack the head, and the woman stopped him with the hand.

The sleeping one had in her hands a true owl and in the other a hawk with open wings wishing to attack the owl. On the walls, there were many paintings of snails, slugs, frogs, wasps, beetles, and other small animals.

The floor was all tiled. In a place by the side of the pit, there was a very big stone with an inscription saying the following:

> Whoever be the first to open this pit
> Will see great things never seen
> Dig in front to resist
> The great fear with the chest to the test
> Do not fear, do not fear, do not show fright
> Go to the bottom, enter by the center
> Because the more you see, the more is inside
> Thing of valor is hidden
> You will find things that will happen
> In the coming ages in which Portugal
> Will again have the royal labarum
> Of the industrious people who know how to win.

They tried to take out the stone, to know what was inside, as the inscription said, but they could not, because it was too big, and digging, they began to till around the stone, where they found the sepulcher of

Montemuro, with bones and a skull, all rotten, as well as some molded books from which not much could be read, and writing everything down, it was ordered to be kept on the city library, where after being taken by the Christians, there was found written many meanings of astrologers about these enchantments; and filling everything with strong alicerces, they built the castle over it, that presently is named "of Giraldo."

A few steps from this place, the king Alvado had a rural property, where he ordered his sepulcher to be made and to be buried when he died.

In that property lived a man named Fausto, who had a very beautiful daughter, with whom fell in love a Moor who was an astrologer and magician, with the name of Matacabel, and kidnapping her, put her into a house outside the city, where a Moor woman lived, also a magician and enchantress, who was named Lagarrona. The Moorish woman had a son named Candabul, who, seeing the Christian woman in the house, fell in love with her, and so kept her from Matacabel, who decided to take her to another place, what was the reason he lost his life, because one day, going with determination, Candabul waited for him in a secret place and killed him, burying him in that place who became known as Matacabel, and today is Matacabello.

The justice, being informed of this case, went out to arrest him, but his mother Lagarrona made him invisible, and that way convinced the justice he was absent. Lagarrona knew through her spells that her son would one day disappear because of the love of a Christian woman and, understanding that she was the one she had under her power, pretended to make her a Moor so her son could marry her. The girl, however, said she would only be happy if she could see her parents, to what Candabul consented, promising to bring her back.

The parents were very happy to see their daughter and determined to marry her quckly, before Candabul came to take her, who knowing this went to his mother Lagarrona, who made certain spells, and Candabul left with them, becoming invisible, to the house of the Christians and, arriving by the time the daughter was married, put the sorceries under the bridegrooms pillow, so when they laid they would sleep deeply. Candabul put into the sleeves of the groom certain materials, what as soon he dressed made him benumbed and speechless; and with everybody coming to help, without profiting from any medicine, he went on consuming for twenty-four hours, until he died.

The parents of the bride were very sad and became determined to marry her again; knowing this, Candabul did the same as he did to the first. And getting married a third time, Candabul did it again, and the groom also died.

Christian did not know anymore how to marry the daughter to someone who would be happy and ordered to be said to the son of the witch to come and receive her, because they did not have other resource, because beside killing the grooms, he caused great damaged to the farms or the Christians.

However, they told the justice to come and arrest him, for the treacherous death he came to Matacabel, what was done to great relief of the Christians, who were with ill forebodings; and so they married the daughter to a Christian named Fabricio, a rich man who had an inheritance nearby; and as the people of that place saw the maiden, they called the lady Forever Bride, because she was married four times, and in a short time, the place became known as *Forever Bride*, as it is until today.

Candabul was sentenced to be hanged and cut into quarters, because he killed Matacabel. Lagarrona, knowing this, prepared herself with her enchantments and Magic to free him.

That night, in the prison, many shadows appeared enveloped in fire, as they were demolishing the prison, to the point the guards had to abandon the post; and reporting to the alcaides, they came to suspect that it was caused by the mother of the convicted, because of the armed giants and fierce animals.

Tying the captive's hands and feet, they took him out to bring him to justice; but when they came to the gallows, there was great thunder and lightning, which scared everyone, and soon dark clouds came, so thick that the air became dark and they could not see each other, and after that, the ground opened, with a lot of smoke and dark shadows walking in the air, with snakes in the hands, fustigating everyone.

Then with a great noise and trembling of earth, the air became as clear as before.

The executioners, then, rushed to take the criminal, and catching him with an arm around his neck, drowned him; and when they went to quarter the victim, they saw him turned into a donkey, with which they were very amazed, and soon they understood there to be enchantments of the Lagarrona, because they saw him running, fleeing through the fields.

When Lagarrona saw her son, she sent him, enchanted as he was, to the Forever Bride, where Fabricio lived with his wife, whilst she prepared certain things to disenchant him and return Fabricio's wife to his power.

The justice ran to Lagarrona to make her hand over her son or pay on his place; but finding her door well closed, they had to use their shoulders to open it, which she did not notice for being so concentrated on doing the sorceries.

When the people of justice came in, the witch was standing with her left hand raised, and with the right, she was moving as if writing in the air, moving it from one point to other. In front of her, there was a mirror in which she saw herself; over the mirror the hand of a man, opened, which was slowing closing, and when it closed, she hit the ground with her feet, and soon it opened again.

On the ground was painted a sign of Solomon, and in the middle, there was a timber which reached the ceiling; the said timber had two rats holding it to keep it from falling, because the timber sustained a big crossbar where a stone was hanging, like a mill's stone with a hole in the middle, which stone got down and up very slowly, until the witch put her head inside the hole, where saying certain words, a bat appeared and flew in the house, and the crossbar lifted the stone again. The Lagarrona repeated her sorceries with the hands and feet, lowering the stone again, and saying the words with her head inside it, and the bat came flying again.

The words the witch said, as Gulpodia, Dicanie, Zurmio and other ancient authors affirm, were the following:

Olenta in pus, nigalaonegabus.Oleolapolaó, merrinhaó, merrinhao, nhão, nhãn, nhão!

When the justice came to see her, there were two bats, and stopping to pry how she did the sorceries, another two bats had come; and not wanting to wait anymore, they got inside and arrested her. And with that the toads which were bleeding the timber [sic], and leaving it, the crossbar fell with the great stone, which, hitting the head of the Lagarrona, killed her, and all the sorceries were unmade.

The justice hanged her in that place, where she remained until she rotted, which was where she lived, and from that on it was called Lagarrona, taking the name of that witch, and changing a letter with time, today is called Lagarrona [sic].

The sorceries the witch was making to disenchant her son, Candabul, were left unfinished, the reason why he remained enchanted, in the Forever Bride, and still today he wanders there, because many times knocks are heard at night in that house of the Forever Bride, where Fabricio lived peaceful with his wife and children, from whom the youngest named Rodrigo, the king Alvado of Evora, took to be the gardener of his propriety.

The Magical Art

Instructions of Cyprian

[GAG]

There are six important things to be observed in this work, but if you neglect but one, it is doubtful you shall succeed in your purpose.

I

The Master must have a firm faith and not doubt his work, for he that doubts his prayers will be answered prays only with his mouth and not with his heart.

II

He must be secretive and not betray the secrets of his Art except to his fellows and to them of his counsel.

III

He must be strong-minded, severe, and not fearful.

IV

He must be clean in conscience, penitent for his sins, never willing to return to them again as long as God gives him grace.

V

He must know the rulerships of the Planets and the Times to meet to do the work.

VI

He must lack none of his instruments. He must speak all things plainly and distinctly. He must make his Circle in clean air and one time.
Whoever observes these six rules by God's grace shall not falter, but shall obtain his purpose.

Exclusion of all evil things, maledictions, bindings, incantations, bewitching, enchantments either by devices or otherwise, which we know or those which we know not.

Author est Saint Cyprian.

Necessary Knowledge to Exercise the Magical Arts

[TDH]

That person, man or woman, who wants to dedicate his spirit to the Magical Arts, shall possess a true calling for this, putting his will and good faith into the exercises and practices. It is very important that he does not forget that the spirits he invokes can read his thoughts. If he does not put himself into the invocation with all his senses and without getting distracted from the work he performs, instead of being properly answered, his invocation will be punished for its audacity by the same spirits that he had disturbed or called to make a pact with.

He also must be aware that the invocations cannot be done in a place where crosses or holy symbols are present. The person who wants to perform these experiments must be completely alone, unless someone initiated in the Art and who made a pact with some spirit is with him.

The place most adequate to make the invocations will be atop a mountain, with a river circulating on its base, ensuring that there is no taller mountain around. If that cannot be, then a place near a river will be searched for, where two ways cross making four paths which go in opposite directions. These paths represent the four cardinal points of the universe, and the spirit being called can come along any of these roads. It is absolutely necessary that the river is close to the place of invocation, because water and air are the elements most suitable for the transmission of thought, and these, together with the metals, play a great role in the exercise of the Magical Arts.

If, due to health issues, or for any other reason, it is not possible to perform the operation outside, it will be necessary to choose a solitary habitation, with all the walls and the roof covered with a black cloth, after which the windows shall be open and the following orison must be said:

> *The place for the experiments is ready: in it there is nothing holy and neither are there any religious symbols: my soul is completely free from the divine spirit and inclined to the pact with the spirits of Hell who I will invoke with all my will and without obeying the mandate or imposition of anyone.*

It is necessary not to feel any fear in that hour nor at the apparition of the spirit, because if you are fearful, you expose yourself to be tormented by the very spirit who appears at your conjuration. The truly initiated must be bold; as a consequence, whoever has fear does not perform the invocation with the true faith that Lucifer requests from those who will make a pact with him. He punishes with innumerable sufferings, and sometimes with death, the impudent who wish to use him as a plaything of his mistakes. There are endless cases of people who fell mute, deaf, blind, or that have other sufferings because of this.

In order that the invocations have real force, it will be convenient to possess some talisman or amulet with the cabalistic signs from the Clavicule and make the drawing of the great circle, not forgetting, however, the previous warnings.

In the section corresponding to the invocations and conjurations, it will be found the explanation and way of executing them.

Essential Qualities to Profess the Magical Arts

[TDH]

Magic, like all Sciences, requires very special conditions from the people who dedicate themselves to its study and knowledge. Because of this, it is useful to undertake a detailed examination of the aptitudes you possess, to achieve the desired result in how many works are done.

In first place, you must have true desire and calling, because if it is not like that, it is futile that you propose to achieve anything, as you will take the subject as a mere entertainment and will not put all your energy into the work.

In second place, it is necessary to put great attention into the preparation of everything you propose to do, because for any missing detail or distraction you have, the result will be the impairment of the work itself, putting you at risk of being unsuccessful.

There is also the need for constant study of the natural world, to be able to arrive at the true knowledge of the supernatural which is the aim and object of the Magical Arts.

Another thing that must be acknowledged is that for no reason should you reveal to someone who is not an adept in these sciences the supernatural things you come to know.

What was just said will be enough for anyone to judge if he is well disposed and if he possesses the qualities required. If he does, and if he has valor and temerity, he will succeed in everything he wishes. But if he lacks faith or valor, or if he does not put his will in the works, then he should not expect any positive result, opening himself up instead to see that which he least expects come to pass.

The true mage then shall be studious, discreet, and constant in his works. He must especially put all his faith and will into the work, and persevere when the work does not go to plan, or when he does not achieve what he searches for.

The spirits do not always show themselves propitious to assist the invocations of the mortals; sometimes it is necessary to repeat the call, conjuring them again to show themselves, obliging then if they do not come with some talisman or amulet which possesses enough power over them.

On the Necessary Qualities

[LSC]

As it happens with any art and with any science, some aptitudes and talent are necessary to realize the true magic. Therefore, I will now show some of the basic necessary faculties that must be possessed by everyone who approaches our studies, and aspires to achieve everything they desire.

The desire and the calling are, without any doubt, the base in which is founded the pillar of magical knowledge; without these, nothing is possible. Whoever takes our science as a mere recreation and amusement to create a distraction from banal life should forget all possibility of achieving his objective, because he will not apply himself with all his desire and calling.

The necessary requisites are the diligence and zeal to prepare everything that is necessary. Each detail has in itself the weight of an entire operation, because there is nothing that is not of absolute importance. Therefore, somebody who is not careful about details, whose attention is easily lost, who is distracted by any triviality, will attract to himself the failure of his operation. It is also of great necessity to apply yourself to the study of natural things, because the comprehension of the supernatural is not possible without the knowledge of the natural.

Silence and secrecy continue our list of requirements. The practitioner of our art is forbidden to communicate his deeds, and the wonders he comes to achieve, to anyone who is a stranger to the occult sciences.

Everything that was said is a necessary step to allow somebody to achieve the knowledge of our science, and if the necessary valor and temerity is taken into account, it is possible to achieve any objective.

He who aspires to be a magician shall put all his endeavor, his knowledge, and his discretion into his objectives. Any failure is especially interesting, because the faith and constancy of the mage is tested through it.

I must add here that, sometimes, the conjured spirit may not present itself to your call, for sometimes it is necessary to repeat the operations, and sometimes to force them with talismans and amulets if it is deemed necessary.

Elemental Knowledge to for Magical Art

[LSC]

Every person who wishes to dedicate himself to the Magical Art, being man or woman, shall always keep in mind that the calling is not everything and that the spirits invoked must be the most important thing in mind. If a mistake is made due to distraction, for not having focused all the senses on the operation, he will be punished for being audacious; the punishment will be inflicted by the same spirits that were invoked to make a pact.

Never, I say, will he perform the invocations or the pacts in places where there are Christian symbols or holy crosses of any kind.

Whoever wishes to perform such operations must find himself absolutely alone, unless his companion is also initiated or has pact with some spirit.

He will always prefer the highest place, if possible the summit of the highest mountain at the side of which runs a river. He will be careful to check that around it there are no higher peaks.

In case this is not possible, the next best place will be a crossroad near a river. Said crossroad must form four roads opposed two to two, representing the four cardinal points, because through any of them he can call the spirit he wishes to invoke.

It is completely and absolutely necessary that the river is present in the vicinity of the place of invocation, as air and water are the elements most pertinent to the mental transmission, which, if I may add, is of the foremost importance in our Magical Art.

If, for other reasons, like health issues, none of the proposed options are possible and you have to operate inside the house, you shall take into account the following conditions.

You will choose an abandoned habitation and will cover it completely with black cloths, including the ceiling and the walls. When it is so arranged, you will open the windows completely, and will say the following invocation:

> *I here have set up the place of my operations; with such objective and end, I dislodged from this place every relic, cross, or any other trace of the Christian religion. My being, my soul, and my mind are free of all divine presence, to fulfill with success my project of making a pact with the beings from Hell. I will invoke and convoke these spirits showing to such effect my iron will, without bending myself before any imposition, unless of free desire and aspiration.*

Fear is the downfall of the sorcerer and his perdition, because in front of the apparition of the conjured spirit, you must never show fear of any kind, or risk being punished by the conjured spirit.

In truth, bravery is the necessary virtue to fulfill our objectives, because fear is considered an insult to the Lord of Hell. No initiate can, nor should, lodge unrest in his inner heart at the appointed hour, because the fear is a lack of faith towards Lucifer, and his derision and just punishment are immeasurable, inasmuch as it can be deadly, or even worse. Nobody has the prerogative of making fun or joking with the infernal spirits.

We could here narrate an infinity of cases about this, in which the boldness of showing yourself irreverent to the infernal figure received as a reply the loss of one or various senses, or becoming maimed by the loss of some member.

With the aim of having a fruitful operation, you should possess some talisman with the powerful cabalistic signs from the *Clavicules of Solomon,* Mage amongst mages, and Wise amongst the wise. It is useful, anyway, to trace the great circle of protection. To do all this, you must employ the correct instruments proper for sorcerers, instruments that I will describe later.

Ceremony of Magic

[LM2]

The magical operations require determined personal preparation, not just preparation of the instruments that the mage needs. Above all he must, instead of helping himself with the power of objects, resort to the highest and most grave secrets of his art to call to himself the celestial and infernal powers, making them faithful servants of his will and of his desires.

Before giving explanations of such mysteries, it is for me a duty of conscience to reveal to the reader the dangers he risks if he does some experiment of this type, disregarding some precaution or being pushed by vain curiosity or lightness of heart, which can make him see the evocations as an object of amusement or pure jest. Keep yourself from committing such imprudence! Nobody with impunity has called or will call at the doors of the supraphysical; once these doors open before you, you must enter into the regions of mystery to win or to be defeated by its terrible guardians, and—do not believe that there is exaggeration in saying this—if you turn back, there is grave danger of losing reason or life.

Personal Preparation

When the magician plans to appeal to the supreme invocation of the celestial powers, for forty days beforehand he will retire to a solitary and quiet place, avoid any encounters and contact with people, particularly women, and he will try to remove mundane thoughts from his mind, extinguishing in his soul the voice of the passions to make it pure, serene, and unalterable at every moment. He will sleep a little and always at the same hours; he will rise at daybreak and will take long walks through solitary places, absorbing himself in the contemplation of nature and in the adoration of the Eternal Creator, to whom he will ask in silent prayer that the celestial lights guide him to the satisfaction of his enterprise. He will eat frugally and without having meat or any other thing coming from animals in his foods; he will not drink wine or liquors, and he will dedicate his time to meditation and study. Every morning, he will bathe in running water, and it is vital that in his internal and external clothes he keeps the most scrupulous cleanliness, not wearing any gift that may have been handled by another person, above all by a woman in her menstrual period.

He will get used to staying awake and well relaxed at a certain hour of the night, so that when it comes, which will be the one of the invocation, he will extinguish the light and stay in the deepest darkness, he will face the Orient and, crossing his hands over his chest, he will invoke the power of God and the celestial powers to help and fortify him so he can face peacefully the presence and oppositions of the terrible *Guardians of the Doors of the Mysteries.* This operation must be repeated every day without fault, in such a way that, if he misses only it once, he must begin the forty days again.

Fifteen days before the appointed end, he must go to the nearest church and give to a priest that he has never met before a scrupulous general confession. In the next day, he will take Communion, and in the remaining days, the mage will submit himself to fasting and to meditation without help of any kind of reading and without breaking the silence that must surround him, not even to talk to himself.

In the following day, he will leave his habitation when the Sun rises, and, placing himself in a place where there is thick vegetation and where he is perfectly sure he will not be seen by anyone, he will remain the entire day in complete quietness, with the mind absorbed in what he will execute and in what he will achieve. When night comes before leaving the place, he will face the four cardinal points, beginning with the Orient, and four times he will ask Heaven for efficacious help from the invisible powers.

In the next day—the day of the magical invocation—he will stay inside his habitation, without taking any food and giving himself to his meditations until the time to begin the magical ceremony.

It is necessary that the mage who does all this has the firm desire to triumph; let him banish from his spirit every doubt; let him make his conjurations with the most unbreakable resolution so that no matter how terrifying the conjurations are they will not intimidate him, and that he will not abandon the magical circle before discharging the spirits even if they do not show themselves visibly: There is a great danger in doing this; let him always be advised against such tricks from the evil powers; let him never establish illicit pacts with them; and, to finish, when he formulates his mandates, let him do it with energy and firmness and without fear or any scruple.

Preparation of the Habitation of the Mage

He will have at his disposal a small room which is situated so that it is away from curious views and inopportune visits: The window will face the fields or some open place from where no one can see the inside of the habitation. Nobody besides the mage will enter the room, particularly women who could make the atmosphere impure with their menstrual emanations.

The most scrupulous cleanliness must reign in the habitation, and all unnecessary furniture and luxuries that can attract the sight must be removed. All that is needed are a table painted in black, a few chairs, and a cabinet to store his instruments and the things proper to the magical ceremonies. This furniture must be new, and if it can be made by the mage, even better. When acquiring any piece of furniture, he will purify them from the contact they had with strangers using proper perfumes and the aspersion of water where there is small branch of rosemary and verbena, picked on Friday at twelve at night, cutting them with a consecrated knife.

In the ceiling of the room will be painted the seal of Solomon with two crossed triangles, one red and the other black, and in the center of the figure will be traced with red characters the Hebraic tetragram of the most sacred name of God.

You will never, in any circumstances, make this room into a place for meals; you can sleep in it, but must have the utmost care to not alleviate your bodily needs—greater or smaller—there, or to leave dirty clothes and things of use or belonging to other people which may be in your power.

When preparing this room, which in fact would be convenient if it were in a new house to avoid as much as possible the personal influences of the previous owners, he will purify it with the water of the magical aspersions thrown with branches of rosemary and verbena against the four walls, ceiling, and floor, saying this exorcism:

> *O Pater conditor, aime siderum, sapientia suma, per omnes fortitudines tuas et virtutes tuas, sanctificare digneris habitationem hanctuo honore preparatam. Exorciso te habitationis, per Deum verum, Deum vivum el æternum qui cuncta fecit ex nihilo et nihil sit in hoc meo opere quod impurum sed virtute plenum.*

On the Instruments that are Necessary to the Magical Arts

[TDH]

This is the most important part of the occult sciences, because if the instruments do not have the proper preparation, or if they are not well engraved with the signs that each one requires, they will lack the sufficient virtues for the works they will perform. Because of this, a great care must be put into their creation and, afterwards, in their storage and use. After making this statement, we will explain in correlative order the name and the creation of each one of the instruments.

Knife of White Handle

On the day of Jupiter, which is Thursday, and when the Moon is full on the horizon, you will take a knife of new steel which has never been used before and will put it into the fire three times. Soon, you will sprinkle over it a mixture of the blood of a mole and the juice of the aromatic plant called pimpernel, which would have been prepared for such purpose. The mole and the plant must be taken during the Full Moon and in the day and hour of Thursday, and in the same fashion you will squeeze the plant and take the blood of the mole in the same day and hour in which the steel is prepared, when the Moon is over the horizon. When bathing the steel with the aforementioned potion, you will cut with it the handle of a goat horn that is white, which would have been prepared a little before so it will possess the necessary virtue. See in the drawing the form of the handle and of the knife. When you have finished the operation of cutting the handle, you will say the following conjuration:

> *I conjure you and form you, instrument, so you will serve me in my works of the Art through the virtue and influence of the planet Jupiter, in whose hour you are created, by the virtue of the elements, of the precious stones, of the herbs, of the snow, of the hailstone and of the winds. It is my desire that you possess all the precious virtues so I can perform those works that I desire with true safety. To you I invoke in this work of mine, oh! Superior Spirits who answer to the names of Damahu Lumech Gadal Pascia, Valoas Marod Lamidoch Ancretón Mitratón and Adonai, to help me in all the works I set myself to accomplish so I can reach the knowledge of the sciences that you possess, the first step of which I make in this solemn hour.*

This being done, you will put the knife into a large pouch of red silk, and you will perfume it with powder of roses and lily of Florence, keeping it safe for when you will use it.

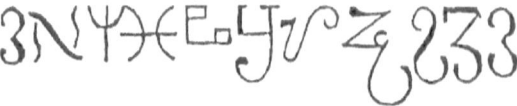

Characters of the white handle, according to the Véritable Magie Noir

Knife of Black Handle

The knife of black handle must be made on the day of Saturn, which is Saturday, following the same procedure used to make the knife of white handle, taking into account that in the conjuration you must say "second step," instead of "first." The handle must be black and of ram's horn. The blood of a black cat with the juice of the herb pimpernel.

The Magical Art

Characters of the black handle, according to the Véritable Magie Noir

The Sword

To make this instrument, you must choose the day of Mars, which is Tuesday, during the reign of Capricorn, which is from the 21st of December to the 21st of January; it will be done in the hours from twelve at night to six in the morning, with the Moon being full over the horizon. A mole must be prepared to be sacrificed in the same day, and bathe the sword with its blood, mixed with the juice of the herb pimpernel. The handle can be made of bone or hazel wood, in this case cutting the bark with the instrument itself. On the sword must be engraved the same inscriptions it takes, if the person who will use it is initiated or a master [sic].

The Poniard

This instrument will be created on the day of Mercury, which is Wednesday, having the blood of a mole and the juice of Mercury; it will have a handle of black goat horn.

Lancet

To this instrument will be observed the same rules for the dagger, but the handle will be of steel.

Needle

The same rules of the dagger and the lancet.

The Wand

This instrument must be created with branches of walnut, which must not have any sprout. It must be cut on the day of the Sun, which is Sunday. The signs must be made on the day of Mercury (Wednesday) with the feather of a male goose. Once finished, the following conjuration will be said:

> *Oh, powerful Adonay! I supplicate your intercession to give this wand virtue and grace forever and ever.*

After that, sprinkle it with clear water from the river, taken on the day of Sunday.

Characters of the wand, according to the Véritable Magie Noir

The Feather of the Male Goose

To acquire the feather of this bird, which possesses all the magical virtues, you must make sure that it is a male, fully grown goose. You will sacrifice it on the day of Jupiter at the hour of twelve of the night, under the light of the Full Moon, and you will say:

> *I sacrifice thee, oh bird without equal!, in this solemn hour and in honor of the powerful and sublime Adonay, to whom I dedicate the first works I do, and to whom I conjure to invest the feathers with the magical gifts necessary to serve well in all my experiments.*

This being said, you will behead the bird with a knife that has never been used before, with which will be made the cuts the feather requires for when there is need to use it. This must be the fifth feather taken from the right wing of the bird.

The Magical Rod

You will find a wild hazel tree that was not cultivated by the hand of men and will look for a branch with the form of the drawing. Once found, you must wait for the day of the Sun, that means Sunday, in the month of June in the days from 2 to 30. You will take the knife of white handle and will stay by the hazel tree so that, when the Sun rises on the horizon, you can cut the branch that you will use. As a following act, you will say:

> *I request thee, oh great Adonay, Eloim, Ariel and Jehovan!, to be propitious in this hour, granting to this rod that I will cut the force and the virtues that Jacob, Moses, and Joshua possessed. I again request to you, oh Adonay, Eloim, Ariel, and Jehovan to adorn it with the force of Samson, the science of Hiram, and the wisdom of Solomon to allow me through your intercession and by the virtues with which you will adorn it to find treasures, metals, waters, and everything that is hidden from my eyes.*

After pronouncing with great faith and ardour these words, you will raise your sight and contemplate the Sun and will make the cut with three strokes. Once having it, you will take it home, put it slightly into the fire to mould the head or will cut it with the same knife, and soon will submerge it in clear river water, saying:

> *Oh rod of rare virtue! You are of greater value than gold, with you I will find treasure and you always will be a rod.*

Repeat it three times. Perfume it and keep it carefully.

Mysterious Rod

To make this rod, you must execute the same operations used for the magical rod and in the same period, but on a Thursday. You will look at the bank of a river that has crystal clear water and a wild rush which must be very full. You must follow the same ceremonies, being careful when saying the invocation up to *"by the virtues with which you will adorn it,"* when you will say, *"to win over every misfortune in this life and all my enemies."* This rod must be four feet long. It is necessary to carve in the biggest part a snake's head with open eyes, and make at the other end the figure of the tail of the same animal. All this must be done in the same day and with the instruments of Art. After it is finished, you must behead a young white lamb. You will make a circle with the rod, joining the two edges, and will attach them with a white ribbon and will put into the circle a new clay bowl, into which you will take care that the blood of the lamb falls to work as a baptism. During this act, you shall say:

> *I sacrifice you, innocent young lamb, in memory of the sacrifice the Israelites made in the times of the Pharaohs, so that the exterminator angel would not maltreat their homes whose doors were bathed in blood. So, I ask in the solemn hour of the sacrifice that the blood I pour over this rod gives me the power to win over all my enemies, corporeal as well as spiritual, and also win over myself and the things that can be harmful to me, which I hope will be granted by the intercession of the higher spirits: Adonay, Bolm, Ariel, and Jehován present in this act.*

Just after this, you will take the rod with the right hand, will wash it in river water and keep it, after perfuming it, according to the indicated rules.

Dagger

This instrument must be engraved only by the master. Its construction is like the sword, only the handle must be of the same steel as the blade.

The Magical Art

Hook

For this instrument, the same rules of the knife of white handle must be observed.

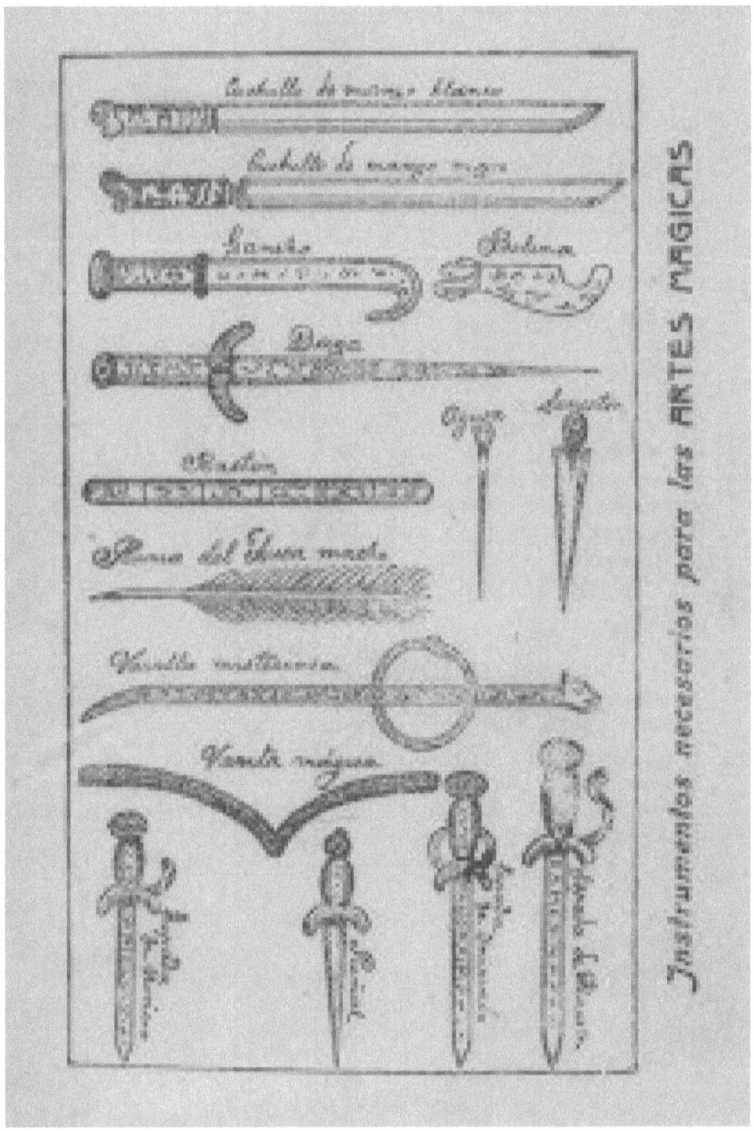

The instruments necessary for the Magical Artes, from the Livro de São Cipriano *attributed to Jonas Sufurino.*

Boline

The boline must be made from boxwood with the same rules as the magical rod, and it will be of use for any operations that must be performed. In the invocation you must say "boline" instead of "rod," and when you submerge it in the water:

> *Receive, oh! mysterious boline, the necessary gifts in order that you can find for me the things which are hidden from my sight and understanding, in order that I may know then.*

You must have great care to imitate the best you can all the drawings and forms of the instruments.

Preparation of the Instruments

[LM2]

The invoker must always have the following ready:
- The sword.
- The knife of white handle.
- The knife of black handle.
- The poniard.
- The lancet.
- The magical needle.
- The magical rod.
- The string with seven knots.
- The consecrated plume.
- The cup of libations.
- The brazier of the perfumes.
- The magical gypsum.

The Sword

Have it done, or buy, a blade of fine temper with a triangular shape and put on it a round handle made of ivory, ending with a pommel of magnetized iron. The cross will be of iron and will be forked in both edges. After it is built, sprinkle it with the water of the aspersions; you will have three

Masses said over it and a priest initiated in the secrets of magic will bless it, and after that will put it in a new and purified sheath, covered with a white silk cloth.

Knife of White Handle

You will have it made with the best steel, with an ivory handle, and will consecrate and keep it in the same way of the sword.

Knife of Black Handle

The blade will be of stainless steel, and the handle of ebony. When you have purified it with the water of the aspersions, you will sacrifice with it a black cat, whose body you must burn in the flames of a bonfire made of branches of willow, cypress, and holy oak, putting the knife to receive the fumes that the fire releases. When you are done, keep it in a sheath of black leather.

The Poniard

Buy a new one of small size, well sharpened and fitted with a ring through which you will pass a red string made by your own hands with seven knots, saying when making them, *"Be my defense against my enemies."* The poniard you will always carry with you tied to the string, which you will pass by your neck, and you will be able to use it after consecrating it magically. To do this, thrust it into the door of the cemetery on a Saturday night at the first toll of midnight, leaving it there until the hour of the dawn. When thrusting it into the door, you will say:

> *Lucifer, Lucifer, Lucifer! by the souls who rest here, by the blessing that this holy ground received, in this hour which*

is the hour of your adorers and of the diabolical spells, I challenge your power and your astuteness and I prepare this weapon which has in its handle a blessed symbol, the cross of the Christian, and its blade a sharp edge ready to sink in your body and in the body of your creations, as it is sank into the wood of this door.

The poniard is the best weapon of the mage, and with it, he can affront every kind of ghost, assured that the wounds on them will be far superior to the ones given by it to a living being with a well-aimed blow.

The Lancet

It is consecrated in the same way as the knife of white handle and the sword, and it is used to extract from the mage a few drops of his own blood when he needs it for any operation of his art.

The Magical Needle

It is not necessary for it to be consecrated; it is enough that it is new and perfectly clean. Use it to sew many things whenever it is needed for the ceremonial magic you are going to practice.

The Magical Rod

(We omitted the original explanation because it is already in one of our previous editions.)[53]

---

[53] Very often, we find in this kind of literature references like that, which are dead ends as the editors do not provide a proper indication of the sources refered to.

The String of Seven Knots

It does not need special consecration, and it would be best to use a string taken from the frock of a Franciscan monk, blessed in the usual way. You will make seven knots with it, saying at the same time the seven words Jesus Christ said on the Cross. It is a powerful talisman that, if it is put in the place where a malign apparition is seen, laid out in a circle, it will trap the apparition and it will not be able to leave, becoming a slave to your desires. Put it around your waist, and it will save you from every attack of the invisible and infernal powers.

The Consecrated Plume

It is used to write the allowable pacts. You obtain it from the right wing of a white hen. You will cut it with the white handle knife, and before using it, you will submerge its tip in the water of the aspersions. You must never use it in any other thing.

The Cup of the Libations

It will be made of bronze with the supports of ivory, and it will have engraved around the border, on the outer side, alternately the names *Deus, Jeová* and *Adonai,* and at the bottom, on the inside, the Solomonic seal with the crossed triangles.

The Brazier of the Perfumes

You will search for a new bowl made of copper, and with the point of the white handle knife, you will write on its contour: *Offering of N. N., be it well received.* You will put it over an iron tripod that you will have made for this. In this brazier, the mage will burn the perfumes required for the invocatory work.

The Magical Gypsum

Buy gypsum that can be used as a bar with which you can write; prepare it at your habitation and keep it wrapped in a piece of white cloth made of new wool, which you will purify with the water of the aspersions. It is used to draw the circle whose figure we will detail later.

Magical Rod

[HEM]

The material from which the rod will be fashioned

The rod will be made from a young and tender branch, less than one or two years old, without protuberances, from the common hazel tree, almond, laurel, or from the artichoke.

How to prepare it

It is essential to make a good rod, that the trunk from where it is taken is cut in half with an iron knife, or a silver knife, new, and pure which has been cleansed beforehand. The operation must be done on a Wednesday at the Full Moon, in the planetary hour of Mercury, between the eleventh and the twelfth hour of night. When you cut the branch, you must say:

> I cut you in the name of Eloim, Mutrathom, Adonay, and Semiforas, so that you have the virtues of the rods of Moses and Jacob to find everything I want to know.

The rod must be two hand spans in length and the thickness of a finger. Soon after you cut it, you will engrave in the cut the sign of the planet ✝ and will write on the upper part the Word *Agla* ✝, in the middle *On* ✝, and on the end *Tetragammaton* ✝, saying:

> *I conjure and cite you mihi obedire, vênias per Deum vivum* ✝ *, per Deus verum* ✝ *, per Deus sanctum* ✝*.*

And you will keep it for when you need it.

The Magical Vestment and the Way to Prepare It

[TDH]

The vestments must be made of white cloth, with a linen lining and the tunic and hood (or cap) made from thin wool. The color of the cap and the tunic must be black, with red silk embroidery of Hebrew characters on the chest and the words in the cap, and with golden and silver threads the stars and the remaining signs.

The shoes will be made from the skin of a white lamb. On them, you will draw with the goose feather indicated in the instruments of art. For this, you will wet the tip of the feather in a solution of cinnabar reduced to powder and mixed with water and gum, which makes the effect of ink.

In the cap, you must also put the following names: *Jehova* on the back, *Adonai* on the right, *Eloi* on the left, and *Gibor* at the front or ahead.

The magician in the circle [TDH]

The Preparation of the Vestments

[LM2]

The invocations of Magic require that the conjurer cover himself with clothes of a particular form and kind, because his ordinary clothes absorb influences and can be made from substances that become a hindrance magically and also a danger because of the pernicious attractions that the evil powers can exercise. These precautions are very old, as Saint Cyprian declares that his masters in the magical arts attributed them to the first men who possessed the great secret of the invocations. In fact, they would not be a means of safe defense when used by somebody who did not know or denied the true God, Lord of the Universe, without whose help nothing can be done.

The mage will prepare a cloth into a tunic of white linen which will cover him entirely, the sleeves will be tight around the wrists, and the tunic will be adjusted on the waist with the string of seven knots. There will be no other interior cloth except a shirt, which must be made of the same cloth; he will use white shoes of velvet, where he will embroider in red over each one the seal of Solomon: Over the head must be placed a white cap of velvet with two crossed triangles in red color.

All these garments, which cannot be made by the hands of women, must be scrupulously clean and without any stain or mark jeopardizing its necessary and perfect whiteness.

When it is prepared, you will place it on a white cloth in the center of the habitation and sprinkle it lightly with the water of the aspersions, making crosses over it and saying the following exorcism:

> *O Pater conditor, alme siderum, sarpientia summa, per omnes fortitudines tuas et virtutes tuas, sanctificare digneris vestem hanc tuo honore preparatam. Exorciso te, vestis, per Deum verum, Deum vivum et æternum qui cuncta fecit ex inhilo et nihisit in hoc meo opere quod impurum sed virtute plenus.*

After, you will incense with the perfume which corresponds to the day and will keep it until you use it.

Magical Perfumes

[LM2]

Each day has its own, so I give for each one precise indications.

Sunday

Dominating Angelic Power
Michael
Perfume
Saffron, red sandalwood, and pure frankincense
Magical Plants
Turnsole, laurel, and litmus

Monday

Dominating Angelic Power
Gabriel
Perfume
White sandal, camphor, aloes
Magical Plants
Yellow ranunculus and artemisia

Tuesday

Dominating Angelic Power
Rafael
Perfume
Pitch and sulfur
Magical Plants
Wormwood and rue

Wednesday

Dominating Angelic Power
Anael
Perfume
Styrax, benzoin, and sweet gum
Magical Plants
Narcissus and almorachy

Thursday

Dominating Angelic Power
Samael
Perfume
Frankincense, amber, and garden burnet
Magical Plants
Pomegranate, poplar, and holly oak

Friday

Dominating Angelic Power
Zacariel
Perfume
Musk
Magical Plants
Violets, roses, myrtle, and olive

Saturday

Dominating Angelic Power
Orifiel
Perfume
Diagridio, field bindweed, alur, sulphur, and asafoetida
Magical Plants
Ash and cypress

Tuesday and Saturday are the most propitious days to evoke the infernal and the maleficent powers. Sunday and Thursday are the best days to evoke the good ones. Friday is proper for any evocatory work which has its foundation in amorous desire and goodness, and Wednesday is propitious for evocations in which the lights of the Region of the Mystery are called about the future and the secrets of knowledge, when these things are asked for with disinterested intention.

The mage should always call in his evocation the power of the corresponding day and will crown himself with branches, flowers, or leaves from the propitious magical plants. In the brazier, he will burn together with the perfumes parts of the vegetables dedicated to the day of the invocation.

Magical Ink

the way to prepare the ink with which you will write the pacts and orisons

[TDH]

The pacts must not be written with common ink. Every time you make a call to the spirit, you must change the ink.

You will put, into a new cauldron filled with river water the powders that I will describe: take the seed of the peach fruit without taking the kernel, put them on the fire to reduce them to burnt coal; after, when they are very black, put them aside with an equal amount of soot from a chimney, add two nuts of the oak apple, four parts of Arabic gum, and, after seiving the said powders, well mixed, through closely-woven material, you will mix them with the river water already indicated.

But now you do not have anything but an ink similar to the usual ones. To make it have magical effects it is necessary to add coal from the branches of the fern taken on the vespers of the Day of Saint John, perfectly squashed; and coal of vine cut in the Full Moon of March. With everything mixed, you will boil it for five consecutive nights, suspending the operation during the day. Every time you start the cooking the supernatural spirits will be invoked. When it is finished, you will expose it at night to the open air, in such a way that the rays from the Moon, waning, fall over the ink and impregnate it with their magical virtue.

When this is done, the ink will be ready for the writing of the pacts, orisons and other documents, through which you will put yourself in communication with the spirits.

When using it, you will add drops of blood from the heart finger of the left hand, which you will take by piercing it a little bit with a pin which is new

The Virgin Parchment

[HEM]

The virgin parchment to be used in the operation mentioned before[54] must be prepared with the skin from animals that have never conceived young. To make the parchment, you must put the animal in a secret place where no one lives; take a virgin stick (a sprout of the same year) and cut it into a knife shape, saying:

> *I conjure you, by the creator of the universe and king of the angels, named Helsadai, for you to have force and virtue to skin this animal, to make the parchment on which I may write the holy name of God, with the intent that everything I later write over it comes to pass, by God almighty who lives and reigns through the centuries. Amen.*

When cutting the stick, you will recite the psalm *Deus judicium tuum regi &c*, and then you will write on the wooden knife these words:

> *AGLA, ADONAY, ELOE make the work of this wooden knife to be accomplished.*

---

54   Psalm 71.

Second, say over the knife, keeping it close to your mouth, these words: *Cara cherma, sito cirua.*

Then, skin the animal with the knife, saying:

> *Adonay, Dalmay, Saday, Tetragammaton, Anereton, Anepaton, Cureton; Holy angels of God be present and give virtue to this parchment; let it be consecrated in your name, so everything written on it comes to a good end.*

After you have skinned the animal, you will take the salt, saying over it:

> *God of gods, bless this salt, so I can sprinkle it over this parchment that I intend to make, so it will have strength, virtue and effect.*

With the salt, you will salt the aforementioned skin and will put it under the sun for fifteen days, taking later a vase made of vitrified clay, onto which you shall write the word *Agla*; on this vase, you will put a large stone of quicklime, with holy water and the aforementioned skin, leaving it there for nine whole days. After that, you will take it back, and with the wooden knife, you will remove hair from the skin; you will put it to dry for eight days, in a shadow, after sprinkling it with salt, saying:

> *In the name of the great and eternal God, I sprinkle you, so you will be purified of every vice and iniquity.*

As soon as it is dry, you will perfume it and will wrap it in a silk handkerchief.

Take great care that a woman who is menstruating does not see this parchment, otherwise it will lose all his valor and virtue.

On this parchment can be drawn pentacles, talismans, amulets, and having all well-kept.

Great Circle of Protection

[LSC]

No one willing to leave safely from an invocation of the most powerful spirits should ignore this chapter. Here is a great tool for protection which was given to us by the sorcerers, and, without it, nobody would be safe facing the infernal spectres.

You must draw a great circle over the earth chosen for your elaborations. You must draw it inscribing a triangle, or any polyhedron, or a Solomonic seal, and its efficacy is such that the most powerful spectres are forced to respect it.

If you wish to invoke a principal spectre from the world of the shadows, some powerful spirit, you must do so with greater awareness, and it will be on according to following.

You will choose the most propitious day to contact the spirit, which will depend on the nature of the spirit. In the day before the eve of the chosen day, and with a knife never used before, you will look for a walnut tree which was not planted by human hand, and in the exact moment when the Sun makes its appearance, you will cut off a branch with which you will prepare a rod.

You will then choose a propitious place to perform such convocation, and you will use to such effect a magnetic stone, two amulets, and two large candles which have been blessed. You must, before and above everything else, take care that nobody will hinder you, because the consequences would be disastrous.

Once you have arranged everything above and arrived at the most propitious moment for the invocation, meaning on its due day, you will speak the following words:

> *Oh Adonai Imperator, aid me in the task to which I am here convoked and grant me to draw this circle which will be my safeguard and protection, to keep me away from every evil.*

You must then take the skin of a goat who was sacrificed on the fifth day of the week, and, laying it on the earth, you will inscribe on it with the magnetic stone, or with a hematite stone, *Lapis Sanguineus* or *Lithos Hæmatitis*, the cabalistic circle. You will draw said circle with five concentric circles and a triangle. You will then inscribe the symbol "**T**," which has often been called *the Way of the Treasure*.

We will not explain here the great significance of this symbol and all of its connotations; it is enough to know that it has been related to expressions like *the route of eternity, the way to Hell, the via to the unknown, to the time, to the esoteric, and a large etcetera*.

Next, you will place the candle holders, in which are the blessed candles, and under said candles, both amulets. Around this must be put three, and always three, wreaths made with basil, flower of elderberry, and vervain. It is essential that all of them are collected on the night of Saint John[55], before dawn, or just one, depending on the nature of the spirit with whom you wish to make the pact. So, it will be necessary that you have a vast knowledge of the spirits before beginning to conjure them.

All these things set out, with the sacred inscription of the letters "**J.H.S.**," and the crosses which accompany them, guarantee the protection of the sorcerer, but his audacity, temerity, or foolishness can bring a bad end to all this, receiving great evils in answer to his boldness.

---

55   In Portugal, it is commemorated on June 24.

With all the preparations complete, you will put on the point of the triangle our metallic censer with its coals, where you will make the fumigation of incense, rue, and laurel.

At that time, the place will be perfectly fit to begin your operation. You will wait for the magical night hour, that is, midnight, at which moment you must put yourself in the middle point of the triangle, the main focus of our preparations, with willful spirit and with courage, holding your rod in your right hand and the *Clavicule of Solomon in* your left. You will have written on paper, or on the parchment if possible, your request and the pact to be made with the spirit, and its dismissal.

The recommendations given to us by Pope Honorius in his unquestionable *Grimoire* must not be deemed of minor importance, in which he urges us to make our magical drawing with coals, blessing the place with holy water, and having at hand to do all this *Lignum Crucis*. It is also required to write certain gospel verses around what was traced.

The possession of impure metals whilst the sorcerer operates is strictly forbidden, because of this, the coins we will use to dismiss the convoked spirit must be of silver or gold. We must add that, if coins made of bronze or any other vile metal are used, the contacted spirit will be offended for reasons that, being obvious, we will not mention.

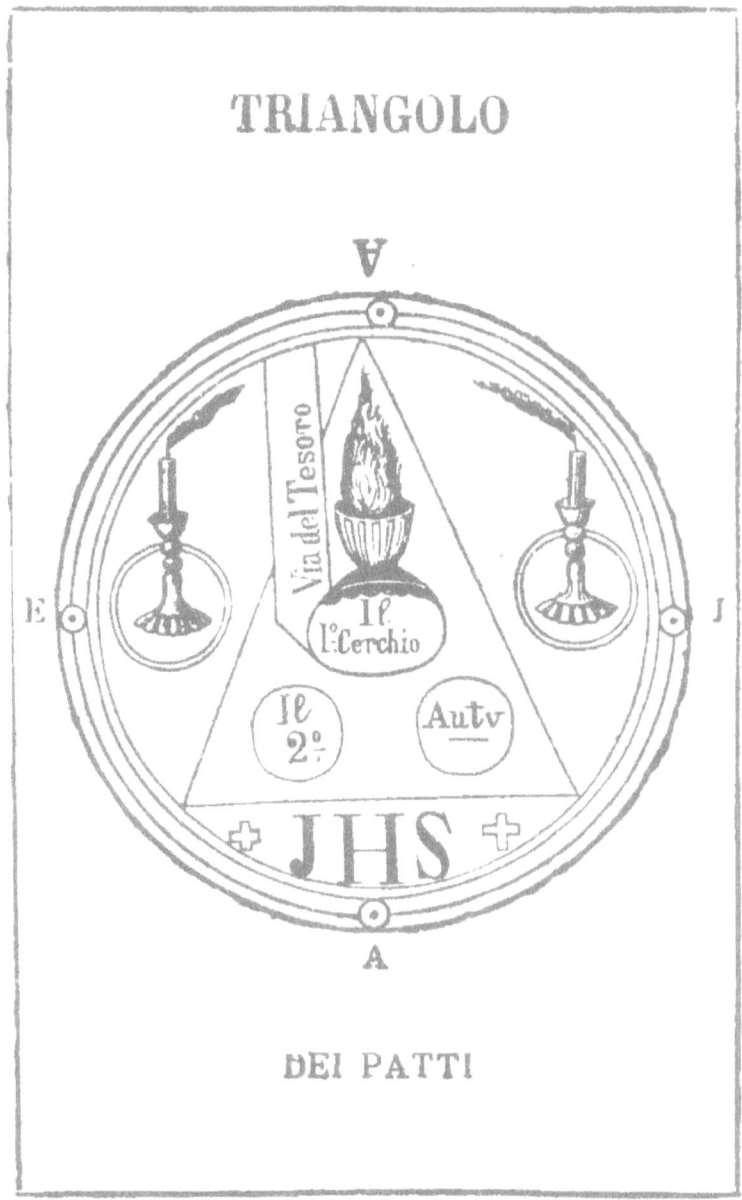

The Triangle of Pact, from an Italian version of the Grand Grimoire. The redactor of this version of Jonas Sufurino's book [LSC] seems to have had his own interpretations about the way the magician must walk when he has to follow the spirit to the nearest treasure.

The Magical Circle

[LM2]

This is the figure the invocator must trace on the floor in the place of invocation to put himself inside the traced lines, becoming protected from the attacks of the maleficent powers who come visibly or invisibly, because in the confines of the magical virtue of the circle, there is raised the highest and strongest battlement. The magical circle can be traced in any place, and so it must be done, because the magician cannot always choose the most convenient place for the invocation. If it can be done out of doors, he will trace the circle on the earth with the tip of the sword or magical rod. If the invocation is done in his habitation or any other building, he will use the prepared gypsum, and if the floor is of white marble, for instance, where the traces made with the gypsum cannot be well distinguished, he can use a piece of coal which has been purified with the water of the aspersions.

To trace the circle, the invocator will be already dressed and prepared, having at hand everything he needs, and as he will need his right hand to do all this, he will have the sword in his left hand.

He will begin marking on the ground or floor of his habitation a very large circular line which must encompass himself and the people who accompany him, in such a way that they have plenty of space. He will make outside another concentric circle, and in the space between both, he will write in a round way, starting at the front:

Veni ✠ per Deum ✠ Sanctus ✠ per Deum ✠ Verum X

In the space inside the two circles, you will draw a triangle with the point towards the front and the base behind your position. In the space between the base of the triangle and the circle, you will write this:

✠ J H S ✠

And in the equal parts on the other sides, you will put two candle holders with a lit candle made of virgin wax in each. In the front point of the triangle, you will put the brazier of the perfumes, which is where the invocator will stand, the other two points being occupied by the people who will assist him.

While the figures of the circle are being drawn, the mage will recite the following conjuration, paying attention to what he is doing so that the conjuration words finish exactly as the figures of the circle are complete.

> *Extator, Nestator, Sitacibor, Adonaij, On, Azozamón, Meechón, Asmodachü, Comphac, Erijonas, Propheres, Alijomás, Conamas, Papiredas, Otiodos, Narbonidos, Almoij, Cacaij, Coanaij, Equevant, Vemat, Deunaij, Comparís, Seier, Serantis, Cosphilados: Angels of God come and be present, because I invoke thee in this operation so this circle will acquire from you your unbreakable virtues and that, through your assistance and help, I can take to a happy end my purposes.*

That being said, the candles will be lit and the perfume will be burnt in its brazier.

The Magical Art

The magical Circle of Saint Cyprian, *graphic art by Asterion Mage*

Magical Ceremony

[TDH]

It is good to perform this part with precision, as it befits that the initiated pass through the three phases, which are "desire," "perseverance," and "dominion." The first belongs to the "initiation" and to the "desire" of learning, the second to the "initiated" who needs the "perseverance" to come to the end, and the third, to the "master," who is the true mage, as he has attained to the "absolute dominion of the air."

It must not be doubted that to attain the desired goal it needs to proceed with absolute devotion and good faith, as if the practices are done with an illegitimate aim, the results will be null and even contrary to what is searched for.

THE CEREMONY TO BE USED BY WHOEVER WILL UNDERGO THE INITIATION

When you have prepared all the instruments of art, the vestments, and other utensils, it will be necessary to prepare a proper place for the experiments you will execute. Do not forget that in that place should not be allowed any person who has not made a pact with some spirit before. You must make sure it has two windows, one to the Orient and the other to the sunset, which must be in the higher part of the house; you will cover its walls with a black cloth, being careful that there is not in it, and neither in any place nearby, any blessed object or symbol or religious figure, and nothing which forms a cross.

To understand the importance of this observation, I will make reference to a well-known occurrence that happened to the famous mage Atothas, which was the cause of his death.

He had a perfectly prepared habitation, with the correct windows, which were well positioned and closed, which he did not open except on the nights he made his conjurations.

It happened that a fight broke out in the city in which he lived, someone was killed, and the killer, to avoid being recognized, threw the dagger away with all his strength, and it stuck in one of the windows of the habitation that the aforementioned Atothas had devoted to his practices. A few days after this incident, he had need to perform some conjurations and invocations, but no matter how much will he put in his work, it did not achieve any result. Desperate and not knowing the cause of this, he had to give up because the Sun was already risen on the horizon. He spent the whole day pondering about it, and at night, he returned to prepare his works with methodical order, and prepared himself with the most powerful talismans, made his conjurations with energy and will; but nothing. The spirits did not attend his calls. Completely desperate, he cursed them all, and before two hours had passed, he was arrested by the authorities and accused of the killing perpetrated by other. His house was searched, and when the sun came, a guard saw the window where the dagger was stuck.

When he was informed of this circumstance, he understood the cause of the futility of his conjurations of the last two nights, because the dagger had the shape of a cross, and it was not possible for the spirits of Lucifer to pass through this obstacle. And because generally in every village and in every time the evil done by others is attributed to the people who dedicate themselves to the mysterious arts of magic, it was not worth poor Atothas trying to prove his absolute innocence, because before getting to the prison, he was executed by the populace of the town, incited by the true murderer to avoid the truth being revealed.

The novice, to be able to perform his experiments, invocations, and conjurations, must in the first place free himself of prejudice and make his imagination clean from every thought which is not dedicated to the work he will execute. He will wash himself with clear water from a river, perfuming himself after with the powders of rose and Florence lily. When washing himself, he will say, *"Purify this water I will use, oh powerful Adonai! So in my turn I will be purified and clean so I can be worthy of contemplating all your majesty and beauty. So be it."*

Once the face and the head are washed, he will dry himself with great tranquillity and repose, and soon will take the powder of rose and lily with the index finger and thumb of the left hand and will pass it over his neck and beard. In the same way, he will perfume the vestments, and when giving every offering, he will say, *"The graces of Adonai be granted over me, with equal will and lovingness I cover my body with these vestments I have prepared with all the rules of the art, to make me worthy of the spirits I will invoke. So be it."*

Once he has dressed all the vestments, he will say, *"On this solemn hour I want to invoke you, with all my will and good desire, exalted spirits who accompany me in my works,* 'Astroschio,' 'Asath,' 'Bedrimuba,' 'Felutt,' 'Anabotos,' 'Serabilem,' 'Gemeri,' 'Domas,' *and* 'Arbatel,' *to be propitious and enlighten me on these things in the ways my human intelligence cannot understand with true clarity, providing for such defects that exist in my work, attending my good desire and will. So be it."* After doing this, he can execute the work he wants.

The invocations are the same for the novice and the initiated and the master; the only distinction is that the novice must use the supplication; the initiated, the persuasion; and the master, dominion or command. That can vary, in fact, according to the character, valor, and energy of the practitioner.

Ecstasy and Abstraction

[TDH]

The phenomenon known as "ecstasy" is very common in these persons who, having an active imagination, are without doubt susceptible to being suggestible. The ecstasy is generally produced by the magnetic influence the spirits work on us. It can be partial or total. In the first case, the person can have his imagination abstracted in a certain way from everything around, and he does not pay attention to the sounds and happenings around him though he does perceive them. When the ecstasy is considered to be total, it is when the person does not perceive anything around him. In this case, it can be considered that the person loses even his sensibility.

Among the Chinese, Indians, and Arabs, very often we find people in such states of abstraction, in which you can pierce the person with a needle without getting any sign of sensibility.

According to science, the ecstasy is produced by a cerebral exaltation, which can be caused by the ingestion of narcotics, moral influence, hypnosis, or religious superstitions.

During the effect, the body remains motionless and insensible to the most vivid pains, burns, thrusts, lacerations, etc.

Sometimes, it also manifests in convulsive movements and hallucinations of sound and sight; as a result, sounds of voices, music, etc., are perceived, and unknown apparitions are seen.

The mystical ecstasy can determine the apparition of saints or devils in a form truly realistic and according to the figures present in the imagination.

All this follows the supernatural causes produced by the good or evil spirits who surround us continually.

Ritual of Invocation

[LM2]

The circle being made, the mage having his Sword, which he will hold with the right hand, having in his left the Magical Rod, the book or notebook where he copied the ritualistic words of every conjuration, and the parchment in which he drew with the magical plume the expression of his desires directed to the corresponding angelic power, the formula of the pact written and signed with his own blood (when he must establish one). He burns the corresponding perfumes and plants, making a cross in the air with the Sword, facing the direction of the Orient and with his eyes raised toward the sky, he will say:

> *I confess myself to you, my God, King of heaven and earth, and I cry my sins, humiliating my face in front of your presence, because I recognize I have yielded to the instigations of pride, avarice, wish for richness, honors, and mundane pleasures. In the same way, I recognize I am guilty of having on some occasion impure thoughts, ignoble ideas, and satisfaction in idle conversations, even harmful ones.*
>
> *All this I confess to you, Lord, and with this solemn act, by your will, I become clean. Becoming pure from*

> *every stain of sin as I must be to face the celestial powers and spirits.*
>
> *Eternal and all-powerful God, loving father of men with clean hearts, grant me in your infinite mercy that my call is heard so all the spirits I invoke attend willing to fulfill my desire, because of such grace they see that You in your infinite greatness granted us, and let my works be, now and forever, lasting chants of praise offered to the greater glory of He who created the world and all creatures, and who is present in every part for all centuries of centuries.*

This being said, you will begin the spoken invocation in the following way, at the same time throwing into the flames your written expression the objective of both:

> *I, N.N., servant of the Highest, in His name I request N., by the image and figure of Our Lord Jesus Christ, who redeemed human kind with his most precious blood, assist me in a way I can see or feel your presence. Help me, N., I do not command, I supplicate by the eternal Kingdom of God ✠! Help! ✠ Help! ✠ Help! ✠ And by Him who put his foot over the asp and the basilisk, who is your and mine Lord, and of everything that exists and can exist; by Him who judged and reduced the ferocity of the lion and of the dragon and raises an insurmountable barrier between hell and the just, I require from you that you receive my petitions so I can see them fulfilled in their every part and immediately! ✠ Appear N.! ✠ God commands! ✠*

If the Power attends in a visible form, the invocator will be able to see in front of himself an angelical figure, serene and beautiful, surrounded by luminous vapors. If it does not take a perceptible form, you will notice in the air around you something indefinable which reveals the presence of the spirit, and in every case, your ears will perceive a very sweet voice, which will suavely exclaim, "*What do you want from me?*" The invocator with his right knee on the ground will formulate his petition and without leaving the reverent posture will ask the spirit, saying:

> *N., I N. N. I give thanks to God and to you: I declare myself from now on your servant and I charge you to never abandon me. Return N. to the celestial mansions where you live* ✠ *God help me* ✠.

It may happen that it will be necessary to repeat the invocation three times. If, despite everything, it does not work, this indicates that the preparations for the magical ceremony did not happen as they should, and if there is certainty that all the requirements were satisfied, then we must believe some cause of higher or divine order is against you performing the evocation. In such cases, it is necessary to repeat it twice on the same day of the week, and if in the third the words of the invocator are still not answered, he will give up his purposes, which evidently the Highest does not sponsor in his infinite wisdom.

When you notice the presence of the Power, even if you do not see it, it is not important that you hear its divine accent; the burnt script takes to the celestial spirit the expression of your purpose, and just the fact that it attended is a certain promise that you will be assisted.

The Art of Invoking the Dead

Necromancy, or the art of evoking the dead

[TDH]

Much has been said about the invocations and consultations about the things to come through the *manes*, and those who made to appear the spirits of the dead, from whose shadows they wanted to consult. This class of divinations was practiced with great fervor between by the Greeks, who received "oracles," which means certain answers about the future. There were magicians who presided over these practices, and these magicians demanded that sacrifices be made to the *manes* of the deceased, to have them propitious, without which they would remain deaf to the questions made to them.

When Saul consulted a necromancer, she made to be seen the shadow of Samuel, to predict all kinds of things. The emperor Basil, who reigned in Constantinople, having lost his son Constantine whom he loved greatly, dedicated himself to Necromancy, and with the counsels of a heretic monk called Santabrenus, he succeeded to make appear a spectre that had a very strong resemblance to his son.

In Salamanca and Toledo, in past centuries, there were schools of Necromancy performed in deep caves, to which not a few sages attended.

To evoke the dead, you must wear the ring of Solomon on the finger of the heart of the right hand, and after elevating the spirit to God, you will put the hand over the heart of the corpse and say:

> *I conjure thee, creature who was but is not anymore, from the part of the spirits whose names this magical and magnetized ring has engraved, to attend my call and answer my questions that I will put to you.*
>
> *For the second and third times, I conjure you so your lips formulate the answers I request, by the wonderful power of this sacred ring, a representation of the one Solomon possessed during his life.*

With your hand over the heart of the corpse, you will ask, and if you are worthy and virtuous, he will obey you immediately.

Hours and Virtues of the Planets

[TDH]

It is very convenient to know the hours in which each planet dominates in the universe and the experiments that must be done according to the ruling planet. With that aim, the following table must be always present, being ordained according to the importance of each one.

Solday (Saturn)	*Saturday*
Zemem (Sun)	*Sunday*
Zehac (Moon)	*Monday*
Madime (Mars)	*Tuesday*
Cocao (Mercury)	*Wednesday*
Zeder (Jupiter)	*Thursday*
Hoyos (Venus)	*Friday*

The experiments must always be performed at night, after the twelfth hour, when dealing with invocations and conjurations.

To find occult treasures, mines, waters, etc., you must use the morning hours between dawn and the rise of the Sun.

The hours of Saturn, Mars, and Venus are good to talk to the spirits. The hours of Mercury, to talk about stolen things, occult treasures, waters, and mines. The hours of Jupiter, to call the souls of the ones who are dead. The hours of the Moon and the Sun have special virtues, but for what it can be said they are useful for general experiments.

It is very necessary to have great faith and absolute will in the time of executing the invocations, or any other divination, checking that no detail is missing, to achieve a well-done operation. We will not get tired of warning that any circumstance, as insignificant as it can look, can fail the magical operation, in which case you will need to start the operation again.

Inauspicious Days

[GLT]

The most inauspicious days in the year, during which sorceries to do good cannot be done, only for evil.

January	1, 2, 3, 4, 5, 6, 7, 8, 9, 10, 11, 13, 15, 16, 23, 24, 26, 30
February	2, 4, 10, 13, 14, 15, 16, 17, 18, 19, 23, 28, 29
March	10, 13, 14, 15, 16, 17, 19, 28, 29
April	3, 5, 6, 10, 13, 15, 18, 20, 29, 30
May	2, 7, 8, 9, 10, 11, 14, 17, 19, 20
June	1, 4, 6, 10, 16, 20, 21, 24
July	2, 4, 5, 8, 10, 13, 16, 17, 19, 20, 27
August	2, 3, 8, 9, 13, 19, 27, 29
September	1, 13, 15, 16, 17, 18, 22, 24
October	1, 3, 6, 7, 8, 9, 10, 16, 21, 27
November	2, 6, 7, 11, 15, 16, 17, 18, 22, 25
December	1, 6, 7, 9, 21, 28, 31

It is necessary to note that the spells made on the days mentioned above do not give result.

They can, however, be made on the other days that are not mentioned here, and they will produce the desired effect.

Talismans and Amulets

The Secret of the Secrets

[TDH]

Speaking to his son Rehoboam about the secret mysteries of nature, Solomon said: "*Know, my son, that I possessed a gift of wisdom unrivalled by anybody else; however, I do not have power enough to give it to you as was my wish.*"

"*And what is the reason,*" asked Rehoboam, "*that I cannot have the same merit as you, to acquire the knowledge of all created things?*"

"*I cannot answer your question, my son, except by saying to you: In the same way as there are not two beings exactly the same in the universe, so there also cannot be two persons with identical faculties. The higher spirits, who were pleased to adorn my intelligence with the knowledge no mortal had ever possessed, did not consider that you are worthy of possessing the true wisdom. Be resigned, then, and accept with humility the arcane mysteries of these spirits that certainly you will never know. Notwithstanding this, I want to make manifest the origin of my great power, in case one day you can find utility in its knowledge. I must manifest all the wisdom I acquired through the exercise of the magical arts, to which I always had great inclination; but if the higher spirits had not gifted me with a clear intelligence, if they had not been so benign to me, like they always were, I would never have reached the height I find myself now. One night—I remember well!—I performed my experiments with great will, requesting from the higher spirits the gift of wisdom and the knowledge of everything. To my requests, the admirable*

Adonai presented himself with all his beauty and splendour, surrounded by other spirits, emanating a wonderful clarity from all his being, and he said to me: 'Oh beloved son Solomon! Your supplications were received with contentment, and because you did not ask for riches, to live long years, nor the ruin or harm of your enemies, but only the wisdom and knowledge of the created things, that is why what you desire will be granted to you, and from this moment, I can assure you that there never was and never will be in the world one who can be compared to you in wisdom as in riches and power.' I gave to the great and beautiful Adonai the greatest demonstrations of gratefulness; my eyes were filled with tears, and when I raised them again to contemplate him, I observed he had vanished, and there remained from that beautiful vision only a luminous blast. From that moment such a change happened in my intelligence that there was not a thing or thought or occult knowledge that I did not see with clarity.

"*Now, son of mine, it remains only to be said to you that, if you should attain the favor of the higher spirits, have in mind that they will grant to you anything you ask with good will and when they understand that you will make good use of your gifts; if they do not grant to you, it will be because they did not find your heart clean and pure enough, or because it is not convenient to their designs to grant it. I, as a father, have the duty of steering you in the direction of acquiring all kinds of knowledge, and so I deliver to you this book which is the one that provided me with the means to acquire the wisdom I possess. Read it with attention, practice faithfully everything indicated on it and maybe you will achieve what you wish. But, if the spirits you invoke do not show themselves propitious to grant you their gifts, do not be sad, because it will be the proof that they do not judge it convenient to grant your wishes, which must persuade you that their infinite wisdom when working that way preserves you from many dangers that could happen to you.*"

This wise advice that the great king gave to his first-born son, when he was at the end of his life, must be constantly engraved in the memory of the ones who follow the study and the practices exposed in the pages of this treatise.

On Talismans

[TDH]

Talismans are magical objects of different kinds which possess wonderful virtues. They are printed, engraved, or chiselled onto stone, metal, or other material and take the seal of a celestial symbol. The metal must correspond to the heavenly body from which you desire to gain the supernatural power. Said talismans must be made by people initiated in the occult sciences in a determined hour and with the soul completely focused on the work at hand, in a place especially devoted to these mysterious works, under a serene and splendid sky, and invoking the mysterious influence of the planet under which the talisman is put. The talismans were invented by the Chaldeans and Egyptians and are innumerable in their variety. The most famed of them all was, no doubt, the ring of Solomon. On this was engraved the mysterious name of God, which only Solomon came to know. Apollonius of Tyana made in Constantinople the figure of a stork which, by its magical virtue, made all birds of its species flee. Other famous talismans of antiquity are mentioned, but, unfortunately, they did not come down to us. Here are some of the properties of the many talismans consecrated to the heavenly bodies:

- The talismans of the Sun, carried with faith and veneration, give the favors and benevolence of the princes: honors, riches, and general appreciation.

- The talismans of the Moon preserve from illness and protect one who is traveling from all dangers.
- The ones of Mars have the virtue of making invulnerable the one who carries them with fervor, granting to them also an extraordinary vigor and strength.
- The ones of Jupiter dispel sorrows and fears, bringing fortune and good outcome to every enterprise undertaken.
- The ones of Venus quench hatred, inspire love, and inculcate affection to music.
- The ones of Saturn make women give birth without pain.
- The ones of Mercury make those who carry them with respect prudent and discreet, give science and a privileged memory, heal fevers, and, when put under the pillow, produce happy and true dreams.

Each talisman must be made in the corresponding color and metal of its planet, in the following way:

Saturn	color black	metal lead
Mars	color red	metal iron
Jupiter	color celestial blue	metal gold
Venus	color green and red	metal tin
Sun	color yellow	metal mercury
Mercury	color green	metal silver
Moon	color white	metal copper and brass

The form of the talismans generally must be circular; they also can be made octagonal, pentagonal, hexagonal, etc.

The names of God have greater efficacy when they are written in Hebrew.

As for their size, it varies according to the taste of the artificer, who can enlarge or make them smaller as long as the cabalistic signs are complete and put in their proper place.

Talismans and Amulets

The talismans play a very important role in the secret sciences because of their wonderful properties, which you will have the opportunity of learning from this treatise.

One of the most ancient is, no doubt, the one entitled "Abracadabra," which generally is engraved on a symbolic stone. It serves to prevent from diseases and sorceries. To make it possess all the magical virtues, it must be made in the following way:

```
ABRACADABRA
ABRACADABR
ABRACADAB
ABRACADA
ABRACAD
ABRACA
ABRAC
ABRA
ABR
AB
A
```

The mystery of this talisman is that the letters of this name, which is formed by Greek characters, represent numbers, and on every side, give the cipher 365, which is the number of days in the year.

After this talisman, which is certainly the most primitive and simple, we will expose the most known and important in order of their merits and virtues.

Magnetic Talismans

[TDH]

It is useful to touch the talismans with the magnetic stone before using them, as it is known that the magnetic stone has the property of attracting all the bodies in nature.

Considering that in the universe everything is ruled by the laws of attraction, this is a circumstance that the cabalistic sages took into account when they endowed talismans with virtue of attraction.

The celestial bodies have these proprieties to the highest degree, because if it were not so, they could not gravitate in space, and it is clearly seen that the power they exert over each other leads them to unite; however, they are equalized by the attraction made by the other planets, which results in them being fixed in a given point without being able to move in any other direction.

That is not enough to make their influence not felt over the universe, and this influence is the one you must search for with greater certainty with the magnetic talismans, which serve to transmit it in turn to all beings, both natural and supernatural. This means that they can attract people as much as animals, spirits, and elements.

This explanation being given, there remains only to indicate the form used by the great Rabbi Yram Radiel, adding to the explanations the wise Solomon gives to us in his sacred *Clavicule*. These talismans are made under the auspices of the seven metals proper to the planets, by which and with the virtue communicated by the magnetic stone, enjoy general properties, who do not possess the qualities of ones made of only metal and under the influences of only one celestial body.

To use them, they are put, like the others, inside a small purse of green satin, putting in also some filings of steel and gold and seven grains of wheat as an offering to the seven planets. This ceremony must be done on Sunday at sunrise, putting it after over the heart, hanging from a small thread of green silk.

Do not forget that the talisman favors the one who carries it, in business as in travels, in games, in love affairs, fights, etc., but to acquire its gifts you must make yourself worthy of deserving them.

The Great Talisman

[TDH]

Great talisman Dominatur or the key of the pacts

Here is shown the true key which opens all the doors of the unknown sciences, to persons who, by their merits and good faith, are worthy of possessing the wisdom, a precious gift that many wish for but few succeed in achieving. The key, or clavicule, serves also in every kind of pact, because with it, all the spirits are compelled to present themselves to the person who uses it in their invocations.

This key or clavicule is known as the great talisman *Dominatur*, or dominator, which is, therefore, the one we shall consider first in the scale of the talismans; Solomon used it to subjugate the spirits, which always humbly attended his mandates.

This key is made with the metals gold, brass, and bronze; it is fabricated on Sunday in the morning at the first hour of the rising sun. It bears the shape of parchment with Hebrew words, and over it is the key. It can be constructed in metal as in the picture, or make a parchment with the engraved words and the key made separately.

To invest yourself with this talisman, you will choose the first hour of sunrise on Sunday; you will add to it a small piece of magnetic stone and say:

By the thrice holy and powerful name of the Supreme Creator of all things, by the name of the Son and the Holy Spirit, one and three, by the grace given to the angels of light, by the light given to me when you formed me as a human being in your image and likeness, by the power you gave to the seven planets, which are Sun, Moon, Mars, Mercury, Jupiter, Venus, and Saturn, to reign, influence, and dominate everything over and under the earth and the waters, by the sacred words it holds, this dominator talisman, by the names of the good spirits Adonai, Eloim, to achieve through its mediation, the absolute dominion of the creatures, spirits, and elements.

After this, put it in a scarlet purse and perfume it with powder of frankincense and myrrh. Every Sunday, at sunrise, you will put in the purse some filings of steel to feed the talisman and seven grains of wheat like in the offerings to the seven planets. When putting it over the heart, you will say:

Oh, mysterious planet who rules and governs in this hour all the destinies of the world and of the created things, taking me under your protection and shelter and favoring me with your gifts until the hour of my death. Amen.

Take it into account that *clavicule* means key, and that it is a word of Hebrew origin, this one being the one that gave the title to the *Clavicule of Solomon*.

La llave de los pactos

On Talismans

[HEM]

Talismans are divided between ordinary and mixed; the ordinary ones are fabricated with a seal, figure, or character of a celestial symbol impressed or engraved onto a sympathetic stone, or over a suitable metal for the celestial body, by someone who has a focused spirit on the work, without being distracted by strange thoughts, in the day and hour of the planet, in a fortunate place, with beautiful and serene weather, when the sky is in a good disposition to attract the influences.

They are fabricated by astromancy and quiromancy and contain the horoscope of the person to whom they correspond, and they lose their magical power and strength when passed to another person. There are many ordinary talismans which can be fabricated to fight certain diseases, which are called *magical rings,* of which I will give some idea with the following.

Constellated Ring against Colic

Fabricate one iron ring, and engrave, on the seventeenth and twenty-first day of the Moon, the sign of the planet Mars, with these mysterious signs:

"Flee, flee miserable animal, the otter found you."

Ring to prevent Epilepsy

This ring must be fabricated from pure and fine gold, and in the middle, mount a piece of the hoof of a moose. It must be fabricated on a Monday during the Spring, in a day that the Moon is in a favorable aspect or conjunct to Jupiter or Venus. Then engrave around the ring the following words:

† *Dabi* † *Habi* † *haber* † *habry* †

And after that, the astrological sign of the planet. Soon after, perfume it with the appropriate ceremonies, and carry it with confidence.

Ring to make yourself Invisible

Take the hair from the head of a furious hyena, and with this hair, make a tress and with it a ring. Soon after, hide it in the nest of the hoopoe for nine days, after which it is perfumed with the correspondent ceremonies.

Ring to destroy Enchantments

Particularly produced under the auspices of Mercury. With lead very fine and pure, in the day and hour of Saturn, you will make one ring, inside of which you will mount the eye of a female weasel that never gave birth more than once. Around the ring, the following words will be engraved:

"*Apparuit Dominus Simoni*"

To make this ring, it is necessary that the chosen Saturday is the day that is in opposition to Mercury; soon after, perfume it three times and then wrap it with a mortuary handkerchief and bury it in the cemetery for nine days, after which you will perfume it three times with the perfume of Saturn and will be able to use it. Its effect is so certain that I can assure on my word of honor, that whosoever carries it will never be enchanted or suffer any kind of witchcraft.

On Mixed Talismans

[HEM]

The talismans called mixed are the ones which are at the same time magical, cabalistic, and astrological. Their mixed nature belonged to the sages who made a profound study in these great sciences.

We will begin this important chapter with the most ancient known talisman.

Abrasax or Abraxas

It consists of a cut and symbolic stone, upon which is a symbol of the body of a man with a crowned head, with two serpents for legs and in one arm a scourge, and he is standing over an amulet,[56] and above the head there is the name *Abraxas* written in Greek, and on one side the word *IAO*, Alpha and Omega in the Greek alphabet.[57]

---

56   As can be seen by comparing the images, the strange sentence "standing over an amulet" possibly came from a misunderstanding from the artist (who horribly drew what possibly originally was the crocodile) and other from the writer (who did not know what to do with the strange image at the feet of the figure).

57   It seems the artist also adapted the motif of the two "serpents for legs" from other Gnostic images attributed to Abraxas. That would explain why the text says, "in one arm a scourge," when the image clearly shows the figure delicately holding a kind of wand or scepter. As it can be seen in the next image, Abraxas' figure, differently from Serapis, has two serpent legs and seems to hold a scourge.

The *Abraxas* is a talisman that carries good fortune everywhere, and more particularly more to the satisfaction of the passions which derive from the soul and spirit, than to the ones that come from the senses.

---

58 This image from [HEM] clearly borrows from Gnostic ideas, as can be seen by the use of the names "Abraxas" and "IAO." The kingly figure most likely was inspired on images of the god Serapis, as we can see in the examples below.

59 "*Serapis or Hermes is sometimes represented as identical with Osiris, and sometimes as a distinct divinity the ruler of Tartarus and god of Medicine.*" From *The age of fable or beauties of mythology*, by Thomas Bulfinch (1897).

60 "Serapis," from *Mosaize Historie der Hebreeuwse Kerke*, by Willem and David Goeree, 1700.

Talismans and Amulets

61

Abracadabra

This is a Greek word which, when repeated several times, or written in a certain way, is a precious talisman to prevent against fever and, generally, from every chronic disease.

To possess its magical virtues, it must be made in the following way. Take a piece of white paper or cardboard and draw upon it a regular triangle. Fold the paper so that the writing is covered and weave a piece of thread in the shape of a cross. Carry it suspended on the neck for nine days, and after that, untie it before sunrise on the bank of a stream of water which flows to the East. The *Abracadabra*, if it is written over paper, is just a simple amulet; but if engraved over metal, it is a precious talisman, even more if put under the influence of some planet.

---

61 "A mystical word [Abraxas] used by the Gnostic followers of Basilides to denote the Supreme Being or perhaps its 365 emanations collectively or the 365 orders of spirits occupying the 365 heavens." From William Dwight Whitney, *The Century Dictionary, an Encyclopedic Lexicon of the English Language*, 1902.

```
ABRACADABRA
ABRACADABR
ABRACADAB
ABRACADA
ABRACAD
ABRACA
ABRAC
ABRA
ABR
AB
A
```

Pantacles

The pentacles must be fabricated on Wednesday, at the waxing Moon at three in the morning, in an aired room, recently whitened, and with no more than one person who will burn many pungent plants. Take a virgin parchment, which also must be blessed, draw upon it three circles which are contained one inside the other, using the three principal colors, gold, red and green; the colors and the plume must be exorcised beforehand. Write after that the sacred names and place it on silk. Take a clay vase in which you put new burning coals, mixing frankincense and aloes, all purified and exorcised. Then, you put all this facing the Orient and read with devotion the Psalms:

"Domine Dominis noster: Coli enerrant gloriam Dei."

Together with:

Most powerful Adonay, Alpha and Omega who made Thy people to cross the sea with dry feet; who elected Abraham to be Yours and blessed in his name all the tribes of earth and multiplied their prudence like the stars. You who gave

Moses the Law upon Mount Sinai, You who delivered to Solomon the pentacles for the safety of the soul and the body, we humbly supplicate that with Thy power you consecrate these pentacles, so they obtain all the virtue against the spirits, through You, oh most holy Lord Adonay, whose kingdom will be without end. Amen.

All that done, perfume again the pentacles with the pungent plants, and put them back on the consecrated piece of silk to be used when needed. They are talismans of great virtue, because they contain the ineffable names of God.

Sixième Pantacle de Jupiter from the *Veritable Magie Noir*.

---

62   This image is derived from the "Sixième Pantacle de Jupiter" (Sixth Pantacle of Jupiter), found in the *Veritable Magie Noir*. In the original book, its position was changed with the image of the Moon. There is no evident connection between it and what is written about the pentacles in this part of the text.

The Book of Saint Cyprian

Seal or Talisman of the Moon

These talismans must be fabricated on Mondays at the 1st, 8th, 15th, and 22nd in the purest silver. It has two faces; in one is engraved the figure of the planet, which is a woman dressed in white clothes, having at her feet a waxing Moon, one star above her head, and a waxing Moon in her left hand. The name *Hecate* will be written in Sanskrit above. In the other face, there is a hexagon polygon, with a magical square with nine divisions[63] with numbers, which mysterious number is 369.

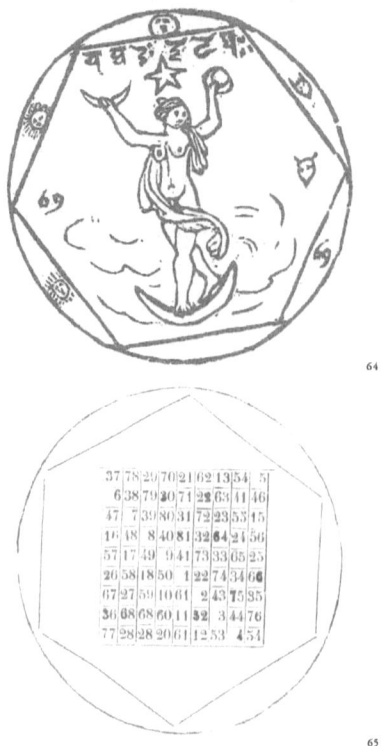

---

63   It means a 9x9 square. See the images below.
64   This figure is most likely a redrawing of the image found in the *Secrets Merveilleus De La Magie Naturelle et Cabalistique du Petit Albert,* which can be seen below. The word "Hecate," "written in Sanskrit" follows the table to be found in this edition in the section "The Book of the Spirits."
65   What we have here in truth is the Magical Square of the Moon, according to Agrippa. The lower/right square should be 45, and not 54. Compare with the other image below.

The operation must be done in the Spring, when it is in the first degree of Capricorn or Virgo[66], in a favorable aspect with Jupiter or Venus. When necessary, wrap it in a piece of white silk. This talisman avoids the epidemic and contagious diseases, preserves travelers against thieves and other disgraces, and specially favors the merchants and farmers in their works.

Image attributed to Paracelsus, in the *Secrets Merveilleus De La Magie Naturelle et Cabalistique du Petit Albert*

Abb. 19.[67]

---

66   I assume it means the position of the Moon.
67   Image from the article by W. Ahrens (of Rostock) about magical squares, published in the September 1915 issue of *Himmel und Erde*.

Talismans of the Saturn

These talismans are fabricated over purified and smooth lead on a Saturday after the first until the ninth hour. Its magical square is the one with three divisions[68] and its mysterious number is 15. Its polygon has eight equal sides.[69] In one face, it has the symbolic figure of time armed with his scythe, in the action of razing, with a sand clock at his side.[70] Other times it is an old man with a great beard, who seems to be digging with a hoe, inclining over a funerary gravestone. Over his head there is a star and with Sanskrit characters the name *Typhom*.

[71]

The talisman must be fabricated in the moment in which Saturnis in a favorable aspect, when the Moon enters in the first degree of Taurus or Capricorn. When it is finished, it is wraped in a piece of black silk. This talisman is used to help the women at childbirth, making them leave with happiness from this state without pain. It prognoses prosperity in everything. If a horseman carries it inside his left boot, his horse will not hurt or be hurt. But it produces the opposite effects if it is fabricated in under bad and unfavorable circunstances.

---

68 It means the square 3x3.
69 However, the figure given has only six.
70 The precision of the description leaves little room to doubt the writer had the image from the *Petit Albert* in mind.
71 The text mentions the "symbolic figure of time armed with his scythe" but did not included it. We are adding here the image from the *Petit Albert*.

Talismans and Amulets

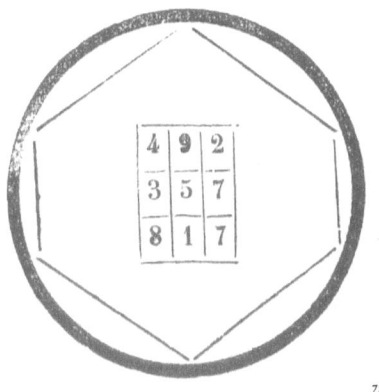

Talisman to prevent against the geniuses and goblin spirits

This talisman is fabricated on a Sunday under the auspices of the Sun. Take a plate of the purest and finest gold and cut it round with the size of two fingers [sic]; after, engrave in the middle a human face with a trimmed beard and long hair falling over the shoulders. Around this head one aureole with 15 rays; 3 rays over it, 5 to the right, and 7 to the left. In each side of the medal put on the right side three Hebrew letters, **J E H**, and on the left **O V A**; inside a double circle around the medal engrave: ✝ *Ecce faciem ejus per quem factæ sunt et cui obedient omnes creaturæ.* Perfume it with the perfumes of Sunday at the hour when you have the plate in a favorable situation under the auspices of Jupiter. With this talisman are obtained the favors of the geniuses who distribute honors and wealth.

---

72 At the center is the Square of Saturn, according to Agrippa. The problem is, the lower/right square is copied wrong, the correct number being 6 and not 7. That completes the presence of all numbers from 1 to 9 in the square, and makes all the sums (vertical, horizontal, and diagonal) equal to 15.

Talismans for the good success of a war and to avoid the wiles of the enemy

This talisman is fabricated under the auspices of Mars with the corresponding ceremonies with perfumes and in the happy hour of this constellation. When Mars is in conjunction with Jupiter or facing favorably Venus. It is engraved over a plate of very pure and polished iron, an arm which comes from a cloud, which seems to be stretching the hand to save someone from danger. Under it, there is the name of Mars in mysterious characters.[75] Around the medal between two circles this inscription: *Deus in adjutorium meum intende Domine ad adjuvandum me festina*.[76] If this talisman is carried with respect, you will defeat your enemies and will have nothing to fear from their weapons.

---

73 The description in the text has some similarity with the "Premier Pantacle" of the Sun in the *Veritable Magie Noir*, which we included here.
74 The description in the text also has some similarity with the "First Pantacle of the Sun" in the *Greater Key of Solomon*, which we included here.
75 This description, and the precedent one about Saturn, gives the impression that such images were supposed to be included in the book but were left out due to some mistake.
76 These words come from the beginning of the Psalm 70. I corrected some misspellings from the original.

Talismans to find out treasons

It is fabricate in Wednesdays under the auspices of Mercury over a plate of solidified mercury. Engrave over it the figure as in the previous one but with the following sentence: *Exsurgat Deus et dissipentur inimici eius et fugiant qui oderunt eum a facie eius.*[77] Prepare the proper perfumes of the planet and at the fortunate hour of the constellation when Mercury is in conjunction or benign aspect with Venus or the Moon. Whoever possesses this talisman and carries it with confidence will be fortunate in the game and in the trade, and if it is carried with veneration, it puts to flight treasons and other plots against the life of its owner.

---

77 Psalm 67, with some misspellings corrected.

Medal

To make anyone who carries it to be safe from sorceries, ligatures, and maleficence

[LM2]

The medal you will carry with you will be fabricated from gold or silver, metals that must be pure; you will put in the middle the Holy Name of God, with the letters Alpha and Omega, surrounded by rays to indicate that His Name reaches everywhere. You will not put it on you without doing a rigorous fasting for nine days, and you will carry it day and night. This medal will free you from the snares of your enemies, and they will not be able to make you suffer any kind of evil.

The Red Dragon and the Infernal She-Goat

[TDH]

The Red Dragon of Moses and Solomon

Moses was the chief of the Hebrews who in the time of the Pharaoh resided in Egypt. Forced to redeem his people, he had to put into practice a series of portentous miracles and, for last, the crossing of the Red Sea, which he made by separating the waters. When the Israelites were safe, he returned the sea to its normal state, drowning the Pharaoh and his troops who had pursued them.

The wise Moses possessed the science of the true magic of the Egyptians and used it to transform a wooden rod into a serpent; he foretold the plagues of Egypt and many more extraordinary happenings. The crossing of the Red Sea was a deed so wonderful that there are still people who doubt it. In fact, there is no way but to surrender to the evidence, because if they did not cross the Red Sea, the Hebrews would not have been able to become established in Judea.

What is ignored, and because of that we want to make it known, is the following story taken from a treatise of the true magic that we are translating.

Moses lived in Egypt, saved from the waters of the Nile in a miraculous way by the daughter of Pharaoh when he was a baby. His natural talent made him excel quickly in all the sciences of the Egyptians; when he was able to give lectures to anybody about anything, he had a desire to learn the magical arts, and to achieve this, he made himself disciple of the high priest Anacharsis, who in his time was the most wise of all the magicians.

Moses was known as "the son of the waters." The magician-priest, seeing his great disposition to the study of the true science, taught him all he knew with great kindness, which Moses put to good use, and soon he found himself in the position of giving lessons to his own master.

The master possessed among his talismans and amulets a small red dragon, a rare object of polished stone in which he had great pride. Moses, when he was initiated in the secrets of magic, was also interested in everything related to talismans and amulets, being permitted to examine at his will the small museum of his ancient teacher. Nothing, however, called his attention so much as the small "red dragon," and, motivated to know its properties, he asked the magician to indicate them. The master did not wait for more, because he really wanted to make his disciple aware of the mystery that the "dragon" held, which he did as follows:

> "My dear Moses," he said, "this 'dragon' that so much attracts your sight is a symbol of your very being."

Moses gave an exclamation of great awe when he heard these words and indicated that he did not understand the relationship that could exist between this talisman and him.

> "It is very simple and precisely this 'dragon' that, as you, is a son of the waters, served me to attract your steps to the temple of the true wisdom. Yes, Moses," he repeated, "you could not imagine that an object like that could have had influence over you since you were thrown in to the Nile,

Talismans and Amulets

until the present hour, and it will be like that until the end of your life."

Moses was enamored with what he heard, even more because he believed that there was not anything in the world capable of causing him admiration. He wanted to know about the relationship he had with the little "dragon" and how it came into the venerable old man's possession.

"You must know," he said, "that in the moment you were thrown into the river by your own mother, fulfilling the mandate of the Pharaoh of killing the firstborn children of the Jews, this small 'dragon' took you under his protection, making the small basket, in which you were thrown into the Nile, float over the waters. Besides this, he influenced the spirit of Thermutis, the daughter of the king so that in that hour she went to the river and had the desire to see what held the small basket that was navigating over the water, and it was him, finally, that gave her the impulse to pick up and raise you, giving to me certain signs of everything it did at your behalf. Now, and after what you now know, you will not find it strange the great influence this little 'dragon' has exercised over your person; it was he too that suggested to you the desire of coming to my house to learn the magical sciences, and it, finally, will give to you the power to learn the magical sciences, so through their virtue you see accomplished one day all you desire, for more extraordinary and wonderful it is. I am very old," he continued, "and I think that because of your kindness and wisdom, you made yourself worthy of my affection, and I want to give to you this precious talisman which will provide an absolute dominion over all the spirits and elements of the universe. With it, there will not be for you anything impossible, as everything will bend to your mandate. What I charge you about this matter is that every day when the sun comes up you say the following words:

'Jobse, Jalma. Afia.'

"This is the invocation to the higher spirit, Who presides over all, and to whom you must give adoration. After saying these words, you will give to the 'dragon' a gram of pure camphor without mixture, in the size of a grain of wheat."

Moses gave to the venerable Anacharsis great demonstrations of gratefulness, and taking the little "dragon," he gave farewell to the elder man promising that from now on all his effort would be put to faithfully fulfilling his advice and teachings and to dedicate all his power to searching for the freedom of the Israelites that were then slaves to the Egyptians, which he achieved after many and wonderful successes.

Where is demonstrated the power and virtue of the talisman named "The Red Dragon"

El Dragón Rojo

Hiriam Abid, son of a Hebrew widow, from the tribe of Levi, was a notable architect and metal engraver. The queen of Thebes, who knew his great qualities, ordered him to present himself to the wise Solomon on the occasion that this great King was preparing the construction of the temple of

Jerusalem, and this same soul also provided all the cedar wood necessary to the edification of the temple.

Solomon gave to Hiriam the position of higher architect and initiated him in the sacred mysteries of the "occult sciences," to which he owned the knowledge of the true wisdom.

As soon as he was initiated in all the sciences, he donated to him a small metallic red dragon, made in such a way that Hiriam, who himself was an excellent engraver, was amazed. Solomon said, "You will have at your disposition three masters, 70,000 companions, and 170,000 apprentices. By the virtue of this dragon, they will obey you blindly, and your orders will be perfectly interpreted by them, but it is necessary that every day at sunrise you say the words that the celebrated magician Anacharsis taught to Moses, which are:

'Jobse, Jalma. Afia.'

"After that, you will give to the dragon a gram of the purest camphor and of the size of a grain of wheat. Then you will put it in a purse of scarlet cloth, saying when putting it:

'Adonai. Almanach, Elochay, your power and wisdom be with me, now and forever. So mote it be.'

"Practicing all this with desire and good faith, your enemies will reconcile with you, and you will be respected by all kings and every people: your wisdom will be immense, your beauty and your youth will be sustained, your riches will increase, and your life will be long."

All these virtues the red dragon possessed, being one of the rarest talismans which existed in Egypt. Moses had it in his power for many years, and it is for this reason that it is believed that all his enterprises were crowned with the most complete success.

This talisman must be fabricated from an alloy of the seven metals which possess the influence of the seven planets.

It must be fabricated on a Thursday when the Moon is conjunct with the Sun, which happens very rarely. In its construction, only the sages initiated in the occult sciences should work.

To use this talisman, it is necessary to wash and perfume the whole body, and at sunrise, the words indicated before must be pronounced with great tranquility. Put in your mouth a gram of camphor and, after putting it in the purse with a magnetic stone, put it by the side of your heart.

Faithfully fulfilling what was said, you can ask whatever you wish, and the doors which are closed will open at your call.

The Infernal She-Goat

Besides the "Red Dragon," known as a talisman, there is another one, named after the Infernal She-Goat mentioned in the beginning of the treatise. The diabolical spirits are accustomed to taking every form of people or animal. The most usual, in fact, are the forms of the dragon or of the she-goat, although sometimes they present themselves in the forms of a cat, chicken, crocodile, etc.

There is no need to fear when doing the invocations of any form in which the spirits present themselves, and the operator must be always prepared to defend himself with the instruments of the art, in case the spirits wish to do some material harm to him, and with the talismans, which can serve you to force them into obedience.

The Infernal She-Goat appears giving doleful bleats like a lost soul, and the Dragon, shouting strong and hoarse howls and throwing fire through its eyes and mouth. Despite the Dragon showing itself so imposing, it is, in fact, to be less feared than the She-Goat, because the latter is the symbol of perfidy and deception. The operator must be always on guard and not let himself be defeated by its more-or-less innocent appearance. The She-Goat represents the most refined dissimulation and astuteness: This is the reason why it is said of this animal that it has "art" and "pact" with the devil.

Talismans and Amulets

Ring of Solomon

[TDH]

This ring must be fabricated from the most pure gold, on Sunday at sunrise and in the month of May. It must have in the center an emerald stone, in which is engraved the figure of the Sun and, on the opposite side of the ring, over the same gold, the Moon. Soon after, engrave also with the burin, made of new steel, the following words: "*Dabi*," "*Habi*," "*Alpha*," and "*Omega*," keeping in mind they must be done with Hebrew characters, because they are more cherished by the spirits whose names it carries. So it can be made exactly, the figure of the ring above is accompanied by another representing the ring extended showing the Hebrew signs to be engraved.

To acquire great magical effects, this talisman must be put into contact with the magnetic stone at sunrise, and you must say the following salutation:

> *I dedicate to you, Powerful Lord Alpha and Omega, substance and spirit of all creation, the daily remembrance of my soul, which awaits your divine protection, in all the works it executes today.*

Having faith, patience, constancy, and observing all the virtues, you can acquire a dominion so great that even the kings will need your help, and never will anyone be able to do any kind of harm to you. You will have a vivacious intelligence to acquire all kinds of knowledge, and you will prosper in all the works you do. This ring is to be put on the finger of the heart of the right hand.

Original image

[TDH]

Magical and Portentous Ring

[GLT]

The person who wishes to be idolized during his lifetime by the individuals of the opposite sex must do the following spell, which is attributed to Saint Cyprian.

Buy a ring with a small diamond and, having it plucked out, give it to a crow to swallow when midnight strikes, keeping the ring in the little finger of the left hand, carrying it until the crow expels the diamond through the excremental way. As soon as this happens, send the ring to have the stone put back and put it again in the finger of the left hand, saying at the same time:

> *By the power of God and by the power that your brilliants have, your brothers, that everything achieve in the world, because have more power than the gold, I ask that you makes me achieve everything I wish related to love. Amen.*
> *P.N.A.M.S.R.*

As was said, whoever carries the ring, being a man and knowing how to present himself, will marry the woman that most pleases him, and even will possess others who arouse his carnal desires. If the one who carries the ring is a woman, it will achieve the same ends; but to these we do not advise it when they want to be faithful, because the talisman makes the person who carries it very fickle.

These are the instructions from the *Inguerimanços.*

History of the Wonderful Ring

[GLT]

The story tells that Candaule, the famed king of Lydia, one day showed to Giges, who was his favorite official, his wife, the queen, completely naked. The charming queen saw Giges and, for love or for revenge, gave order to this official to kill her husband, promising as a reward for this crime her hand and her court. Giges became, for this reason, after making the killing, the king of Lydia, in the year of 718 before Jesus Christ.

Plato tells differently about this usurpation. He says that, opening the earth, Giges, the king's shepherd, descended to the bottom of the abyss, and there he found a great horse. Mounted on this horse was a man of Herculean forms, who had in his index finger a magical ring, gifted with the great virtue of making someone invisible. Giges took the ring from him and used it, without any risk, to kill the king Candaule, and substituted him in his throne.

We will give here a brief outline of the precious talisman. It had two mountings: In one, in the shape of the Sun, there was a big topaz; in the other, in the shape of the Moon, an emerald. The ring was made of silver and had cabalistic signs, engraved around it.

Until today, the great sorcerers try to find the magical words that were pronounced to make the individual invisible with the help of this ring. If they come, as we wish, to our knowledge, we will not wait to transmit them to our readers, as soon as this book be printed again, in this edition in three volumes.

In Portugal, there was a fanatic, almost ninety years old, still working incessantly to find the necessary words, to make easy that enchantment. Unhappily, he died without achieving what he desired.

Secret to make yourself invisible

[LM2]

Giges was the friend and favorite of the king of Lydia, Candaule, who, desirous that the physical perfections of his wife could be appreciated by his favorite, let him see her completely undressed. Such an affront to her modesty, the queen took it so seriously that she threatened Giges with an appalling death if he did not consent to be the killer of his friend the king. Candaule was killed, and Giges received as reward the hand of the widow, and with her the crown.

Plato makes a reference to the story that, when Giges was the king's shepherd, he found in the body of a bronze horse the famous ring which made invisible the person who carried it. Using the ring, Giges killed the king Candaule and took possession of the crown by virtue of his marriage with the queen.

According to what was told by diverse authors who dealt with the invisibility, this famous ring showed two faces or precious stones; at one was seen the image of the Sun engrave in a topaz, and in the other, the Moon engraved in an emerald. The ring was made of silver and had around it certain cabalistic signs. Without doubt, it was necessary to recite some magical words to make, by the virtue of the ring, its possessor become invisible; the ring and the words were lost, but the cabalists preserved the secret of its preparation; here it is:

Under the auspices of Mercury, on a Wednesday in the months of Spring and when the mentioned planet is moving in the sky in conjunction with the Moon, with Jupiter, with Venus, or with the Sun, make the ring with fixed and purified mercury, in a size enough to wear on the finger of the heart. In the ring, you will mount one stone that is found in the nest of the bird called *Bori* by the Chaldeans and *Isan* by the Greek. Around the ring, engrave these words and crosses: *"Jesus passing* ✠ *between them* ✠ *he went."* After that, put the ring over a plaque of fixed mercury and fumigate it with the perfume of Mercury; wrap it with a piece of silk in the color corresponding to the mentioned planet, and you will leave it for nine days in the nest from where the stone was taken. Finishing at the appointed time, perfume it again and keep it in a small box containing fixed mercury until the time to use it comes. Here is another way to make the *ring of invisibility* taught by Porphyry, Iamblichus, Peter and Apona and Agrippa. Take three hairs from the upper part of a hyena, and with them make a ring, which must be left for nine days in the nest of the mentioned bird and fumigate it according to described way.

Great Talisman of the Constelations

[TDH]

This talisman will be constructed from the seven metals associated with the seven planets, trying to make the drawings like the engravings. It must be fabricated on a Friday, between the tenth and twelfth hours of the night, when the sky is very clear. When making it, you will say the following invocation:

> *Receive, oh admirable metal, the planetary influences of all the celestial bodies, and in particular from Venus, so you will possess all the graces and virtues necessary to give me fortune, power, and glory as is my wish in this hour. So mote it be.*

This invocation must be repeated every night for thirty days, exposing the talisman to the benefic influences of the planets. To use it, observe the initial rules for the Ring and the Red Dragon.

Image attributed to Paracelsus, in the *Secrets Merveilleus De La Magie Naturelle et Cabalistique du Petit Albert*

---

78 This image was also taken from the *Petiti Albert*, as it can be seen in comparison with the next image.

Celestial Talisman

[TDH]

Like the one before, it is made with all the metals, and its only difference is that, as the other must be white with the silver dominating over the other metals, so this one must be yellow because the gold is the dominant metal. Its construction should be on a Sunday at dawn, and it must be finished when the sun has risen.

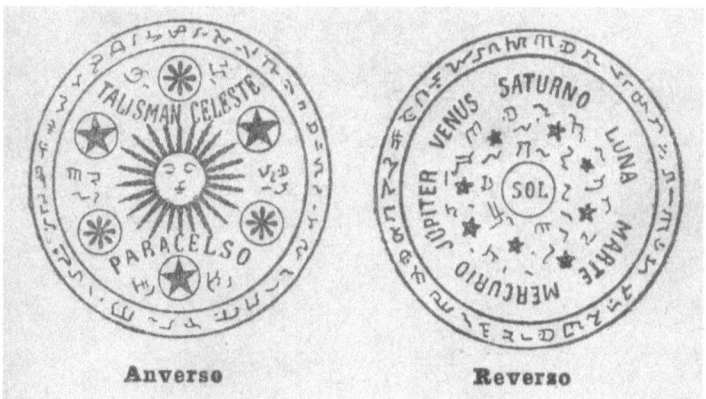

The invocations will be made as in the one before, but instead of Venus, the Sun will be named. To expose it to the planetary influences, you will choose the hours between the first break of dawn and the Sun being fully risen, for one week, ending on Sunday. To use it, follow the indicated procedures.

Talisman Exterminator

[TDH]

This talisman will be fabricated on a Saturday night between 10 and 12 on the occasion of the Moon being in the center of its path and the sky being serene and clear. For this invocation Saturn will be named. Its predominant metal will be lead, but it will have all the metals. It will be exposed to the planetary influences every night from 10 to 12. For its use follow the rules indicated. The wonderful power it possesses over bad spirits is very great, by the virtue of the Cross of Caravaca, and the scorpion and the cabalistic circles it contains. Whoever uses this talisman will be able to impose his will on the spirits, and if you put it over the person possessed by a demon, in the same moment he shall be free.

Talisman of Isis

[TDH]

Isis, known by the name of "The Good Goddess," was a benefactor deity of the Egyptians. Her main attributes were the four-leafed clover, one of the rarest occurrences in the vegetable world, as rare as the happiness which this Isiac emblem gives. The four-leafed clover is not a different species, but the same common clover (*trifolium pratesse*) which, by Isis's will, exceptionally has a fourfold leaf. The plant which possesses this divine accident never flowers and because of this cannot reproduce itself.

Among the Egyptians who consecrated a special cult to Isis, no one that was initiated in the mysteries before has found a four-leafed clover: The finding was, in the eyes of the patriarchs, an evident proof of the goddess's protection.

During the solemn ceremony of initiation, the neophyte offered to Isis, in the moment of the sacrifices, the leaf he had found and received in return from the hands of the great priest a silver four-leafed clover, a sacred talisman, fortunate gift, which plays an important role in the acts of existence.

Happiness follows this talisman. The bridegroom offers it to the bride as a gift of love; the mother puts it around the son's neck as a preservative against the adversities of life, and within the family, it is passed from parents to children as a sacred symbol of prosperity. It was also put in the sarcophagus as a pious testimony of trust in its efficacy even into the next life.

To have the exact idea of the great importance given by the Egyptians to the four-leafed clover, it must be mentioned that they carved it in monuments and hieroglyphs. The four-leafed clover appears upon the London obelisk, called "Cleopatra's Needle," and upon the larger part of the funerary books. It is seen in the famous Isiac table representing the mysteries of Isis, in the royal gallery of Turin, which the priests of this goddess attached to their purple tunics with a pin with the shape of a four-leafed clover, attached on the shoulders.

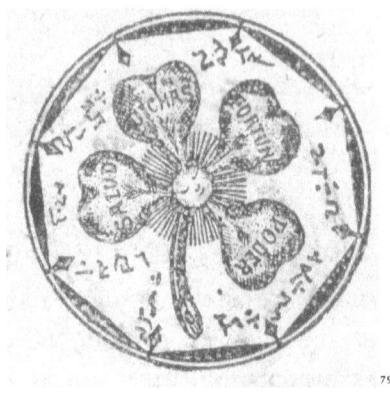

For its fabrication will be used the metals silver and platinum, choosing the hours from 9 to 11 at night, on a Monday and on the occasion that the Full Moon is over the horizon, which is the beginning of its path. The invocations will be made in the following way:

> *Oh, solitary celestial body, who eternally walks in that limitless space, flowing your melancholic light over this planet called Earth, I, the most humble of the mortals, ask you in this solemn hour to fix your rays and mercies over this metal carrying your image, endowing it with the necessary magical virtues, so with its mediation I can achieve happiness, fortune, health, power and love during the course of my life upon this planet. If you attend to*

my supplication, I promise in gratitude for your favors to remember you every hour of my life.

This invocation will be repeated for 30 nights at the same hours, from 9 to 11. To use it, follow the mentioned procedures.

The previous talismans were indicated as truly special, and now there remain to mention the most current and usual.

Ordinary Talismans

[TDH]

The very "great and unique talisman" is dedicated to Mercury, and because of this, it must be made of green and red metal. Carrying it with you, and being pure of heart, it is used against the dangers of the world. Showing it to the spirits, they will obey you in everything.

---

80 The source of this talisman is the *Véritable Magie Noir*. The original description says, "The Very Great Pantacle, carried over your you without sin: protects against the dangers of the world and against the weapons; if you write this circle, and show it to the spirits, they will obey you in everything."

LES TRÈS GRAND ET UNIQUE

PANTACLE,

De couleurs verte et rouge, correspondantes au signe de Mercure ☿.

Le très-grand Pantacle, étant porté sur soi sans péché : vaut tout contre les périls du monde et contre les armes ; si vous écrivez ce cercle ; et le montrez aux esprits, ils vous obéiront en tout.

The "great and unique talisman" in its original version from the Veritable Magie Noir. Courtesy of Joseph H. Peterson.

Talismans and Amulets

The "great and unique talisman" published in the "Cipriano el Temeroao." Courtesy of Felix Castro Vicente.

To Saturn corresponds the seven talismans in black color. The principal is the one used to call the celestial spirits, to chase away the guardians of treasures, and to make you win at every kind of game.

Another of the talismans dedicated to Saturn is the one used to prevent earthquakes, through the virtue of the spirits expressed in this talisman with the names *Noni, Chori, Josmondichi*.

Also to Jupiter correspond another seven talismans formed from celestial blue metal, the distinctive color of said planet.

One of the most important talismans consecrated to Jupiter is the one used to know the spirits that correspond to its nature, and principally the one whose name is written on this talisman, among which is found

---

81 "Primer Talisman de Saturno" in [TDH]. We here substituted it for the identical original image from the *Véritable Magie Noir,* for better quality. In the *Véritable Magie Noir* it is listed as the "Cinquième Pantacle de Saturne" (Fifth Pantacle of Saturn).

82 "Segundo Talisman de Saturno" in [TDH]. We here substituted it for the identical original image from the *Véritable Magie Noir,* for better quality. In the *Véritable Magie Noir* it is listed as the "Septiéme Pantacle de Saturne" (Seventh Pantacle of Saturn).

Talismans and Amulets

"*Parosiel*," who is the lord of treasures and the one who teaches how to acquire them.

To Mars, six talismans are consecrated in the color red, within which the principal has great efficacy so that, carrying it with you, nobody can hurt you, but the shots from firearms will turn against those who directed them; when you find yourself at war, it will be very necessary and will give you the victory.

It also exerts a sovereign dominion over the troops and over the multitude, being great its virtues to attract the spirits linked to the planet it represents.

With what was indicated about the talisman of Mars, it will be understood that its use is useful to the military in general and to all those people who, through the ill-fortunes of life, are involved in revolutions and wars. This does not mean that the rest of the mortals should abstain from these, just that, in general, they fit better to the ones that feel themselves inclined to wars, fights, mutinies, and revolutions.

In the center of this talisman is found a small dragon with eight claws and its face turned to the right, and on the other side, there is the figure of a person.

---

83   "Talisman de Jupiter" in [TDH]. We here substituted it for the identical original image from the *Véritable Magie Noir*, for better quality. In the *Véritable Magie Noir* it is listed as the "Premier Pantacle" (First Pantacle), in the chapter with the pantacles of Jupiter.

The Book of Saint Cyprian

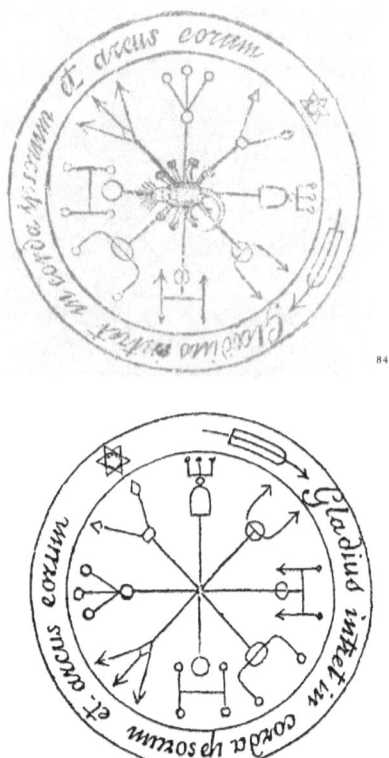

Cinquième Pantacle of Mars from the *Veritable Magie Noir*.

Quatrième Pantacle of Mars from the *Veritable Magie Noir*.

---

84 This talisman shows some "creativity" as it mixes the Cinquième Pantacle of the *Veritable Magie Noir* with the image of the scorpion (TDH says, "a small dragon with eight claws") from the Quatrième Pantacle.

Talismans and Amulets

Seven are the talismans consecrated to the Sun, and they will be made in the color yellow.

One of the principal spirits of this talisman is the one which possesses the wonderful virtue of acquiring and conquering kingdoms and the domains of others. It is proper to the kings and great sovereigns of the earth. Alexander Magnus carried it in his warrior enterprises. This talisman can be used like the previous one of Mars, because its properties in certain ways are the same, because of which it can be said that they complement each other.

Another of the most important talismans consecrated to the Sun is the one which possesses the virtue of invisibility, and if someone is in prison, having irons on the feet and hands, if he had acquired the supreme perfection and carried this talisman, in the same moment the chains would break and he would be free.

There are many known wonderful cases of persons unjustly persecuted, who were released through the virtues of this talisman.

---

85 "Primer Talisman del Sol" in [TDH]. We here substituted it for the identical original image from the *Véritable Magie Noir*, for better quality. In the *Véritable Magie Noir* it is listed as the "Troisième Pantacle" (Third Pantacle), in the chapter with the pantacles of the Sun.

The Book of Saint Cyprian

To Venus, five talismans are dedicated, in green color.

One of the most wonderful is the one that is used to attract the spirits from Venus to win the person you desire or to make her desire you. Such is its virtue that if she is retained in a way she cannot come to see you, by invoking the talisman and commanding it with true will, it will make the beloved person come to your side, and immediately you will achieve your desire. However, you must be aware that if you are guided by self-interest and not by love, you will achieve nothing. The talisman and the characters will be made with three metals, silver, copper, and brass. You will bless and exorcise it, carrying it with you day and night.

If the person that possesses it is worthy of its gifts, and if the talisman is endowed with all its magical virtues, you can be sure that he will achieve love when he wishes it.

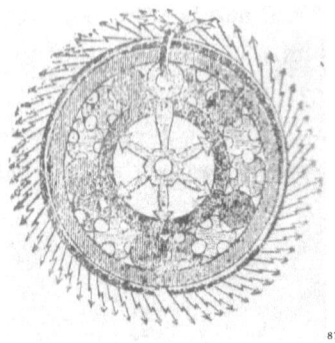

---

86 "Segundo Talisman del Sol" in [TDH]. We here substituted it for the identical original image from the *Véritable Magie Noir*, for better quality. In the *Véritable Magie Noir* it is listed as the "Septiéme Pantacle" (Seventh Pantacle), in the chapter with the pantacles of the Sun.

87 "Talisman de Venus." Differently from the other images in this section, this talisman does not appear in the *Veritable Magie Noir*. Its source remains unknown.

Mercury also possesses five talismans in the colors red and green, among which the most powerful is the one used to acquire science and knowledge of all created things, both terrestrial as celestial, to know the most occult secrets and to send the spirits to any place you want.

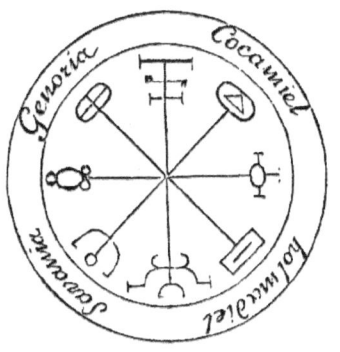

Six talismans are consecrated to the Moon, the principal being the one that is useful to travelers. It is wonderful against the dangers of the water.

---

88   "Talisman de Mercurio" in [TDH]. We here substituted it for the identical original image from the *Véritable Magie Noir*, for better quality. In the *Véritable Magie Noir* it is listed as the "Troisième Pantacle de Mercure" (Third Pantacle of Mercury).

89   *This is in truth the* "Quatrième Pantacle of Venus" from the *Veritable Magie Noir*. It is also upside down.

Useful Explanations about the Talismans

[TDH]

In his *Magical Archidoxes,* Paracelsus explains that it is worthy of note that the planets never exert so well their influences but through an intermediary of the seven metals which are proper to them and that have sympathy with their substances.

In truth, the wise cabalists, having recognized through the sublime penetration of their sciences which are the proper metals to the planets, attributed gold to the Sun and Sunday, silver to the Moon and Monday, iron to Mars and Tuesday, quicksilver to Mercury and Wednesday, the tin to Jupiter and Thursday, copper to Venus and Friday, and lead to Saturn and Saturday.

On this foundation the ancient philosophers, among them Moses and Solomon, established the skies of the planets. If for any reason it is not possible to acquire the proper metals, it will be enough to use others of the same or similar colors if they have a part corresponding to each planet and the talisman is formed under the influence of the same.

It is convenient to know also that the wonderful effects of a talisman can only be modified through the influence exerted over it by other talismans of greater virtue and force or by the qualities and virtues possessed by the person who has it. It must be said that, if someone is worthy of the talisman he possesses, it will favor him much better than the one who is not worthy of it. So everyone who uses a talisman must make himself worthy of its gifts, which he will achieve by being modest, humble, and virtuous.

Magical Amulets

[TDH]

Since primitive times, the priests of every known religion made use of magical amulets as an efficient preservative against malefactions and infirmities. The Arabs kept this tradition in such a way that there is no one between them, being woman, man, or child, who does not carry an amulet on the left arm or over the heart.

This custom is not just being transmitted from parents to children not by the Arabs, as we can for say for sure that there is not one single known point in the world where we cannot find someone making use of it, be it in the form of a stone, or any other, once they all have the same purpose.

The effects of the amulets, like the talismans, must be wonderful and supernatural every time they are built in the proper way and have special virtues. Moses owed to them the wonders he worked in Egypt: the crossing of the Red Sea, the feeding of the Hebrew people in the desert. Through their virtues, he could also make water flow from a stone, talk on Mount Sinai with the great spirit of God, Alpha and Omega of the cabalistic sciences, and finally win and submit the people he found in his path.

The wise king Solomon was, without any doubt, after Moses the one who succeeded in possessing talismans of great power and virtue, and to them he owed the great domain he exerted over all the creation and his infinite wisdom.

Using them with faith, they protect from sorceries and enchantments, which comes from their mysterious power that no evil can destroy. Because of this, you must make sure to place it over children, to protect them from malign influences and make them receive the virtues and benign influences of the amulet, which, operating over their infantile imagination, gives to them pleasant dreams, forming them into a tranquil and kind character.

ON THE WAY OF PREPARING THE AMULETS

To obtain good amulets, it is necessary to know firstly the different ways to create them. Among the Arabs, the most used is the one employed by the sage Alaka Bajamet Alaja, who lived in Mecca. This celebrated magician was constantly at the altar of the offerings, sitting upon a carpet, according to the customs used by them. There, under the auspices of the great priest Mahometalit, he wrote and engraved amulets, which he made, upon a piece of virgin parchment, taken from the skin of a small white lamb.

The ink he used in the drawings was prepared with the blood he extracted from the veins of the virgin priestess, to which he added the sap of holy plants and mineral ink. The mineral ink was made with the seven metals which have the influence and representation of the seven planets. Once he had engraved and drawn the cabalistic signs, he perfumed and put them over the altar of the seven sacrifices: Then, they were folded in four and wrapped in white paper containing verses from the Quran written in Arabic. To this was added a medal, passed first through the sacrificial fire with cabalistic signs, and everything was put into a small purse made of scarlet silk. Next, it was perfumed with the sacred and odoriferous plants sacred to the prophet. The medal is the symbol of abundance, receiving the protection of the great Nakir, the greatest of the prophets, who consecrated their lives to the study of the magical sciences and to the progress of humanity. The amulet must be put on the left arm or over the heart, saying the following invocation:

Talismans and Amulets

"Boas, Tubaliaon, Eluar, Adonay, jarua; Menaart, be propitious and deliver me from every evil, in my body as in my soul."

The indicated way is the most current among the Arabs, some amulets having such rare virtues that the mortal who possesses them acquires the gift of fascinating animals like serpents, lions, panthers, etc., do, exerting over them a kind of magical enchantment which permits them to completely dominate.

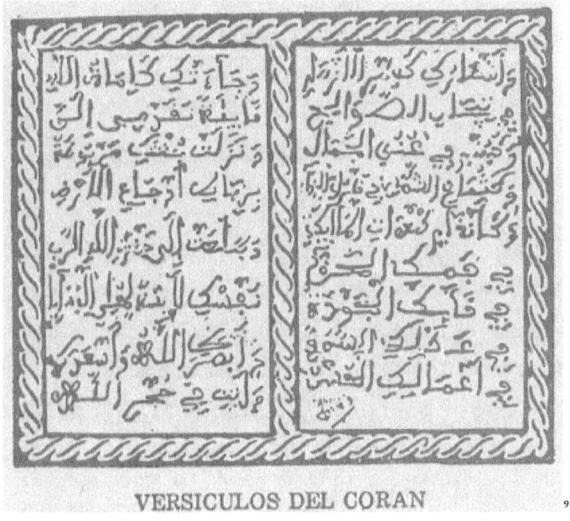

VERSICULOS DEL CORAN

CONSTELLATE AMULET

This amulet is made with a piece of virgin parchment on which you must draw with scarlet ink a big circle, and with silver ink mixed with Arabic gum, another one smaller. Inside these circles make 12 divisions with two rays in each one, and inside the division one of the zodiacal signs. In the center make a star tracing each of its rays with one of the colors of the rainbow and also writing over them the names of the planets. These names, and the names of the metals that go into the rays, must each be written with the ink of the planet they represent. In the center of the star draw the image of the Sun, this one and its rays will be made with gold ink or reddish yellow.

The entire indicated operation must be made at night, and in the hour of each planet, draw it and the name of the metal that represents it. The drawings in the center must start on Monday with the Moon, to be able to finish on Sunday with the Sun. After that, add a sheet of silver and one of gold or a small plate or coin of each metal, put them inside, and fold the parchments four times, wrapping with white paper with the verse from the Quran shown in the drawing.

All that, carefully wrapped, is put into a small purse of green silk and exposed to the influences of the celestial bodies, as will be said in the next chapter, which deals with the way to acquire to the talismans and amulets the good influences of the planets. Some add a magnetic stone, a tooth of a hanged man, or the clove of garlic etc., with which greater virtue is acquired, but it is not of absolute necessity, and these objects cannot always be acquired.

With this amulet, the person is free from being hurt by a firearm, because the bullets turn against whoever is firing, or the shot does not work.[92]

91
92 About this effect, we will mention the following case, described by an English traveler who witnessed this: An Arab chief pitched his amulets against shots from rifles, and these did not fire, even with the trigger pressed. When aimed by the other side, the shot

TALISMANS AND AMULETS

EVANGELICAL AMULET

The use of this amulet, made as a small book containing printing of the four Gospels, is very common among Christians. These must be read in the presence of a boy by a priest, blessing it with exorcized water. Put the little book in a purse of satin, green or blue, and weave it into the boy's clothes, over the left side, in the inner part. It is very useful at guarding the boy against malefic influences like enchantments, sorceries, the evil eye, etc., which produce the same incurable infirmities and sometimes death.

---

came with a great noise. A similar happening is referred to in China, which many of our readers know about.

On the Way of Making the Amulets and Talismans Possess Virtues and Efficacy

[TDH]

To endow the talismans and amulets with the necessary virtues, it is good for the person who will use them to dedicate, for thirty nights, the hour between ten and eleven to the contemplation of the celestial bodies, exposing the talisman over a new small dish, to receive the beneficial influences. Half of the time, which means after half an hour, you will expose one side, and in the other half, the other side. Each night, you will recite for this hour the following preaching with the right hand over the talisman or amulet and your gaze fixed on the starry heavens:

> "Direct your emanations, oh sovereign stars, unto this piece of metal (or parchment) which represents you on this planet called Earth, and endow it with all the virtues and qualities that are necessary to have absolute Power to dominate the good and bad spirits, according to my wish; that it can through your favor and mediation win over all the obstacles of life, acquire riches and power, to not be molested or defeated by persons or spirits, be free from malefaction, spells and other enchantments. That nothing

can cause me any evil or harm and possess an absolute dominion over the stars and the elements of earth, spirits and people. I supplicate too the spirits of light, Adonai, Ariel, Jehová and Metraton to adorn it with the gifts of wisdom, so through its magical virtues I achieve everything I propose myself to.

"For the second time I ask the stars, elements and created spirits, to hear my supplication in this solemn hour, and to endow it with grace so through its means I achieve the many wonders I propose myself to, always for my well being and that of my fellow men."

If it is necessary to achieve the desired benefits by means of the talismans and amulets, make yourself worthy of them, which is achieved by fleeing from vices and acquiring the supreme perfection through the constant practice of virtues. To that end, it is useful to leave any laziness aside, making yourself diligent; luxury must be changed into chastity or the moderate use of pleasures; vanity and pride will be exchanged for patience and humility and so on. As we correct your defects, we go forward in the way of the supreme perfection which is what will make us worthy of acquiring the gift of dominating ourselves and subjugating our will and free will over everything that creation holds, in the spiritual as in the material.

We must not forget the warnings made to be patient and long-suffering, because lacking these virtues, the possession of the secret science and the true wisdom, which are only achieved through persevering on the investigation of the natural and spiritual things, will be difficult.

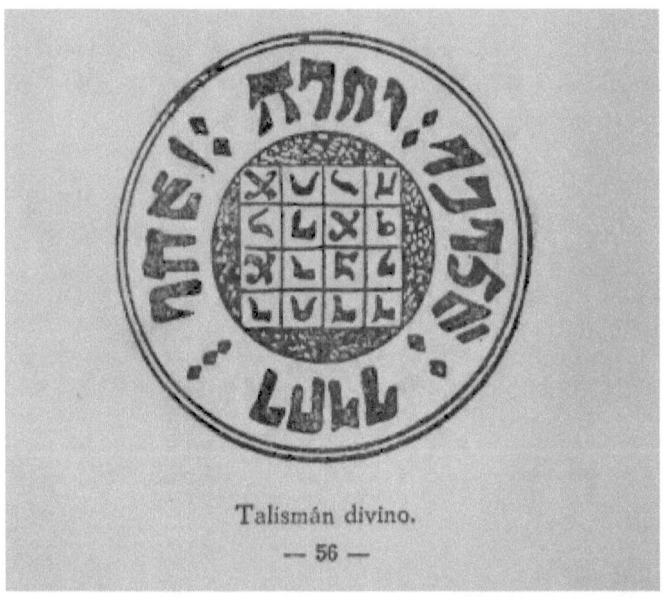

Talismán divino.
— 56 —

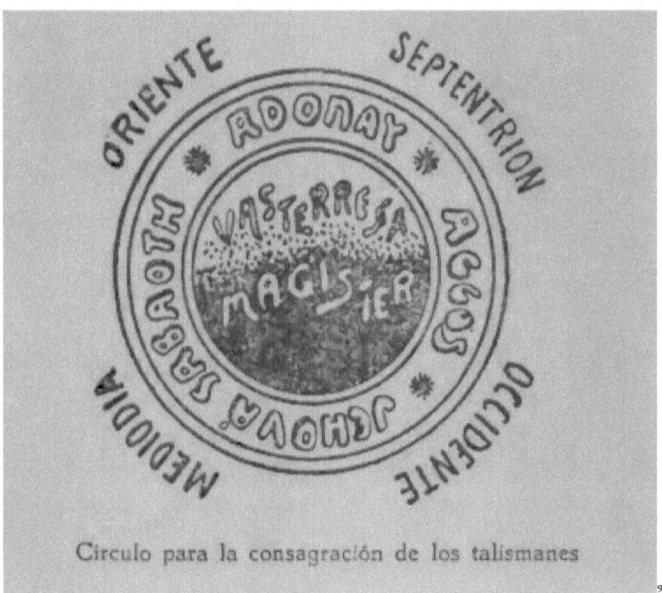

Círculo para la consagración de los talismanes

---

93 I could not find any immediate source for these two last images. The modern style of the drawings inclines me to think they were made for this edition.

The Book of Spirits

Invocations Pacts and Exorcisms

[TDH]

To the reader:

Do not forget, whoever tries to put into practice the experiments that here will be revealed, that you must be clean from impurities, put all your faith and will in the ceremonies and conjurations, that it is necessary to be daring to the utmost degree, not being convinced if some malevolent spirits tell you to quit your enterprise. He who has faith and temerity will achieve the domain of the wonderful things, but whoever is fearful and lacking in courage exposes himself to torment and mortification without achieving any benefit.

This declaration being made, which is also a prologue, we move on now to explain the different categories of supernatural beings with which we necessarily have to deal if we put into practice the instructions to be found in the course of this work.

On the spirits in general

The spirits are divided into many categories, their faculties and conditions being diverse.

The Supreme Spirit or Creator rules and governs everything, and to him all the things created are subject in an absolute way, the spiritual as well as the material.

Under his immediate command, and as the principal chiefs, we found the superior spirits which are followed, according to their categories, by the middle and inferior spirits. Each spirit gathers distinct qualities and understandings. There is the celestial, aerial, terrestrial, and infernal, being named, according to their conditions, of protection, mercy, temptation, of good, and of harm.

Each one has its own special mission in the universe, and all of them render worship and obedience to the Supreme Creator and Sovereign Spirit. It is the general rule all over the world to accept as fixed truth the existence of spirits both good and evil, creating antagonism between them. This cannot be accepted by the sacred science of the true magic for the reason that good and evil are the complement of everything. In the same way there is no pleasure without pain, so in all creation necessarily must exist the absolute and the relative, which is its complement. It can be assured, therefore, that good is joined with evil, good fortune to unhappiness, suffering to joy, life to death, spirit to matter, soul to body, heat to cold, light to obscurity, and on this point, we could enumerate infinite subjects.

The spirits can be, individually, good or bad, of light or of darkness, but all of them necessarily carry out their missions according to the laws they were given at their creation. So we understand that the spirits of temptation dedicate themselves to tempt, the spirits of mercy and protection to protect, etc. The ones called celestial reside in the sky, the aerial in the air, the terrestrial in the earth, and the infernal in their lairs.

Besides the fact that everyone has his mission, as it was said, all of them, without exception, own respect and obedience to the Supreme Spirit, whose name is Jehovah in Hebrew, Alpha and Omega in Chaldean, Allah among the Moors, and Deus among the Christians. In the works, you can invoke all of them but must call only the ones of one or other quality, according to the type of petition you are going to make.

That means, when the conjuration is of temptation, you will call the ones who tempt; when it is of tenderness and love, the ones who please; if it is a conjuration for good, you call the good ones; if it is for evil, the evil ones, or the ones who do harm; and so on.

The good spirits dominate always the bad ones, and not the latter over the former, because this is how the Sovereign Creator made it, to whom all render absolute obedience. Always have present the sign of the cross, called the Sign of Redemption, as it has such a virtue and force over the bad spirits that they cannot resist its sight, and only when sheltered inside someone or inside an impure animal, or forced by the power of a conjuration or invocation, can they stand in its presence.

To invoke the spirits of light or celestials, you should not also use the sign of the cross, because it is for them a sign of great veneration and respect, the result being that its contemplation enraptures and subjugates them without allowing them to pay attention to anything else. That is why it was indicated that the cross must be removed from every magical ceremony and can only be used in the experiments or in the invocations made to the principal superior celestial spirits.

After these warnings, we will indicate the different hierarchies and names of spirits which must be invoked according to the experiments someone wishes to execute.

On the hierarchy of the spirits

The Supreme Spirit

The Supreme Spirit is the Creator of everything that was created, over whom nothing has command and to whom everyone owns obedience, submission, and respect. It is so immense and great that there is not one atom in all of creation where this mysterious energy does not reach.

From the Supreme Spirit, all the other spirits derive, as these are nothing more in reality than parts of the great all. For this reason, the magical science demonstrates that if the spirits are divided into many categories, all of them as they proceed perfecting themselves, and once the mission the Supreme Creator commended to them is fulfilled, they once again identify themselves with him. The entire universe constitutes one single life, animated by the Divine Spirit, and nothing exists in reality that is not fed by him.

We can very well, therefore, come to the absolute affirmation that the Supreme Spirit is eternal and infinite, that he rules and disposes everything, being the cause and principle of everything created.

For him, there is no time, space, or measure, and although it is difficult to express his greatness, we will make some observations to give us a small idea of its immensity and of the work and wonders of creation.

Imagine for a moment, reader, that you propose to undertake a journey through infinite space. Very well: Admitting as a base the speed of light, which travels with a velocity of 77,000 leagues per second, and taking Earth as the starting point, pretend to go to a point in space. In the first second, you will have covered 77,000 leagues, in the second 144,000, and after 100 seconds, 770,000. With this wonderful speed in a minute of travel you will be at 4,420,000 leagues of distance from Earth.

Following this, march for days, months, years, and centuries, and you will have covered thousands of millions of leagues, to which calculus there is no possibility of determining, but even with this amazing result, after the space covered and still continuing with the same speed for millions of years, you would never reach the limit of the infinite, for the simple reason that the infinite does not have a limit. So we must imagine the sovereign spirit, as it is eternal, and the eternal does not have a beginning or end. Because of this, and having demonstrated that this spirit fills and vivifies everything, it can be calculated how difficult it must be for men to express and understand its immensity. The words "infinite," "eternity," and "Supreme Being," completely escape human comprehension, because our intelligence is too limited to be able to define them.

Goethe to Eckerman said, "The Supreme Being is incomprehensible to men; they do not have of Him anything more than a vague feeling, an approximate idea, which does not prevent us from being so identified with the deity that it can be said that it sustains us; that in it we live and breathe. We suffer and we enjoy, according to eternal rules, in the face of which we represent at the same time an active and a passive role. It cares little if we recognize it or not. The child savors the candy without disturbing herself about what she did, and the little bird pecks the cherry without thinking about from what it sprouted. What we know from the idea of God, and what this narrow intuition we have of the Supreme Being definitively means, even if we would designate it, like the Turks do with a hundred names, it would remain infinitely below the truth; so innumerable are its attributes! ... As the deity manifests not just to men, but also equally in the entire nature and in the happenings of the world, the idea we can form of it, is anyway insufficient."

After making this brief explanation, we will discuss the celestial spirits, according to their importance and hierarchy.

To have a better understanding of the successive chapters, we will show later the tables containing the figures of the principal spirits of light and the symbols used to make their pacts with men.

The Superior Spirits

The Superior Spirits are the ones we consider first in category and which have the power of command over the rest which are found on the inferior scale.

The first of all is Adonay, called Angel of Light, who receives directly from the Supreme Being the orders he will transmit to the rest.

At his immediate service and with identical power, there are other two, whose names are Eloim and Jehovam, who have the mission of fulfilling the mandates that Adonai receives and that they transmit in their turn to the spirits in charge of their execution.

Next in the hierarchy follow Mitraton, Azrael, Astroschio, Eloy, Milech, Ariel, and Zenaoth, who also have at their command other spirits who render to them great and absolute obedience.

From this, we deduce that they go ascending in category in spite of being considered superior spirits, for which we can describe them as first, second, and third magnitudes, being the principal of the great Adonay, or Angel of Light, as it was said.

In the continuation, we give an approximate idea of the celestial spirits, which can be said to form true armies, for their organization as for the obedience with which they execute the orders they receive from their superiors.

On the Celestial Spirits

We call Celestial Spirits the ones who inhabit the firmament and the celestial bodies which turn around through space. Their functions are to preside over the destinies of each mortal and to direct the happenings which concern them, according to the will of the Divine Creator. Because of that, the Celestial Spirits are sheltered from every ambush from the harmful genius.

Each celestial spirit cannot work except with the coordination of its corresponding celestial body and according to what allows it the divine omnipotence, because God gives to it only the power to work. For this reason, said spirits cannot undertake anything but under divine direction and only to a good end, as the history of the world confirms since its creation.

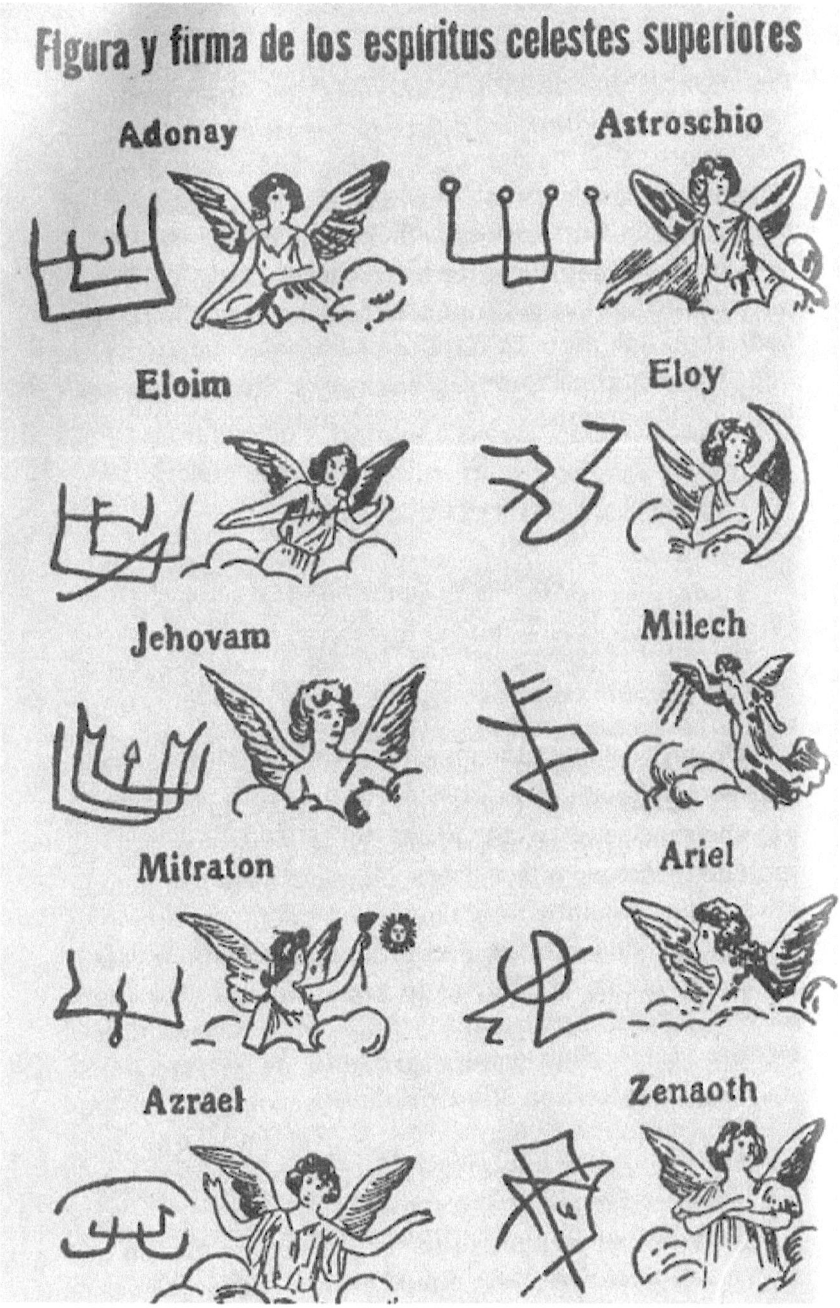

The Book of Spirits

Figura y firma de los espíritus celestes superiores

Adonay

Astroschio

Eloim

Eloy

Jehovam

Milech

Mitraton

Ariel

Azrael

Zenaoth

[TDH]

There are seven governors with different functions. Their visible stars are: Aratron, Bethor, Phaleg, Och, Hageth, Ophiel, and Phul, to whom are attributed the following conditions:

> ***Aratron*** has the power to change instantly stones into gold and to do the opposite, for instance, convert coal into gold and vice-versa; he teaches Alchemy, Magic, Physics, how to make beings invisible and give long life.
>
> ***Bethor*** bestows high dignities, brings to men spirits which give exact answers, transports objects from one place to another, gives precious stones, and prolongs life indefinitely if God allows.
>
> ***Phaleg*** belongs to the attributes of Mars, establishes peace, and elevates to the higher military hierarchies whoever receives its mark.
>
> ***Och*** presides under the attributes of the Sun and gives long life and health, distributes wisdom, teaches Medicine, and gives power to change everything into pure gold and into the most precious stones.
>
> ***Hageth***, under the influence of Venus, gives great beauty to the women who honor its protection, distributes to them all graces, changes copper into gold, and does the opposite.
>
> ***Ophiel*** possesses the power of metallic transmutation, and under the planet Mercury, it gives the means to transform silver into gold, a transformation upon which is founded, according to Alchemy, the great philosophical stone.

Phul governs the lunar regions, and its potency extends to the cure of infinite infirmities. It changes every metal into silver, protects the man who travels, and gives a long and powerful life.

It must never be forgotten that everything is possible to whomever has faith and will, and that nothing will be achieved by whomever lacks both things. There are no greater obstacles than the ones operated by bewilderment, inconstancy, frivolity, disorderliness, and disordered passions.

Whoever wishes to possess the gift of Magic must first of all be an honorable, virtuous man, constant in his words and in his actions, firm in every work, prudent and avaricious only of his wisdom, and a loyal believer in the enterprise he undertakes.

This ulterior digression made, because we consider it of good use, we move on to discuss the gnomes.

The gnomes

After the specifications made about all the categories of the spirits, detailing the elements which populate them, the properties and functions commended to their innate instincts imposed by the King of the Confines, the way to supplicate their help in our magical enterprises, etc., we are now going to discuss other beings that are also spiritual but who, disconnected in everything from the former, form a new legion and work and act with absolute freedom in relation to the others.

Gnomes—the name of these spirits is defined by Arbatel[94] in the annals of Magic, to the knowledge of his fellows, in the following way: the spirit guardians of treasures, intimate with humanity, of which they are an integral part, they are invulnerable to our most subtle charms. This annotation, written in Arbatel's own hand, has been generally ill-interpreted in one of its most significant parts, due to the lack of comprehensive

---

94   Although the text treat the name 'Arbatel' as if refering to a person, the source of the name probalby is the ***Arbatel de magia veterum*** (English: *Arbatel of the magic of the ancients*) is a treatise on ceremonial magic written in Latin, first published in 1575 in Basel, Switzerland, whose author is unknown.

knowledge of the geniuses who have been treating such an uncovered branch of knowledge, and it is, concerning the beginning of the verse mentioned before, because I must warn that the sentences and maxims written in the Red Book, Arbatel's masterpiece, are in Arabic, and I give the translation to whomever, not acquainted with the secrets of this mystery, cannot by themselves, with the help of a conjuration, use the original, rare book, written on sheets of parchment, which Olympiadoro and Sinesio tried to copy, for the simple reason that, as long they wrote, the letters went on vanishing [sic]; in fact, such was the endeavor of both in knowing it, that they managed to retain in their memory some paragraphs, which were very useful in their experiments in Alchemy, managing to artificially make gold and diamonds. But, leaving aside the digressions, we will say that the qualification of guardians of treasures we mentioned before is hyperbolic and in a figurative sense, because its author not only made reference to treasures which are hidden in the form of minerals, precious stones, minted coins, etc., but also to the intelligence of men which, well understood, is the greatest treasure we mortals are endowed with, and of which they become the most faithful guardians, directing it through the road of supreme perfection.

We must, however, give a succinct explanation to the incredulous who doubt the free will of these spirits toward the matter, and to this effect we expose the following:

The spirit, said the doctor Herman Scheffer, is nothing else than a force from matter, resulting immediately from the nervous activity: But we object with Flammarion, from where comes this nervous activity? What is it if not the spirit from which comes such power? Is it the soul who obeys the body, or is it the body which submits to the soul?

These are dogmas to which we must not pay attention, even if supported by eminences like Laugel, Maleschott, Bücher, and other famed professors.

It must be stated that our spirit is constituted in such a way that into its composition enters an immensity of small spirits, who work constantly in the development of our ideas, and these in direct relationship with the gnomes are the ones who produce in our soul sensations of pleasure, joy,

The Book of Spirits

valor, fear, sadness, and many others which, without us giving a clear account of their origins, take us over completely.

These spirits are so tiny that to compare we should say they look like atoms[95], which is not an obstacle to their being precise in the fulfilment of their duties, that as soon as we appear upon the face of the earth and inhale the first breath of life, we are already victims of their benefic invasion, which accompany and direct us to the end of the fate that providence signalled to us beforehand.

So complex, large, and important is this role they perform that we can almost say that we depend on them, without fearing regret and, for obvious reasons, they are the ones we should know to be able to explain many phenomena that happen to us and that until now lacked categorical explanation.

The residence of the gnomes is the aerial waves, and like their abodes, they are never at rest. Besides this, they also have the property of penetrating through every pore of the earth and even infiltrating the heart of the mountains.

They have absolute power over the imagination of man; they are his aegis in danger, his inspiration in doubt, his horoscope of the future; from there come the preoccupations we have, which are usually right [sic].

The zephyr is the transmitter of orders, demands, or the supplications of men between them and their spirits, and such is their conviction about good and evil that, if the voice they carry to its destiny is harmful to rational beings, they take great care to get rid of their possible charge, hitting against obstacles they find in their path. This way they ruin the power of the non-congener spirits, which can do nothing to counteract their righteous impulses, because as we have said, the gnomes have as their principal mission to watch over the balance of the talents threatened by the vexing wonders of the maleficent spirits.

We also must note that the influence or action of the gnomes is exerted over the brain, and because of this, they are the ones who engender the illusion of the senses. They wish man well and give to him an immaterial life, make him dream, and teach him to feel, because it is false, as it is

---

95 Veja-se o capítulo seguinte, que trata "do infinito."

believed, that the dream is nothing more than a retroaction of thoughts already impressed in our encephalic mass; no, the imagination is as incessant as the same gnomes who incite it to work, being ready to create at any moment, and if it was not for this mechanic, matter would be confounded until the moment it reached its total transformation, which would not take long.

There can be different degrees of mental activity or relative rest only in relation to the kind of cells that vibrate in our understanding; we can affirm that the more the object or the image is in contact with the material and mundane, the cause of the physiological moment, the more agitated the nervous system is, due to a larger number of nerves from the remarkable fabric of our organisms being under tension.

Do you think perhaps that these immense mountains of granite whose geognosy is, in larger part, made of small crystals of quartz, feldspar, mica, and orthoclase, which are elevated an infinity of meters above the sea level, remain motionless and at absolute rest? No! They vibrate in their every molecule, due to the cohesion and expansion of the atoms in which the ether imprints its movements, and you will now vacillate if I tell you that living matter is always in flux when even the masses, apparently inanimate, are not? Even more, if you confess that organized matter is constantly in movement, what would you say about the spirits in which are synthesized these qualities, and a powerful one that the rest of the elements of the universe lack?

Nothing is more beautiful than to abandon yourself to these spirits which give to us pleasures that perhaps are Platonic, because our being does not enjoy the soul in unity, but the soul is purified and learns to think on the divine and supernatural when we transport these gracious spirits on the wings of desire to the unknown regions and make us experience a thousand sensations which startle us with respect, making grow in our mind vague ideas like the hint of a desired happiness, which we start to achieve.

They make us believe in possible utopias, start to clarify with their germinating light, and we enjoy a beautifying ecstasy, elevating us each time to the splendid sun of the truth, the one which shines in the immense space of the Supreme Good.

Angels of misfortune fight against wickedness, making its progress impossible, even if they cannot destroy it as they obey the laws of nature [sic].

Easily, we observe the interference of these spirits in our designs, because we are intimately connected with them; that is why if we do some harm, because of an interior vacillation, we feel remorse, and if it is about a good we feel the ineffable enjoyment of a good fortune united with the frequent satisfaction of a soul manifest for a work done. How can we explain to ourselves this joy and this grief, *"sui generis,"* that we sometimes see ourselves possessed by, without a visible cause that awakens it, if not by the gnomes who engrave in our nervous system the echoes of a close happening? It is they who warn us, not to incite our lack of control or dejection, but to protect us from a sudden impression and make us become accustomed, little by little, to the temptation we will suffer, making us this way superior to ourselves.

Is it not true that, when we talk about someone we did not see for some time, that person suddenly appears before our eyes? To what can we attribute this if not to the gnomes? This ill-feeling that assaults us when we face a stranger who looks at us, this antipathy or sympathy which is born at first sight between two people, and this benevolent pre-disposition we have toward the magnanimous stars, what is all this if not examples of these spirits who put themselves in contact?

Yes, a hundred times yes; they are inherent energies, our inseparable companions during the transit which, sooner or later, we all suffer, and we have to search to make ourselves worthy of their help, which lies in the reflection of our acts, taking care that when they call we submit to their inclinations; then we will arrive on a straight path to the summit of wisdom which is promised by the Highest to his chosen.

On the Infinite

You will find the infinite in matter, in space, in movement, in the stars which stud the celestial vault, and in so many things that you direct your attention or your gaze. Man must be proud of the explorations he makes into the unfathomable spaces, from which, thanks to his wisdom, many secrets from nature were revealed.

It is necessary, in fact, to keep yourself from studying the moral contained in the neglected writings of a multitude of systems, produced by fits of imagination, by the disquiet of men exaggerated with the idea of achieving great and quick celebrity.

All the works created with this character must be dispelled, and only the ones reputed and accepted by all peoples must be sheltered, the ones which will reveal to us the secrets of the infinite, magical words which embrace an unalterable series of wonderful and unknown mysteries.

In the infinite must be appreciated, firstly, the space, which can be said to be the world of extraordinary powers and mysteries, which are produced constantly in front of us, though we cannot have the slightest understanding of them.

The space is populated by an innumerable multitude of beings with a slightly sinister appearance, but who, in reality, are docile; these beings are lovers of the light, subtle, loyal to ingenious and wise men, but they are hostile to the foolish and ignorant.

The beings of this who populate the air are called "sylphs," the ones who populate the seas and rivers are called "undines," and the ones found to populate the earth from within are called "gnomes," and they are the guardians of the metals and stones.

The gnomes, as has been said, possess in the highest degree the virtue of being generous towards wise and ingenious men, giving to the ones adorned with these qualities treasures of stones and metals, without any other reward than being dutiful.

In the inflamed center of the earth, which is the region of fire, live the salamanders, propitious to the philosophers.

There is also another category of invisible beings called "familiar geniuses." Socrates, Pythagoras, Plato, Celsus, Zoroaster, and many others who shone in the highest spheres of philosophy, dominating in the highest branches of human knowledge, owe to their "familiar geniuses" their relevant wisdom, and, in the same way as these reputed personalities, everyone, even the most vile, has a genius who inspires him. The existence of this genius cannot be proven by the senses, but it is this genius who positively influences every judgment a man makes, even though it is not so efficacious and active when it influences a vile man than when it does it with an intelligent one.

Besides the already mentioned, we could enumerate other beings, like the imps and goblins, which dedicate themselves to molesting men with blows, noises, and other manifestations, which serve to make us know their existence.

Matter constitutes the entirety of creation. There is not a single point of the universe lacking this substance. It forms the worlds, the water, the air, and, as the Supreme Spirit, fills and vivifies everything with its divine essence, matter creates the elements that manifest in a tangible way before our eyes.

It is not possible for men to destroy the smallest part of matter, and taking as an example a simple sheet of smoking paper, it will be seen that, even if it is burnt or kneaded, it can never be completely destroyed.

The atom is the lowermost part of matter.

To build a grain of sand the size of a pin head, it would be 8,000,000,000,000,000,000,000 atoms, and it would have to be made at the rate of a thousand per second, and, if we suppose as Grandin said, that we wanted to count sixty thousand per second, it would take—be amazed reader!—250,000 years to finish counting them. Who can explain, after this calculation, the number of atoms of created matter?

Complete Hierarchy of the Infernal Spirits

It is very useful to the neophyte to know the hierarchy of the Infernal Spirits he will have at his disposition through the pact:

Lucifer, emperor; Belzebut, prince; Astaroth, great duke.

These are the principal spirits of the infernal kingdom.

After, come the superior spirits which are subordinate to the former, and they are as follows: Lucifugo, first minister; Satanachia, great general; Agaliareth, great general; Fleuretty, lieutenant general; Sargatanas, brigadier; and Nebirus, field marshal.

The six great spirits we just mentioned direct with their power all the infernal potency which was given to other spirits.

At their immediate service, and as special emissaries, we find three superior spirits, whose occupation is to transmit the orders they receive; their names are Mirión, Belial, and Anagatón.

They have at their service eighteen more spirits subordinated to them, to know:

BELZEBUTH	LUCIFER	ASTAROTH
1 Bael		10 Bathin
2 Agares		11 Pursan
3 Marbas		12 Abigar
4 Pruslas		13 Loray
5 Arimon		14 Balefar
6 Barbatos		15 Foran
7 Buer		16 Ayperos
8 Gustatan		17 Nuberus
9 Botis		18 Blayabolas

After the names of these eighteen spirits, who are inferior to the first six, it is useful to know the following:

Lucifer commands the first three, named Bael, Agares, and Marbas.

Sanatachia rules over Pruslas, Arimon, and Barbatos.

Agaliaroth rules over Buer, Gustatan, and Botis.

Fleuretty rules over Buthin, Pursan, and Abigar.

Sargatanas, brigadier, has the Power to grant invisibility.

Nebiros rules over Aypcros, Nurebus, and Glassyabolas.[96]

Lucifer, Beelzebut, and Astaroth. Illustration from the book attributed to the diabolical monk Jonas Sufurino.

And although there are millions of spirits who are subordinated to the former, it is useless to name them because they are not used unless it pleases the superior spirits to make them work in their place, because they have them as servants and slaves.

In this manner, make the pact with one of the seven principals, for it should not matter which spirit is serving you; in fact, always ask the spirit

---

96 There are several discrepancies on the names used in the original, and we opted for keeping the names as they are in the source.

with whom you make the pact that one of the three principal spirits subordinated to him be put at you service.

Here are the powers, knowledge, arts, and talents of the spirits already mentioned so that the person who wants to make a pact can find in each one of the talents of the six superior spirits the one he needs.

The first is the Lucifugo Rofocale, the first infernal minister; he has the power of Lucifer who gave him power over all the riches and over all the treasures of the world. He has under him Bael, Agares and Marbas, and many more thousands of demons or spirits, who are all subordinated to him.

The second is Satanachia, great general; he has the power to submit to him every woman and make with them all he wishes. He commands a great legion of spirits and has under him Pruslas, Ammon, and Barbatos.

Agaliareth is also a general; he has the power to discover the most occult secrets and reveal the greatest mysteries; he commands the second legion of spirits. At his command are Buer, Gusatan, and Botis.

Fleuretty, lieutenant general, has the power to perform the desired work at night; he can also make hail fall wherever he wants. He commands a considerable body of spirits. Under his orders and at his service are Bathin, Pursan, and Abigar.

Sargatanas, brigadier, has the power to make us invisible and transport us to any place, to open any locks, to make us see everything that happens within houses, of teaching us all human shrewdness; he commands many brigades of spirits. He has at his service Loray, Balefar, and Foran.

Nebiros, field marshal and general inspector, has the power to cause harm to whomever he wants, to teach the qualities of metals, of minerals, of vegetables, and every pure and impure animal; he possesses the art of predicting the future, being one of the main necromancers of the infernal spirits. He goes everywhere having charge of the inspection of the armies of hell. He has at his service Ayperos, Nebirus, and Glasyabolas.

The next table presents the figures and the signatures of the principal infernal spirits.

The Book of Spirits

In which the invocations are treated

The secret name that human effort cannot find without a revelation resides in a secret being, and to the spirits, it is permitted to be revealed.

The secrets refer to the divine and natural or human things. It is necessary before doing the invocation to define the nature of the secret you wish to penetrate and know whom you will ask for the revelation.

Seven are the greatest secrets, which, in general, are most useful to man to know.

The *first* is to cure all infirmities in the space of seven days, be it by the means of natural objects, or be it by concourse and help from the superior spirits.

The *second* is to conserve life at will and for an undetermined time, no matter what the age of the person.

The *third* consists of making yourself obeyed by the beings who populate the elements under the form of purified spirits, like the pygmies, gnomes, etc.

The *fourth* lies in obtaining an understanding with all spirits visible or invisible, invoking in each case the one who can give the desired revelation.

The *fifth* consists of coming to know the special purpose for which everyone was created.

The *sixth* is to identify yourself as much as possible with the superior spirits, getting closer to a higher human perfection, which is the foundation of all well-being and prosperity.

The *seventh* consists of obtaining the protection of the superior spirits and, with and through it, of achieving the benefits of supernatural life under the most perfect form.

All the writers reputed to be serious who treated on these questions have reunited the medley of sacred and profane, avoiding with this devaluing the true nature of the invocations, which must be done based on the spirits, using for this the words and ceremonies of the true magic, without appeal to the formulas of strange sects.

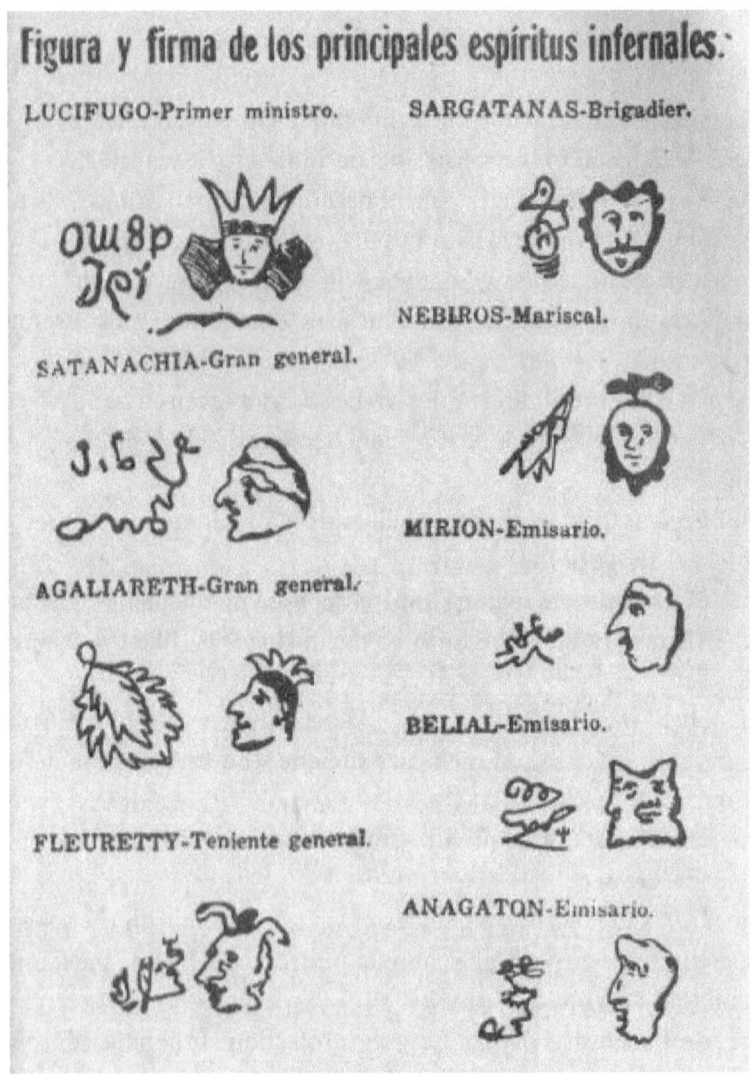

Source of the image: [TDH]

Invocation of the Gnomes

To make them propitious

[TDH]

The gnomes exert an important role in every invocation. They are the spirits who serve to transmit our petitions to the ones we direct them. Their intelligence is such that it can cause harm to us by disturbing our senses, or because, when the apparition happens, it can make us scared and cause our death through fright; or because we were not discreet enough to keep secret the wonderful or celestial apparition that we witnessed, and when we mention the occurrence it can make people think we are insane, ignorant, or demonic, so many people would lose respect for us, which could bring a countless number of grievances to us; or for causes hidden from our understanding, it is the case that sometimes the spirits do not show themselves propitious to support us in our enterprise, making it absolutely difficult to see achieved our desire.

To ensure that their benefic influence is shown to us in a positive way, it is good to first make the invocation to the spirits, whose apparition or help we ask, addressing the gnomes asking for help, reciting with all our heart the following orison:

"To you I appeal, oh admirable and incomprehensible geniuses! With blind faith and humble heart, I deliver myself to your mercy, hoping that as you direct our steps and actions from the moment we appear on this planet until the one in which, finished with our mission, you pick our spirit to accompany you through the sidereal worlds to the place the Supreme Creator has reserved for us in its inscrutable designs, in the same way you provide your help, faithfully transmitting the petitions I want to make to the Celestial Spirits (or Infernal), without changing my words or intentions. Observe well the purity of my feelings, my great desire and trust, my discretion and reserve; appreciate all the qualities I possess and do not pay attention to the defects I did not wish for, and do not make cause to not give me your cooperation; work constantly in perfecting me from every impurity, in making me worthy of the gifts the Deity bestows to its chosen, and I give thanks with all my soul and during my time on this planet, for the favor I receive from you. Amen."

Invocation of the Superior Celestial Spirits

[TDH]

Sermon

*B*e always praised the Holy Name of the Supreme Creator, who I humbly revere in this solemn hour.

To you, sublime Adonay, I direct my most fervent prayers, supplicating you be propitious to me and grant me the honor of sending me one of your most humble messengers, so I can, through its mediation, achieve that which with great respect and veneration I ask of you. Do not see in me a boastful person nor a skeptic who dares out of pride to harass you. See, in me, oh powerful Adonay, the smallest of the beings which in creation live and dwell, humbly prostrated before the Divine Majesty of his God and Creator, to whom he submits with true and great desire, to be able to know through mediation of his spiritual messengers a glimpse of your immaculate glory.

May my supplications also reach to all the superior celestial spirits, so they intercede for me before the glorious throne of the Highest, Sovereign Creator of all the created, so he deigns by the powerful intercession of the angels of light, Eloim and Jehovam, to attend this humble appeal of mine.

I have tried to make myself the most perfect possible in this poor and never-satisfied human condition, so you judge me worthy of the power of contemplating you glorious loftiness. Forgive me the defects that I did not wish for and do not make them cause of your anger and severity.

I come to invoke you again, and generally the powerful Adonay, Eloim, and Jehovam, so my desire can be satisfied in this hour, the stars which exert their powerful influence over the starry firmament being witness.

Let your radiant light come in the form of the glorious messenger, and receive through its mediation the gifts of wisdom, of honor and glory, until I, purified of every impurity of the flesh inherent to the weaknesses of humankind and always defective nature, can contemplate you in all your Sovereign Majesty and glory. Let my humble supplication be well received, and eternally my sincere and thankful heart will give adoration and homage to you.

This invocation or preaching must be repeated four times for four nights, elevating the soul to God under the starry firmament.

On the last night, and after finishing the final invocation, a very sweet and melodious music followed by celestial choirs will be heard. A translucent vision will be seen, which will grow in clarity, soon becoming the celestial vision of the form of an angel of light, of incomparable beauty, surrounded by infinite celestial spirits who incessantly accompany him, forming a true guard of honor. With the sweetest and most sonorous voice, he will say this or similar words:

> "I am sent as a messenger of the Divine Majesty. Your supplications were attended, but to achieve his mercies, it is necessary to be worthy of them. Do not forget, wretched mortal, that the Deity only grants these gifts that its infinite wisdom judges convenient, according to the degree of perfection in those beings that appeal to its infinite kindness in humble supplication. Follow the way of absolute perfection, with which you will achieve all those benefits to that you deserve. If you do this, you will always have me at your side in an invisible form, but serving as a tutelary

angel on your journey upon the planet where you live and dwell with permission from God. And now I momentarily separate myself to return again to the place I must stay, awaiting the orders deigned to be transmitted to me."

In that moment, the vision will vanish, only a luminous glow remaining which will fade little by little.

To the angels of Light, there is no need to make to them any petition with words, because God and the superior spirits will give those gifts to which we become deserving, and they know perfectly our thoughts, desires, and actions.

After the celestial vision is vanished, recite with great fervor the following orison in thanksgiving for the favor received:

"Oh, eternal and infinite God! I, the most miserable of mortals, was favored with the visit of your celestial messenger. How could I, my God and Creator, express with words how thankful I am for the kindness with which you have deigned to favor me. My soul, seized with joy and gratefulness, does not find words to express how much love and veneration it professes. Receive, Lord, all that I am and value, and the most sincere affection from my soul, heart, and senses, until I, dispossessed from this human containment, become part of the beings who in eternal harmony intone celestial chants in honor of admirable loftiness and glory. Amen."

The Chiefs of the Six Legions

[HEM]

Before we proceed with this chapter[97] we must initiate the reader in the profound mysteries of the occult sciences of writing the magical, and the astrological, and the cabalistic. These writings form what is cabalistic called a *magical book*.

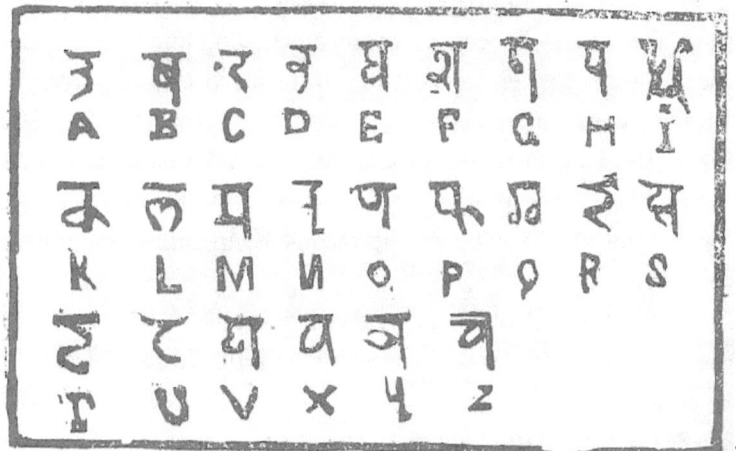

---

97 This chapter and the following, about the "influences of the stars," come from the original chapter "Chiromancia Astrologica." I left out the instructions on palm reading.
98 The drawing of the Sanskrit letters and the correlation with the Latin alphabet in this table are not in agreement with the information to be found in the article on Sanskrit to be found in the Wikipedia. It is more likely a free adaptation made by the writer of the text.

The Book of Saint Cyprian

We begin with the cabalistic alphabet. This alphabet came to us from the Indians, and it is inspired in the one that the Brahmin use until today.[99] As under each sign I already put the letters they indicate, I will not occupy myself with them. I will talk about the 16 magical characters.

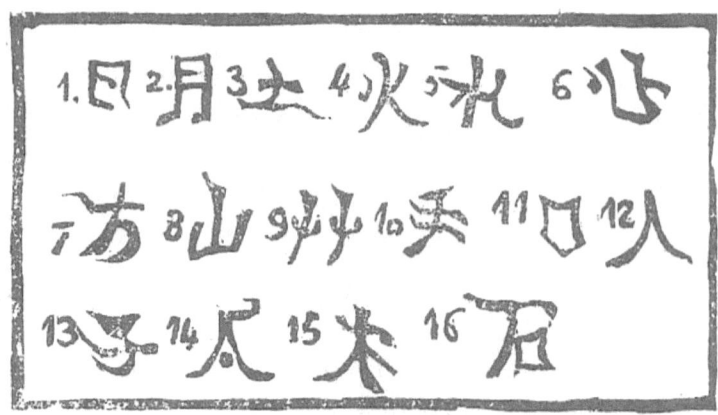

The number 1 means the Sun, element of fire, and as consequence the energetic passions although generally nobles.

The 2. The Moon—it means calm and melancholy and all sweet passions.

The 3. Earth. Element of humility; it means vassalage, slavery, work, penalties and concerns.

The 4. The Fire. Element: it means violence, devastation, ferocity, irreparable evils.

The 5. The Water. Element: it means temperance, mobility, travels overseas.

The 6. The Heart. Noble and generous passions.

The 7. Cultivated land. Prosperity, wealth through work, ambition, avarice.

The 8. The Mountain. Elevation, grandeur, dominion, pride, superiority in the diverse things.

The 9. A Plant. Innocence, infancy, much protection, intelligence.

---

99 I will give the original writer some credit, and understand what he says as meaning that he created a "cabalistic" version of the Sanskrit alphabet, as the letters in the table are imperfect and the correlation with the Latin letters does not follow the ones I checked.
100 These 16 characters seem to be freely based upon Chinese symbols.

The 10. A Hand. Charity, help, assistance, work.
The 11. A Purse. Loquacity, gluttony.
The 12. A Man. Power, authority.
The 13. A Child. Whims, lies, and meanness.
The 14. A Woman. Beauty, sweetness, chastity, love.
The 15. A Tree. Force, nobility, dignities, protection, majesty.
The 16. A Stone. Death, war, grave wound, infirmity.

With these 16 figures, we have the means to fight all the human Passions, but it is necessary to combine then in a certain way, as it will be explained in the treatise about the talismans.[101]

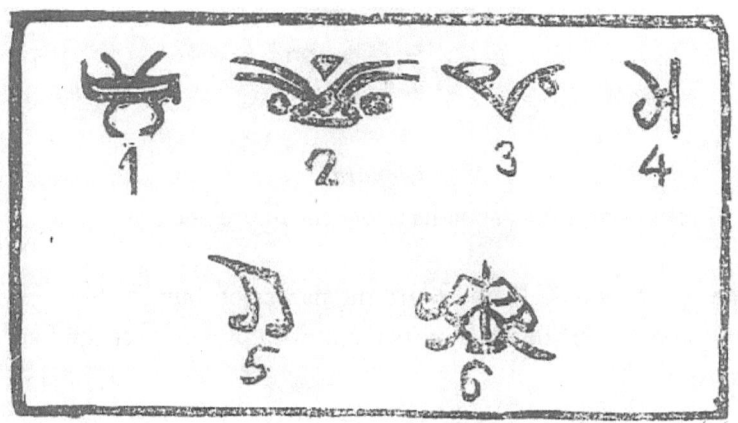
[102]

The six signs in this table are the names of the chiefs of the six legions of geniuses and dark spirits, with whom we can enter into direct communication.

---

101 The chapter on talismans, however, does not mention this.
102 This table was printed upside down in the original book.

1

Beelzébuth
Commands all demons.

2

Léonard
Presides over the Sabbaths under the figure of a black goat.

The numbers 3, 4, 5, and 6 are the names of four chiefs of geniuses, who serve better the aims of men and who preside over the four elements, Arabic.[103]

3

Nicksa
The queen of the waves and ruler of the ones who inhabit the seas and the great lakes.

---

103 Although the sentence is not clear in the original, it seems the writer is saying that the following spirits (or their names) are Arabic.

The Book of Spirits

4

Gob
The chief of the gnomes who inhabit the inner parts of the earth and guard the metals and hidden treasures.

5

Paralda
The queen of the sylphs who inhabit the air.

6

Djin
Chief of the salamanders who live in fire, and their main occupation is to found the metals making the volcanoes happen.

Influences of the Stars

[HEM]

Habitations of the Dark Geniuses

The house of *Beelzebuth*, and the principal sign of his legion, evil star; it is in the heart of Scorpion.

The house of *Baalberith*, the great master of dreams, dreamers, and sleepwalkers, evil star: it is in Cancer.

Habitations of the Wise Geniuses

good or bad according to the circumstances

The house of *Niksa*, the queen of the undines; it is generally good and mainly protective of sailors and fishermen, but she is vindictive towards those who despise her, fearing storms under a clear sky[sic]; it is in Aries and it is a good star.

The house of *Gob*, king of gnomes, has *Kobold* as minister; often, he favors those who search for mines and hidden treasures. Sometimes, he is vindictive, creating intrigues and revolutions with the gold he takes from the entrails of earth; it is in Cancer and is an evil star.

The house of *Peralda*, queen of the sylphs, protects innocence and chastity; it is in Virgo and is good star.

The house of *Djin*, king of the salamanders, protector of the warriors; it is in Sirius and is a good star.

The following constellations have less importance than the six former, but we will give an explanation to show their influence, treating them constellation by constellation.

Constellation Aries, house of *Fatua* or *Fressina*, queen of the faeries, always good, but sometimes she looks like she is evil; she presides over the birth of people, tries to balance the moral and physical qualities and compensate for them with some flaws: For instance, she give riches, balancing them with pride; beauty, balancing it with fatuousness and coquetry; wisdom and chastity, balancing them with murmuring; science with pedantry, etc. She has a propensity towards great men. Star more good than evil.

Belonging to the same constellation is the house of *Melusine*, who every Saturday covers herself with scales from the waist to the extremity of the feet. She is a lover to mysterious people, she is discreet, and she teaches how to keep a secret. Good star.

Constellation of Taurus, the house of imps, domestic demons and sorcerers, presided over by *Aldebran*; rules the superstitious, imbeciles, the credulous, and the dreamers. Evil star.

Belonging to the same constellation is the house of *Salvania*, queen of the *suelvas*, a kind of sylphid. She watches over agriculture and helps the husbandmen in their works. His protection is very good.

Also belonging to it is the house of *Dexgar*, sovereign of the mountains. He protects hardworking men and helps them in their works, but he demands from them submission and respect. Good star, but unfortunate.

Constellation Geminis, house of *Deoinehia*, chief of the meadows. He presides over work, knowledge of cattle, especially horses, and inspires concord and peace. Excellent star.

To the same constellation belongs *Deer Foot*, queen of the incubus. She appears as the figure of a beautiful woman, but hiding under her large vest are the feet of a deer. Protects the hunters but exposes them to filthy loves. Evil star.

Constellation of Cancer, house of *Robin of the Woods*, chief of the hunter spirits of the night. He rules the thieves of the roads, the furtive hunters, and evil men. Evil star.

Constellation of Leo, house of *Alfheino,* chief of the white spirits. Guides men in the thorny feelings of honor and virtue. Excellent star.

To the same constellation belongs the house of *Svvart*, great master of the spirits of the night. He directs the spirits of the great, the governors, and blinds them to seeing the misery of the peoples. Evil star.

Constellation of Virgo, house of *Hodeken*, white genius, who does not descend from his star except to help virtuous and chaste people. Very good star.

Constellation Libra, house of *Follet*, chief of the vagabond spirits, who are perfidious, inconstant, voluble, and capricious. Evil star.

In the same constellation is the house of *Tomptogobe*. He rules braggarts, making the boasters strong and heard over all people who make noise. This star promises many beatings, blows with cubs, and long life.

Constellation of Scorpio, house of *Grisu,* general of the evil gnomes. He sends these geniuses through all kinds of obstacles to miners, or through collapses or floods, and makes them show themselves in horrible forms; they rule the avaricious, the selfish, the ungrateful, and the parent-killers. Very evil star.

Belonging to the same constellation are *Kelpic*, under the form of a horse and *Norickar,* who appears in human form. He inhabits the lakes, seas, rivers, and streams. He is declared the enemy of fishermen, sailors, and every man who has work on water. Very evil star, announcing a disgraceful end.

Constellation of Sagittarius, house of the great sorcerer *Nicneven,* who marches ahead of all the sorcerers and changes their luck from good to bad. Evil star.

To the same constellation belongs *Nika*. She is the great master of the *gynos*, a kind of good genius, who are pleased in guiding men by the paths of honor. Good star.

Also belonging to the same constellation is *Amadria,* queen of the *periscious;* intelligent, kind beings who like to dance under the Moon in fields full of flowers; they rule doctors and direct them to choose the best herbs to cure infirmities. Good star.

Constellation of Capricorn, house of *Oldnick,* protector of pirates, of the contrabandists whom he later abandons to disgraceful luck. Evil star.

To the same constellation belongs *Dobia,* the master of ghosts and specters. She walks through solitary roads, ruins, and uninhabited houses. She inspires fright and cowardice. Evil star.

Constellation of Aquarius, house of *Galdrakina* or *Striga,* instructor of sorcerers in the art of creating philtres. She rules poisoners, the love providers, and the lost women. Very evil star.

Belonging to the same constellation is *Geirada,* a good genius who frees the people he rules from charms, witchcraft, and other magical weapons used against them. He loves truth and detests superstition and lie. Good star.

Constellation of Pisces, house of *Annaberge,* evil genius, appears on Saturdays in the form of a goat with horns of gold and as a horse snorting fire through its nose. He makes incessant war against the young who direct a trade without talent and ability. Evil star.

To the same constellation belongs the house of *Puck,* the marriage broker from hell, because of the love he has for men, especially the young to whom he render his services. Although he is a devil, it is a good star.

Hour, Month, Season

presided over by the Angels

[HEM]

The Hours

I	*Yayn*	Miguel
II	*Lanor*	Anael
III	*Nasnia*	Rafael
IV	*Salla*	Gabriel
V	*Sadedali*	Cassiel
VI	*Thamus*	Sachiel
VII	*Ourer*	Samael
VIII	*Thanir*	Arael
IX	*Neron*	Cambiel
X	*Jaya*	Uriel
XI	*Abai*	Azael
XII	*Natalon*	Zambael

The Months

January	Gabriel
February	Basquiel
March	Maquidiel
April	Asmodel
May	Ambriel
June	Muriel
July	Verchiel
August	Hamaliel
September	Vriel
October	Barbiel
November	Aduaquiel
December	Harael

The Seasons

TALVI	GASMARAN	ARDARAEL	TALIAS
Spring	*Summer*	*Autumn*	*Winter*
Espugliguel	Gargasiel	Torcuaret	Albarib
Caracasa	Tubiel	Targuum	Amabael
Commisors	Tariel	Quabarel	Crarari
Amatiel	Gabiel		

CELESTIAL SPIRITS AND INFERNAL SPIRITS

[LM2]

The seven angelic powers of the week are the Celestial Spirits of Ancient Chaldean Magic, to whom the government of the Universe belongs by a mandate from God, and of all human acts according to their kind. One, then, of the great deeds of the Celestial Spirits is to work the destiny of creatures and to direct the happenings that correspond to them, according to the will and the designs of the Creator. So it happens that these occurrences are sheltered from the ambushes that the harmful spirits do to the human beings, and no adverse fate they can achieve, *quod reponet in protectione Domini*. It must be taken into account that every Celestial Spirit will never do anything opposed to the influence of the celestial body that had influence over the deed and will always follow the divine mandates, because from God they receive all their power and only to Him universally obey the beings from the supracelestial regions, sublunar and infernal. In consequence, nothing must be done if not under divine protection if you want to take the matter to a good conclusion, as the history of the world proves since the creation until our days. Peace to the virtuous men *et pax uno est impiis!*

There are seven governors that have in their office seven different functions; their names and powers are, according to the teachings of the

Magic of the wise Arbatel, *Aratron, Bethor, Phaleg, Och, Hageth, Ophiel,* and *Phul*, to whom is attributed:

To *Aratron*, the power to change instantly stones into gold and to do the opposite, for instance, converting coal into gold and vice-versa; he teaches Alchemy, Magic, Physics, how to make beings invisible, and give long life.

To *Bethor*, the power to bestow high dignities, bring to men spirits which give exact answers, transport objects from one place to another, give precious stones, and prolong life up to seven hundred years if God allows.

To *Phaleg*, the attributes of Mars; governs peace and elevates to the highest ranks of the army the people who receive his mark or sign.

To *Och*, the presidency of the attributes of the Sun; gives long life and health, distributes wisdom, teaches Medicine, and gives power to change everything into pure gold and into the most precious stones.

Hageth, under the influence of Venus, gives extraordinary beauty to the women whom he honors with his protection and adorns them with numerous charms and changes copper into gold and gold into copper.

To *Ophiel*, the power of transmutation of metals, under the influence of Mercury; transforms mercury into gold, a transformation upon which is founded, according to Alchemy, the great philosophical stone.

To *Phul*, the government of the lunar regions. His power is sovereign in the cure of dropsy. He transforms all metals into silver, and protects the man who travels. He grants three hundred years of life.

Arbatel adds: *"Everything is possible to those who have faith and will; everything is impossible to those who lack both. There are no greater obstacles than the ones created by lack of consideration, lightness, inconstancy, frivolity, a life of intoxication, passions and lack of submission to the divine word. Whoever wants to be a magician, will be, before anything else, an honored, virtuous person, constant in his words and in his deeds, firm in his trust in God, prudent and avaricious of possessing the wisdom."*

In the same way that there are seven Celestial Spirits, patrons of every work of benefic magic, there are six others who are the infernal princes, protectors of the wonders of malefic magic, and in the same way that the former governs the world to fulfill everywhere the will of God, these ones from the abyss go out to spread harm, shrewdness, and perverse judgments that Satanaz uses to bring men to the ways of wickedness and crime, which leads the soul to its eternal condemnation.

The number 1 is *Belzebut,* or *Beelzecuth,* chief of all demons and special protector of every witchery and all the lineage of malefactions; his passion is hate; his color is black; his favorite places are places of pain, tears, and death; his hour, midnight of a New Moon; his plant is hemlock; his perfume, the perfume of pepper burnt in the bonfire of the invocations.

The number 2 is *Leonardo,* owner and lord of the sorcerers and sorceresses. He appears on the Sabbath as the figure of a goat. He is the protector of malefic philtres and of the erotic excesses where incest, sodomy, and bestiality happen; his passion is luxury, also cholera; his colors, greyish-brown or greyish-red; his favorite place, where bloody scenes happen or have happened and of the most repulsive liberties; his hour, one after midnight on Tuesdays and Fridays, in a place not reached by the brightness of the stars, for example beneath the thickest branches of the woods; his plant, the mandrake; his perfume, the blood of any animal whose skin is black.

The number 3 is *Nieksa,* who rules over the liquid elements and promotes floods, inundations, sea catastrophes, and many sinister happenings where water is the cause, the place where they happen; his passion is envy; his colors, bluish-green and greenish-grey; his favorite place, the rocks on the coast and solitary beaches; his hour, the dawn of Saturdays; his plant, poisonous mushrooms; his perfume, pine resin.

To *Gob* corresponds the number 4, which dominates the element of Earth and subterranean things; he promotes sinking, devastating commotions of the soil, the expansion of asphyxiating and deleterious gases; he gives mortal properties to the venomous substances, presides over the development and propagation of plague and other epidemics, and intervenes in the disgraceful happenings of human life, fomenting the passions of avarice, pride, and cruelty; his passion is avarice; his color the one of dirty earth, greenish but also reddish; his favorite place, the subterranean and the galleries of mines; his hour, the nightfall of Mondays; his plant, poisonous roots; his perfume, leaves of rue, bryony, and aconite.

The number 5 is *Peralda,* and he dominates the air. He promotes hurricanes, cyclones, and combined with *Nieksa, he* creates torrential rains; with *Gob,* he spreads infectious diseases and makes certain places inhabitable; and with *Djin,* he directs the sun into places and things where it can spread destruction and death. His passion is cholera; his color the dirty bluish-grey; his favorite place, the solitary summits of mountains facing North and the sunset; his hour, late afternoon on cold and cloudy days when the wind blows violently; his plant, aconite; his perfume, the so-called apples of cypress.

To *Djin* corresponds the number 6; he is the infernal lord of fire. He promotes, in union with *Gob,* earthquakes with the release of flames and burning lava, as well as volcanic eruptions; he is the cause of fires, of explosions, and he instigates men to war, by which he amuses himself with scenes of slaughter; he protects and directs the arm of the murderer and profits from the occasion of imprudence to make firearms shoot and the ones made of cold steel harm the victims of those wretched accidents, which can only be attributed to chance; his passion, the destruction of everything alive; his color, yellowish and bluish-red; his favorite place, where fire is, and above all the summit of volcanoes; his hour, midnight on Tuesdays, preferably with storms; his plant, the o *enformio*; his perfume, gunpowder.

Cover of one of the oldest of the Brazilian editions of the Book of Saint Cyprian, published by Editora Quaresma, in the beginning of the XX century.

The Prayers of Saint Cyprian

Prayer of Saint Cipryan

[LAE]

Arabic Version

Praise to God, one in his essence, triple in his person.

This is the prayer of the spiritual saint, Saint Cyprian, who, although being a magician, believed in the Lord Jesus the Messiah: his conviction was so strong he deserved to become bishop of Carthage; after he was judged worthy of martyrdom. This is a sword to the patience and a shield that repels demons and the evil eye; it was translated from Greek into Arabic.

Let the salvation of God be with all of us. Amen.

Praise to the God of the sky and salvation over the earth and between men, to whom write it three times. On Sunday, the day the Lord sanctified and blessed, all evil action was turned aside. I, Cyprian, servant of the Lord Jesus the Messiah, directed my intelligence and my thought to the Lord Jesus; I directed to him a demand and a petition and said to him:

Lord, you are the God all powerful, you possess everything, you are the master of all, the sovereign light, the Messiah. A long time ago, you knew the conduct of your servant; I was under the command of Satan. I ignored your name. I bound the sky, and the rain did not fall upon the earth, and the earth did not give crops; the trees did not give fruit anymore.

Every time I passed by a flock of sheep, I caused them to miscarry what was in their wombs; in the same way, I made conjurations against the pregnant woman, and she could not deliver; I used to stop the fish of the sea from passing through the water; so great were my secrets and my sins. That is what happened.

Presently, my Lord and my God, I learnt to know your name, to love your vision without macula; I come to you and to your command. I demand and supplicate to you, by the lasting and complete love that your only and beloved Son has for all human beings, let the sky open, let rain pour over the earth, let earth give forth its crops, and let the trees give forth their fruits; let all pregnant women bring their children into the world safely and let the children have the milk of their mothers; let the fishes of the sea and from the rivers be freed; in the same way, the birds of the sky, the beasts of the earth, and every man under attack. Let everyone be sheltered from everything done against them, be it sorcery, be it the practice of enchantments, be it binding by your holy name; let every dire demon flee away from them; let the one for whom I recite this prayer be sheltered from every evil; let his affairs, his soul, his body, and everything associated with him remain intact. Lord, protect him against the devil and all his powers, by your holy name, powerful and glorified in the heavens and over the earth. As the rock which opened and the water came out and the Israelites drank it, so, oh Lord, stretch out your hand full of mercy over so-and-so, son of so-and-so [mother], and over anyone who possesses this writing in their homes.

Lord, as in the beginning you established paradise in Eden, as you put a great fountain divided into four rivers—the Pishon, the Gihon, the Tigris, and the Euphrates—to water all the earth, which no one can resist, no one can stop, so let the dire and damned demon become impotent and let neither conjuration, nor magic, nor evil eye come before all this. Remove from your servant, so-and-so son of so-and-so [mother], every evil and every corruption. Amen.

The Prayers of Saint Cyprian

Lord, expel far away from your servant those who oppose him among the seventy and two diverse languages: Let Legion be damned with all its armies, its forces, and its works; expel them from before your servant; keep his life in a state of purity, his conduct, his body, and all his vestures, by the virtue of God all powerful, by the virtue of the Holy Ghost, by the sixty and six angels who descended in the city of Aghounas, by the name of the Cherubim and Seraphim who praise God before the living and glorious throne. I freed and I free you from every sorcery, from every magical bond, from every evil eye, from every evil, by the prayers of the angels spread all over the world: Let this formula serve to protect this house and everyone who inhabits it from the evil workings of the wicked. I freed and I free by the name of God who sits beyond the Cherubim who serve before the august throne; let the damned demon be unable to stand in front of him in any of his forms, neither by night, now by day: Let Legion be damned and anathema with all his forces and his armies, by the curse of Simon the curator, chief of the apostles. Amen.

I freed and I free by the name of God, who is beyond the Cherubim, your servant, carrier of this writing, so-and-so son of so-and-so [mother], from every sorcery, from every magical bond, from the evil eye, by the prayer of the superior beings, by the supplication of the humble; by the perfection of the saints; by the tears of foreigners; by the sacrifice of Abel, by the love of Seth, by the beauty of Enoch, by the purity of Cainan, by the lamentations of Lamech, by the humility of Malalel, by the salvation of Noah; by the birth of Shem, by the faith of Abraham, by the succour of Isaac whom God saved from the immolation with a lamb, by the priesthood of Melchizedek, by the prophecy of Jacob, by the beauty of Noah, by the submission of Job, by the flight of Jacob, by the purity of Joseph, by the love of Benjamin, by the submission of Moses, by the force of Joshua son of Nun, by the priesthood of Aaron, by the prayer of Phinehas, by the Psalms of David, by the tears of Elijah, by the inspiration of Elisha, by the love of Japheth, by the prophecy of Isaiah, by the lamentations of Jeremiah, by the death of Zechariah, by the prophecy of the prophets; by the vigil of the ones who do not sleep at night, by the congregation of people who do not sin, by the depth of the abyss, by the voice of thunder; by the clash of the masses of water, by the glaring radiance of lightning, by the movement of the clouds, by the echelon of the angels, by what Moses saw, by the vision of the light of the stars, by the holiness of the Apostles, by the prayer of prisoners; by the birth of Jesus the Messiah, by his baptism ministered by John, by the voice who spoke from the heights of heaven, saying: *This is my beloved son, in whom I rejoice, hear him;* by he who transformed water into wine, who fed thousands in the desert, by he who expelled Legion, by he who resurrected the son of the widow, who made Lazarus rise from his tomb, by he who made the waves firm under the feet of Peter the apostle, who was crucified and buried, who resurrected from the dead on the third day, who ascended to the heavens; by the praise of the angels, by the thousands of myriads who rise to heaven; by the fasting of the Apostles without blemish, by the isolation of the solitaries, I prescribe and adjure you, dire spirit, guilty thoughts, do not come closer to the carrier of this writing, so-and-so son of so-and-so [mother], neither during the day, nor during the night, nor during his sleep and nor during his vigil, neither when he comes in, nor when he goes out, neither at his home, nor appearing in any form, nor at any moment; let him not have over him any power, neither over the place where this prayer is found; let every dire and evil action flee far away from there and extinguish like the fire in the oven; let the spirits of evil flee like the Philistine fled from before the prophet David; let them fall as the walls of Jericho fell before Joshua son of Nun. If you lie and transgress this word and this oath, if I ever find you where this writing is placed, harm will come to you... To the glorification of the cohorts of angels, by the sound of the trumpet that will resound, by God full of glory who stands upon the mount Sinai shining in his light, by he who spoke to Moses and who gave to the Israelites a book which made known his august name powerful and holy; by he who knows all, by the miracles and the extraordinary powers of him whose power I will not be able to describe, by he who trusts to Gabriel the unshakeable ranks, and to Michael [lacuna]; prayer of the three courageous youths Hananiah, Mishael, and Azariah, by he who descended between them, untied their bonds and saved them from the fire of the furnace without even one of hair on their heads being burned, in the same way, let every malefaction, every magical binding,

The Prayers of Saint Cyprian

every evil eye be expelled from this house and from everyone in it; by the crown of Saint Stephen, the first martyr, by the heart of our master and savior, Jesus the Messiah, by the walls of the holy Church, by his blood shed over the wood on Golgotha, by the tomb where he was captive, by his resurrection, by the right hand of the Saints, by the diadem of King David, by the blood of the venerated martyrs, by the chariot Ezekiel saw, by the four venerable beings below the august and praised throne; one with the face of man, the second with the face of lion, the other with the face of an eagle, the last with the face of a bull; I removed and I remove, from the carrier of this writing, so-and-so son of so-and-so [mother], every malefaction, every evil eye, and let God open the door of his mercy before all the sons of Adam and Eve, let him serve as a lesson to the world. Amen. Let him not be touched neither by witchcraft nor by magical bindings, nor by evil eye, nor by the fatal gaze, from any of the seventy and two nations spread across the entire world; let no dire and damned spirit, let no wickedness be sustained before the formula of liberation that today I pronounce; I preserved and I preserve by the word directed by God to Adam in paradise, by the hand which separated the waters before Moses, there where the Israelites crossed, by the voice which cried to Lazarus to rise, by the sighs of foreigners, by the faith which could not be found to be false, let the carrier of this writing, a so-and-so son of so-and-so [mother], be sheltered from every magical binding and every sorcery, from every envy, from every evil eye and every secret and evident wickedness; by the power of God, creator of the universe, by the word pronounced by the Messiah over the wood of the Cross: "Eli, Eli, why have you abandoned me?" by the name of God, powerful and glorious.

If there is sorcery or magical binding or wickedness by iron, by gold, by silver, by bronze, by lead, by tin, let it be unmade and be no more, as if it existed in a thread, from silk, from cotton, from flax, threads of silk, in the remains of wool, let it be unmade; if it is made with human bones, with the bones of a quadruped, or of birds, of fish, let the enchantment be undone. If the enchantment or the magical binding was made with the help of wood or any other created plant, let it be undone. If it exists in a book, in a beam, in a stone, in the tomb of an orthodox, of a Jew, of a pauper, of a foreigner, or of a hermit, in ruins, inside the corpse of a murdered man, in a coffin, in the bone of a dead man, in the water, in a point of infiltration of water, in a spring, in a fountain, in a river, in the sea, in a brook, let it be removed from the carrier of this writing, so-and-so son of so-and-so [mother]: If the enchantment exists in a high room or in low room, in a purse, in a field, in an orchard or in a tree, in a rosebush, in a narrow place, or in a grotto, let it be undone and frustrated. If it is made under a star, at a crossroad, among ruins with the image of a martyr, in beeswax, in a fava bean, or anything of the kind, let it all be undone. If it is in the wall or in the hinge of the door, in the ashes, in the atrium, in the oven, let everything be powerless against the carrier of this writing, so-and-so son of so-and-so [mother], as everything wicked I mentioned and the ones I did not mention that will be tried against him, by the name of Abraham, of Isaac and Jacob, by the name of the king powerful and glorious: Let all be in vain against so-and-so son of so-and-so [mother]; let every wickedness be without force against him, let the doors of affection and mercy be open for him before everyone.

Let his desires be realized by the light emanated from the Messiah over the Djebel and the Tour when he manifested himself to his disciples in the conversation of Elijah and Moses, by the cloud which surrounded them, by he who made the lame walk, who revived the eyes of the one who was born blind, who walked over the sea, who restrained the violence of the winds, who raised Peter when he was about to drown, by the moment when he cured the possessed and the leper, where he healed the one who touched the cloth of his vestments, the woman who suffered from a flux of blood for eighteen years; by the rays of the Sun, by the light of the Moon, by the rows of the stars, by the four evangelists, Matthew, Mark, Luke, and John, by the intercession of immaculate Our Lady, Mary, mother of light, virgin without blemish, by the twelve holy apostles, by the congregation of the apostles and the totality of the prophets, of the Saints and of the martyrs, of whom the first was Stephen, by Sergius, by George, by Theodore, by Christopher, by the forty martyrs who were executed in Samaria, by Bartalâtalâ, by Nicholas and Basil, by Claudius, by Cyril, Niq^qnyous, Cyriaque, by Ras'alân, by Mâr Ephrem, by the commentator of the divine

The Prayers of Saint Cyprian

book, by all the Saints we mentioned, and the ones we did not mention, by the names of the women who carried the perfumes, by Zarah, by Helen, by Samona, by the seven prophetesses, by all the holy women, by the blood of the faithful, by the death of all the perfect martyrs, by the faith of the 318 holy fathers of the council of Nicaea, we finish this writing by the force of the right hand of God living and vivifying, by the holy Cross, dispenser of life, by the consecration of Peter, the chief of the apostles, by John the regretful, by Simon the magus, and his mother Martha, by Simeon the first Stylite; by the intercession of Anthony, chief of the monks, by Daniel, by James the intercessor, by Zachariah, by the prayers of all the prophets, of all the apostles, of all the faithful martyrs, I freed and I free the carrier of this writing, so-and-so son of so-and-so {mother], from all magical binding, from all the sorcery, from every evil eye, from every wickedness, from every evil and every work of Satan, in the name of the Father, of the Son and of the Holy Ghost, from today to eternity. Amen.

I adjure you and I conjure you, dire and damned spirit; I conjure you by the name of God all-powerful whose royalty is extended over the whole earth, whose throne rests over the clouds, who marches on the wings of the winds, before whom there are always angels with their thuribles, turning their faces to avoid the august and terrifying vision, and the river of fire that runs before him, where the souls of the guilty are burned; by he in front of whom the fire descended and who stopped the water; by the power of this God who is the sovereign God, the master of masters, the king of kings, vade retro! By he who strengthened the feet of the lame and said: *"Rise, take your bed and go to your home"* and also *"sin no more,"* being that for thirty and eight years he was stretched out. I freed and I free, by he who opens the heavens and makes the rain upon the earth which offers its harvests; I freed and I free by he who descended from heaven, who unbound the chains of Saint Paul; so, I release the carrier of this writing, so-and-so son of so-and-so [mother], and I remove from him every magic, every evil, every malefaction, from him as from his sons, from his daughters, from his wife, from his cattle and from everything he owns, because it is written: *The heavens will change, but my word will not* (Matthew XXIV:35; Mark XIII:31). Anyone who pronounces against him the wicked formulas,

God will annul them; if anyone tries against him any evil thing, it will fail thanks to God who is Emanuel, Ahia, Cherahia, Sabaot, El Chaddai, Adonai. Oh, my God, you will be a treasure to the carrier of this writing, so-and-so son of so-and-so [mother]; you will be a support, a protection, a succour, a shield against every wicked action, past and future, by our Lord, our God, our Savior Jesus the Messiah, I beg you and I supplicate, by the prayer of every Saint who constantly enjoys your affection and your contentment, let every wickedness flee and go away from this house, from everyone who lives here and from the carrier of this writing, so-and-so son of so-and-so [mother].

In the same way the wax melts before the fire, so disappear the dire spirits and all of you, forces of Satan, wicked enemy, before whom is this writing which contains this prayer. In the name of the Father, of the Son, of the Holy Ghost, from today through the centuries to eternity. Amen. Praise God continually and perpetually. We finish this writing by the force of the right hand of God living and vivifying, by the holy Cross, dispenser of life, by the seal of Peter, chief of the apostles. Amen.

The book of the prayer of Saint Cyprian is finished; let his blessing be with you. Amen.

Orison

†

[GLT]

I, Cyprian, servant of God, whom I love with all my heart, body, and soul, feel such grief for not having loved you since the day you gave me life. However, my God and my Lord, you always remembered your servant Cyprian.

I thank you, my God and my Lord, with all my heart, for the benefits that I am now receiving from you; so now, oh God of the heights, give to me the force and faith to unbind everything I have bound, for which I will invoke always your most Holy Name. In the name of the Father, of the Son, and of the Holy Spirit. Amen.

You who lives and reigns through all the centuries, amen. It is right, Our Lord, that now I am your servant Cyprian, saying to you: God strong and holy, be you praised forever.

You who saw the malices of your servant Cyprian and such malices by which I was put under the power of the devil; but I did not know your Holy Name. I used to bind women, bind the clouds in the sky, bind the waters of the sea so fishermen could not sail, to not allow them to catch fish for the maintenance of men; by my evil and my great iniquity I used to bind pregnant women so they could not deliver, and all these things I did in the name of the demon. Now, my God and my Lord, I know your name, and

I invoke and invoke again so the sorceries and witcheries be undone from the machine or the body of this creature (so and so). So I call you, oh powerful God, so you can break all the bindings from men and women. ✠ Let the rain fall over the face of the earth so it gives its fruit and women deliver their children, free of every binding done to them; unbind the sea so fishermen can fish. Free from every danger and unbind everything which has been bound by this creature of the Lord; let it be untied, unbound from any form. I unbind, unpin, tear, put and take out everything, such as the doll which is in some well or taken, to dry this creature (so and so), so every damned devil and everything be delivered from evil and from all the evils or bad deeds, sorceries, enchantments or superstitions, and diabolical arts! The Lord destroyed and annihilated all of them; let God from the height of heaven be glorified in heaven and on earth as Emanuel, which is the name of the powerful God. As the dry stone opened and cast water which the sons of Israel drank, so, Lord most powerful with a hand full of grace, free this your servant (so and so) from every malefaction, sorcery, binding, and enchantment in part and in everything made by the devil and his servants. And as soon as you have this orison over you and carry it or have it at home, be with it before the earthly paradise from which come the four rivers Pishon, Gihon, Tigris, and Euphrates, by which you commanded to lay water in the entire world, by which I supplicate my Lord Jesus Christ, son of the Most Holy Mary, that whoever creates sadness and harm with a malign spirit will make no enchantment, plot, or evil deed, or move anything bad against this your servant (so and so), but all things here mentioned be obtained and annulled to which I invoke the seventy and two languages which are split all around the world; let any of its opposition be annihilated by their searches, by the Angels; let this your servant be absolute (so and so), with all his house and the things that are inside it, be all of this free from every malefaction and sorcery, by the name of God the Father who was born in Jerusalem, by all of the Angels and Saints and by all who serve before Paradise or in the presence of the high God all-Powerful, so there the damned devil does not have power to hinder any person. Any person who carries this orison with him or has it read or where there is some sign of the devil day or night, by the God of Isaac and Jacob, let the damned enemy be expelled; I invoke the communion of the holy Apostles, of our Lord Jesus Christ, of Saint Paul, by the orisons of religious women, by cleanliness, the beauty of Eve, by the sacrifice of Abel, by God united to Jesus, his Eternal father, by the chastity of the faithful, by their kindness, by the faith of Abraham, by the obedience of Our Lady when she delivered God by the prayer of Magdalene, by the patience of Moses; let the orison of Saint Joseph serve to undo the enchantments. Saints and Angels avail me, by the sacrifice of Jonah, by the tears of Jeremiah, by the orison of Zachariah, by the prophecy and by the ones who do not sleep at night and are dreaming with God our Lord Jesus Christ, and by the prophet Daniel, by the words of the Evangelists, by the crown he gave to Moses in tongues of fire, by the sermons the Apostles made, by the birth of Our Lord Jesus Christ, by his baptism, by the time it was heard from the Eternal father, saying: *"This is my chosen son and my beloved; I am very pleased because everyone fears him and because he assuages the sea and makes the earth give fruit."* By the miracles of the Angels who are with him, by the virtues of the apostles, by the coming of the Holy Spirit who descended over them, by the virtues and names that are in this orison, by the praise of God who made all things, by the Father ✠, by the Son ✠, by the Holy Ghost ✠, (so and so), if any witchery is made against you by the hairs of the head, cloth of the body or of the bed, in the footwear or in cotton, silk, linen, or wool; in the hair of Christian, of Moor, or of a heretic; in bones of human creature, of birds, or of any other animal; in wood, books, or in a sepulchre of Christians or Moors, in a fountain or on a bridge, altar or river; in a house or in a wall of lime; in a field or in solitary places; inside the churches or at the division of rivers; in a house made of wax or marble; in figures made of cloth, inside a frog or inside a saramaganta[104]; in animal of the sea or of the river; in a slough or in food or drink; in soil taken from the left or from the right foot, or in any other things by which a sorcery can be made...

---

104 The gold-striped salamander, golden-striped salamander, *saramaganta* or *píntega rabilonga* (*Chioglossa lusitanica*) is a species of salamander in the Salamandridae family. It is the only species of the genus *Chioglossa*. It is found in the north west of Iberia at an altitude of up to 1,300 m.

All these things be undone and unbound from this servant (so and so) of the Lord, the ones I, Cyprian, have done, as much as the ones made by these witches, servants of the demon; all this be turned back to what it was before, or in its own figure, or in the one in which God created it.

Saint Augustine and all the Saints, by holy names, make all creatures be free from the evil of the demon. Amen.

New Orisons for the Open Hours

[GLT]

To the Noon
Oh Virgin of the sacred Heavens,
Mother of all-redeemer
Who among all women has the victory,
Bring joy to my life
Which wails full of pain,
And come to pour on my lips
Words of pure love;
In the name of the God of the world
And also of the beloved son
Where the supreme good exists,
Be forever praised
In this blessed hour. Amen.

To the Trinities
Let the Most Holy Trinity
Always accompany my steps,
And extend to me its friendly arms
In the hours of unhappiness.

Let the Eternal Father help me,
And bless me Jesus.
Let the spirit give me light
Against the temptations from hell.
Let me pass the whole of existence
Always practicing the good,
And the Most Sacred Trinity
Guide me on the earth. Amen.

For the Midnight
Oh my good Guardian Angel,
Be by my side now.
And come always by this time
Release me from the bad visions;
And let God keep my soul
From some mortal sin,
And avoid dreams and ideas
That to my brothers cause harm.
Oh my good Guardian Angel,
Ask the Virgin our Mother,
To keep me away from sin
For all this life. *Amen.*

Magical Orison of Saint Cipryan

[HM]

According to the legend, St. Cyprian was Bishop of Antioch, but ecclesiastical history says that his seat was that of Carthage. It matters little, for the rest, whether the personalities are the same; the one belongs to poetry, while the other is a father and martyr of the Church. There is extant among the old grimoires a prayer attributed to the St. Cyprian of legend, who is possibly the holy Bishop of Carthage: Its obscure and figurative expressions may have given credit to the idea that prior to his conversion he was addicted to the deadly practices of Black Magic. It may be rendered thus:

> *I, Cyprian, servant of our Lord Jesus Christ, have prayed unto God the Almighty Father, saying: Thou art the strong God, my God omnipotent, dwelling in the great light. Thou art holy and worthy of praise, and Thou hast beheld in the old days the malice of Thy servant and the iniquities into which I was plunged by the wiles of the demon. I was ignorant of Thy true name; I passed in the midst of the sheep and they were without a shepherd. The clouds shed no dew on earth; trees bore no fruit and women in labour could not be delivered. I bound and did not loose; I bound the fishes of the sea, and they were captive; I bound the*

pathways of the sea, and many evils did I encompass. But now, Lord Jesus Christ, I have known Thy Holy Name, I have loved Thee, I am converted with my whole heart, my whole soul and all my inward being. I have turned from the multitude of my sins, that I may walk in Thy love and follow Thy commandments, which are henceforth my faith and my prayer. Thou art the Word of truth, the sole Word of the Father, and I conjure Thee now to break the chain of clouds and send down on Thy children Thy goodly rain like milk, to set free the rivers and liberate those who swim, as also those which fly. I conjure Thee to break all the chains and remove all the obstacles by the virtue of Thy Holy Name.

The antiquity of this prayer is evident, and it embodies a most remarkable memory of ancient things belonging to Christian esotericism during the first centuries of this era.

ORISON TO THE CUSTODIAN ANGEL

[Dialogue between the Devil and the Custodian Angel]

[GLT]

This orison is destined to release from enemies, envy, and sorceries

The orison of the Custodian Angel was taught to Saint Cyprian by Saint Gregory, his companion, a virtuous man who preached frequently in those temples, announcing the virtue and the proceeding of Saint Cyprian and his great regret from that life full of iniquities. Says Saint Gregory: "*Behold, my brothers, the happy day has come in which I, with my orisons, have won over Satanaz and saved Cyprian, who for three days is the slave of Our Lord God, and I have all the certainty that he will not be again slave to the demon!*"

"How could Cyprian be saved?" the people said.

"With orisons!" answered Saint Gregory.

"Go to mount Zion, in the place of the Hermitage; there you will see the place where the demon, taking the body of Cyprian, hurled him down into the depths of hell; the virtue of that damsel who he, with his sorceries, tried to conquer and convince for his friend [sic]."

But the virtue of that damsel was not lost, and she not only forgave Cyprian, but also asked God not to punish him and to also forgive him.

The orison of the Custodian Angel is so effective that every creature that says it once a day is not only delivered from the power and astuteness of Satanaz, but also creates an obstacle that within the distance of twelve leagues no creature can enter. Because of this, every faithful Christian must learn it by heart, to better say it whenever he wants.

Lucifer and the Angel

"Custodian Angel, my friend, do you want to save yourself?"

"Yes, I want, and … I am the Custodian Angel, your friend, am I not?"

"Do you want salvation?"

"Yes, I want."

"And what are the principal virtues of the sky which can save you?"

"They are:

I

The sun clearer than the moon.

II

The two tablets of Moses, where Our Lord put his sacred feet.

III

The three persons of the Most Holy Trinity
and the entire Christian family

IV

It is the four evangelists, John, Mark, Matthew, and Luke

The Prayers of Saint Cyprian

V

It is the five wounds of Our Lord Jesus Christ, who so
much suffered to break your forces, Lucifer!

VI

It is the six blessed candles, which illuminated the sepulchre
of Our Lord Jesus Christ, and which illuminate me, to deliver
me from the astuteness of Lucifer, the god of hell

VII

It is the seven sacraments of the Eucharist, because
without them nobody has salvation

VIII

It is the eight beatitudes

IX

It is the nine months during which
the Virgin Mary carried in her womb
her beloved Son Jesus Christ,
by this virtue we are free from
your power, Satanaz!

X

It is the Ten Commandments of the Law of God, because
whoever believes in them does not enter the infernal depths

XI

It is the eleven thousand virgins, who incessantly ask
God on our behalf

XII

It is the twelve Apostles who always accompanied Our Lord Jesus Christ
until the day of his death and after his eternal redemption

XIII
It is the thirteen rays of the Sun, which eternally
Esconjure you, Satanaz!
São os treze raios de Sol, que eternamente

On this occasion, Satanaz submerged, accompanied by thunder and lightning sent by God Our Lord.

We warn that this orison must be said in its entirety and, if necessary, repeated three times.

Orison to Assist the Sick at the Time of Death

[GLT]

This orison is so efficient that Saint Cyprian says no soul is lost when it is said with devotion and faith in Jesus Christ.

Saint Cyprian says, in chapter XII, that this orison has such virtue that all the sick to whom he read it he took a hair of his head and threw it in a glass of water, and used this water to wash the open wounds of the sick, whose maladies were incurable by other medicine; he threw at them a drop saying, "I, Cyprian, heal you in the name of the Father, of the Son, and of the Holy Ghost. Amen."

ORISON

Jesus, my Redeemer, in your hands, Lord, I commend the soul of this servant so you, Savior of the world, take him to heaven in the company of the Angels.

Jesus, Jesus, Jesus, be with me so I can defend you; Jesus be in your soul, so you can settle yourself; Jesus be before you to guide you; Jesus be at your presence to guard you; Jesus, Jesus reigns, Jesus dominates, Jesus from every evil defends you. This is the cross of the divine Redeemer: flee,

flee, absent yourself enemies of the redeemed souls, with the most precious blood of Jesus Christ.

Jesus, Jesus, Jesus; Mary, Mother of grace, Mother of mercy, defend me from the enemy and support me in this hour. Do not forsake me, Lady, plead for this your servant (so and so), to your Beloved Son, so by your intercession he escapes free from the dangers of his enemies and their temptations. (Sprinkle holy water.)

Jesus, Jesus, Jesus; receive the soul of this your servant (so and so), look at him with the eyes of compassion: open these arms to him, support him, Lord, with your mercy, because he is the work of your hands, and the soul is your image.

Jesus, Jesus, Jesus; from you, my God, will the remedy come to him; do not deny him your grace in this hour, because I (so and so) call you, oh Powerful God, to come without delay to receive this soul in your most holy arms; come, Lord, come to help me, as you came to help Cyprian when he was in the battle against Lucifer.

Jesus, Jesus, Jesus! I believe, Lord, firmly, in everything that the Roman Catholic Apostolic Church commands to believe; fortify, so, the soul of this your servant (so and so). Come, Jesus, oh true life of all souls! Free him, Lord, from his enemies; as sovereign physician, heal all his infirmities; purify him, Jesus, with your precious blood, because prostrated at your feet I claim your mercy.

Jesus, Jesus, Jesus! Oh Most Holy Mary, Mother of Our Lord; now, Lady, it is time you show that you are Mother of him and of all of us. Help us in this dangerous hour, because in your hands we have put the important business of our salvation.

Take him from this conflict and agony in which he sees himself, and put his soul in the presence of your Beloved Son.

Jesus, save him; Jesus, help him; Jesus, support him; oh my God, my Lord, have compassion for all of us; free us from everything, as the deer desires the fountains of water, my soul desires you, Jesus. When will you call for me? Oh! My ears now hear the words from your sacred mouth: *Enter and come, soul of mine, in the enjoyment of your Lord.*

Jesus, Jesus, in your hands, my God, I offer and put my spirit; it is right that we return to you what we received from you; be, then, for our soul, just, and save it from the darkness.

Defend it, Lord, from all combats, so it goes to sing eternally in heaven your infinite mercies.

Mercy, most sweet Jesus; mercy, most kind Jesus, mercy and forgiveness to all your sons, for whom you suffered on the cross. It is just then that we are saved. Amen.

Useful Orison to Heal All Diseases

even if they are natural, which must be said with great respect for Jesus Christ, with whom we are talking

[GLT]

(make the sign of the Cross)

In the name of the Father, of the Son and of the Holy Spirit. Amen. Jesus, Mary and Joseph.

I, (so and so), as a creature of God, made in his image and likeness and redeemed with his blood, put faith in your sufferings, as Jesus Christ did to the sick from the Holy Land and to the paralytic of Sidon; because I, (so and so), ask you, my Lord Jesus Christ, that you have compassion with this your servant (so and so); do not allow, Lord, that he suffer more tribulations in life! Throw over this your servant your Most Holy Blessing, and I, (so and so), will say with authority from our Lord that all your sufferings cease. Most Kind Lord Jesus, true God, that from the bosom of the Eternal Omnipotent Father was sent to the world to absolve sins, absolve, Lord, the ones this miserable creature has committed; you who were sent to the world to redeem the afflicted, release the incarcerated, congregate the vagrants, conduct to their homeland the pilgrims; because I, (so and so), supplicate to you, Lord, to conduct this sick man to the way of salvation and of health, because he is truly regretful, consulate, Lord, the oppressed and the distressed; deign to free this servant from this disease from which he is suffering, from the affliction and tribulation in which I see him, because you received from God the Almighty Father the human form; and men being made in prodigious way, you bought the Paradise with you precious blood, establishing a complete peace between Angels and men. So then, deign, Lord, to establish a peace between my humors and soul; so (so and so) and all of us may live in happiness, free from diseases, both of body and of soul. Yes, my God and my Lord, resplendent then be your peace, your mercy over me and over all of us; as you practiced with Esau taking from him all the aversion he had against his brother Jacob, extend Lord Jesus Christ, over (so and so), this creature of yours, your arm and your grace, and deign to free him from everyone who hates him, as you freed Abraham from the hands of the Chaldeans; his son Isaac from the conscience of the sacrifice; Joseph from the tyranny of his brothers; Noah from the universal flood; Lot from the great fire of Sodom; Moses and Aaron, your servants, and the people of Israel, from the power of the Pharaoh and from the slavery in Egypt; David from the hands of Saul and from the giant Goliath; Suzanne from crime and false testimony; Judith from the arrogant Holofernes; Daniel from the den of lions; the three young men Shadrach, Meshash, and Abednego from the fiery furnace; Jonah from the belly of the whale; the daughter of the Canaanite woman from the vexation of the demon; Adam from the penalty of hell; Peter from the waves of the sea and Paul from the prison of the carcer; so, then, most kind Lord Jesus Christ, Son of the Living God, attend me too, (so and so), your creature, and come with promptness to aid me; by your incarnation; by your birth; by the hunger, the thirst, the cold, the heat, the works and afflictions, by the spittle and the slaps in the face, by the whips and the crown of thorns; by the crucifixion nails, the gall and the vinegar; by the cruel death you suffered; and by the lance which trespassed your chest and by the seven words that you said in the cross, first to God the Almighty Father: *Father, forgive them, for they do not know what they do.* Then to the good thief, who was with you crucified: *Truly, I say to you, today you will be with me in paradise.* Then to the Father: *Heli, Heli, lamma sabatani?* which means: *My God, My God, why have you forsaken me?* Then to your Mother: *Woman, behold your son.* After to the disciple: *Behold your mother* (showing that you took care of your friends). *I am thirsty,* because you wanted our salvation and that of the holy souls, who were in Limbo. You after said to your Father: *Father, into your hands I commit my spirit.* And at last you exclaimed, saying: *It is…finished.* So were concluded all your works and pains. Deign, then, Lord, that from this hour on this creature (so and so) will never suffer from this malady that mortifies him, so I implore by all these things, and by your descent into Limbo, by your glorious resurrection, by the frequent consolations you gave to your disciples, by your admirable ascension, by the coming of the spirit, by the tremendous day of judgment, as also by all the benefits I have received from your kindness (because you created me out of nothing, and gave me your holy faith); so by all this, my Redeemer, my Lord Jesus Christ, I humbly ask you to throw your blessing over this sick creature.

Yes, my God and my Lord, have pity on him. Oh God of Abraham, oh God of Isaac and God of Jacob, have pity on this your creature (so and so); send to his aid, your Saint Michael Archangel, to give him health and to defend him from this misery of flesh and spirit. And you, Saint Michael, Saint Archangel of Christ, defend and heal this servant of the Lord, because you deserved from the Lord to be blessed and free creatures from every danger.

Here is the cross of the Lord, who wins and reigns.

Oh Savior of the world, save him; Savior of the world, help us, by your blood and by the Cross you redeemed me, save us and heal us from all diseases, both of body and of soul; I, (so and so), ask all this by all the miracles and steps you gave on this earth when you were man.

Oh Holy God! Oh strong God! Oh immortal God! Have mercy on us. Cross of Christ, save me; Cross of Christ, protect me; Cross of Christ, defend me in the name of the Father, of the Son, and of the Holy Spirit. Amen.

(Kneeling, say the Creed and the Salve Regina to Our Lady
and put holy water on the malady of the sick person).

WARNING

This orison can be said to anyone who suffers from any malady, it being for any suffering, especially erysipelas, fire, worms; finally, to every misery of life.

NB. — While the religious understand that every malady is not always sorcery or devilry, it is good also to read the Orison of Saint Cyprian, because the sick person is more satisfied and the faith he becomes possessed by helps a lot in his cure. So Cyprian says in his book, Chapter I.

ORISON OF THE JUST JUDGE

[GLT]

†

Just Judge of Nazareth, son of the Virgin Mary, who at Bethlehem was born in the midst of idolatries, I ask you, Lord, by your sixth day, that my body be not captive, nor wounded, nor killed, and not in the hands of justice wrapped, *Pax Tecum, Pax Tecum, Pax Tecum*. Christ so said to his Disciples: If my enemies come to arrest me, they will have eyes but will not see me; they will have ears but will not hear me; they will have mouths but will not speak; with the weapons of Saint George, I will be armed; with the sword of Abraham, I will be covered; with the milk of the Virgin Mary, I will be sprinkled; with the blood of my Lord Jesus Christ, I will be baptized; in the ark of Noah, I will be taken; with the keys of Saint Peter, I will be closed where they cannot see me, nor hurt me, nor kill me, nor blood from my body take. I also ask you, Lord, by those three blessed Chalices, by those three clothed priests, by those three consecrated Hosts, which you consecrated on the third day from the doors of Bethlehem until Jerusalem, that with pleasure and joy I be so well guarded at night, as Jesus walked in the womb of the Virgin Mary, God in front, peace in guidance, God give you company, that God always gave to the Virgin Mary from the holy house of Bethlehem until Jerusalem, God is your Father, the Holy

Virgin Mary your Mother, with the weapons of Saint George you will be armed, with the sword of Saint James you will be forever guarded. Amen.

(Although this orison is not from Saint Cyprian, we published it here because it is very miraculous.)

Orison Which Preserves From Lightning

[GLT]

Tie a white ribbon around the arm, neck, and waist of Saint Barbara, as soon as the thunderstorm begins, and light a candle which lasts twelve hours.

This being done, every hour, after have rinsed the mouth three times with water, you will say:

> I ask you, Lady, that you intercede for me with Him who died for us. Like this ribbon I girded on the neck, I have a pure soul and pure intentions. Deliver me, Lady, who is worthy of your protection, from the terrible effects of the lightning. Amen.

Prayer to Saint Expedite

Patron of urgent causes and quick solutions

My Saint Expedite of the urgent and just causes, please intercede for me with Our Lord Jesus Christ. Help me in this hour of affliction and despair, my Saint Expedite.

You who are a warrior saint, you who are the Saint of the afflicted, you who are the Saint of the desperate, you who are the Saint of urgent causes. Protect me, help me, give me strength, courage, and serenity. Hear my appeal.

> *(Express very clearly what you want, and ask him to find a way of obtaining it for you.)*

My Saint Expedite, help me to prevail through these difficult hours, protect me from everyone who wants to prejudice me, answer my appeal with urgency. Bring me back to the state of peace and tranquillity, my Saint Expedite.

I will be grateful to you for the rest of my life, and I will talk about your name to everyone who has faith.

Amen.

> *(Say one Lord's Prayer, one hail Mary, and make the Signo of the Cross.)*

Orison to Saint Expedite

Oh glorious Saint Expedite! By the merits of your unbreakable faith, concede to us that in imitation of you we know to prefer celestial delights to the fleeting goods of this world; speed up by your intervention the entrance into heaven of the blessed souls who suffer in Purgatory, and concede to us your patronage in urgent cases. Be it so.

Prayer

Saint Expedite, valiant defender of the Church of Christ, pray for us.

Saint Expedite, popular image.

Another Prayer to Saint Expedite

May the intercession of the glorious Martyr, Saint Expedite, recommend us, oh my God, to your kindness, so your protection may obtain for us what our merits are incapable of obtaining.

Amen.

We supplicate to you, Lord, to inspire by Your grace our thoughts and actions so that, You being their principle, we can, by the intercessions of Saint Expedite, be conducted with courage, fidelity, and promptitude, in the proper and favorable time, and come to a good and happy end, through our Lord, Jesus Christ.

Amen.

Saint Expedite, honored by the gratitude of those who invoked you in the last hour and for pressing causes, we pray to you to obtain from the all-powerful goodness of God, by the intercession of Immaculate Mary, (today or in such day) the grace that we solicit with all submission to the Divine Will.

Amen.

Orison

to everyone who reads it, be safe from sorceries, bindings and malefactions

[LM2]

The following orison is useful to deliver people from evils done and from sorceries, and from backbiting, from bindings and enchantments, so all of them are untied and unbound, and from pestilence and corrupt air; the orison must be read three times thrice a year on three different Sundays, saying:

> You who are God strong and powerful, who resides on the great summit and who are holy and elevated at all times, God and Lord, I know Your Holy Name, and I love it powerfully, and multitudes are formed with my ills. Today all my firm and pure heart and all my will I put in Your love and in Your commandments so you keep me and send Your love and mercy to break and untie all the bindings of men and women so that the rain falls upon the earth and it gives its fruit, and women give birth to their children without any malady, and they suck the milk of the breasts of their mothers; and unbind at their time the fishes of the

sea, and every animal that walks on the earth, and all other things, and every man and woman to whom sorceries were done by day or by night be unbound; by Your Holy Name let every enemy flee from those who place this orison over themselves or have it read for them, thrice a year on three different Sundays, and with it delivered and unbound from every evil and from all evils done, let them profit from their work, and You, Lord, keep them day and night from the Devil and his power, and from all his snares, by the Holy Name of God glorified and praised in heaven and on earth. And for loving him who is the Word of God, as the stone was opened and gave water, and from it drank the sons of Israel, so the Lord Almighty put his hand full of grace over this Your servant ✠ and over whomever brings this orison or has it at home, be always with him, Lord, as You put into the earthly paradise four rivers, which are the Pishon, Gihon, Tigris, and Euphrates, which You command to irrigate the entire world, for which things I supplicate that neither in thought, neither in malice, can the damned Devil nor the malign spirit, nor binding or evil deeds be made, nor envy against this Your servant ✠ and furthermore, let all evil things be abated and annulled, that none of the seventy and two languages which are divided by the world damn them, and any opposition that wishes to do harm to them be damned, and by the orisons of the good angels, be these Your servants ✠ with all their house, and everything inside and outside it, and by Emanuel and by all the Holy Names of God our Lord and the other things here named, be untied and unbound these your servants and be separated from them all the sorceries and every kind of malefaction that against them try the power of the Devil; and by You, my God, let these your servants be separated from every evil deed, sorcery, bindings, and every evil venture. Amen.

Cypriani Citatio Angelorvm

[VJL]

Angelical Citation of Cyprian

I cite, call down, demand, and exorcise you now: O Almaziel, Ariel, Anathamia, Ezebul, Abiul, Ezea, Ahesin, and Calizabin, most holy angels of God, by all Dominions, Thrones, Powers and angelic Principalities, and all the assembly of the Saints, and by the ineffable delight with which the angel proclaimed to the shepherds the incarnation or rather the birth of the Savior, and with which they themselves perceived. By the twenty-four elders who sing unceasingly before the throne of God: Holy, Holy, Holy is the Lord our God! and by the uncreated angel of the Covenant, namely Jesus, and by the cherubim and seraphim, and all the archangels, and by the infinite omnipotence of God within the perceptible circle, who created one and all with a word, that you would help me in this arduous business in the same way that you helped Lot and Abraham when they were entertaining you as a guest, and no less than Jacob, Moses, Joshua, Samson, and many others whom you have deemed worthy to visit. So come, oh you angelic ones, in beautiful form, full of dignity and brightness, and do all that I have requested, in the name of the threefold Jehovah, whose praises all spirits sing ceaselessly giving honor to the all powerful who is your Lord as he is mine. Amen.

Dimissio Cypriani

[VJL]

Now I conjure you oh human spirit! By the omnipotence, wisdom, and justice of God the Father; by the omnipotence of God the Son; by the immensity of His mercy and charity towards men; by the omnipotence of the Holy Spirit, by his infinite wisdom, and unfathomable principle. By the holy Archangel Michael, and all the host of Heaven, without lightning, terrible rattling, and uproar, without rain or thunder, and in one word: without danger or injury to our bodies or souls. I command you to depart from this place and not appear again unless I summon you. May the peace of the threefold God be with us now and preserve us. O God, be with us and have mercy upon us. O God, turn this spirit (so and so) to the path of righteousness and give us peace! Amen!

Orison of the Miraculous Black She-Goat

Miraculous Black She-Goat who climbed the mount, bring me (name of the woman/man you desire), who disappeared from my hand. (Name of the woman/man you desire), as the cock cackles, the ass neighs, the bell rings, and the she-goat bleats, so you will walk after me.

As Caiaphas, Satanaz, Fierabras, and the Maioral of Hell, who gave dominion to all, make (name of the woman/man you desire) be dominated, to come to me as a lamb, captive under my left foot.

(Name of the woman/man you desire), money in the vat and in my hand will not be lacking; neither you nor I will die from thirst; neither you nor I will be caught with a knife or shot; my enemies will not see me.

I will win the fight, with the powers of the miraculous She-Goat. So and so, with two I see you, with three I fasten you, with Caiaphas, Satanaz, Fierabras.

This prayer is done with a knife and three virgin candles.

The giant Fierabras, engraving from the 1497 edition of
Jehan Bagnyon's Roman de Fierabras le Géant

EXORCISMS

Vade Retro Satana

"*Vade retro satana*" *is a medieval Catholic formula used as an exorcism, registered in a manuscript from 1415 in the Benedictine Abbey at Metten, in Bavaria, and later in an Austrian manuscript from the middle of the XIV century. This powerful prayer remains as part of the ritual of the Roman Catholic Church.*

    Crux sancta sit mihi lux
    Non draco sit mihi dux
    Vade retro satana
    Numquam suade mihi vana
    Sunt mala quae libas
    Ipse venena bibas

    (Let the Holy Cross be my light
    Let not the dragon be my guide
    Step back Satan
    Never tempt me with vain things
    What you offer me is evil
    You drink the poison yourself)

The medal of Saint Benedict, with the initials of the *Vade Retro Satana* prayer in the back. From the treatise written by Dom P. Guéranger (1805–1875), Abbot of Solesmes.

INSTRUCTION TO THE RELIGIOUS THAT WILL TREAT ANY MALADY

Rule that every religious person must study to know if the maladies he will treat are or are not the work of sorcery or of the devil

[GLT]

We must not easily believe that all maladies are sorceries or arts of the demon, because we see, all the time, people who suffer from natural maladies, but when the sickness prolongs itself and does not have a cure, they attribute it to sorceries when it is, in fact, the opposite.

They have the custom of going to the house of certain women and certain men, who know a little about what is natural or supernatural, who begin to make conjurations and sometimes to curse spirits that are not guilty at all. These impostors become damned by God, as Saint Cyprian says in his work, chapter XVI.

So I pray with all my heart that they study with attention these instructions so that they do not expose themselves to the damnation of the Creator; so, we must note that everything we do is in the name of Jesus Christ, and for this reason, we must not offend him, but instead invoke his Holy Name to assist us in the hour we are praying for the sick, to avoid being deceived about whether the malady is or is not the work of sorcery or of infernal spirits. At the end of these instructions, I will cite a prayer in Latin to be read by the sick three times, because if it is sorcery or benign spirits or malign spirits they will talk, declaring that they are inside the creature, because soon she begins to convulsively be afflicted. That being the case, you have certainty that the malady is supernatural and not natural, and so then you must say:

> *I supplicate to you, spirit, in the name of God Almighty, that you declare to me why you are molesting this body (here you pronounce the name of the sick), because I conjure you to say to me what you wish to lay claim to from the corporal world. Here is the protector who will supplicate to God for you, so you be purified in the realm of Glory.*

At the end of this invocation, the religious will soon understand if the spirit walks the world searching for charity, because as soon as it is said to him, *"I will supplicate for you,"* the sick person begins to calm down and stays tranquil. If it happens like that, everyone must kneel and say together the following orison:

ORISON FOR THE GOOD SPIRITS
TO BRING THEM TO GOD
AND LEAVE THE CREATURE

When it is said to the spirit, *"You calm down so that I may pray to God for you,"* if the person becomes even more afflicted, it demonstrates that the spirit he has inside him is evil.

The conjuration of Saint Cyprian must then be done.

But, my good reader, I ask you, in the name of God, not to treat any malady before first studying these rules well. It is necessary to note that each one of the orisons that this book contains has a specific application,

Exorcisms

and one that is used for one thing is not useful for another. There are five orisons to be found in this book:

1. To supplicate to God for the good spirits.

2. To conjure the evil spirits.

3. To heal maladies, even natural, without them being the work of sorcery or devilry.

4. To conjure the enchantment or enchanted treasures.

5. To close a place in an open body, so the spirits do not return to enter into that body.

These are the main orisons, but beside that, this book contains many curious things, with which the reader, certainly, will identify himself.

Signs that there is Malefaction in a Creature

Orison that is read to the sick to know if the malady is natural or supernatural, which the religious must study well in chapter I and in the instructions; without this, they cannot provide good services to the sick.

[GLT]

This orison must be spoken in Latin, so that the sick cannot use deceit; if the sick person does not know when he must move or be quiet, he cannot deceive the religious.

We give in sequence the orison in English, with the same end.

Signs that there is malefaction in the creature:

If the religious person understands that it is a demon or a lost soul, say the litany; after saying it, put on him the precept that follows in English:

> *Praecipitur in Nomine Jesus, ut desinat nocere aegroto, statim cesse delirium, et illuo cordinat discurrat. Si cadat, ut mortuus, et sine mora surget ad praeceptu. Exortistae factu in Nomine Jesus. Si in pondere assicitur, ut a multis himinibus elevaret non aliqua parte corporis si dolor, vel tumor, et ad signo Crucis, vel imposito praecepto in*

nomine Jesus cessat. Si side causa velit sibi morte inserre, se praecipite dure. Quando imaginationi, se praesentat res inhonestae contra Imagines Christi, et Sanctorum, et si eorem tempore sentiant in capit, ut plumbum, ut aguam frigidam, vel ferrumignitem, et hoc fugit ad signum Crucis vel incovato Nomine Jesu. Quando Sacramenta, Reliquias, et res sacros edit; quando nulla praecedente tribulation, desperat, se dilacerat. Quando subito patenti lumen aufertur, et subito restitutur; quando diurno tempora nihil vidit, et nocturno bene vidit et sine fuce lugit epistolam: si subito siat surdus, te postae bene audiat, non solun materialia, sed spiritualia. Si per septem, vel novem dies mihil, vel parum comelens fortis est, et pinguis, sicut antea. Si loquitur de Mysteris ultra suas capacitatem, quando nun custat de illius sanctitite. Quando ventus vehemens discurrit per totum corpus ad mudum formicarum; quando elevatur corpus contra volutatem patientes, et non apparet a quo leventur. Clamores, scissio vestium, arrotatines dentium, quando potiens non est stultus: vel quando honro natura debilis non potest teneri a multis. Quando haber liguem tumidam, et ni gram, quando audiuntur rugitus leonum, balatus ovium, latra tus canun, porco-rum grumitus, et similium. Si vairepraeter naturam vident, et audiunt, si homines maximo odio perseuntur; si praecipitis se exponunt, se oculos horribiles habent, remanent, sensibus destituti. Quando corpu talibenedicti, quando ab Aeclesia fugit, et aguam benedictan non consentit: quando iratos se ostendune contra Ministros superdonentes Relíquias capiti (eti occulte). Quando Imagines Cristi, et virginis Mariae nolunt inspicere sed conspuunt, quando verba sacra nolun, profere, vel si proferant, illa corrumpunt, et balbat cienter student prefere. Cum superposita capiti manu sacra ad lactionem Evangeliorum conturbatum aegrotus, cum plusquam solitum palpitaverit, sensus occupantum, gattaes sudoris destuunt, anxietates senta; stridores usque xxx ad Caelum mittit, sed posernit, vel similia facit. Amen.

PRECEPT

To the demon or demons so they do not mortify the sick during the time of the conjuration

This precept must be repeated many times, especially to pregnant women, so that they do not vomit with the strong attacks that the demons cause on this occasion.

> *I, as a creature of God, made in the greatest likeness and redeemed by your most holy blood, put this precept on you, demon or demons, so you stop your deliriums so that this creature is not again tormented by you with your infernal furies.*
>
> *Because the name of the Lord is strong and powerful, it is by this that I cite and notify you to be absent from this place. I bind you eternally in the place that God our Lord destined to you; because with the name of Jesus, I step on, beat back, and displease you even from my heart out. Oh Lord, be with me and with all of us, absent and present, so you, demon, can never torment the creatures of the Lord. Flee, flee, opposing forces, because the lion of Judah and the race of David wins.*
>
> *I tie you with the chains of Saint Paul and with the towel which cleaned the holy face of Jesus Christ, so you can never torture the living.*

Following this, make an act of contrition.

After that, the orison of Saint Cyprian must be said to unmake all kinds of sorcery and conjurations of demons, malign spirits, or bindings made by men or women, or to pray in a house believed to be possessed by malign spirits and even for anything related to supernatural maladies.

In this orison must be said many times, "*I, Cyprian, servant of God, unbind all that I have bound.*" But the religious must not pronounce the name of the saint, but only speak in his name saying:

I… unbound all that is bound.

The Saint is invoked, but his name is not pronounced, because in this first part there is only the life of Saint Cyprian, extracted from the holy book written by him, in which there are restrictions about this. In the other two parts of the work, however, the reader is informed about everything that interests him.

First Conjuration

[GLT]

This conjuration must be performed by the religious with all respect and faith, and when he sees that the sick person is afflicted and the demon or the evil spirit does not want to leave, he must read to him again the precept of chapter IV, or the one written in Latin, at the end of the litany.

> I, Cyprian (or I, so and so), from the part of God Our Lord Jesus Christ, absolve the body of (so and so) from all the evil sorceries, enchantments, spells, bonds that men and women made, and require it in the name of God Our Lord Jesus Christ, the God of Abraham, God very great and powerful! Glorified be you, forever let them be destroyed in your most holy Name, unmade, unbound and let all the ills that this your servant (so and so) suffers be reduced to nothing; let God come with his good help, by love of mercy let many men and women who are the causes of these evils be touched right now in the heart to not continue in that damned life anymore!
>
> Be with me the Angels of heaven, principally Saint Michael, Saint Gabriel, Saint Raphael, and all the Saints, and angels of the Lord, and the Apostles of the Lord,

Saint John the Baptist, Saint Peter and Saint Paul, Saint Andrew, Saint James, Saint Matthias, Saint Luke, Saint Simon, Saint Anastasius, Saint Augustine and all orders of the Saint Evangelists John, Luke, Mark, Matthew and all the cherubim and seraphim Migueis [sic], created by the work and grace of the divine Spirit. By the seventy and two languages that are distributed across the world and by this absolution and by the voice that called Lazarus from the sepulchre, by all these virtues, let everything be returned to the proper state it had before or to the health it enjoyed before being taken by demons, because in your Almighty name I command that all the supernatural disarrangement stop.

Even more, by the virtue of those most holy words by which Jesus Christ called: "Adam, Adam, Adam, where are you?" By these most holy words we absolve, by the virtue from when Jesus Christ said to the sick, "Rise and go to your home and do not sin again," the infirmity of which had been three years, so may God absolve you, ✠ he who created the heaven and the earth, and let him have compassion for you, (so and so), by the prophet Daniel, by the holiness of Israel, and by all the Saints of God, absolve this your servant (so and so) and bless his house ✠ and let everything else be free from the power of demons, by Emmanuel, so be God with all of us. Amen.

By the Most Holy name of God Our Lord Jesus Christ, let all things here named be unbound, unbewitched, unpinned from all the bindings formed by the art of the demon or by his companions; be it all destroyed, because I command from the part of the Omnipotent so that now those I have not named also be unbound and untied, all the evil sorceries and bindings, and every evil venture by Christ our Lord. Amen.

Second Conjuration

[GLT]

I conjure you, excommunicated demons or baptized evil spirits, so that evil ties, sorceries, enchantments of the devil, of envy, be they made of gold, silver or lead, or in solitary trees, be all destroyed and untied, and do not hold anything to the body of (so and so) or his house, because from now on if the sorcery or enchantment is on some celestial or terrestrial idol, it will be destroyed from the part of God, because all the infernorium or all the language, I trust in Jesus Christ, joyous name; as Jesus Christ put apart and expelled from the earth the demons and their deeds, so by these most joyous names of Our Lord Jesus Christ let all demons, ghosts, and all malign spirits in the company of Satanas and his companions flee to their abodes that are in hell, where they will be perpetually in the company of all the sorcerers who made sorcery against this creature (so and so) or in this house; and to everything this house contains, be undone and null, be conjured, broken and abjured, under the power of the Most Holy Obedience, by the power of the I Believe in God the Father and the Three Persons of the Most Holy Trinity and of the Most Sacred Sacrament of the Altar. Amen.

With the whole Holiness, I conjure and exile you, damned demons, malign spirits, and rebels to my and your Creator!

So I bind you and bind again, fasten and tie to the waves of the curdled sea, where neither chicken nor cock sing, or to your destiny, or places that God Our Lord Jesus Christ destined to you.

I raise, break, abjure, and conjure all the requirements, stalemates, precepts, and obligations that you did to this body of (so and so). From now on be cited, notified and obligated, you and your companions, to follow the way that Jesus destined to you, that without appellation nor aggravation by the power of God Our Lord Jesus Christ and of Most Holy Mary and of the Holy Ghost and of the Three Divine Persons of the Most Holy Trinity, which is only one true God in whom I firmly believe and by whom I raise the plagues and rages, revenges and fears, hates and evil visits; I break and abjure all the requirements, embargoes, stalemates, precepts, and obligations by the power of the Holy Incarnated Word, by the virtue of the Most Holy Mary and all Saints, angels, Cherubim and Seraphim, created by work and grace of the Holy Ghost. Amen.

When the religious finishes what is written above, the demon screams and says, "*I am not Satanas but a lost soul; however, I still have salvation.*"

The religious asks him, "*Do you wish for us to pray for you?*" The soul answers, "*Yes, I wish it.*" After that answer, everybody kneels and says the Orison for the Good Spirits, which appears in this book, because many times it happens that we are conjuring a soul who needs orisons and not conjurations.

The reader must study well the instructions of the chapter 1, so he does not commit one of the mistakes I just mentioned, because this service is not an entertainment, but a work, to God as much as to the good spirits.

Third Conjuration

[GLT]

Here is the cross ✠ of the Lord; flee, flee, absent yourselves, enemies of Nature!

I conjure you in the name of Jesus, Mary, Joseph, Jesus of Nazareth, king of the Jews. Here is the cross of Our Lord Jesus Christ. Flee, enemy parts, the lion of the tribe of Judah and the race of David has won.

Hallelujah, Hallelujah, Hallelujah, exalted be the Lord, bless us, keep us, and show us your divine face, turn to us with your divine face and have pity on us. The king David came in peace, as when Jesus made himself man and lived among us and was born from the Holy Virgin Mary by his blessed mercy.

Holy Apostles, blessed of the Lord, pray to the Lord that Saint Cyprian might help me, so I can destroy all I have done.

Saint John, Saint Matthew, Saint Mark, Saint Luke, I ask that you deign to deliver us and keep us free from the work of demons.

We wait for all that live and reign with the Father and the Holy Ghost, forever and ever. Amen.

The blessing of the Omnipotent God, Father, Son, and Holy Spirit descend upon us and bless us continually.

Jesus, Jesus, your peace and your virtue and your Passion, the sign of the Cross ✠, the wholeness of the blessed Virgin Mary, the blessing of the Saints chosen of God, the title of our Savior on the Cross. Jesus of Nazareth king of the Jews, be triumphant today and every day among your visible and invisible enemies, against all the dangers of our lives and of our bodies, and in every time and place. I will have supreme enjoyment and happiness in God my Savior.

Jesus, Jesus, Jesus, be for us. Jesus, Jesus, Creator and understanding, Jesus will put the evil ones of the universe into the hells and will impede the demon's torment of his creatures. Jesus, Son of Mary, Savior of the world by the merits of the Blessed Virgin Mary and of the Holy Angels, Apostles, Martyrs, Confessors, and Virgins, so the Lord be with you to defend you and be inside you to keep you, guide you and accompany you, and be over you to bless you, He who lives and reigns in a perfect unity with the Father and the Holy Spirit, forever and ever. Amen.

The blessing of the Omnipotent God, Father, Son, and Holy Spirit descend upon us and remain continually.

Most Holy Virgin, Our Lady of Protection, I, the greatest of the sinners, ask you to pray to your beloved Son to break all the forces of the demons so they never again can torment this creature.

I bring an end to this holy orison and will end the maladies in this house caused by the sickening of the malign spirits.

Orison to the Lord, or praises for having delivered
the sick from the power of Satanas or his allies,
which must be prayed on the knees and with devotion

My Lord Jesus Christ, I give to you infinite graces, because by the merits of your Most Holy Passion, of your precious Blood, and by your infinite goodness, you deigned to deliver me from the demon, or sorceries and its malefactions; and

Exorcisms

so I ask, and pray now to you, to deign to preserve me and keep me so the demon from now on cannot molest me in any way; because I want to live and die under the protection of your Most Holy Name. Amen. P.N.A.M.

WARNING TO THE RELIGIOUS

When at the end of all these orisons the sick does not become entirely free, the religious, after three days, must ask about the ameliorations of the sick. When he sees that he is still possessed by the demon (and to know it must read again to him the signs that are in Latin, certain that there are malefactions), then, in this case, it is an open dwelling and must take care soon to close it in the way that follows, after reading again to him the orison of Saint Cyprian.

The Way to Close a Dwelling

[GLT]

Take an iron key, a small one, and bless it as follows:

The Lord throws over you his Most Holy blessing and his Most Holy power to give you the efficacious virtue, so that the entire house or the door by which Satanas enters be closed by you; never the demon or his allies can enter through it, so may it be blessed, in the name of the Father, of the Son, and of the Holy Ghost. Jesus be with you.

[Sprinkle holy water over the key]

Most holy words that the religious must say when closing the dwelling. The key must be upon the chest of the sick as if they are closing a door.

Oh Omnipotent God, who from the bosom of the Eternal Father came to the world for the salvation of men, deign, Lord, to put rules upon the demon or demons, so that they no longer have the power or insolence to enter this dwelling.

Let its door be closed, as Peter closes the doors of heaven to the souls who want to enter there, first expiating their faults.

(The religious person pretends he is closing a door in the chest of the sick.)

Deign, oh Lord, to allow Peter to come from the heavens to the earth to close the dwelling into which the damned demons want to enter whenever it pleases them.

Because I, (so and so), by your Most Holy name place rules upon these spirits of evil so that from today to the future they cannot make a dwelling in the body of (so and so), and this door will be perpetually closed to them, as is closed the one of the realm of the pure spirits. Amen.

At the end of said orison, write on a piece of paper the name of Satanas and burn it, saying, "Go, Satanas, disappear as the smoke of the chimney disappears."

At the end of all that was said, if the sick is still unhealed, say again the orison of Saint Cyprian.

Exorcism to Expel the Devil from the Body

[GLT]

This Exorcism was found in a very ancient book, written by the friar Bento do Rosário, religious from the order of Saint Augustine.

In the name of the Father, of the Son, and of the Holy Spirit; in the name of Saint Bartholomew, of Saint Augustine, of Saint Cajetan, Saint Andrew Avellino, I forswear you, evil angel, who pretends to introduce yourself inside me and pervert me. By the power of the Cross of Christ, by the power of your divine wounds, I conjure you, damned, so you cannot tempt my quiet soul. Amen.

This must be said three times, and at the same time the sign of the cross over the breast must be made.

Why God Allows the Demon to Torment Creatures

[GLT]

I

So that this man, obstinate in his faults, serves as a terror and example to other men.

II

So that the ones who are not obstinate are chastised only in this world by their faults.

III

So that men, seeing himself being chastised by the demon, flee from offending God.

IV

To punish some light fault, which is needed to quickly satisfy the justice of God.

V

To ensure that the ones who are in grace do not fall from it.

VI

To make sinners repent, seeing with their own eyes the scourge of divine justice.

VII

To manifest the power of God.

VIII

To show the holiness of some creatures.

IX

To increase the merits of corrupted creatures.

X

To purify more his chosen.

XI

So that creatures can undergo purgatory in this world and are confounded, seeing that from their evils good results for others.

Why God Allows the Demon to Torments Creatures

[TDH]

I

So that this man, obstinate in his faults, serves as a terror and example to other men.

II

So the ones who are not entirely evil receive the punishment in this world for the faults they commit.

III

So the person who sees himself punished by the demon recognizes God and humbles himself before him.

IV

To punish minor faults and look for correction.

V

To correct men, seeing with their eyes the truth of the divine justice.

VI

To appreciate the great Power of God.

VII

To show the great holiness of some creatures.

VIII

To increase the merits of corrupted creatures, turning them back to the good way.

IX

To purify more in every sense.

X

So creatures may undergo purgatory in this world and correct themselves seeing that from so many evils can come so many goods.

Names of the Demons

who torment the creatures, and why God consents that they mortify them; how many castes there are of demons or corrupted creatures

[GLT]

There are the obsessed, the possessed, and the accursed. From those, some are accursed and possessed, others are accursed, possessed, repetitious, pythonic, lunatics, and fascinated.

The obsessed are the ones who the demon torments, being outside the body.

The possessed are the ones who have demons inside the body.

The accursed are the ones who the demon pesters or molests with pains and maladies through the work of sorcery.

The possessed accursed are the ones who are enchanted and jointly possessed by the demon.

The possessed accursed are the ones the demon persecutes from outside.

The repetitious are the ones the demon suspends or snatches in the air, who are the ones who have a pact.

The pythonic are the ones who have a divination spirit.

The lunatics are the ones that are tormented during the waxing and the waning of the Moon.

The fascinated are the ones the demon moves to work or to speak without knowing what they say.

On Ghosts

On ghosts which appear at the crossroads, or souls from the spiritual world, who on mission from God come to this corporeal world in search of orisons to be purified from the mistakes they committed in this world against the Lord our God

[GLT]

What are ghosts?

They are visions that appear to certain individuals of weak spirit who believe that the souls of the ones who have already left existence can return to this world. As such, the ghosts appear only to these believers in spiritual beings and not to the unbelievers, since from this they do not profit, but instead receive curses.

Ah! What will become of those that work like that, unhappy, in this world, who did not do anything beyond mocking the servants of the Lord, who come to this world in search of relief and to find penance? Their torments are doubled.

Ah! What will become of you in the day you are sentenced? If you do not have good friends who pray for you to the supreme Judge, if you do not have friends, you will be punished with all the rigor of Justice.

So, cultivate, cultivate good friends, so that on that tremendous day there are good friends praying to the Creator on your behalf; act like the farmer who, to harvest a lot of fruit on the day of Saint Michael, put into the soil good things.

Note well, brothers, that these words are not the work of the beak of the quill, but are inspired from the depths of the heart! When a vision appears to you, do not conjure it, because then it will curse you, will disturb all your businesses, and everything will go awry for you; however, when you feel a vision, resort to the orison that is mentioned in this book with the title *Orison for the Good spirits,* because you will soon relieve that beggar who searches for alms from charitable people.

Note, brothers, that the Devil, on a very few occasions, appears as a ghost, because the demons were once angels and do not have bodies with which to clothe themselves; because of this, I recommend that, when you see a ghost in animal form, it is certainly a Demon, and you must conjure it and make a ✠. But, if the ghost is a human figure, it is not Demons, but certainly a soul who seeks relief to its penances. You must quickly say the orisons that appear in this small book: You will not lose anything by it, because this soul that you delivered will be always with you whenever you call it. Do not trust me; perform the experiment and you will see.

Pray, pray for these wretched spirits, and invoke them in all your business and in everything as it pleases you; then you will be successful, I swear.

Happy is the creature who is persecuted by spirits, because it is certain that he is a good person, whom the spirits persecute so he might pray to the Lord for them, because he is worthy of being heard by the Creator. It is for this reason that some are more persecuted by ghost than others. Now, there are many spirits that do not adopt the system of appearing as ghosts, but appear at the houses of their parents, making noise at night, dragging chairs, tables, and everything inside the house: One day they kill a pig, on the other a cow, and so everything runs backwards in that house for lack of intelligence from the inhabitants, because if they resorted quickly to the orisons, they would be delivered from the spirits and would do a charitable work, and, in the last day of their lives, the gates of heaven would be open for them. Note, brothers, these words, and consecrate them in your heart, that I claim that, because of this work, many souls will be saved, and I claim that mistakes are not committed.

Exorcisms

Orison to Ask God for the Good Spirits

who come to this world seeking orisons to be purified from the evils they committed in this world, and to restitute some debt or theft

[GLT]

This orison must be said in any place where it is needed, or in which a spirit or ghost wanders. At the end of this orison the Creed and the Act of Constriction are said.

Leave, Christian soul, this world in the name of Almighty God, the Father who created you; in the name of Jesus Christ, Son of the living God, who suffered for you; in the name of the Holy Spirit, who abundantly communicated to you. Go away from this body or place where you are, because the Lord receives you in his kingdom; Jesus, listen to my orison and be my shelter as you are the shelter to the Holy Angels and Archangels; to the Thrones and Dominations, to the Cherubims and Seraphims; to the Prophets, to the Holy Apostles, and to the Evangelists; to the Holy Martyrs, Confessors, Monks, Religious, and Hermits; to the Holy Virgins and wives of Jesus Christ, and to all the Saints of God, who concedes to give you a place of rest, and the enjoyment of the eternal peace in the holy city of Sion, where you will praise him through all the centuries. Amen.

LET US PRAY

Merciful God, clement God, God who, after the greatness of your infinite mercy forgives the sins of this spirit who is in pain for having committed them and who gives him the liberal absolution from past faults and offences, put the eyes of your compassion on this your servant who wanders in this world in penance; open to him, Lord, the doors of heaven, be propitious when you listen to him and grant him the absolution of all his sins, because with all his heart he asks this from you through his humble confession. Renew and repair, oh most merciful father, the breaks and ruins of this soul and the sins he made and acquired by weakness or by cunning and the deception of the devil. Accept him to become part of the body of your Triumphant Church. As a living member of your Church, freed by the precious blood of your Son, have compassion, Lord, to his moans; let his tears and sobs move you; let his and our entreaties touch you. Shelter and help he who had put his hope only in your mercy, and instate him in your friendship and grace, by the Love you have for Jesus Christ your beloved Son, he who with you lives and reigns through all the centuries of the centuries. Amen.

Oh, soul who wanders atoning for your faults, I entrust you to God Almighty, brother of mine most dear, for whom I ask God to give shelter and favor as a creature of his, so that paying with death the punishment of this life you come to see the Lord as the sovereign creator, he who formed you from the dust of earth; when your soul leaves from the body, the shining army of Holy Angels will come to escort you, defend you, and celebrate you; let the glorious college of the Holy Apostles favor you, being defender judges of your cause; let the triumphant legions of invincible martyrs shelter you; let the most noble company of the illustrious confessors receive you in their midst, and with the gentle perfume of lilies and of the white lilies they bring in their hands, symbols of the perfumed smoothness of their virtues, let them comfort you; let the choirs of the happy and content Holy Virgins receive you; let all that blissful company of celestials and courtiers with tight embraces of true friendship give you entrance into the glorious bosom of the Patriarchs; let the face of your Redeemer

Jesus Christ present itself to you pitiful and pleasant, and let him give you a place among the ones that forever assist in his presence. Never let you experience the horror of the eternal darkness, or the noises of its flames, nor the penances which torment the condemned. Let the damned Satanas surrender with all his allies, and when you pass by him, in the company of the Angels, let the miserable tremble and fearfully retreat to the dense darkness of his dark abode.

Go, soul; let your martyrdom be finished because you no longer belongs to this corporeal world, but to the celestial. Let God who favors you free you and disband all enemies who abhor you; let them flee from your presence; let the rebellious and damned demons disappear like the smoke in the air and like the wax in the fire; and let the just and content sit in safety with you at the table of your God. Let the infernal armies confuse themselves and, affronted, retreat, so the ministers of Satanas will not dare to hinder your way to heaven. Let Christ free you from hell, he that was crucified for you; free yourself from these agonies in which you walk in this world, tormenting and being tormented.

Christ, who gave his life for you, let Christ, Son of the living God, place you in the fields and forests of Paradise, which never dries or withers, and as the true shepherd, he will recognize you as a lamb of his flock. Let him absolve you from all your sins and sit you at his right hand among the chosen and the predestined; let God make you so joyous, that forever assisting in his presence you shall know with blissful eyes the manifest truth of his divinity, and in the company of the courtiers of heaven, you will enjoy the sweetness of his eternal contemplation through all the centuries. Amen.

Visions and Apparitions

[TDH]

There are few people in the world who did not witness or have not heard about some fantastical incident happening in their family, village, or place where they live. Such apparitions are much more frequent than some believe. Sometimes, it is a beloved one who presents herself after death in a spiritual form once or twice. Sometimes, it is a virtuous person who by divine permission is allowed to be seen by those who invoke or remember her in his thought. Sometimes, finally, there are those who, having done harm to another person, receive the order from the Supreme Spirit to appear to their relatives so they can amend the injuries they caused, or even to whom they caused harm, in search for forgiveness.

These last are the ones who generally are called lost souls, who beg forgiveness from their fellows so they can rest in peace in the mansion that the Sovereign Maker appointed for them.

Apart from these apparitions that we can call personal, there are others that, although more rare, are as true as the others. In many traditions, there are references to cases of some people who were visited by virgins, holy women, damsels, or ladies with translucent appearance, and also by malign spirits, which after appearing and addressing them, vanished without leaving any trace of their presence.

The apparitions can be natural or provoked. The natural ones are those that, like it was said, are produced without the person playing any part in the incident that we can call psychic or psychological, and the provoked ones are those which happen through a particular disposition of our senses, and most especially through the sensations of the imagination, which can produce in certain cases the phenomenon of the double view.

To come to produce these apparitions, it is necessary first to put to use a powerful will and make the imagination constantly occupied with the idea of the spirit that is desired to be invoked. Any minor distraction would make the desired apparition absolutely impossible; on the contrary, if you succeed in concentrating the imagination as we propose, the result will not be delayed, because the spirit will be forcefully attracted by the magnetic current that develops between it and the person who solicits its apparition.

It can be said then that the person with clear intelligence, great faith, and powerful will is able to see it, something that the distracted and the obtuse will not achieve, because they cannot concentrate on the required mental work.

As a demonstration of this truth, we could cite an infinite number of cases that occurred to people who, because of their affections and feelings toward their loved ones that were already dead, by force of thinking about them and keeping them constantly in their imagination, succeeded in making the spirit appear, but in the same image it had when living with them.

We are not going to finish this chapter without mentioning, even if briefly, the visions. These are distinct from apparitions because their action is faster, because as soon as the vision is presented to our sight, it disappears, as if by enchantment. The visions appear usually on roads, ways, crossroads, or in ruined places. There are mentions about entire processions of friars, monk women and funeral processions, and, finally, of celestial spirits which appear and disappear with the speed of the lightning.

Exorcisms

And on the way to know if a person suffers from sorceries or from natural infirmities

[TDH]

Exorcisms serve to expel spirits when they possess someone, whom they make suffer horribly with temptations and torments. Sometimes they suggest to the possessed strange thoughts and repulsive words, and force him to say blasphemies and furious screams.

It is convenient to know before proceeding with the healing if the infirmity is caused by sorceries or if it is natural, because sometimes it happens that a disease which is unknown to doctors is attributed to supernatural causes. When that happens, we can avoid any doubts by doing the following: Ensure that someone possessing an exterminator talisman puts his right hand over the head of the sick, saying to him with faith and will:

> *I ask and command, unknown spirit, in the name of the Supreme Being and of the admirable Adonay, that you declare the motives for which you are tormenting this body that I cover with my hand. I also want to know what you intend by doing this. I offer you, if you obey me, to pray to*

God for you so you can be purified and transported to the place where the celestial angels live.

The objective of this orison is to know if the spirit is wandering in this world in search of charity and orisons, because at the moment when it is said to him, *"I offer you, if you obey me, to pray to God for you,"* etc., the sick will become quiet and tranquil; but if this does not happen, everyone present will kneel and, elevating their soul to God, they will recite again the given orison.

It must be warned that in the same fashion good, but not perfect, spirits can be lodged in our body, as can the evil or harmful ones, and because of this, when the sick is found tranquil by virtue of the previous orison, we must suppose that he will be released by the prayers that every day are directed to the Most High in search of the forgiveness and purification of the spirit, which in gratefulness will stop molesting you; but if this spirit is evil or harmful, it will be known that, when hearing the orison, he will cause more torments and maladies to the sick. In this case, it must be expelled by the use of exorcisms. If the sick cannot perceive any change, it is proof that his infirmity is purely natural.

PRECEPT OR CONJURATION TO THE DEMONS TO NOT MORTIFY THE SICK DURING THE TIME OF THE EXORCISMS

I, as a creature of God, made in his likeness and redeemed with his blood, oblige you by this rule, demon or demons, so that your delirium stops and you no more torment with your infernal luxuries this body that serves as your dwelling. A second time I cite and notify in the name of the Sovereign Lord, strong and powerful, that you leave this place and go out, nevermore coming to occupy it. The Lord be with us, present and absent, so you, demon, cannot torment the creatures of the Lord anymore. Flee, flee, or else you will be tied with the chains of the Archangel Michael and humiliated with the orison of Saint Cyprian, dedicated to unmaking all kind of sorceries.

Next, you will say the following:

ORISON TO SAINT CYPRIAN

As a servant of God and creature of yours, I unbind from the malign spirit all that he has bound. In the name of the Divine Creator whom I have loved since I knew him, with all my heart, soul, and senses, and whom I promise to adore eternally, and also to whom I give thanks for the benefits that, like a loving father he concedes to me without measure or restraint, I command you, spirit of evil, to separate yourself right now from this body that you are tormenting and let it be free from your presence so it can with dignity receive the aspersions of exorcised water that, like the rain, falls over him, saying: In the name of the Father, of the Son, and of the Holy Spirits (do like that), who live eternally by the virtues possessed by the superior spirits, Adonay, Eloim, and Jehovam, whose presence and fortitude I invoke in this act. Amen.

All these invocations must be done with great faith and love of God, and it is certain that Satanas will not wait until the end of the following exorcism to deliver the possessed sick person.

EXORCISM TO DELIVER PEOPLE FROM THE EVIL SPIRITS

In the name of Saint Cyprian and from the part of God thrice holy, by the power of the superior spirits Adonay, Eloim and Jehovan and Mitraton, I, N., absolve the body of N., so it is freed from all evil sorceries, enchantments, and witchcraft, be they produced by men or women, or by any other cause. God be praised and glorified and deign to dispose that all witchcraft be unmade, destroyed, unbound, and reduced to nothing, so that the body of N. be free of all the ailments it suffers. Great and powerful God! Let your name be glorified, that by your sovereign intercession the spirits that have dwelled in this body of N. be forced to retire, ceasing now the witchcraft that the causers of this harm used. I conjure and command you to disappear without ever being able to enter this body over which I make three crosses[105], and I bless him with exorcized water in the name of the Father, of the Son, and of the Holy Ghost, that they support and protect N. so he will never again be tormented.

When saying these words, sprinkle him with holy water. It is convenient to know that he who executes the exorcism must be at the right side of the sick, and that the crosses are made precisely from the left to the right.

---

[105] Make, with the thumb of the right hand, a cross over the face, another over the chest, and another over the belly of the sick.

Exorcisms

EXORCISM TO DELIVER THE HOUSE FROM TEMPTING SPIRITS

> *I conjure you, rebel spirit, indweller and ruiner of this house, that without delay or pretext you will disappear from here, dissolving any malefaction that you or one of your helpers have done: I by myself dissolve them, counting on the help of God and the spirits of light Adonay, Eloim, and Jehovan, and I also want to tie you with the formal rule of obedience, so you cannot stay, nor return, nor send another, nor disturb this house, under the penance of being eternally burnt with the fire of melted pitch and sulfur.*

The whole house will be blessed with exorcized water and crosses will be made on all walls with the knife of white handle, saying:

> *I exorcize you, house-creature, so you be free from the tempting spirits who made you their dwelling.*

It is good to know that when malign spirits show themselves in houses making noises and giving blows without attacking people, it is because they do not have domain over them, because their hands carry the mark of the cross of Saint Bartholomew or because the spell only allows them to molest without touching people.

EXORCISMS AGAINST THE OS CONTRA LOS PEDRISCOS AND HURRICANES

The conjuration, as the crosses, must be repeated four times in the directions of the four cardinal points.

I conjure you, clouds, hurricanes, hailstorms, hailstones, and torments, in the name of the great living God of Eloim, Jehovan, and Mitraton, to dissolve you as salt in water without causing any harm or damage.

After saying this, take the knife of white handle and make four crosses in the air as if you cut from top to bottom and from left to right.

How to Prepare the Blasting Rod to Punish the Devil

[GLT]

Cut a stick from a hazel tree, large enough to hold three nails of three centimetres, after the said stock is prepared, that is, without the nails.

HOW TO PREPARE THE NAILS

Kill a small virgin lamb with a steel knife, and as soon as the lamb is dead, take the knife to a smith, who will make with it three nails, and thrust them into the stick, one in one end and two in the other, all three in the middle, and this way you can punish the demon easily.

We declare that the knife must be put into the fire with the blood of the lamb. The chains to fasten the demon can be the horns of a ram or, better, the blessed string of Saint Francis, or a stole blessed by a priest during Mass, at least eighteen times.

Orison to Place Rules upon Demons

[GLT]

This orison is made when conjuring for a pregnant woman, because some harm can happen to her due to the great convulsions. It is also good to place this precept for anyone who is attacked by a malady, so it does not continue.

> *I command, by the virtue of the Most Holy Name of Jesus, the demon or demons who cause such-and-such infirmity, affliction, or pain (name it) to stop moving it and desist, leaving the humors, that from any part they move, or have been moving equally, with all the other operations be free to serve my good God. And if such affliction is moved by any humor, even if it is natural or elementary, by the virtue of the Most Holy Name of Jesus, with all my faith, I command you to compose yourself and cease your disorder, so without this affliction and pain I can serve and praise, with all my heart, my God and Lord Jesus Christ, for whose love alone I live, and I want health as the health of my Redeemer.*
>
> V. Omnis, qui invocavit nomem Jesu.
> R. Ilic in tribulatione salvus erit.

True Orison to Expel the Demon from the Body

[GLT]

The importance of this orison, in some cabalistic combinations, is known by everyone who dedicates themselves to the study of the so-called occult sciences.

We are going to repeat it here, with all its purity, with all its exactitude and truth:

> *Immortal, eternal, ineffable, and saintly: Father of all things, who in a rolling chariot travels incessantly through these worlds that turn in the immensity of space: dominator of the vast and immense fields of ether, where you raised your powerful throne which sends light and light, from which your tremendous eyes discover everything and your large ears hear everything! Protect the children you have loved since the beginning of the centuries, because long and eternal is your duration. Your majesty shines above the world and the stars! You elevate yourself above them, oh scintillating fire; and enlighten and conserve yourself through your own resplendence, from your essence coming out inexhaustible currents of light which feed your infinite spirit! This infinite spirit produces all things, and*

constitutes the undying treasure of matter, which cannot fault to the generation it encircles with the thousand forms it is surrounded by, and with which you clothed and filled the beginning. From this spirit also comes the origin of those most holy kings who are beside your throne and who compose your cohort; oh universal Father, oh unique Father of the blessed mortals and immortals! You have, in particular, powers that are wonderfully equal to your eternal mind and to your eternal essence. You established them superior to the Angels who announce to the world your wills. Finally, you created one more third order of the sovereigns of the elements.

Our practice every day is to praise you and adore your will. We burn with desire to possess you. Oh Father! Oh Mother! Tender Mother, the most tender of all mothers! Oh Son, the most precious of the sons! Oh form of all forms! Soul, spirit, harmony, names, and numbers of all things, keep us and be propitious to us. Amen.

Diabolic Spirits

which infest houses with noises, and the ways to avoid them

[GLT]

CHAPTER I

Experience has shown that some places and houses are infested by spirits which disquiet them with noises, apparitions, and other importunities.

In history, too, there is no lack of examples, referred to by serious authors, to whom due credit cannot be denied. Saint Augustine, in the book 22 of the City of God, and in chapter VII, mentions that those spirits brought sickness to animals and people who inhabited the house of a certain man called Hesperus, who exercised the office of tribune.

John the Deacon, in the life of Saint Gregory, chapter LXXXIX, says that this holy pontiff was very often molested by a malign spirit. With that objective, when he saw him praying, the spirit took the horses from the stables, having suddenly startled two of them, appeared in the form of a cat to two religious men who were at the Saint's home, trying to scratch them, and other times as the figure of a Moor, trying to wound them with a spear.

Plutarch, in the life of Dionysius of Syracuse, tells that one afternoon he was thoughtful, and a woman of extraordinary greatness appeared to him, with a terrible and dreadful visage, as if she was some infernal fury, and began to very quietly sweep the floor of the room. Dionysius was very scared by this visit, called his friends and told them of the vision, and asked them not to leave him alone that night, fearing the monster would repeat the visit, which was not repeated [sic]; however, a small son of Dionysius, on a childish and brief accident, fell from the highest part of the house and died.

The father Possevino, from the Society of Jesus, also made reference in the life of Antonio Barreto, senator of Tolosa, that to his wife, a very spiritual matron, appeared a woman of high stature, whose visit gave her such a fright that for the space of 24 hours she was continually trembling, without being able to sustain the movement which agitated her.

Cardan in book 16, chapter LXXIII of the *Rerum Variet,* says that the noble and principal family of the Torrelles in Perma possesses a fortress where it is seen, on certain occasions, in the chimney of the house, an old lady, appearing to be a hundred years old.

More notable is the history referred to by Johannes Trithemius, in the description of the monastery of Hirsau. He says that around the year of 1132, at some place in Saxony, there was seen a little man without his hat on the head, who for this reason was called by the Saxons *Hudekin,* which in the Latin language means *Pileatus,* and must have been what in our language we call *fradinhos de mão furada.*[106]

Many notable things were told of him: that he liked to talk with men, to whom he appeared in peasant clothes; other times, invisibly, he made big bruises and pulled pranks. He gave important warnings to high people and was not averse in helping with the work of the servants. He served in the kitchen of the bishop, and recommending to him a certain man that kept his wife during his absence, he served him with punctual diligence,

---

106   Literally, "small friar of the perforated hand"; a kind of familiar spirit in Portugal, who can be beneficent or mischievous according to the circumstances.

keeping away whoever could unquiet her honesty. He did harm to none, unless provoked, because then he felt it and took revenge.

There was a lad who was a servant in the kitchen of the bishop, who got very familiar with this spirit, and with much trust told him some insults. He complained to the kitchen master to reprimand him, but seeing that he did not mend with heedfulness, drowned him and cut the body into slices and roasted it in the oven, and by other means offended the master of the kitchen and other servants of the bishop. Here it is seen how harmful it can be to the body and soul to have any familiarity with disguised demons.

Alexander ab Alexandro, in chapter IX of *Dierum Genial,* tells that in Rome a man had a very particular friend, who by reason of a certain infirmity was forced to take the baths at Puçol. They both took to the road, and with the disease becoming graver, the sick man died in an inn. The friend buried the cadaver and, having completed his pious office, he continued his journey to Rome. Being in a store, he laid in a bed to sleep, and whilst he was still awake, he saw coming into the house the same dead man with a pale and emaciated visage, like in the time of his sickness.

Terrified by this spectacle, he asked who he was, but the figure, without answering, came closer to the bed, took the clothes he appeared to carry, and lay in the bed in the action of trying to embrace the living friend. This one, afflicted with dreadful anguish, threw him away with force, and the dead man took again his clothes and looked at him with a scowling face, left, and disappeared, but after this incident, the friend experienced a very grave and dangerous infirmity. He used to say, after, that when touching the feet of the deceased, when he pushed him away, he felt it colder than the snow.

Gordian, another person known to the same author, walked with a servant to Arezzo, and after getting lost on the road came to some brushwood, large and uncultivated, where there were no houses, cottages, or any sign of human presence.

They wandered by many rustic bushes, with great fear caused by that dreary solitude, until, at the end of the afternoon, they sat down to rest from their fatigue. They thought they could hear far away the voice of a man, and supposing that it could be someone to show the way, they came closer. At the top of the hill, they saw three horrible figures of extraordinary height, with dark and long tunics, with long hair and beards and dreadful visages.

The travellers called out to these men, who drew closer until they could see them better: They were greatly gigantic, and between them another one was naked, jumping around, and making indecent gestures.

Agitated by excessive fear, the travellers fled at maximum speed, until after running over many trails and mountainous precipices, they found a cottage of a farmer where they took shelter.

About himself, the same author says that, being sick in Rome, and waking up on one occasion, he saw before him a woman of elegant presence whom he watched for a long time, considering if it was a trick of his own imagination. Finding out that his senses were perfect and his muscles vigorous, he asked the woman who she was. She repeated the same question with a sneering smile and vanished as if by magic.

André Tiraqueau, in the notes he made to the aforementioned Alexander, put these incidents down to dreams, but it is not impossible or unbelievable that demons use such tricks, with which they always search, with deceit, to do harm, to make us fall with some mistake or sin, as is shown by their ridiculousness as they seem to enjoy afflicting and prejudicing the souls of creatures so much.

Nonnulus, says Cassiano Callat: *Immundorum spiritum quos etiam. Faunnus vulgo appellat, ita seductores.*

See also the very learned priest Manuel Bernardes, from the Oratory of Saint Philip Neri, in his *Floresta*, book 1, title 10, where with his usual erudition he treats similar subjects and refers to many cases of demonic spirits.

CHAPTER II

REMEDY AGAINST THE SPIRITS

On the subject of remedies, the heathens used many useless and vain superstitions to be freed from these works, which the devil perhaps complied with to further confirm the same superstitious diligences and mistakes of men.

Apollonius of Tyana convinced himself that saying insults to these spirits caused them to go away or become quiet, stopping their hindrances.

But he was mistaken, because offensive words do not have by themselves such force, and nor did God give them this operative power, only giving that power to the words that the Church uses in the correct exorcisms to cause a fear of God in demons and to constrain them to obey the priest.[107]

In the same fashion, the ones who pretend to expel these spirits by the force of arms are mistaken, as if these incorporeal substances could be mistreated with iron.

It seems they want to follow the advice of Sybil, who said to Aeneas when he entered hell, as Virgil narrated, to take the sword to defend himself from the Stygian shadows.

Others considered that it was very important to have a flame or lit fire.

The flame favors somehow the experience, which shows that more commonly these spirits mistreat men in the darkness of night than in daylight, although at this time the stories refer to some hindrances.

In favor of the fire seem to be some happenings that Paulinus refers to in the *Life of Saint Ambrose*.

The empress Justine tried, by several means, to take the life of the Saint doctor and decided, at last, to talk with Innocent, a sorcerer, so that he could take it by the art of the demons. He set some demons to the task, which returned, saying that they could not reach even the doors of the

---

107   Read the first part of the *Great Book of Saint Cyprian*.

house of the Saint, because an impassable fire surrounded and defended the whole building in which they burned. However, this fire we can understand to be divine protection, which surrounded Saint Ambrose and caused torment to the demons so they did not dare to come to him and offend him.

Leaving, then, some superstitions used by the ancients that Alexander and others refer to, the true and efficient remedies are the ones used by the church; these are the sign of the Holy Cross ✠ and the invocation of the Most Holy Names of Jesus and Mary, the exorcisms of the church, fasting, orisons, conjurations, relics of the Saints, blessings upon houses, aspersions of holy water, and others like this.

But, be warned, that it is not always malign spirits that appear as dire figures and cause noises in houses.

They can originate from different principles, as can be seen in the following examples.

In Athens, there was a group of spacious houses belonging to one family, but they were uninhabited because of the well-known rumors spread about them.

When the silence of the night came, it could be heard in them, as if from far away, the dragging of irons and chains; then it sounded nearer, and at last, a shadow or figure appeared of an old man with a squalid aspect, emaciated face, long beard, unkempt hair, with his hands fastened in chains and his feet in the fetters he dragged.

When this vision began the residents passed grievous nights and vigils, and were pierced with fear, which brought sickness and even death to some of them.

For this reason, they stopped, completely, inhabiting the houses, but the owner wanted to see if could find some profit, by sale or rent from someone who ignored the defect, and so put writings on the houses offering a limited rental. To Athens came the philosopher Athenodorus, who read the writings and quickly became suspicious of the houses. He asked around and, discovering the reason, for that very reason decided to rent the properties.

Exorcisms

Once inside, he ordered to be put on the table a light and an inkpot, and telling his servants to retire to the inner houses, with all application of his disposition and sight, began to write, to avoid the unemployed imagination pretending vain things.

By this time, nightfall began, and soon he started to hear the noises of iron and the dragging of chains, but he did not raise his eyes or drop the quill, and just listened.

The sound grew even louder and was already felt in the room, and here Athenodorus raised his eyes and saw the figure people talked about, which stopped and made with its hand a beckoning gesture.

In the same fashion, Athenodorus made a gesture to wait and, inclining again to the table, continued to write.

The shadow came closer, making a greater noise over his head. The philosopher got up, took the light and followed his steps, which were slow, as of someone loaded with chains.

When they came to a backyard of the house, suddenly the shadow disappeared, so Athenodorus gathered some herbs and leaves and put them, as a sign, in the place where the shadow disappeared.

After some time without the shadow chasing him, he called the magistrate to have the place he had marked dug up, and they found the bones of some person, covered in chains, bones only because soil and time had already consumed the flesh.

The bones received public and sacred sepulchre, and after that, there were no more noises heard in the houses.

This case is referred by Pliny the Younger, book 7, and his credibility seems to confirm other cases.

Saint Germanus, bishop of Auxerre, was walking in the height of winter, and with the night drawing in, he was looking for to take shelter, to rest from the journey that had tired him. Not far away was a house without a roof, almost entirely ruined, where for a long time nobody had lived, and because of that there was born a bush of thistles and nettles within it.

It seemed to him better to stay in the fields than to retire to such habitation, especially because two old practicers from the area claimed to him that in that house ghosts used to appear, for which reason it was uninhabited. However, the Saint prelate wanted to stay there for the night. He ordered his luggage to be put in one of the rooms leaving his companions there, who were taking a light meal, and went to another room with one of his clerics, whom he ordered to read a spiritual book.

After some time had passed, as the Saint was tired from the road and had not eaten anything, he slept, and suddenly there appeared to the lector cleric a horrible figure, and he heard a loud noise like big stones knocking against those ruined walls.

The cleric, frightened by this apparition, gave a loud shout which awakened the Saint, who, getting up and invoking the name of Jesus with an intrepid spirit, commanded the shadow to say who it was and what it wanted.

The shadow, with the humble voice of someone who begs, answered that it was the shadow or figure of the deceased buried in that house, with another companion of his, and that it disturbs other people, because they cannot rest, and then he asked if they wanted to help them through their orisons and suffrages the church does for the deceased.

The Saint felt pity for them and, with the light on, followed the shadow to be shown where the bodies were buried, which were found in the appointed area, with the chains with which they were killed when they were put into the grave.

They were given a decent burial, with the usual orisons of the church, and that habitation became quiet, without the noises being heard anymore.

This case is referred to in the *Life of Saint Dominic,* brought by Soeiro Gomes, on the 31 of July, chapter 7.

NECESSARY PREVENTION

To avoid and fight these apparitions, you must go to Mass every Sunday, and when entering the church, wet your right hand in the font of holy water, and cross yourself with it, besides what is exposed.

When leaving the temple, you must take a portion of holy water and always have it by the head of your bed, using every morning two drops to wash your face.

Prayer of Saint Michael against Satan and the Rebel Angels

This prayer was added in 1886 to the Leonine Prayers which in 1894 Pope Leo XIII ordained to be said after the Missa Lecta (Low Mass).

Sancte Michael Archangele,
defende nos in proelio;
contra nequitiam et insidias diaboli esto praesidium.
Imperet illi Deus, supplices deprecamur:
tuque, Princeps militiae Caelestis,
satanam aliosque spiritus malignos,
qui ad perditionem animarum pervagantur in mundo,
divina virtute in infernum detrude.
Amen.

Saint Michael the Archangel,
defend us in battle;
be our protection against the wickedness and snares of the devil.
May God rebuke him, we humbly pray:
and do thou, O Prince of the heavenly host,
by the power of God,
thrust into hell Satan and all the evil spirits
who prowl about the world seeking the ruin of souls.
Amen.

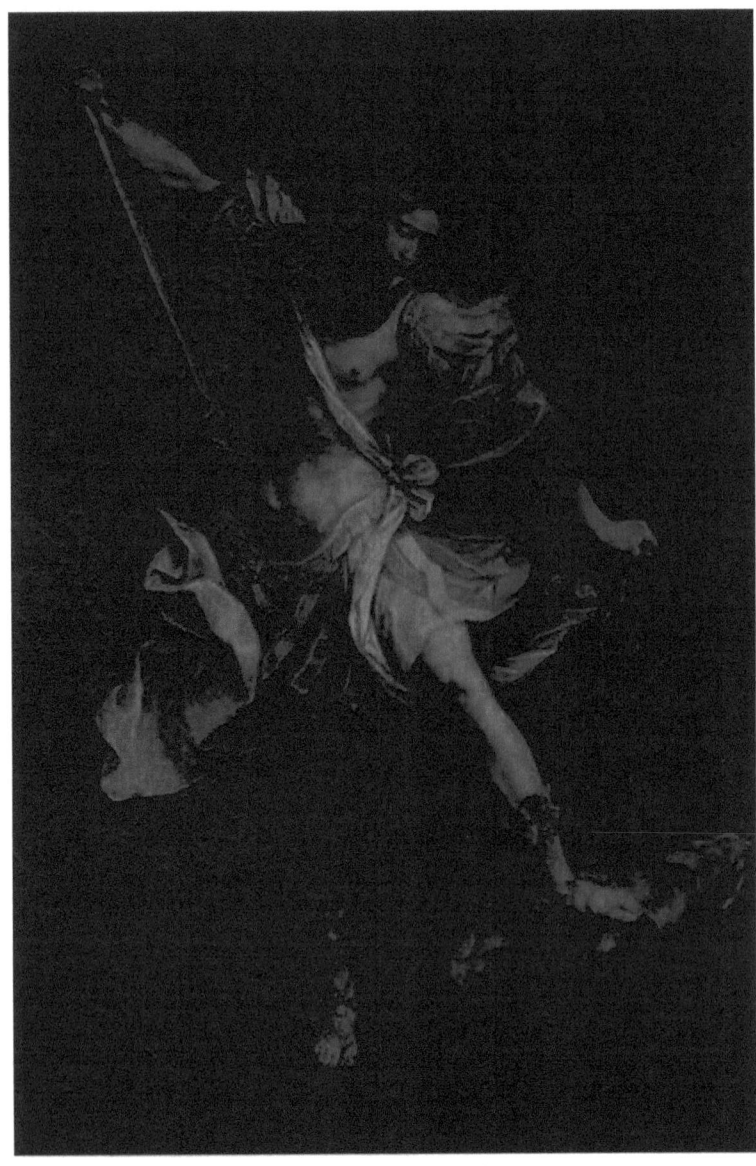

Michael the Archangel, de *Guido Reni*, Santa
Maria della Concezione, Rome, 1636.

ANOTHER PRAYER OF SAINT MICHAEL

This prayer was approved by the Catholic Church in 18 of May of 1890, twenty years after the capture of Rome. This prayer was included to precede the series of prayers of exorcism of the Roman Ritual.

O glorious Archangel St. Michael, Prince of the heavenly host, defend us in battle and in the struggle which is ours against the principalities and Powers, against the rulers of this world of darkness, against spirits of evil in high places. Come to the aid of men, whom God created immortal, made in his own image and likeness, and redeemed at a great price from the tyranny of the devil. Fight this day the battle of the leader of the proud angels, Lucifer, and his apostate host, who were powerless to resist thee, nor was there place for them any longer in Heaven. But that cruel, that ancient serpent, who is called the devil or Satan, who seduces the whole world, was cast into the abyss with all his angels.

Behold, this primeval enemy and slayer of man has taken courage. Transformed into an angel of light, he wanders about with all the multitude of wicked spirits, invading the earth in order to blot out the names of God and Christ, to seize upon, slay, and cast into eternal perdition souls destined for the crown of eternal glory. This wicked dragon pours out, as a most impure flood, the venom of his malice on men of depraved mind and corrupt heart, the spirit of lying, of impiety, of blasphemy, and the pestilent breath of impurity, and of every vice and iniquity.

Lord, together with the holy angels, as already thou hast fought

These most crafty enemies have filled and inebriated with gall and bitterness the Church, the spouse of the Immaculate Lamb, and have laid impious hands on her most sacred possessions.

In the Holy Place itself, where has been set up the See of the most holy Peter and the Chair of Truth for the light of the world, they have raised the throne of their abominable impiety, with the iniquitous design that when the Pastor has been struck, the sheep may be scattered.

Arise then, O invincible Prince, bring help against the attacks of the lost spirits to the people of God, and bring them the victory.

The Church venerates thee as protector and patron; the holy Church glories thee as her defense against the malicious powers of this world and of hell; to thee has God entrusted the souls of men to be established in heavenly beatitude.

Oh, pray to the God of peace that He may put Satan under our feet, so far conquered that he may no longer be able to hold men in captivity and harm the Church. Offer our prayers in the sight of the Most High, so that they may quickly conciliate the mercies of the Lord; and beating down the dragon, the ancient serpent, who is the devil and Satan, do thou again make him captive in the abyss, that he may no longer seduce the nations.

Exorcisms

This prayer was replaced in 1902, a year and a half before the death of Pope Leo XIII, by a much shortened prayer:

> O glorious Archangel St. Michael, Prince of the heavenly host, defend us in battle and in the struggle which is ours against the principalities and Powers, against the rulers of this world of darkness, against spirits of evil in high places. Come to the aid of men, whom God created immortal, made in his own image and likeness, and redeemed at a great price from the tyranny of the devil.
>
> The Church venerates thee as protector and patron; to thee has God entrusted the souls of men to be established in heavenly beatitude.
>
> Oh, pray to the God of peace that He may put Satan under our feet, so far conquered that he may no longer be able to hold men in captivity and harm the Church. Offer our prayers in the sight of the Most High, so that they may quickly conciliate the mercies of the Lord; and beating down the dragon, the ancient serpent, who is the devil and Satan, do thou again make him captive in the abyss, that he may no longer seduce the nations.

Exorcism

To oblige the demon to return the writing wherein the pact has been made with any person

[LM2]

Clementissime Deus, cujus potentiæ non, est finis, qui omnes creaturas tuas et res earum suprmeum habes sem perque retines dominium ita ut nihil sit quod tuo etiam per apostasiam eximi possit império; peccavimus in te tuamque provocavimus justissimam iracumdiam quando tuis mandatis non obedimus, atque tunc máxime quando ab imicitia tua et Domino fugientes te abnegavimus et impiorum dæmonum consortio nos adjunximus; el quasi non sufficeret abnegase te, etiam per scripturan nos dæmonibus obligavimus, et chirographum illud voluntariæ obligationis contra te illi tradidimus asservandum. Verum, clementisseme Domine, quia misericordiæ quoque tuæ non est numerus, et tibi proprium est misereri semper et parcere; hæc tua creatura quæ te abnegato se dæ monibus tradito chirographo obligavit, in se infinita tua bonitate reversa, suam detestatur impietatem, et timore tuo compuncta, abnegato rursus dæmone, tibi vero Domino subdi, atque in gratiam tuam recipi contrito corde desiderat. Scimus, domine, te cor contritum et humiliatum nunquam despicere, neque chirographumillid misericordiæ tuæ ullum impedimentum ponere posse ideoque supplices te deprecamur, ut abundantia pietatis tuæ non tantum h'ujus peccati impietatem per Sanguinem Filii tui domini nostri Jesuchristi remittas, sed et dæmonem ad restituendum chirographum obligationis et traditionis illius verbo vertitis tuæ acompellas: ne de sua tyrannide glorietur, ne jus aliquod prætendat in hominem, quem per Filium tuum peccatorum suorum vinculis adsolvi deprecamur, Per enmdem Dominun nostrum Jesum Christum Filium tuum, Exorcizo te, impie Satan, qui cum tuo excideris principatu tyrannicum in homines semper affectas imperium. Exorcizo te per Jesum Christum, qui venit in hun mundum peccator es salvos facere, ut ad hac creatura, quæ tuis fraudibus decepta se tibi traditit omne Tum imperium festinus amoveas. Ex hoc enim rursus te deserens, divinæ misericordiæ se committit, ut ei serviat, cui se totam debet, quique servientibus sibe æternæ vitæ mercedem promisit. Exorcizo te per pretiosum Sanguinem Jesu Christi, quo deletum est chirograplan decreti quod erat nobis contrarium, ita ut suscipiente Jesu peccatorem in gratiam suam adversus eum nihil amplius debeas præsumere, ut chirographum, que hæc creatura se tibi obligavit, cum per Sanguinem Christi abolitum sit, hic restituere non moreris.

Audi, maledicte Santam Dei servus nullan habet postestatem, ut invito Domino suo alterius se subjiciat servituti: unde tu frustra in vano isto gloriaris chirographo: ac proinde in nomine Domini tibi præcipio ut illud restituas, nec penes te diutius serves: ut omnibus constet, Deo pecatorem in gratiam recipienta, nullum tibi in animan ejus restare imperium.

Adjuro te per cum qui te cum in átrio tuo tamquam fortis armatus gloriareis eaque quæ posidebas in pace tenere procesumeres, infinitis partibus fortior superveniens vicit, et atrio te ejecit, tuaque arma, in quibus Vane confidebas, abstulit, et spolia distribuit. Redde igitur nunc chirographum, quo hæc Dei creatura stulte seibsam tibi traditi inservitutem: redde inquam, in nomine ejus a quo es devictuar: et cum tuam tyrannicam potestatem Just amiseria non præsumas illius vanunm chirographum dintius retinere. Iam enim per pœnitentiam hæc Del creatura vero suo Domino se restituit et tyrannidem tuam spernit, atque in Dei misericordia adversus tuas impugnationes sperat invenire protectionnem, adjuvante sanctissima et gloriosissima virgini Dei genitrice Maria, cuyus intercessione, quod per se consequi digna non est, a Filio ejus Jesu Christo obtineat. Per eumdem Dominum nostrum.

Magical Treasures

Way of using the Rod

To find hidden things

[HEM]

The Method to Hold the Rod

There are many methods to hold the rod, and they vary according to its form. The most usual is to hold it with both hands gently to allow it to turn, holding it in a way that the back of the hands are turned toward the ground. This rod must be crotched, so the end of the crotch will point forward and the rod is parallel to the horizon.

Another Method

The other method is to have the end of the crotch pointing up.

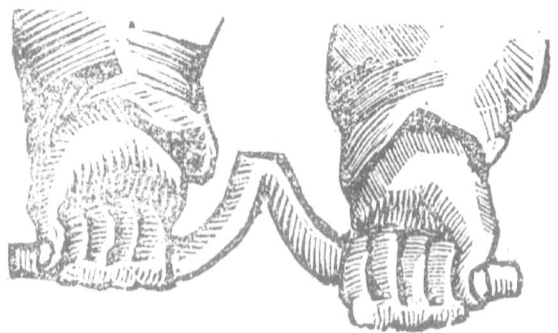

Another Method

It is to have the end of the crotch pointing downward. In all these cases, the back of the hands must always face the soil, as it is seen in the figures.

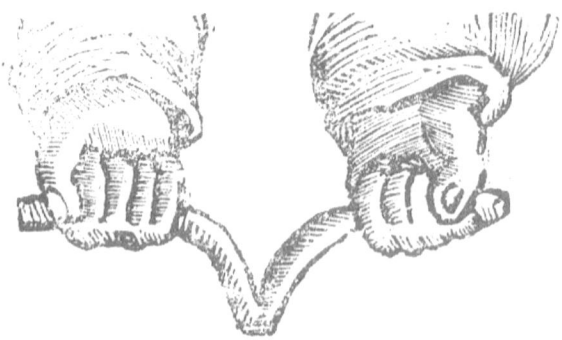

Other Method

The other method is to carry the horizontal rod on the palm of the hand, as a piece of wood is naturally carried.

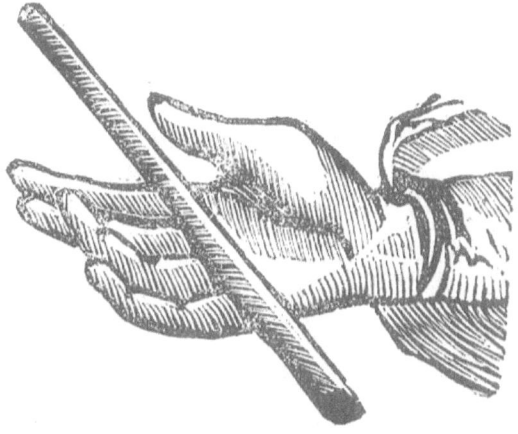

Another Method

The other is to take a sprouting without knots from one of the mentioned trees, break it into two equal halves, making a point on the end of one of the picks, to graft into the other.

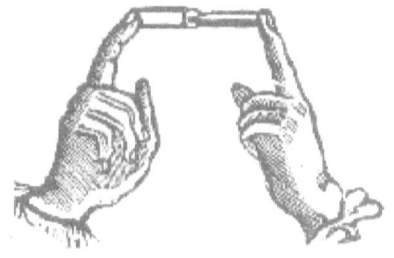

And, at last, it is with the hand extended so the palm faces the soil, and with the horizontal Rod balanced on the back of the hand.

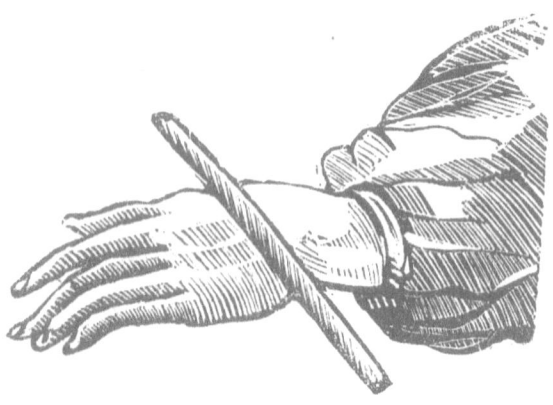

These are the more general methods of holding the rod with which I have executed a great amount of experiments that never failed.

The Way to Operate to find hidden things

To search for hidden things, like treasures, coins, waters, and everything lost, operate in the following way. Hold the road with your hands as has been described before, and walk step by step over the place where there are supposed to be mines, coins, treasures, etc. It is important to not rush or walk fast, because then the vapors or exhalations that rise from the place where the things are could impregnate the rod and make it turn.

Magical Treasures

When walking recite the psalm *De profundis... Credo videre hona Domini in terra viventium.* When you pass over the place where the sought after thing lies, the rod turns in A. B. A.

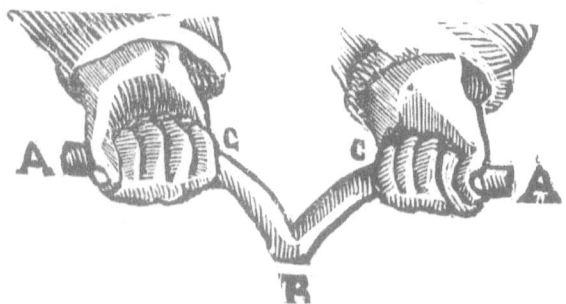

But, if the extremities of A.A. stand still, because you have the rod too tightly held in the hands, it will infallibly turn in C., because it will not be able to turn in other way because it is too tightly held. That will happen principally if the thing searched for is situated near the surface of the earth.

On the way the things over which the rod turns are identified

If you want to know if there is water when the rod turns when you pass by a certain place, then operate in the following manner. Wet a piece of cloth and wrap the rod in it. If it still moves, it is a sign that there is indeed water there. If metals, coins, etc., are searched for and the rod turns when you pass by the place where it is supposed to be hidden, to convince yourself that it is metal or coins, put on the holder of the rod some coin or metal, and if it still moves it is an infallible sign that in that place is hidden metals or coins, because the subterranean vapors which rise when finding metal; if it is metal that is searched for, or the humidity of water if it is water, make the rod insist on moving and give an evident certainty of the thing searched for. Then, if you have stopped walking, because when walking by another place the rod remains quiet, it is an indication that you have already found what is searched for.

If the vapors which rise from the earth where the objects are hidden move with speed in a way that the turn or movement of the rod is very perceptible, it is a sign that they are near the surface of the earth, and so it will be easy to take and find them. On the contrary, if the vapors leave slowly in a way that the movement of the rod is not very perceptible or impressive in the hands, it is a sign that the depth to the hidden things is great.

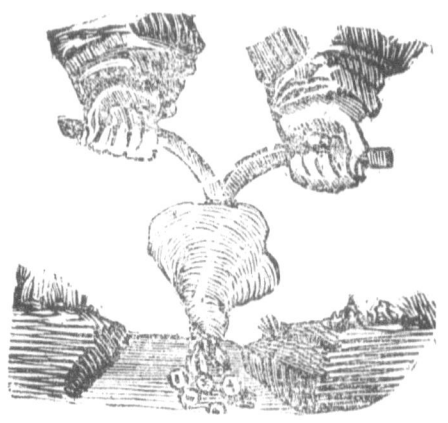

Magical Treasures

Sometimes the accumulation of hidden objects is such that it produces a very clear movement with the rod; then you should dig the place and observe the movement of the rod, and by the depth you dig, it will be known and you will be able to predict that the amount of the hidden thing is a great amount, because the more you dig the earth, more and more perceptible is the turning movement of the rod.

One of the most essential things when searching for hidden objects is that the feet are not dressed with materials containing metals, like iron nails or other materials made of metal, because it would prejudice notably the finding, and especially the distinction of the hidden things, so it is necessary to wear shoes made of materials entirely different from the object for which the experiments are searching. The shoes must be light and simple, woven with thread of pure hemp, and the sole or part which touches the earth should be made of cow leather, without any other matter on it. Because a shoe with edges of metal prejudices notably the movement of the rod, deviates the vapors which rises from the hidden things, and produces a result totally contrary to the purpose of the experiment. It is interesting to have present these rules, because from them come the good outcome of the operation.

When you want to know more or less the depth of the hidden treasures, operate using two branches of hazel with two sprouts, whose trunk is one year old and the sprouts from the same year, cutting these rods in a crutch like an Y, the branch being a foot long more or less, and the two sprouts prepared as we said before. To practice this operation, hold two branches or rods, one in each hand, pressing them against the chest one against the other in a straight line, leaving them to move freely when they want or when they began to move. When you pass over the place where treasures or coins are and observe its movement, you must return and begin anew the experiment, until the rods cross and incline downward or upward, which is a sign that you are directly above gold, silver, etc.; if they cross upward, it is a sign that treasures are hidden in the deep of the earth, but on the contrary, if they cross downward, they are closer to the surface of the earth.

Sometimes, the treasures or hidden things are hidden in rocks; then the rods must be held putting a rod above the other in an opposite position with their crutches parallel to the horizon, and if the treasures, coins, etc., are hidden in two places, one rod will point to one place and the other to the other place.

To know if the hidden metal is gold, silver, or any other, you must be aware that the rod produces a stronger movement when it is gold, less perceptible when it is silver, weaker when it is copper, weaker when it is lead, etc., being less perceptible as the metal is of inferior quality.

The person who is dedicated to search for hidden or secret things must possess a fine and sensitive touch; the mound of Mercury on his hand must be very marked, he must not be distracted by anything, must be a deep observer, and all his attention, his thought, and his sight must be fixed on the rod, because a little distraction will be the cause of losing time and not finding what is searched for.

Hidden Treasures in Enchanted Places

[HEM]

It happens many times that the rod does not have a movement and neither causes any sensation, no matter how much you pass by a place where treasures, coins, and hidden things are, and this is produced by an enchantment, which makes it so that no matter how much you try and walk according to all the rules said before, no result is achieved. Then you must operate first disenchanting the place in the following way.

First, you will draw over the place a magical circle with pure coal and, sprinkling it with holy water, say the following orison:

Lord, I appeal to your virtue, Lord, confirm this work because what we work is like the dust that the wind disperses; and being present the angel of the Lord, the darkness disappears, and the angel of the Lord always seeks after the Alpha, Omega, Ely, Elohe, Elbium, Zebaot, Elion Saday. Here is the victorious lion of the tribe of Judah, origin of David. I will open the book and its seven seals. I saw Satanas like a light fell from heaven. You are He who gave the power to reduce under our feet the dragons and scorpions and your enemies: Nothing will damn us, Eloy, Elohe, Zabahot, Elion, Esarchia, Adonay, Jah, Tetra, Gramaton, Saday. The land and all who inhabit it belong to God, because He made it above the seas and put on it the rivers. Who is the one who will climb to the mountain of the Lord? The innocent with pure hand and heart, who did not receive his soul in vain and did not swear hate to his fellow, will be blessed by God and will enjoy from His mercy for his salvation. This the generation of the ones who desire Him. Prince, open Your eternal doors and the king of glory will enter. Who is this king of glory? The all-powerful Lord, the Lord victorious in combats, princes, open your doors; raise the eternal doors. Who is this king of glory? The Lord all powerful; this Lord is the king of glory.

When the magical circle is ready, as was said, enter it, without taking any impure metal with you, only gold and silver, to throw the coin to the spirit. Wrap it in white paper on which nothing is written; it is thrown to the spirit to stop him from causing any harm; when he inclines to fetch it in front of the circle, say the following conjuration:

Demons who dwell in this place, or in any part of the world in which you are, and any power which was given to you by God and by the holy angels over this same place; demons, of any order who are dwellers of the Orient, Occident,

> *Noon and Septentrion on all parts of the earth, by the power of God the Father and creator who formed us from nothing, I command and oblige you of good or of ill will to declare your names and leave me in peaceful possession of this place: and from every legion to which you belong, and from any part of the world you dwell; by the power of the living and holy God, I unchain you, spirits who dwell in these places, and send you to the deepest of the infernal abysses. Go, then, damned spirits and be condemned to the eternal fire which is prepared for your companions; if you are rebellious and disobedient, I conjure you by the same authority, I call and command you by the sacred names of God, Hasin, Lon, Hilay, Sabaot, Helim, Radiaha, Ladicha, Adonay, Jehova, Ya, Tetragammaton, Saday, Macias, Agios, Ysquiros, Alfa and Omega, who are in the deepest abysses of fire justly established, in order that you do not have again the power to reside and dwell in this place, and I ask you to do this by the virtue of the said names, and let the archangel Michael throw you in the deepest infernal abyss. So mote it be.*

As soon as the conjuration is concluded, perfume the place with pure incense, not mixed with any other strange thing, because it would not produce the desired objective, three consecutive times, with an interval of a quarter of an hour between each time, and the place will be free from malefactions and enchantments.

If what is searched for is hidden inside a building or inside a cavern, and those are enchanted, you shall do the following. First, disenchant the place before going inside the building or the cavern as said before, and then you will enter the building or cavern and begin to disenchant it in the following way. Make three circles, one inside the other, the larger having nine feet of circumference: Put one inside the lesser, in which will be written the names of the angels who preside over the hour, the month, and the season. After writing the names in the circle, sprinkle with holy water, saying:

> God of Abraham, of Isaac and Jacob, deign to bless and sanctify these perfumes, so that its smell restrains the spirits I want to chase away.

Put the perfumes inside a vessel of new clay and say:

> I exorcise you, perfume, so your noxious ghosts flee from me.

You will take a virgin parchment on which you will draw crosses, calling from the four corners of the world the angels who preside over the air with these secret names, *Agla, On, Tetragammaton*, commanding them to help, and say the conjuration as it was said before. For all these operations, it is necessary to be purified for nine consecutive days. The perfumes mentioned must be made of equal parts of pepper, good herb, and palm of Christ.

If the treasures are hidden in a dark place, the light used must be composed of pure bear fat, of pure goat fat, and oil of alligator. With all these, make a candle whose fuse must be made of the toothache plant, and it will be useful in the case mentioned before.

I conclude this treatise recommending much valor, much prudency, to not step back because of any noise you hear, because these operations must be done at midnight, and whoever does not have valor should not expose himself, unless he searches for a talisman or amulet against the enchantments, although in these cases it is good to look for one; then, do not fear, because with it I defeated all the spirits and dominated all their ambushes and malefactions.

You must have present all the rules I gave, because any of them lacking, you will not succeed in what you want. Nature itself already indicates the persons who are apt to operate, through Chiromancy, Astronomancy, etc., which will be consulted, and ruled by these sublime sciences, you will have knowledge of the persons predestined to these ends.

Way to Disenchant Treasures

[LM3]

When in some place there are hidden riches kept by enchanted arts, in order to reach them you must first remove them from the enchantment that guards them.

The researches made will be useless if you do not proceed with the disenchantment first, because many men during many years could dedicate themselves to searching for the place where the treasure is and never be given to them the secret to putting their hands on it.

That is why first you must draw the magical circle, in the way described before, and once the conjurer and the persons who accompany him are inside it, the three must prepare themselves mentally for the operation to be executed, putting all trust in God and in his supreme mercy.

This requirement being fulfilled, the conjuror and the companions will get on their knees, always inside the circle—under no circumstances must you leave the circle, with the objective of not exposing yourselves to very grave dangers—and will pray aloud the following orison, which is the

First Conjuration

Unbinding of the Earth

Earth, you will create everything and you will eat everything—said our Lord God.

Ladainha dos Santos

Litaniae Sanctorum

[See next section - GLT]

Second Conjuration

[See next section - GLT]

When finishing the conjuration, dreadful ghosts may appear around you to infuse you with fear and to make you abandon, terrified, the enterprise without achieving your aims. Do not be afraid; these visions can do no harm to you and will disappear fleeing to their abodes as soon as you say the following:

Imprecation

Satanaz, go back to the deep hells, and you, damned ghosts, vanish. Jesus! Jesus! Jesus! defend me against all that surrounds me to stop me achieving my desires. Jesus! Jesus! Jesus! Come Lord to my aid, and you, Satanaz, retreat because you are already defeated. Your astuteness I destroyed with the holy power of Our Lord Jesus Christ. Your ghosts, enemies of human creatures, I conjure by the miraculous name of Saint Cyprian, by the virtue of the Lignun Crucis on which Our Lord Jesus Christ died for the men, by this sublime cross I command you, Satan, and make you my servant. Retreat Satanaz, make retreat the ghosts, enemies of human beings. Amen.

Disenchantment of Treasures

[GLT]

Everyone who assists the disenchantment of the treasure must be inside a triangle, as represented by the gravure above, which must be drawn on the floor, because being inside it, no harm can happen to them.

The Book of Saint Cyprian

Orison and Conjuration to disenchant the Treasures

First, pray the Litany of the Saints in a loud voice. If it can be said on the knees, it will be even better.

First Conjuration and unbinding of the earth

Earth, everything you will give and everything you will eat—said the Lord my God.

Litany of the Saints
Litaniae Sanctorum

Latin and Greek (original)	**English (translation)**
V. Kyrie, eléison.	V. Lord, have mercy.
R. Christe, eléison.	R. Christ, have mercy.
V. Kyrie, eléison.	V. Lord, have mercy.
V. Christe, audi nos.	V. O Christ, hear us.
R. Christe, exáudi nos.	R. O Christ, graciously hear us.
V. Pater de cælis, Deus.	V. O God the Father of heaven.
R. Miserére nobis.	R. Have mercy upon us.
V. Fili, Redémptor mundi, Deus.	V. O God the Son, Redeemer of the world.
R. Miserére nobis.	R. Have mercy upon us.

V. Spíritus Sancte, Deus.	V. O God the Holy Ghost.
R. Miserére nobis.	R. Have mercy upon us.
V. Sancta Trínitas, unus Deus.	V. O Holy Trinity, one God.
R. Miserére nobis.	R. Have mercy upon us.
V. Sancta María.	V. Holy Mary.
R. Ora pro nobis.	R. Pray for us.
V. Sancta Dei Génetrix.	V. Holy Mother of God.
R. Ora pro nobis.	R. Pray for us.
V. Sancta Virgo vírginum.	V. Holy Virgin of virgins.
R. Ora pro nobis.	R. Pray for us.
V. Sancte Michael.	V. Saint Michael.
R. Ora pro nobis.	R. Pray for us.
V. Sancte Gabriel.	V. Saint Gabriel.
R. Ora pro nobis.	R. Pray for us.
V. Sancte Raphael.	V. Saint Raphael.
R. Ora pro nobis.	R. Pray for us.
V. Omnes sancti Angeli et Archangeli.	V. All ye holy Angels and Archangels.
R. Orate pro nobis.	R. Pray for us.
V. Omnes sancti beatórum Spírituum ordines.	V. All ye holy orders of blessed Spirits.
R. Orate pro nobis.	R. Pray for us.
V. Sancte Joánnes Baptista.	V. Saint John the Baptist.
R. Ora pro nobis.	R. Pray for us.

V. Sancte Josephe.   V. Saint Joseph.
R. Ora pro nobis.   R. Pray for us.

V. Omnes sancti Patriárchæ et Prophetæ.   V. All ye holy Patriarchs and Prophets.
R. Orate pro nobis.   R. Pray for us.

V. Sancte Petre.   V. Saint Peter.
R. Ora pro nobis.   R. Pray for us.

V. Sancte Paule.   V. Saint Paul.
R. Ora pro nobis.   R. Pray for us.

V. Sancte Andrea.   V. Saint Andrew.
R. Ora pro nobis.   R. Pray for us.

V. Sancte Jacobe.   V. Saint James.
R. Ora pro nobis.   R. Pray for us.

V. Sancte Joánnes.   V. Saint John.
R. Ora pro nobis.   R. Pray for us.

V. Sancte Thoma.   V. Saint Thomas.
R. Ora pro nobis.   R. Pray for us.

V. Sancte Jacobe.   V. Saint James.
R. Ora pro nobis.   R. Pray for us.

V. Sancte Philippe.   V. Saint Philip.
R. Ora pro nobis.   R. Pray for us.

V. Sancte Bartholomæe.	V. Saint Bartholomew.
R. Ora pro nobis.	R. Pray for us.
V. Sancte Matthæe.	V. Saint Matthew.
R. Ora pro nobis.	R. Pray for us.
V. Sancte Simon.	V. Saint Simon.
R. Ora pro nobis.	R. Pray for us.
V. Sancte Thaddæe.	V. Saint Jude.
R. Ora pro nobis.	R. Pray for us.
V. Sancte Matthia.	V. Saint Matthias.
R. Ora pro nobis.	R. Pray for us.
V. Sancte Barnaba.	V. Saint Barnabas.
R. Ora pro nobis.	R. Pray for us.
V. Sancte Luca.	V. Saint Luke.
R. Ora pro nobis.	R. Pray for us.
V. Sancte Marce.	V. Saint Mark.
R. Ora pro nobis.	R. Pray for us.
V. Omnes sancti Apóstoli et Evangelistæ.	V. All ye holy Apostles and Evangelists.
R. Orate pro nobis.	R. Pray for us.
V. Omnes sancti Discípuli Dómini.	V. All ye holy Disciples of the Lord.
R. Orate pro nobis.	R. Pray for us.
V. Omnes sancti Innocéntes.	V. All ye Holy Innocents.

R. Orate pro nobis.	R. Pray for us.
V. Sancte Stephane. R. Ora pro nobis.	V. Saint Stephen. R. Pray for us.
V. Sancte Laurénti. R. Ora pro nobis.	V. Saint Lawrence. R. Pray for us.
V. Sancte Vincenti. R. Ora pro nobis.	V. Saint Vincent. R. Pray for us.
V. Sancti Fabiane et Sebastiane. R. Orate pro nobis.	V. Saint Fabian and Saint Sebastian. R. Pray for us.
V. Sancti Joánnes et Paule. R. Orate pro nobis.	V. Saint John and Saint Paul. R. Pray for us.
V. Sancti Cosma et Damiane. R. Orate pro nobis.	V. Saint Cosmas and Saint Damian. R. Pray for us.
V. Sancti Gervasi et Protasi. R. Orate pro nobis.	V. Saint Gervasius and Saint Protasius. R. Pray for us.
V. Omnes sancti Mártyres. R. Orate pro nobis.	V. All ye holy Martyrs. R. Pray for us.
V. Sancte Silvester. R. Ora pro nobis.	V. Saint Sylvester. R. Pray for us.

V. Sancte Gregóri.	V. Saint Gregory.
R. Ora pro nobis.	R. Pray for us.
V. Sancte Ambrósi.	V. Saint Ambrose.
R. Ora pro nobis.	R. Pray for us.
V. Sancte Augustine.	V. Saint Augustine.
R. Ora pro nobis.	R. Pray for us.
V. Sancte Hieronyme.	V. Saint Jerome.
R. Ora pro nobis.	R. Pray for us.
V. Sancte Martine.	V. Saint Martin.
R. Ora pro nobis.	R. Pray for us.
V. Sancte Nicolaë.	V. Saint Nicholas.
R. Ora pro nobis.	R. Pray for us.
V. Omnes sancti Pontifices et Confessores.	V. All ye holy Bishops and Confessors.
R. Orate pro nobis.	R. Pray for us.
V. Omnes sancti Doctores.	V. All ye holy Doctors.
R. Orate pro nobis.	R. Pray for us.
V. Sancte Antoni.	V. Saint Anthony.
R. Ora pro nobis.	R. Pray for us.
V. Sancte Benedicte.	V. Saint Benedict.
R. Ora pro nobis.	R. Pray for us.

V. Sancte Bernarde.
R. Ora pro nobis.

V. Sancte Dominice.
R. Ora pro nobis.

V. Sancte Francisce.
R. Ora pro nobis.

V. Omnes sancti Sacerdótes et Levitæ.
R. Orate pro nobis.

V. Omnes sancti Monachi et Eremitæ.
R. Orate pro nobis.

V. Sancta María Magdalena.
R. Ora pro nobis.

V. Sancta Agatha.
R. Ora pro nobis.

V. Sancta Lucia.
R. Ora pro nobis.

V. Sancta Agnes.
R. Ora pro nobis.

V. Sancta Cæcilia.
R. Ora pro nobis.

V. Saint Bernard.
R. Pray for us.

V. Saint Dominic.
R. Pray for us.

V. Saint Francis.
R. Pray for us.

V. All ye holy Priests and Levites.
R. Pray for us.

V. All ye holy Monks and Hermits.
R. Pray for us.

V. Saint Mary Magdalene.
R. Pray for us.

V. Saint Agatha.
R. Pray for us.

V. Saint Lucy.
R. Pray for us.

V. Saint Agnes.
R. Pray for us.

V. Saint Cecilia.
R. Pray for us.

V. Sancta Catharina.	V. Saint Catherine.
R. Ora pro nobis.	R. Pray for us.
V. Sancta Anastasia.	V. Saint Anastasia.
R. Ora pro nobis.	R. Pray for us.
V. Omnes sanctæ Vírgines et Víduæ.	V. All ye holy Virgins and Widows.
R. Orate pro nobis.	R. Pray for us.
V. Omnes Sancti et Sanctæ Dei.	V. All ye Holy, Righteous, and Elect of God.
R. Intercédite pro nobis.	R. Intercede for us.
V. Propitius esto.	V. Be thou merciful.
R. Parce nobis, Dómine.	R. Spare us, Lord.
V. Propitius esto.	V. Be thou merciful.
R. Exáudi nos, Dómine.	R. Graciously hear us, Lord.
V. Ab omni malo.	V. From all evil.
R. Líbera nos, Dómine.	R. Good Lord, deliver us.
V. Ab omni peccáto.	V. From all deadly sin.
R. Líbera nos, Dómine.	R. Good Lord, deliver us.
V. Ab ira tua.	V. From thine anger.
R. Líbera nos, Dómine.	R. Good Lord, deliver us.
V. A subitanea et improvisa morte.	V. From sudden and unrepentant death.
R. Líbera nos, Dómine.	R. Good Lord, deliver us.

V. Ab insídiis diaboli.

R. Líbera nos, Dómine.

V. Ab ira, et ódio, et omni mala voluntáte.
R. Líbera nos, Dómine.

V. A spíritu fornicatiónis.
R. Líbera nos, Domine.

V. A fulgure et tempestáte.
R. Líbera nos, Dómine.

V. A flagello terræmotus.

R. Líbera nos, Dómine.

V. A peste, fame et bello.

R. Líbera nos, Dómine.

V. A morte perpetua.
R. Líbera nos, Dómine.

V. Per mystérium sanctæ Incarnatiónis tuæ.
R. Líbera nos, Dómine.

V. Per advéntum tuum.
R. Líbera nos, Dómine.

V. From the crafts and assaults of the devil.

R. Good Lord, deliver us.

V. From anger, and hatred, and all uncharitableness.
R. Good Lord, deliver us.

V. From the spirit of fornication.
R. Good Lord, deliver us.

V. From lightning and tempest.
R. Good Lord, deliver us.

V. From the peril of earthquake, fire, and flood.
R. Good Lord, deliver us.

V. From pestilence, famine, and battle.
R. Good Lord, deliver us.

V. From everlasting damnation.
R. Good Lord, deliver us.

V. By the mystery of thy Holy Incarnation.
R. Good Lord, deliver us.

V. By thine Advent.
R. Good Lord, deliver us.

V. Per nativitátem tuam.	V. By thy Nativity.
R. Líbera nos, Dómine.	R. Good Lord, deliver us.
V. Per baptismum et sanctum jejunium tuum.	V. By thy Baptism and holy Fasting.
R. Líbera nos, Dómine.	R. Good Lord, deliver us.
V. Per crucem et passiónem tuam.	V. By thy Cross and Passion.
R. Líbera nos, Dómine.	R. Good Lord, deliver us.
V. Per mortem et sepultúram tuam.	V. By thy precious Death and Burial.
R. Líbera nos, Dómine.	R. Good Lord, deliver us.
V. Per sanctam resurrectiónem tuam.	V. By thy holy Resurrection.
R. Líbera nos, Dómine.	R. Good Lord, deliver us.
V. Per admirábilem ascensiónem tuam.	V. By thy glorious Ascension.
R. Líbera nos, Dómine.	R. Good Lord, deliver us.
V. Per advéntum Spíritus Sancti Paracliti.	V. By the coming of the Holy Spirit the Comforter.
R. Líbera nos, Dómine.	R. Good Lord, deliver us.
V. In die judícii.	V. In the day of judgment.
R. Líbera nos, Dómine.	R. Good Lord, deliver us.
V. Peccatóres.	V. Even though we be sinners.
R. Te rogamus, audi nos.	R. We beseech thee to hear us, Lord.

V. Ut nobis parcas.

R. Te rogamus, audi nos.

V. Ut nobis indulgeas.

R. Te rogamus, audi nos.

V. Ut ad veram pœniténtiam nos perducere dignéris.
R. Te rogamus, audi nos.

V. Ut Ecclésiam tuam sanctam regere et conservare dignéris.
R. Te rogamus, audi nos.

V. Ut domnum Apostolicum et omnes ecclesiásticos ordines in sancta religióne conservare dignéris.
R. Te rogamus, audi nos.

V. Ut inimícos sanctæ Ecclésiæ humiliare dignéris.

R. Te rogamus, audi nos.

V. That it may please thee to spare us.
R. We beseech thee to hear us, Lord.

V. That it may please thee to pity and pardon us.
R. We beseech thee to hear us, Lord.

V. That it may please thee to give us true repentance.
R. We beseech thee to hear us, Lord.

V. That it may please thee to rule and govern thy holy Church.
R. We beseech thee to hear us, Lord.

V. That it may please thee to preserve the Apostolic Lord, and to keep all orders of the Church in thy sacred religion.
R. We beseech thee to hear us, Lord.

V. That it may please thee to overthrow the enemies of thy holy Church.
R. We beseech thee to hear us, Lord.

V. Ut régibus et princípibus christiánis pacem et veram concordiam donare dignéris.
R. Te rogamus, audi nos.

V. That it may please thee to bestow on all Christian kings and princes true peace and concord.
R. We beseech thee to hear us, Lord.

V. Ut cuncto pópulo christiáno pacem et unitátem largiri dignéris.

R. Te rogamus, audi nos.

V. That it may please thee to give to all Christian nations both peace and unity.
R. We beseech thee to hear us, Lord.

V. Ut omnes errántes ad unitátem Ecclésiæ revocare, et infidéles univérsos ad Evangélii lumen perducere dignéris.
R. Te rogamus, audi nos.

V. That it may please thee to restore unity to thy Church, and to lead all unbelievers into the light of thy holy Gospel.
R. We beseech thee to hear us, Lord.

V. Ut nosmetípsos in tuo sancto servítio confortare et conservare dignéris.
R. Te rogamus, audi nos.

V. That it may please thee to strengthen and preserve us in true worshipping of thee.
R. We beseech thee to hear us, Lord.

V. Ut mentes nostras ad cæléstia desidéria erigas.
R. Te rogamus, audi nos.

V. That it may please thee to endue our hearts with heavenly desires.
R. We beseech thee to hear us, Lord.

V. Ut ómnibus benefactóribus nostris sempitérna bona retríbuas.

R. Te rogamus, audi nos.

V. That it may please thee to bestow on all our benefactors thine everlasting benefits.
R. We beseech thee to hear us, Lord.

V. Ut ánimas nostras, fratrum, propinquorum et benefactórum nostrórum ab ætérna damnatióne erípias.
R. Te rogamus, audi nos.

V. Ut fructus terræ dare et conservare dignéris.

R. Te rogamus, audi nos.

V. Ut ómnibus fidelibus defunctis réquiem ætérnam donare dignéris.

R. Te rogamus, audi nos.

V. Ut nos exáudire dignéris.

R. Te rogamus, audi nos.

V. Fili Dei.
R. Te rogamus, audi nos.

V. Agnus Dei, qui tollis peccáta mundi.
R. Parce nobis, Dómine.

V. That it may please thee to deliver from eternal damnation our souls, and those of our brethren, kindred, and benefactors.
R. We beseech thee to hear us, Lord.

V. That it may please thee to give and preserve to our use the kindly fruits of the earth.

R. We beseech thee to hear us, Lord.

V. That it may please thee to bestow upon all thy faithful departed rest eternal.

R. We beseech thee to hear us, Lord.

V. That it may please thee graciously to hear our prayer.

R. We beseech thee to hear us, Lord.

V. O Son of God.
R. We beseech thee to hear us, Lord.

V. O Lamb of God, that takest away the sins of the world.
R. Spare us, Lord.

V. Agnus Dei, qui tollis peccáta mundi.	V. O Lamb of God, that takest away the sins of the world.
R. Exáudi nos, Dómine.	R. Graciously hear us, Lord.
V. Agnus Dei, qui tollis peccáta mundi.	V. O Lamb of God, that takest away the sins of the world.
R. Miserére nobis.	R. Have mercy upon us.
V. Christe, audi nos.	V. O Christ, hear us.
R. Christe, exáudi nos.	R. O Christ, graciously hear us.
V. Kyrie, eléison.	V. Lord, have mercy upon us.
R. Christe, eléison. Kyrie, eléison.	R. Christ, have mercy upon us. Lord, have mercy upon us.
Pater noster (secréto usque ad):	Our Father (which words are said aloud, and the rest secretly to):
V. Et ne nos indúcas in tentatiónem.	V. And lead us not into temptation.
R. Sed líbera nos a malo.	R. But deliver us from evil.
Psalmus 69. Deus, in adjutórium	Psalm 69. Deus, in adjutórium
1 Deus, in adjutórium meum inténde: * Dómine ad adjuvándum me festína.	1 HASTE thee, O God, to deliver me; * make haste to help me, O LORD.
2 Confundántur et revereántur, * qui quærunt ánimam meam.	2 Let them be ashamed and confounded that seek after my soul; * let them be turned backward and put to confusion that wish me evil.
3 Avertántur retrórsum, et erubéscant, * qui volunt mihi mala.	3 Let them for their reward be soon brought to shame, * that cry over me, There! there!

4 Avertántur statim erubescéntes, * qui dicunt mihi : Euge, euge.

5 Exsúltent et læténtur in te omnes qui quærunt te, * et dicant semper : Magnificétur Dóminus : qui díligunt salutáre tuum.

6 Ego vero egénus, et pauper sum : * Deus, ádjuva me.

7 Adjútor meus, et liberátor meus es tu : * Dómine, ne moréris.

8 Glória Patri, et Fílio, et Spirítui Sancto.

9 Sicut erat in princípio, et nunc, et semper, * et in sǽcula sæculórum. Amen.

V. Salvos fac servos tuos.
R. Deus meus, sperántes in te.

V. Esto nobis, Dómine, turris fortitúdinis.
R. A fácie inimíci.

V. Nihil profíciat inimícus in nobis.
R. Et fílius iniquitátis non appónat nocére nobis.

4 But let all those that seek thee be joyful and glad in thee: * and let all such as delight in thy salvation say always, The Lord be praised.

5 As for me, I am poor and in misery: * haste thee unto me, O God.

6 Thou art my helper, and my redeemer: * O LORD, make no long tarrying.

8 Glory be to the Father, and to the Son, and to the Holy Ghost.

9 As it was in the beginning, is now, and ever shall be, world without end. Amen.

V. O God, save thy servants.
R. That put their trust in thee.

V. Be unto us, O Lord, a tower of strength.
R. From the face of the enemy.

V. Let the enemy prevail nothing against us.
R. Nor the son of wickedness approach to afflict us.

V. Dómine, non secúndum peccáta nostra fácias nobis.	V. O Lord, deal not with us after our sins.
R. Neque secúndum iniquitátes nostras retríbuas nobis.	R. Neither reward us according to our iniquities.

V. Orémus pro Pontifice nostro (Nomen).

V. Let us pray for our Pope (Name).

R. Dóminus consérvet eum, et vivíficet eum, et beátum fáciat eum in terra, et beátum fáciat eum in terra, et non tradat eum in ánimam inimicórum ejus.

R. The Lord preserve him and keep him alive, that he may be blessed upon earth; and deliver not thou him into the will of his enemies.

(Vacante Apostolica Sede, Versus cum suo Responsorio præteritur.)

(If the Holy See is vacant, the above Versicle with its Response is omitted.)

V. Orémus pro benefactóribus nostris.

V. Let us pray for our benefactors.

R. Retribúere dignáre, Dómine, ómnibus, nobis bona faciéntibus propter nomen tuum, vitam ætérnam. Amen.

R. Vouchsafe, O Lord, for thy Name's sake, to reward with eternal life all them that do us good. Amen.

V. Orémus pro fidelibus defunctis.

V. Let us pray for the faithful departed.

R. Réquiem ætérnam dona eis, Dómine, et lux perpétua luceat eis.

R. Eternal rest grant unto them, O Lord; and let perpetual light shine upon them.

V. Requiéscant in pace.
R. Amen.

V. May they rest in peace.
R. Amen.

V. Pro frátribus nostris abséntibus.	V. Let us pray for our absent brethren.
R. Salvos fac servos tuos, Deus meus, sperántes in te.	R. Save thy servants, O my God, that put their trust in thee.
V. Mitte eis, Dómine, auxílium de sancto.	V. Send them help, O Lord, from thy holy place.
R. Et de Sion tuere eos.	R. And from Zion deliver them.
V. Dómine, exáudi oratiónem meam.	V. O Lord, hear my prayer.
R. Et clamor meus ad te véniat.	R. And let my cry come unto thee.
V. Dóminus vobíscum.	V. The Lord be with you.
R. Et cum spíritu tuo.	R. And with thy spirit.

Oremus. (Oratio)

Let us pray. (Collects)

Deus, cui proprium est miseréri semper et parcere: súscipe deprecatiónem nostram; ut nos, et omnes fámulos tuos, quos delictórum catena constringit, miserátio tuæ pietátis clementer absolvat.

O God, whose nature and property is ever to have mercy and to forgive: receive our humble petitions; and though we be tied and bound by the chain of our sins, yet let the pitifulness of thy great mercy loose us.

Exáudi, quæsumus, Dómine, supplícium preces, et confiténtium tibi parce peccátis: ut páriter nobis indulgéntiam tríbuas benignus et pacem.

We beseech thee, O Lord, mercifully to hear the prayers of thy humble servants, and to forgive the sins of them that confess the same unto thee: that they may obtain of thy loving-kindness pardon and peace.

Ineffábilem nobis, Dómine, misericórdiam tuam clementer osténde: ut simul nos et a peccátis ómnibus exuas, et a pœnis, quas pro his meremur, erípias.	O Lord, we pray thee, shew forth upon us thy servants the abundance of thy unspeakable mercy: that we may be delivered from the chain of our sins, and from the punishment which for the same we have most righteously deserved.
Deus, qui culpa offenderis, pœniténtia placaris: preces pópuli tui supplicántis propítius réspice; et flagélla tuæ iracúndiæ, quæ pro peccátis nostris meremur, averte.	O God, who art wroth with them that sin against thee, and sparest them that are penitent: we beseech thee to hear the prayers of thy people that call upon thee; that we, which have most justly deserved the scourges of thine anger, may by thy great mercy be delivered from the same.
(If the Holy See is vacant, the following Collect is omitted.)	(If the Holy See is vacant, the following Collect is omitted.)
Omnípotens sempiterne Deus, miserére famulo tuo Pontifici nostro (Nomen), et dírige eum secúndum tuam cleméntiam in viam salútis ætérnæ: ut, te donante, tibi placita cupiat, et tota virtúte perfíciat.	Almighty and everlasting God, we beseech thee to have compassion upon N., our Pope, and by thy mercy govern him in the way of everlasting life: that, being endued with thy grace, he may ever seek those things that are pleasing unto thee, and with his whole strength perform the same.

Deus, a quo sancta desidéria, recta consília et justa sunt ópera: da servis tuis illam, quam mundus dare non potest, pacem; ut et corda nostra mandátis tuis dedita, et, hóstium subláta formidine, témpora sint, tua protectióne, tranquilla.	O God, from whom all holy desires, all good counsels, and all just works do proceed: give unto thy servants that peace which the world cannot give; that our hearts may be set to obey thy commandments, and also that by thee we being defended from the fear of our enemies may pass our time in rest and quietness.
Ure igne Sancti Spíritus renes nostros et cor nostrum, Dómine: ut tibi casto corpore serviamus, et mundo corde placeámus.	Grant, O Lord, we pray thee, that the fire of thy Holy Ghost may in such wise cleanse our reins and our hearts: that we serving thee in pureness both of body and soul may be found an acceptable people in thy sight.
Fidélium, Deus, ómnium conditor et redemptor, animábus famulórum famularumque tuárum remissiónem cunctórum tríbue peccatórum: ut indulgéntiam, quam semper optavérunt, piis supplicatiónibus consequántur.	O God, the Creator and Redeemer of all them that believe: grant unto the souls of thy servants and handmaidens the remission of all their sins; that, as they have ever desired thy merciful pardon, so by the supplications of their brethren they may receive the same.
Actiónes nostras, quæsumus, Dómine, aspirándo prævéni et adjuvándo proséquere: ut cuncta nostra orátio et operátio a te semper incipiat et per te cœpta finiátur.	Prevent us, O Lord, in all our doings with thy most gracious favor, and further us with thy continual help: that in all our works begun, continued, and ended in thee, we may glorify thy holy Name, and finally by thy mercy obtain everlasting life.

Omnípotens sempiterne Deus, qui vivórum domináris simul et mortuórum, ómniumque miseréris quos tuos fide et ópere futuros esse prænoscis: te supplices exorámus; ut, pro quibus effúndere preces decrevimus, quosque vel præsens sæculum adhuc in carne retinet vel futúrum jam exutos corpore suscépit, intercedéntibus ómnibus Sanctis tuis, pietátis tuæ cleméntia, ómnium delictórum suórum véniam consequántur. Per Dóminum nostrum Jesum Christum, Fílium tuum, qui tecum vivit et regnat in unitáte Spíritus Sancti, Deus, per ómnia sæcula sæculórum.

Almighty and everlasting God, who hast dominion both of the quick and the dead, who likewise hast mercy upon all men, whom by reason of their faith and works thou hast foreknown: we commend unto thee all those for whom we now do offer our prayers, whether in this world they still be held in the bonds of the flesh, or being delivered therefrom have passed into that which is to come; beseeching thee that at the intercession of all thy Saints they may of thy bountiful goodness obtain the remission of all their sins. Through our Lord Jesus Christ thy Son, Who liveth and reigneth with thee in the unity of the Holy Ghost, God, world without end.

R. Amen.

R. Amen.

V. Dóminus vobíscum.
R. Et cum spíritu tuo.

V. The Lord be with you.
R. And with thy spirit.

V. Exáudiat nos omnípotens et miséricors Dóminus.
R. Amen.

V. May the Almighty and Merciful Lord graciously hear us.
R. Amen.

V. Et fidélium ánimæ † per misericórdiam Dei requiéscant in pace.
R. Amen.

V. And may the souls of the faithful departed, † through the mercy of God, rest in peace.
R. Amen.

Antiphon

Ne reminiscaris, Domine, delicat nostra vel parentum nostrorum, neque vindictam sumas de peccatis nostris propter nomem tuum. Pater noster, etc. Et nenos inducas in tentationem. Sed libera nos a malo. Amen.

Second Conjuration

Ecce crucem Domine viest seu Radix do vielin nomine Jesu omne genus tutantor coelestum terrestrum infernorom it omnis Língua Confititur quiadoemonus Jesu Cristuns in gloria est Dei patri viest Deus ille crucem Domine te tribu Judá Radix David fugite partes adversæ veribilium in nomine Jesu omne genus tutantur coelestum terrestrum infernorum omnia Língua Confitiur quia Dominos Jesu Cristus in gloria est Pater, amem; o Senhor seja comigo e com todos nós: Amen.

Jesus, Mary, and Joseph, in the name of the Father God, the Son God, and the Holy Ghost God. Amen.

By the virtue of the Holy Father God, three persons distinct and only one true God, by the virtue of the Virgin Mary and all the Holy Evangelists, Apostles, Patriarchs, Prophets, Martyrs, and Confessors, by the virtue of the Saint Ubalde Francisco, I, creature of Our Lord Jesus Christ redeemed with his most holy blood and made in your likeness, on your most holy name I disenchant this treasure which is before me buried; I command you under the holy power of obedience, that the earth open now where the treasure is deposited that the Moors buried here; I, by the sight of these lights, command that all the treasures that are here under the earth under the power of Lucifer and his companions, commanding now in the name of Saint Cyprian, that be delivered to me under the power of Our Lord Jesus Christ, Jesus, Jesus, Jesus, be with me, come to aid me! Jesus, Jesus, hear my orison, and come to your ears the prayer of this great sinner, Jesus, help me, Jesus, help me! Jesus, come again to aid me. Jesus, Jesus, a thousand times Jesus, be with me, Jesus, without you I can do nothing, Jesus, I with your Most Holy power command that this treasure be open now.

I command in the name of all the Saints, of the God of Abraham, of the God of Jacob, and of the God of Isaac, and in virtue of all of them be untied and unbind all the things in this world, in order that I find what I search for. Amen.

Whoever reads this orison, God will appear to him through the doors of mercy, accompanied by the archangel Raphael and all others Saints and Archangels, Principalities and Virtues from heaven; and under God's orders are the blessed Saint John the Baptist, Saint Thomas, Saint Philip, Saint Mark, Saint Matthew, Saint Simon, Saint Jude, Saint Martin, and all Saints that are in heaven; all the orders of the martyrs, Saint Sebastian, Saint Cosmas, Saint Damian, Saint Fabian, and Saint Cyprian. Be with me Saint Dionysius with his companions by all the orders of the Virgin Martyrs, Confessors of God and by the crowning of the king David and by the four Evangelists John, Mark, Matthew, and Luke, and by the four columns of heaven, which do not hinder them in any way, and by the 72 languages which are divided throughout the world, and by this absolution, and by the one Our Lord gave when he called Adam, saying, *"where are you?"* and by this virtue by which Adam got up when he said to him, *"Get up and take your frock, go from here and do not sin anymore,"* and from that infirmity he was paralytic for 28 years, saved by Our Lord whom all Saints praised, because everyone received charitably from his fruit by the hand of Jeremiah the Prophet and by the humility of Joseph, and by the patience of Job, and by the grace of God, and more by all the Saints of God, absolve him then, God, from all evil things and be praised Emanuel, for being God with us and by the Most Holy name of God and all the things that are here named and are now untied and unbound to be seen, and get away from the ill fortune and from all evils made by the Moors or by the demons; retreat Satanaz from here out because I command you with all the power I have, that is greater than yours.

Go to the depths of hell! Open the earth now; Jesus, Jesus, defend me from these ghosts that are surrounding me to hinder me from attaining what I desire; Jesus, Jesus, come to my aid. Retreat, Satanaz, because you are defeated!

I break your astuteness with the holy power of Our Lord Jesus Christ. Retreat, ghosts, enemies of human nature; I conjure you in the name of the miraculous Saint Cyprian and by the Holy Wood of the Cross on which Our Lord Jesus Christ was crucified; by this same Cross I command you: Retreat, Satanaz, ghost enemy of God and men.

Prevention

At the end of this orison, there will appear immense ghosts, to try to get you to leave the riches and flee, but do not have any fear, because when the Demon sees that you do this, he will soon flee and leave everything at your disposition.

After taking the riches, command in the name of Jesus and Saint Cyprian that everything returns to its natural state, and at the end, distribute the riches without arrogance, because it was given by God and Saint Cyprian.

Magical Secrets

During the thirty years Cyprian was servant of the demon, he acquired a just reputation as an expert magician, for the good as much as for the evil. After knowing what the men of his time knew about these things, the pact he made with the demon made him the owner of secrets with which he could give satisfaction to his tastes, and Satanaz much gladdened himself, because in such a way his victim was heaping sins which assured irremediably to the great sorcerer the eternal infernal penalties.

God, in his wisdom, arranged the events in a way not predicted by Lucifer. Cyprian repented, and from humble servant converted himself into despotic owner of the devil. In this manner, a glorious soul could be saved, and the magical secrets of Saint Cyprian that follow stopped being an infernal mystery.

[LM2]

SPELLS OF CYPRIAN

[GLT]

FIRST MAGIC

The occult power or way to obtain the love of women

In the life of Saint Cyprian, as in the "Miracles of Saint Bartholomew," it is told that for a man to make himself loved by women, whoever they are, he needs to take the heart of a virgin pigeon and feed it to a snake, and keep the serpent confined for fifteen days. The snake, as you see, does not resist for a long time.

As soon as it dies, cut off her head and dry it over a burning coal or embers and put onto it 30 drops of Hanoverian laudanum; after that, crush everything and put it into a flask of new glass. As long it is conserved like this, the owner of the flask can be sure that he will be loved by however many women he wants.

THE WAY TO USE IT

Rub the hands with a small portion, saying the following words:

Izelino Belzebuth, canta-galen-se-chando-quinha, é a própria xime, é golote.

This magic is so strong, that to attract one creature to another, it is more than admirable.

The reader, be they man or woman, can use it without scruples, because here does not enter sin, because Saint Cyprian himself taught it to his servants, whom he freed from the power of Satanaz, who with his damned fascinations disgraced an entire city.

In the second part of this book, it is shown, more clearly, the cause of occult powers.

SECOND MAGIC

The occult power or secret of the rod from the hazel tree

This magic must be very admirable: so admirable are the wonders it does, that the blood freezes in my veins in publishing it, not because it offends the All-Powerful, but for fear that some foolhardy person might use it without first vesting himself with courage.

Yes, we say courage, because with fear many grave consequences can happen to him. Because of fear and nothing more; because here the power of the demon does not enter into the creature; because in this book we do not treat about having communication with demons, but about getting rid of them with our kindness.

That is why we do not reveal this secret.

THIRD MAGIC

The occult powers of enchanted money

A coin of good silver, put under the altar stone for three days, so that three Masses are said over it, without the priest knowing about it (only the one who deposits the coin there must know and no one else), can be changed or spent anywhere, that when returning home he will find it in his pocket; such is the enchantment that it would be better if the reader does not try it; only for fun.

The months most favorable are February, April, June, September, and December.

The reader that is doing the operation must not fear, seeing whatever he sees, and command to be done what he thinks fit, according to his ideas, and when finished, say with his eyes raised to the sky: *Be at peace!* Amen.

True Treasure of Black and White Magic

or Secrets of sorcery

[GLT]

The Cross of Saint Bartholomew and of Saint Cyprian

In a book esteemed and unknown, even to the major part of studious people, which has for a title *Life and Miracles of Saint Bartholomew*, we find the way to make the cross of this Saint and also the way to use it.

The explanations we are going to give to the readers deserve entire faith, not just because they are extracted from a book full of mystical unction, but because they have already been practiced by people of our knowledge, with the most satisfying results.

WAY TO MAKE THE CROSS

Cut three pieces of cedar wood, one larger and two shorter, to make the arms of the cross; cover then the three arms with rosemary, rue, and celery, and put in each arm, above and below the larger part, a small cypress apple; leave it in holy water for three consecutive days, and take it from the same water at midnight, saying the following words:

> *Cross of Saint Bartholomew, the virtue of the water in which you were, from the plants and woods you are made of, free me from the temptations of the evil spirit, and bring over me the grace that the blessed enjoy. In the name of the Father, of the Son, and of the Holy Ghost. Amen.*

These words must be said almost imperceptibly and must be repeated four times.

WAY TO USE THE CROSS

This cross can be carried inside a small bag of black silk, blessed, or even be carried against the body, hanging around the neck by a thread of black spun silk. The person who carries it must do his best to hide it from everyone; and when suspecting someone of seeing it, throw at him the *evil eye*, and must, on the occasion of going to bed, kiss three times the cross and say the kind of orison we already indicated in the *Way to make the cross*.

When getting up, he must also kiss three times the cross and pray one Lord's Prayer and one Hail Mary.

Magical Secrets

I

Great magic of the broad beans

Kill a black cat, bury it in your backyard, and put a fava bean in each eye, another under the tail and another in each ear. After all that, cover it with earth, and water it every night, at midnight, with just a few drops until the broad beans, who will have sprouted, are mature, and when you see that they are like that, then cut them at the base.

After being cut, take them home and put them one by one in the mouth. When, however, it seems to you that you are invisible, it is because the fava bean you have in the mouth has the precise magical force, and so, if it pleases you to enter into any place without anyone seeing you, put first the broad bean in your mouth.

This works by an occult virtue, it not being necessary to make a pact with the demon, as the witches do...

WARNING TO WHO WILL MAKE USE OF THIS MAGIC

When you go to water the broad beans, many ghosts will appear to you, with the aim of scaring you so you do not achieve your intent. The reason for this is very simple. It is because the demon envies whoever will use this magic, without first giving himself to him body and soul, as the witches do, who are called women of virtue. However, do not be scared because they will not do any harm to you, and to them you must first make the sign of the Cross and, at the same time, say the Creed.

II

Magic of the bone from the head of the black cat

Boil water into a pan with white vines and willow firewood, and as soon as the water is boiling, put into it a cat and cook it until the meat becomes loose on the bones. After all that being ready, filter all the bones through a linen cloth and put them in front of a mirror; put the bones in your mouth one by one, it not being necessary to put them in entirely, but just between the teeth, in a way that when you disappear in front of the mirror keep the bone you have between the teeth because this is the one which has magic. When you want to go to any place, without being seen, put the aforementioned bone in your mouth and say: *I want to be in such place now, by the power of the liberal black magic.*

III

Another magic of the black cat

When a black cat is with a female cat of the same color, which means, united in carnal copulation, you must have ready a scissor and cut some hair from the cat and some from the female cat. Mix then the hairs, burn them with lantana, take the ashes, put them into a glass flask with some spirit of ammoniac salt, and close well the glass flask to keep the spirit always strong.

After all that being ready, you must take the glass flask with your right hand and say, then, the following words:

> *Ashes, with my own hand you were burnt, with steel scissors you were cut from the cat and cut from the female cat, everyone who smells you with me will become friends. This by the power of God and of the Most Holy Mary. When God be not God anymore is when all this will fail me; and to golão, bring matão, goes from the pauto chião and molitão.*

As soon as all that is done, the glass flask will have a spell force, magic and enchantment, that when you desire that any girl have friendship with you it is enough to open the glass flask and under any pretext give it to her to smell.

Let's suppose an individual wishes that his girlfriend take the smell of said glass flask, but cannot find a proper way to make it happen. In that case, he begins to talk about anything, in a way to make mention of the Cologne waters. That made, take the glass flask from the pouch and say with all seriousness:

Do you want to see such a pleasant smell, girl?

Now, in general, women are very curious, so she smells immediately the content of the glass flask and you can count with her love. It must be noted that this enchantment has the same virtue for a man doing it to a woman as a woman doing it to a man.

IV

Another magic of the black cat to cause evil

Let's put into our idea that someone wants to take revenge on an enemy, but does not want the enemy to know about the revenge that is being prepared for him. He can take revenge easily, doing as prescribed in the following way:

Take a black cat, one that does not have one single white hair. Tie his legs and hands with a rope of esparto (the ones used to make carpets). After this operation being executed, take it to a large crossroads and as soon as you arrive there say in the following way:

> *I, so and so, (must say the name of the person), from the part of God Omnipotent, command the demon to appear here now, under the saint penance of obedience and superior precepts. I, by the power of the liberal black magic, command you, demon or Lucifer, or Satanaz or Barabbas, to get inside the body of this person to whom I wish ill, and from there do not leave until I command you, and do to me everything I propose to you during my life.*

(Here say whatever you want him to do to the creature.)

Oh great Lucifer, emperor of everything which is infernal, I fasten and bind you in the body of (so and so), as I have fastened this cat. At the end of you doing all that I want, I offer thee this black cat; I will bring it here when everything is done.

WARNING

When the demon has conducted himself accordingly with the obligation you imposed unto him, go to the place where you requested it, and say twice:

Lucifer, Lucifer, here you have that I promised you.

These words being said, release the cat.

V

Another magic of the black cat, and the way of generating a little devil with the eyes of the cat

Kill a black cat, and after it is dead, take his eyes and put them inside the egg of a black hen, but, taking note that each eye must be separated inside each egg. After this operation is done, put it into a pile of horse manure, and it is necessary that the manure is very warm to generate there the little devil.

Saint Cyprian says that you must go every day to said pile of manure for one month, as this is the time that the little devil takes to be born.

Magical Secrets

WORDS THAT MUST BE SAID BY THE PILE OF MANURE WHERE THE LITTLE DEVIL IS

Oh great Lucifer, I deliver unto you these two eyes of a black cat, so you, my great friend Lucifer, be favorable in this appellation that I do at your feet. My great minister and friend, Satanaz and Barabbas, I deliver unto you the black magic so you put on it all your power, virtue, and astuteness that were given to you by Jesus Christ; because I deliver to you these two eyes of a black cat, so from them a devil will born to be my companion eternally. By black magic, I deliver you to Maria Padilha and all her family and to all the devils in hell, the lame, weak-sighted, crippled, and to all that is infernal, so from this two devils are born to give me money, because I want money by the power of Lucifer, my friend and companion from now on.

Do all this that we just indicated, and at the end of one month, a day less or a day more, two little devils will be born to you, with the figure of a small lizard. As soon as the little devil is born, put it into a small tube of ivory or boxwood and give to him iron or ground steel to eat...

When you are the owner of the two little devils, you can do whatever pleases you; for instance, do you want money? It is just to open the tube and say like that: *I want now money here.* It will immediately appear to you, with only one condition, that you cannot give alms to the poor and neither pay for Masses to be said, because it is money given by the demon.

Readers: It is not possible to describe in this second part of the *Great Book of Saint Cyprian* or *Treasure of the Sorcerer* all that happened to this Saint, because to do it, we would need to make a great volume, which would not affordable by all classes of people as a consequence of the high price it would cost.

We limit ourselves, then, to teach you all the sorceries Saint Cyprian used during his life as a sorcerer, and you, readers, will well understand what a creature can achieve having the wonderful power of the magical art.

VI

The way to obtain a little devil making a pact with the demon

THE WAY TO MAKE A PACT

Take a virgin parchment, and then make the contract giving your soul to the demon, with your own blood.

You must do it in the following way:

> *I, with my own blood from my little finger, make a contract to Lucifer, emperor of hell, so he will do everything I desire in this life, and if he fails me in this, I will not belong to him anymore.*

Name

After writing all that on said parchment, take the egg of a black hen covered by a cock of the same color, and write on said egg the contract you made on the parchment.

After all is done, make a small hole in the egg and put inside it a drop of blood from the little finger of your right hand, and then wrap the egg in lengths of cotton and put it into a pile of manure or under a black hen. From this egg, a little devil will be born; after you put it inside a silver box, with powder of the same silver, every Saturday you must introduce your little finger into the box for him to suck.

After you possess him, you can have everything you want in this world.

But, about this practice, Saint Cyprian says, in chapter XLV of his holy book:

> "Every son of God who delivers his soul to the demons will be in the same hour cursed by he who created him and gave him his being, who was our Lord Jesus Christ."

It is necessary to declare that we do not expose these diabolical recipes for readers to put them into practice; we leave them here because we understand that it is useful to know everything that is good and evil, so the ones who take the bad way can deviate from it in time and thank us for the good intention that we make appear through the pages of this good book, and we also harbor the hope that God will bless our work.

VII

Sorcery to be done with two dolls, as did Saint Cyprian when he was sorcerer and magician

Prepare a doll or a poppet made with linen or cotton cloths; after they are ready, you must unite then one to the other in a close embrace.

After that operation, take a skein of white threads and begin to wrap them around said dolls saying as follows, giving first the name of the person you want to bewitch:

> I bind you and I tie you in the name of Our Lord Jesus Christ, Father, Son, and Holy Ghost, so that under this holy power you cannot eat nor drink, nor be in any part of the world without being in my company (so and so). I, (so and so), here bind you and tie you, as they bound Our Lord Jesus Christ on the wood of the Cross; and the rest you will have all the while you do not turn to me will be one the souls in the fire of purgatory continually suffer by their sins in this world, and like the one that the wind in the air has, the waves in the sea, always in continuous movement, the tide rising and lowering, the sun which rises in the mountains and sets on the sea. That will be your rest that

I give to you all the while you do not turn to me with all your heart, body, soul, and life; under the holy penance of obedience and superior precepts, you stay bound to me, as these two dolls stay tied one to the other.

These words must be repeated nine times, at noon, after praying the orison of the "Open Hours," which is in the first part of this work.

VIII

Enchantment and magic of the seed of fern and its properties

Here is told what is necessary to fetch the seed of a fern on the night of Saint John.

On the night of Saint John, at midnight, put a towel under the fern, where you must have already made a sign of Solomon, drawn under the fern, which you must bless in the name of the Father, of the Son, and of the Holy Spirit, so the demon cannot enter into said drawing.

After doing the same operation, you must put inside the drawing, which must have the precise breadth of the persons who will assist the ceremony.

We warn the persons who pretend to the said seed that they must say the *Litany of the Saints*, which is published in the first part of this work. The Litany must be said in a loud voice, to make the demons that will come to frighten you retreat; but, singing the entire Litany, soon the demons will retreat. In the end of this operation, split said seed, without arrogance or contention, otherwise the seed will stay without any virtue.

Magical Secrets

WORDS THAT ALL MUST SAY WITH THE FACE OVER THE SEED OF FERN

Seed of fern which on the night of Saint John was plucked at midnight. You were obtained and fell over a sign of Solomon, so you will serve me to all qualities of enchantments; and as God is a divine point of Saint John the Father, and a human point of Saint John the Cousin, so everyone touched by you will be enchanted with me.

And all that will be fulfilled by the great Omnipotent God, by whom I, (so and so), cite and notify you that you will not fail me and this by the spilled blood of Our Lord Jesus Christ, and the power and virtue of the Most Holy Mary, be with me and with you. Amen.

At the end of these words, say the creed and make a cross over the seed; that means making crosses with the right hand over said seed. In this way, the seed gets all the power and virtue. After that, pass it in a baptismal font with holy water.

After all that being done, put it into a glass flask, but it must be well closed.

EXPLANATION OF THE VIRTUES AND WONDERS THAT ARE GIFTED TO SAID SEED

1st – Every creature who obtains this seed, if he touches another person with it with evil intention, will mortally sin by the reason of serving his own ends with a divine mystery, contracting offenses against humanity, like touching any woman married or single, to take her to any place with bad intention.

2nd – Any person who with this seed touches another creature in order to trouble his business or enchant his works for ill incurs the penance of excommunication.

3rd – The seed has virtue over any evil spirit of which a creature is possessed, when touched to said creature with living faith in Jesus Christ.

4th – The seed has virtue to cure any infirmity, touching the infirm with said seed, but with a most lively faith in Jesus Christ.

5th – The seed has the virtue of defending us from the enemy and his astuteness if we carry it with us.

6th – The seed has an occult virtue, which operates by an almost divine power, and it is like this: Suppose that there is a girl that the individual is attracted to, but that the innocent girl does not feel any affection for him. It is very easy for the aforementioned girl to fall in love with him, working in the following way:

> When talking with her, throw at her three grains of seed of fern, and you will see that this girl will never refuse to make many caresses to him and obey him in everything.

7th – The seed of fern has an occult virtue, to which only he who obtained it can give credit, and which is as follows:

> When passing by any person, touch her with said seed so that she will follow you, and when you want her to stop following, touch her again.

8th – The seed of fern has so many properties that cannot be explained. Only he who possess said seed can give explanations.

And for now, gentle readers, we think it reasonable to stop with the explanations about the seed of fern and will say to conclude:

This wonderful seed holds virtue in everything that the possessor wishes to achieve.

IX

The magic of the four-leafed clover, plucked on the night of Saint John at midnight

Readers, the four-leafed clover have the same virtues that the seed of fern, so it is not necessary to bother you more about this subject.

We understand that this will be enough for you be convinced and know of the virtues of the four-leafed clover.

To obtain the clover, do as follows:

On the eve of Saint John night, search in the fields for a shrub of clover with four leaves. As soon as you find it, make a sign of Solomon around it and leave it until the night. When, however, the bells sing at the Most Holy Trinity, return to it and say the following orison.

Begin by making the creed in cross over the clover, which means to say the creed whilst making crosses with the hand over said clover.

ORISON

I, creature of the Lord, redeemed by his Most Holy Blood, which Jesus Christ shed on the Cross to deliver us from the furies of Satanaz, have a most lively faith in the edifying powers of Our Lord Jesus Christ. I command the demon to retreat from this place and I bind and tie you in the curdled sea, not perpetually, but yes until I pluck this clover, and as soon as I have plucked it, I unbind you from your prison. All this by the power and virtue of Our Lord Jesus Christ. Amen.

PREVENTION

When you are binding the demon in the curdled sea, if he appears to you that moment and says, *"Living creature, son of God, I ask you not to bind me, tell me what you want as a reward,"* then you answer to him, *"Retreat, Satanaz, ten feet away and be absent from me."*

The demon, having retreated and then asking what you want, will do anything for you so as not to be bound. After saying to him what you want him to do, oblige him to make a vow, otherwise you will be cheated, because the demon is the father and mother of lies; but vowing to you, he cannot fail because God does not allow him to deceive a baptized creature who has been redeemed with his Most Holy Blood.

After all this is well executed, take possession of the clover with which you can do everything you want, because so it is written by the Saint Cyprian, in his book, chapter CXLV.

X

Magic or sorcery to be made with two dolls to cause harm to any person

Observe with attention what we will teach, to be sure this magic is well done.

Take two dolls, one of them signifying the creature to whom you are going to do the spell, and the other signifying the one who is going to cast the spell.

After said dolls are ready, you must unite one to the other, in a way they are tightly embraced. After all that is done, tie both with a sewing thread around the neck as if you are strangling them, and after this operation is done, fix five nails in them, in the indicated parts:

1st – In the head, piercing through both.

2nd – In the chest, in the same way.

3rd – In the belly, piercing from one side to the other.

4th – Through the legs, piercing from one side to the other.

5th – In the feet, in a way that drills from one side to the other.

In this way, the creature will suffer the same pains as if the nails were fixed in his own body.

There is also one more condition, that is, that the nails are fixed, with the saying of the following invocations in the different places where they are fixed:

1° nail – *So and so, I, so and so, nail you, bind, and pierce your body, as I pierce, tie, and nail your figure.*

2° nail – *So and so, I, so and so, I swear under the power of Lucifer and Satanaz that from now to the future you will not have even one hour of health.*

3° nail – *So and so, I, so and so, swear under the power of ill-wishing magic that from today to the future you will not have one hour of peace.*

4° nail – *So and so, I, so and so, swear under the power of Maria Padilha that from today to the future you will be possessed by all spells.*

5° nail – *So and so, I, so and so, bind and tie you from the feet to the head by the power of sorcerous magic.*

This way the ensorcelled creature will never more have one hour of health.

Readers, do not be scared with this, because God, as He gave to men power and wisdom to make spells, also gave medicine to fight against them, as it is explained in the first part of this work, which teaches how to unmake all kinds of sorcery—which is the life of Saint Cyprian, when he was Saint, and this is why we recommend every Christian to have this book

DECLARATION

In order that you do not doubt what you just read, it will be good to give you an explanation, and it is the following:

> It needs to be two dolls united one to the other, the one who will be ensorcelled and the one who ensorcells, meaning, the one who ensorcells is embraced to the ensorcelled wanting to kill him or pierce him with the nails.

XI

Magic of the black dog and its properties

A black dog has much magical force: so says Saint Cyprian in chapter CXLV. Now, there are many persons who say that magic is done with magical words; however, this is false—there is no magic which is worked by word. What can be said is that without words nothing can be said; however, not even the words have value without certain things that have the force of magic, and neither the same value nor more.

Here is the first magic of the black dog:

> Begin with the eyes of the dog: When a dog is dead, take his right eye, without crushing it; then, put it into a small box and carry it inside the pocket, and when passing by a dog, take it from the pocket and show it so that said dog will follow you wherever you go, even if its owner does not

want it to. When you want the dog to leave, wave to him three times with the said box.

XII

Second magic or sorcery of the black dog

With a black dog, you can make one of the strongest sorceries; so asserts Saint Cyprian in chapter CCL, volume XII.

Make it in the following way:

> Cut the eyelashes of a black dog, cut its nails, cut some hair from his tail, gather these three things and burn them with lantana. After having this reduced to ashes, put them into a glass flask very well closed with a cork for nine days, after which the spell is ready.

WAY TO APPLY

Let's suppose that there is a creature, man or woman, who wishes to love another creature, with good or bad intent, and cannot achieve it for any reason. He will easily satisfy his intent.

Take the three objects already mentioned and mix them with a small portion of tobacco and make a cigarette, which must be strong; when you are talking with the person whom you wish to ensorcell, blow some smoke on her, and you will see that the person becomes ensorcelled; this must be done three or five times, or seven, or nine, or more, but the sum must always be odd.

We also declare that if it is woman and she cannot do the sorcery because she does not smoke, make it in the following way.

> Take any item from the person you want to ensorcell and wrap said things we already spoke of inside a newspaper,

then with a thread of green spun silk begin to wrap it around said item, saying the following words:

(First, give the name of the person you want to ensorcell.)

> *I bind you and tie you with the chains of Saint Peter and Saint Paul, so you do not have peace or rest, in any part of the world, under the penance of obedience and superior precepts.*

After saying these words nine times, the person is ensorcelled; but, if this sorcery we just taught you is not enough to obtain what you wish, do not be afraid because of this, and neither should you lose the faith, because many things are not done because of the lack of a most lively faith.

You must know well, readers, that many creatures are not affected by sorcery, because of some orison they say every day when they go to bed and when they wake up.

Mysteries Of Sorcery

extracted from one **Manuscript of Black Magic** *thought to be from the time of the Moors*

[GLT]

Proceeding with some excavations in the village of Penacova, in the year of 1410, it was found there a manuscript in perfect state of conservation.

In this precious parchment, many curious things were found, some of which we will present to the readers, convinced that we are providing them a good service.

It was this parchment, today kept in the library of Evora, which gave subject to a book of spells much accepted today in Brazil, entitled the *Book of the Sorcerer.*

Here we have part of these mysteries.

I

Recipe to oblige the husband to be faithful

Take the marrow from the foot of a black dog, one of the hairless race, and fill a wooden needle-case with it. Wrap later the needle-case with a piece of scarlet velvet, perfectly adjusted and sewn. After unsewing the part of the mattress which lies between the husband and the wife, introduce the needle-case, but in such a way that it will not disturb during the night.

That being done, the woman must become very affable and condescending with the husband, agreeing to everything with his supreme will. She will try to smile when he perhaps is sad, promising to help him if his luck be adverse, and must be resigned if she suspects that he has a lover, pretending even that she does not know it.

At night, in the hour of going to bed, and in the morning, she will give him some food with lots of cinnamon and clove, and some more with chocolate with a great portion with vanilla, clove, and cinnamon.

She will sleep completely naked, leaning as much she can her body against her husband's to transmit heat and sweat to him.

Every time he comes home, she will give him something and will say that she thought about him. The gift may be a fruit or a sweet he likes, a flower, or, in the absence of these things, a hug with a kiss.

If he has an ill temper and is rude and coarse, she must never contradict him, but be tender. If he is kind, but inconstant, she must always present herself as superior to him in all acts of life and in all feelings.

This recipe, if the formalities we described are observed with attention, is of an indisputable effect.

If the reader performs this experiment, we will see her time well employed.

II

Recipe to oblige the ladies, single or even married, to tell everything they have done or want to do

Take the heart of a pigeon and the head of a toad, and after drying them well and reducing them to a powder, fill a small bag that will be perfumed, adding to the powder a little musk.

Put the bag under the pillow of the person when she is sleeping, and after a quarter of an hour, you will know what you want to discover.

As soon as the person stops thinking, or a few minutes after, take the little bag from under the pillow to not expose the person to a cerebral fever which can cause her death.

III

Recipe to be happy in the things undertaken

Take a living toad, cut off its head and feet, soon after the full moon of the month of September, and put these pieces to soak for 21 days in sap of the elder tree, taking it out after this time when the bell tolls midnight; expose it later for three consecutive nights to the rays of the Moon, let it calcinate in a pot of clay that has never been used before, and mix, after, an equal amount of cemetery earth, but from the place where someone from the family of the person this recipe is destined for is buried.

The person who possesses this can be sure that the spirit of the deceased will watch over him and over everything he undertakes because of the toad which will not lose from sight his interests.

IV

Recipe to make yourself loved by the woman

Before anything, it is convenient to study, even if just a little, the character and mind of the woman you want to acquire and regulate and direct your conduct and manners according to the knowledge acquired about the subject.

It is useless to recommend, according to the resources of each person, a suit, so I will not say that it must be elegant or rich, but it should always be of impeccable cleanliness. The soiled man cannot enrapture women. The cleanliness of the clothes is, then, indispensable, and we even more strongly recommend it about the private parts of the body, which demand special cleanliness.

As soon as this first condition is observed, take, six months later, the heart of a virgin pigeon and feed it to a snake. The snake will eventually die; take her head and dry it in embers or over a very hot iron sheet, over a temperate fire. Afterwards, reduce it to powder, crushing it, adding some drops of laudanum; and when you want to use the recipe, rub your hands with a portion of this preparation, as we already taught to our readers in the first part of this work.

V

Recipe to be make you be loved by men

The recipe advised to men to make themselves loved by women, which came before this one, is, in every point of view, the one that women should employ first if they want to make themselves loved by men; however, the efficacy of this recipe depends on certain practices that must not be despised or forgotten.

We will indicate them:

The woman will try to get from the man she chooses a coin, medal, pin, or any other object or fragment, as long as it is made of silver and that he has carried with him for at least 24 hours.

She will come closer to the man, having the silver in the right hand, offering with the other a chalice of wine in which has dissolved a small ball the size of a grain of corn, with the following composition:

Laudanum	two drops
Head of eel	one
Seeds of hemp	one thimble

As soon as the individual has drunk a chalice of this wine, he will, forcibly, love the woman who gave it to him or who ordered it to be given; it not being possible for him to forget her whilst the enchantment lasts, the effects of which can be renewed without any inconvenience.

Magical Secrets

If, however, the man is so strong that he resists the action of the medicine, or if the medicine does not make him fall in love immediately, the woman, then, if she has him with her, alone, should give to him to drink a cup of chocolate, in which she will put, when mixing the eggs:

Cinnamon powder	two doses
Cloves	five
Vanilla	ten grams
Nutmeg, scraped	a small dose

After all is ready, take the cloves and put:

Tincture of Cantharidin[108]	two drops

If the individual wants to ask for something to drink, preferably give to him sponge cake.

Sometimes, and if the woman is not in a hurry to bind the man, the chocolate with the cloves, vanilla, and cinnamon is enough.

The chocolate can be substituted for coffee; however, in that case, prepare the coffee with fennel, and add, simply, one drop of tincture of cantharidin.

We will not hide from the reader that the individual will soon get suspicious that someone wants to ensorcell him.

If the woman is afraid that the man will escape her, and wishes to keep him in love for a long time, she will repeat the first medicine every fifteen days, and in the intervals, inviting him to lunch or supper, must give to him:

At lunch, poached eggs or omelette prepared in the following way: mix the eggs very well, then put them on top of your naked spinal column,

---

108 Cantharidin (etymology: Greek *kantharis*, beetle) is a powerful irritant vesicant (blister-inducing) substance obtained from many blister beetles, and sometimes given the nickname "Spanish fly." Cantharidin is claimed to have aphrodisiac properties, as a result of its irritant effects upon the body's genitourinary tract, and can result in poisoning if ingested. It is a poisonous substance, acting as a blister agent, and can cause severe chemical burns, but these same properties make it effective as a topical medication. Source: Wikipedia.

and catch them below, where the spinal column ends. Then make the omelet, and put it on the table still hot.

At dinner, slicing and crushing the meat into meat balls, put scrambled eggs, and after, before bringing the patties to the oven, pass one by one, across the sweating body, across the chest, back and belly, leaving them for some time under the armpits.

The coffee, if given at lunch and at the end of the dinner, must be filtered through the interior shirt of the woman; in this shirt, she must have slept at least two nights.

I was assured that this recipe has helped in the happiness of many women.

VI

Magic of the grapes and its properties

This magic is very interesting, as Saint Cyprian says on page 14 of his work.

Satanaz is the most astute of all demons, that is, the prince Belzebuth, the wisest of all his companions.

This magic, discovered by the demon, is very simple to do and must be executed as follows:

Take a bottle with a very large belly. After preparing said bottle, put inside it a deciliter and a half of virgin olive oil and put the bottle in a plant with bunches of grapes sprouting, and put one of the bunches inside the neck of the bottle and attach it to the vine the best you can, in a way that the bunches come to ripeness inside the bottle with the olive-oil.

It is necessary to note that the bunch must not touch the oil.

As soon as the bunches are matured, cut the one inside the neck of the bottle, and the operation is done.

Explanation of the virtues and properties
of this oil and of the bunch inside the bottle

Magical Secrets

1st – Lighting a flame with said oil, all the trees around the plant from which said bunch came appear and mature grapes appear and some people are seen, who by chance were at the same place where the bunch was cut; finally, all the objects from that place appear: houses, fruit trees, birds, trees, and everything that was near the bunch.

Warning to this condition: When the fruit and the bunches appear, do not cut them to eat, otherwise you risk being slapped by the demon. As soon as the light is off, all the trees and objects disappear.

2nd – The oil has the virtue to heal any wound new or old, putting on it a drop of oil and some threads of linen.

3rd – This oil has the virtue and power of releasing souls from purgatory to come and talk to the person who calls them at the door of the church, at midnight. Light the flame and say, *"I, by the power of this flame, command that the souls who are in purgatory talk to me, the ones whose bodies are buried in this house."* Immediately the souls appear, but it is necessary to have great courage, otherwise from this can result the death of the person who calls.

4th – The oil has the virtue and power to make a sorcery against another person, as did Saint Cyprian, in the city of Cartagena to a girl named Adelaide.

VII

Way to prepare the magical oil

Gather all the small animals[109] that you can (the ones more poisonous are the ones with more magic); after they are all trapped, put them alive into a frying pan which must have a pint and half of virgin olive oil; make it boil until half of the mixture remains, then keep the remaining oil and light a flame with it, and all persons who are present, on this occasion, are so scared that they cannot move from the place.

The reason of the fright is that great ghosts appear, there are shakings of the earth, and the boiled animals appear, also, giving great shrills and trying to sting the persons there; however, you must not be afraid, because all this is because of the flame that is burning.

VIII

Sorcery made with a toad to blige to love against the will

It is very simple to make this spell, being one which has power over all spells, Saint Cyprian affirms in his work, page 84.

In the book of his life, when he was sorcerer, he says that the reason why the toad has great force of magic and sorcery is because the demon has part of it, because it is the food Lucifer gives to the souls who are in hell.

For this reason, you can make with the toad any kinds of sorceries that you want, according to what we teach here.

---

109 The reference here is to insects, spiders, and the like.

IX

Sorcery of the toad with sewed eyes

Take one of the largest toads you can find, and if the sorcery is towards man, make sure the toad is male.

Holding it tightly with your right hand and passing it under your belly five times, say the following words:

> *Toad, little toad, as I pass you below my belly, so (so and so) will not have peace or rest as long as he does not turn his heart, his body, and his life to me.*

After saying the words above, take one of the thinnest needles, thread it with green spun silk, and then sew the eyes of the toad taking care not to hurt its pupils, or else the person you want to ensorcell will be blind. Just sew the eyelids together, in a way that the eyes of the toad are hidden without being hurt.

Words to say to the toad after its eyes are sewed

> *Toad, I, by the power of Lucifer, the prince Belzebuth, sew your eyes, which I do to so and so (the name of the person), so he (or she) has no peace nor rest in any part of the world without my company and walks blind to other women (or men). He will see only me and his thoughts will be on me only.*

Put the toad into a large pan and say:

> *So and so (give the name of the person), here you are bound and tied without seeing the sun or the moon, as long as you do not love me. I will not release you; here you are bound and tied as is this toad.*

PREVENTION TO WHOMEVER MAKES THIS MAGIC

The pan or basin where the toad is must have water which will be renewed every day with fresh water.

X

Sorcery of the toad with the mouth sewed with black spun silk when you want the sorcery to do harm and not good

Here is the recipe to make this spell:

Take a toad, sew his mouth with black spun silk, and after the mouth is sewed say the following words:

> *Toad, I by the power of Lucifer, of Satanaz, Barabbas, Caifaz and of the lame devil and, principally, in the name of the prince Belzebuth and Robert the Devil, by all these I beseech you, that so and so (say the name of the person whom you want to ensorcell) does not have one more hour of health, and your life I bind inside the mouth of this toad, and as it goes dying and losing health, so it happens to you by the same power of Lucifer.*

This way the sorcery is done. Trap the toad inside a pan where he does not have anything to eat.

WARNING OF GREAT IMPORTANCE

Let's suppose that after you have prepared the sorcery you repent of applying it. Easily you can unmake everything: Take the toad out of the pan and give it cow's milk to drink, for five days, with the book unsewed. It is only in this way that the sorcery is unmade.

XI

Sorcery of the toad to make someone love against her will, or to make marriages

Let's suppose that a girlfriend wishes to marry with her boyfriend as soon as possible, but the boyfriend is not in a hurry to marry, because he does not want to be captive yet or because he does not want her as a wife. Easily the girlfriend obliges him to marry her with the most brevity possible.

Do it the following way:

Take an object from the boyfriend or from the girlfriend and tie it around the belly of a toad; after making this operation, tie the feet of the toad with a red ribbon and put it inside a pan with earth mixed with some cow milk. After all these operations we talked about are done, say the following words, with the pan over the pan:

First give the name of the person.

> *So and so, as I have this toad trapped inside this pan, without seeing the sun or the moon, so you will not see any other women, married, single, or widowed. You will only have thoughts for me; and as the toad has its legs tied, so you have yours, and can only walk to my door, and as this toad lives inside a pan, consumed and mortified, so you will live whilst you do not marry me.*

When the words above have been said, close the pan tightly so the toad does not see the light of the day; then, when you receive [what you want], release the toad in the bush, in a way that you do not hurt it, otherwise the person to whom the sorcery was made will be hurt.

XII

Recipe to win at games

Order a figa[110] to be made from jet, and we especially recommend that it is carved with a new knife of fine steel.

Take the figa soon afterwards to the sea, hanging from a Saint Lucy ribbon, and pass it three times, seven times, or twenty and one times over the foam of the waves.

Whilst proceeding like that, pray three times the creed, with a very low voice, almost imperceptibly, and offer to Saint Lucy a twelve-hour candle.

The player must carry the figa around the neck when playing, having, however, the care not to allow himself to be blinded by ambition, nor to be dragged by greed, to obtain a satisfactory result from this recipe.

XIII

Talisman that allows the maker to return soon to their homeland, rich and happy

It is still the jet figa from the previous recipe, only with the difference that the individual must remain chaste, as long as he can, or in an extreme case, he will only be together with the wife after six months, or each three months, if his health does not allow to make the sacrifice longer.

Every three nights, when going to sleep, on his knees by the bed, he will send to God three Lord's Prayers and two Hail Marys.

---

110 A figa is an amulet in the shape of clenched fist, with the thumb between index and middle fingers. It has an Italian origin, being called *Mano Fico*, and was used by the Etruscans since the Roman age. *Mano* meant "hand" and *Fico* or *Figa* indicated the female genitalia. It was associated with fertility and eroticism, and today with good luck and apotropaic virtues.

XIV

Recipe to turn the good spell into the evil

Take a black toad, whose mouth you will sew with black spun silk.

After that, tie one by one the fingers of the toad with thick sewing thread, also black, making a figure like a parachute, and tie the main sewing thread inside the chimney, in a way that the toad hangs with his belly up.

At midnight, call the devil at each of the twelve chimes of the bell, and then, making the toad turn, say the following words:

> *Unclean animal, by the power of the devil, to whom I sold my body and not my spirit, I ask you to not allow (say the name of the person) to enjoy a single hour of happiness on this earth; his health I trap inside the mouth of this toad; and as it wastes away and dies, the same happens to (say the name of the person), whom I conjure three times in the name of the devil, devil, devil.*

The next morning, put the toad into a clay pot and seal it tightly. To undo the effects of this sorcery, when, for instance, the person comes to pity the ensorcelled, take the toad from the pan and give it fresh cow's milk to drink for seven days, but with the mouth unsewn.

XV

Recipe to make a man have pleasure only with the woman with whom he lives, or vice versa.

Take a toad and sew his eyes with black spun silk but in a way that does not hurt the pupils of its eyes. Do the same as in the previous recipe, substituting, however, the pronounced words, which are these:

> *Unclean animal, in the name of the devil, to whom I sold my body and not my spirit, I sew your eyes, which I should have done to (the name of the person), so he (or she) does not like any other person but me and walks blind to other women.*

After that, hang the toad in the chimney for twelve hours, putting it after that still alive into a pan, which must be sealed tightly.

The words to be pronounced, whilst this is prepared, are the following:

> *So and so (say the name of the person) is here bound and tied, and will not see either the light of day or the dim radiance of the moon without loving me. Stay, devil, devil, devil.*

In this recipe as in the other, the toad will be refreshed every day with water.

XVI

Recipe to hurry marriages

Take a black toad and tie around its belly any object from the boyfriend or from the girlfriend, with two ribbons, one scarlet and the other black; put, after that, the toad into a clay pot, and pronounce these words with your mouth near the pot lid:

> *So and so (the name of the person), if you love someone else and not me, or direct to another your thoughts, to the devil, to whom I consecrated my luck, I ask to enclose you in the world of afflictions as I have here enclosed this toad, and that from there you do not leave unless to be united to me, who loves you with all my heart.*

These words being pronounced, close the pan tightly, refreshing the toad every day with some water, and on the day that the marriage is settled, release the animal by a marsh, and with all caution, because if it is mistreated, the marriage, no matter how good it was supposed to be, will become intolerable; it would be a disgraceful union, to the husband as to the wife.

XVII

Way to predict through magic or through magnetism

When someone is sleeping and is dreaming, put your hand over their heart and ask all you want to know.

If it is a woman and the husband puts his hand over her heart, in this case, he can ask if she has been faithful or not; finally, you can ask everything that comes to your thought.

PRECIOUS PREVENTION

The person who is doing the operation above must be very careful to watch the person who is dreaming to ensure they are not having convulsions, in other words, to make sure she is not afflicted, and if that happens, the person must quickly take her hand, wake her up, and give her fresh water.

If you do not do this, it can cause the death of the person.

The reason for this danger is that the demon, in that case, is at her side to see if he can snatch the soul of the sleeping person, because it is a risky situation.

XVIII

Magic with holly and its virtues or force of enchantment, cut on the night of Saint John Baptist (June 24)

At midnight, cut the holly with a steel knife, and after cutting it, bless it in the name of the Father, of the Son, and of the Holy Spirit; after that, take it to the beach and pass it over seven waves of the sea; and whilst doing said operation, you must say the Creed seven times, always making crosses with the right hand over the waves and the holly.

VIRTUES AND PROPERTIES OF THE HOLLY

1. Whoever carries the holly with him has good fortune in every business he undertakes and in everything that gives happiness to men.

2. Whoever carries the holly with him and touches another person with it, with the lively faith that the person touched will follow him immediately—said person will follow him everywhere he wishes.

3. This secret we have experimented with a few times and we were always successful; of this, we are very remorseful because of certain circumstances that are not mentioned here.

4. The holly has power over everything his owner wants. Any shop owner who possesses the holly and hangs it in his store must every morning say when entering the store, *"God save you, holly, created by God,"* and this way the shop will have very good fortune. This is the system that has enriched many merchants in Portugal and Brazil.

†

XIX

Magic of the enchanting glass flask

WAY TO PREPARE THE GLASS FLASK

Prepare a glass flask of small size so that it is more comfortable to whomever carries it on the pouch; put into it the following ingredients.

1° - Spirit of salammoniac
2° - Granite
3° - Rosemary
4° - Fennel
5° - Marble stone
6° - Fern seed
7° - Mallow seed
8° - Mustard seed
9° - Blood from the little finger
10°- Blood from the thumb and the same from the left foot
11°- A root of hair from the head
12°- Clippings from the nails of the feet and from the nails of
the hands
13°- Pieces of the bones of a dead man, if from the skull even better

When everything above is ready, put it into the glass flask, in a way that it is only half full. We declare that all the ingredients we talked about must be in the smallest possible portion, because it produces a better effect.

After the glass flask is prepared, say the following words:

You, sacred flask, that by my own hand was prepared, my blood inside you is confined and tied to the root of my hair and inside you was spilled. Every person who is touched by

> *you will be enchanted with me. A.N.R.V. Ignoratus tuum vos assignaturum meo.*

After everything is done, exactly as we just explained, keep the flask very well hidden and then you can enchant anyone you please. Giving it to any creature to smell will cause them to follow you to any place you want.

We declare that said flask not only has the power to enchant but also to do evil.

It all depends on the thought of the person who gives it to be smelled: If it is for good, good happens to her; if it is for evil, evil happens to her.

XX

The magic of the needle passed three times in the corpse of a deceased man

This magic is very simple, and Saint Cyprian affirms in chapter XXI of his work that it was discovered by a demon or pythonic spirit in the XII century.

Pass a sewing thread made of Galician flax through a needle, and pass the needle through the skin of a deceased man three times, saying the following words:

> *So and so (say the name of the deceased), this needle in your body I will pass, so it will have the force to enchant.*

After said operation is done, keep the needle, and with it, you will work the following sorceries:

1. When passing by a girl and wishing her to follow you, it is enough to sew a knot in her dress, or in any other part of her clothing, and leave a loose edge of the sewing thread; she will follow you everywhere you go.

When you wish said girl to stop following you, you must remove the sewing thread that was attached to the cloth.

It is necessary to keep a great secret about this magic to avoid happening to you the same that happened to me, as I had serious problems for making said magic and declaring the way I did it; because of this, you should never reveal to anyone this secret.

2. When you want to ensure your girlfriend does not stop loving you and does not love another, do the following: Take an item belonging to said girlfriend or boyfriend and make three knots in the shape of cross, saying the following words (first call the name of the deceased through whom you passed the needle). *First knot:* "So and so (name of the deceased), when you speak is when so and so (name of man or woman) will leave me." *Second knot:* "so and so, when God ceases being God is when so and so will leave me." *Third knot:* "So and so, as long as these knots here remain, and your body remains in the grave, so and so will not have peace or rest until he is in my company."

This way, you can ensorcell or enchant all the people you wish.

We declare that this sorcery has not just the power to do good but has also power to do evil. It all depends on the words of the person; instead of saying, *"When this deceased speaks is when you will leave me,"* say, *"When this deceased speaks is when you, so and so, will live with health,"* and all the rest like that. Chapter XXXVII

XXI

Magic of the enchanted black female pigeon

Raise a black female pigeon at home, giving to it to eat nothing more than floating seeds and holy water to drink.

After it is grown up and ready to fly, write a letter to any person, containing or asking for anything you like.

This operation being done, put the letter in the beak of the pigeon and smoke it with incense, myrrh and asafoetida. Then put your thoughts to the person to whom you want the letter to be delivered and release the pigeon.

We affirm that said pigeon will take the letter to where it is destined and will return to the house of its owner and that the person who receives the letter will forcibly solve whatever is asked of him.

Note that you must not send the pigeon except between 10 o'clock in the morning and 2 o'clock in the afternoon.

XXII

Magic of the egg, to be done on the night of Saint John the Baptist (June 24)

On the night of Saint John the Baptist, leave in the open air an egg of a black hen. The egg must be broken into a glass of water; in the morning, when the sun is rising, you will see your fortune and the works you must endure.

In the same way, you can do this magic on the nights of Saint Anthony and Saint Peter.

XXIII

Sorcery to be done with five nails taken from the coffin of a dead man in his grave

Enter a cemetery and bring from there five nails from the coffin of a dead man, but always with the thought fixed on the sorcery you are going to do.

After that, draw upon a wooden board a sign of Solomon, and you must have an item from the person you are going to ensorcell; this item must be nailed to the sign of Solomon.

THE WAY YOU MUST FIX THE NAILS AND THE
WORDS YOU MUST SAY WHEN FIXING THEM

1. *nail* – (Say the name of the person you are ensorcelling) so and so, I beseech you, in the name of Satanaz, Barabbas, and Caifaz, so you may be bound to me, as Lucifer is bound in the depths of the hell.

2. *nail* – So and so, I bind and tie you inside this sign of Solomon; as the cross of Jesus Christ inside this sign was buried and the blood of Jesus upon it was spilled, so I, (so and so), cite and notify so you will not fault to me on this, by the spilled blood of Jesus Christ.

3. *nail* – So and so, I bind you to me, eternally, as Satanaz is bound in hell.

4. *nails* – So and so, I, so and so, bind you and tie you inside this sign of Solomon, so you do not have peace or rest unless when you are in my company, this by the power of Satanaz and of Maria Padilha and all her family.

5. *nails* – So and so, only when God stops being God and the deceased whom these nails previously served speaks, is when you will leave me.

We declare that, when the last word is said, you must give a great strike upon the nail.

At the end of all this, keep the wooden board, and when you want to undo the sorcery, burn it.

XXIV

Recipe to bind sweethearts

Go to a shop and ask for a piece of ribbon. Leave looking to the sky, and say:

> *Three stars in the sky I see, and a fourth one of Jesus, and this ribbon to my leg I tie, so so and so cannot eat, nor drink, nor rest until he marries me.*

This must be said three consecutive times.

†

XXV

Infallible recipe to get married

This orison must be said for six consecutive days, and the boyfriend will come on the last day to ask his darling for her hand in marriage.

> *So and so, Saint Manso,[111] Saint Manso make you meek and like the meek lamb, so you cannot drink, nor eat, nor rest, as long you are not my true companion.*

If it is possible, when saying this, hold the portrait of the person you have in mind.

XXVI

Way to petition the souls in purgatory to oblige them to do what you wish

On a Tuesday, at midnight, you must go to the door of a church, and as soon as you arrive there, give three knocks at the door, saying in a loud voice these words:

> *Souls, souls, souls! I oblige you, from the place of God and the Most Holy Trinity, to follow me.*

These words being spoken, walk three times around the church, but do not look back because it can result in a great fright to you and you may be disabled of the power of speech forever.

After making the three rounds, pray a Lord's Prayer and one Hail Mary, and you can leave.

---

111 *Manso* means "meek"; although there is no such Saint in the known lists, Saint Manso is a recurring name in popular Portuguese sorceries.

You must make this petition nine times, and in the last, the souls will ask you:

- What do you want us to do?

We observe once again that you must never look back, and must not be afraid of anything, otherwise the operation cannot produce a good effect.

XXVII

Sorcery made with a bat to make someone love

Let's suppose that a girlfriend wants to marry her boyfriend with great brevity. Do as follows:
Take a bat and pass through its eyes a needle with a sewing thread.
After this operation, the needle and the sewing thread acquire a great force of sorcery.

WAY TO ENSORCELL

Take an object of the person you want to ensorcell and make five cross shaped knots, saying the following words:

> *So and so, I ensorcell you by the power of Maria Padilha and all her family so that you do not see neither the sun nor the moon as long as you do not marry me, this by the power of the sorcerous magic of the middle ages.*

After all this is done, as it is written, the ensorcelled person will not have one hour of peace until he marries.
If perhaps you do not want to marry the ensorcelled person anymore, you must burn the object with which the sorcery was made.

XXVIII

Another magic of the bat

Kill one male bat and one female bat in a way you can profit from their blood, and then put together the blood of one with the other, mix with some spirit of salammoniac, and put everything inside a very small glass flask, which you must always carry in a pouch.

When you want to enchant a girl or when a girl wants to enchant her lover, it is enough to give the flask to them to be smelled.

This way, the person who smelled the flask is enchanted and can never leave him or her.

XXIX

Sorcery to be made with mallows plucked in a cemetery or in the churchyard

Pluck three mallow plants, take them home, and put them under the mattress of your bed, saying every day when going to sleep:

> *So and so, (give the name of the person you want to ensorcell), as these mallows were plucked in the cemetery and are put under me, so (so and so) to me will be bound and tied under the power of Lucifer and of liberal magic, and only when the corpses in the cemetery or in the church from where these mallows came speak, is when you will leave me.*

The words that are mentioned here must be repeated for nine consecutive days, to produce a good effect.

XXX

Wonderful sorcery made with sprouting potatoes left on the open air.

When a lady is suspicious that her husband or lover is lost through bad ways with other women, and wants to deviates him from this, she does not need to do more than what follows:

Take six potatoes, which have at least four sprouts each, and after blessing yourself with them, one by one, put them in a glass bowl that has not been used before, cover them with holy water, and put virgin olive oil over it, saying:

> *Satanaz, by the virginity of this olive oil, I petition your great power so my man returns to have the same old friendship with me*

Leave the bowl outside in the open air for three nights, and if there is moonlight, this magic will have even more power.

After three nights, cook the potatoes and stew them with a virgin young pigeon, and then give them to the husband or lover to eat with *brocelos* or bulbs peppered well.

When going to bed, put into the boot of the ensorcelled the head of the pigeon with its intestines in its beak.

This magic comes in the 3rd book of Abrahão Zacutto, a Jew who practiced admirable sorceries in the XV century.

XXXI

Remedy against humpbacks

To avoid your business going wrong, if in the morning you meet some hunchback, Saint Cyprian says to do as follows:

> *Dolphin, hunchback, who crooks towards, vac, vac, diligent, and leave me in peace. Dolphin, dolphin, do not chase me: there goes a figa, do not look back.*

With this, make a figa with the left hand and extend the right arm with the hand open, making the motion of catching a butterfly.

Then, you keep walking with the closed hand until you find one of these fellows:

> Another humpback
> One municipal soldier
> One white horse
> One lame man
> One one-handed person
> One black cat
> One black dog
> One albino man

As soon as you find one of these fellows, open the hand, saying in a continuous act:

> *Go in the name of Maria Padilha and all her family to where you cannot bother neither a rich nor a poor man, nor anyone covered by the sky.*

This conjuration is infallible; we have used it on many occasions and we always avoid walking past hunchbacks, as it is bad luck to see them, although they do not intend it to be so.

IMPORTANT PREVENTION

To make sure this recipe produces a good effect, it is necessary to not have hate toward the hunchback, otherwise everything will go wrong for the person.

Occult Powers of Hate and of Love

discovered by the MAGICIAN JANNES and practiced by CYPRIAN

[GLT]

I

Sorcery of the owl[112] to the women to captivate the men

The owl is the prophetic animal of excellence, and because of this fact, it must not be evoked within six months of someone in the family dying, otherwise the figure of the relative can appear to you. A woman can use this recipe, which is proven to work, but her menstrual flow must have ended at least four days previously.

Obtain a white owl and dress it in flannel, in a way that only the neck is exposed, for 13 days, and then on the 13th day, which is prophetic, severe

---

112 Here it is meant the true or typical owl (family *strigidae*) and not the barn owl (*tytonidae*).

the neck with a single blow over a tree stump, and put the head in alcohol until the 13th day of the next month.

When that day comes, cut the beak off and burn it with coal that will be used to make the supper of the person you wish to bind. On this occasion, the two eyes of the owl must be by the oven or stove, one on each side, and the woman who does this operation must fan the fire with a fan made from her inner shirt in which she must have slept for at least five nights.

It is necessary to advise that this operation must be done on the knees, saying the following orison:

> *By the Wounds of Christ, I swear that I do not have reason to complain (so and so), and if I do this is because of the love that I consecrate to you and so that you do not have affection with other woman. P.N.A.M.*

After this is concluded, you must take care that the man does not suspect but sleeps peacefully, in order for the sorcery to produce the effects that the Saint always got from it with this practice.

II

Magic of the porcupine[113]

When a man is angry with the woman he likes, and does not want to look for her, take a porcupine and after removing its skin of all the thorns, sprinkle it with juice from the devil's weed[114] and, carrying it with him, the woman will appear to him everywhere, asking with humbleness for him to be her friend, and she will do anything he asks. The charmer, to make this have a good result, must say every day when rising from bed, this orison:

---

113 The original says "ouriço cacheiro," what may indicate a species native to South America, the Brazilian porcupine (*Coendou prehensilis*).
114 This is probably *Datura stramonioun*, a plant with medical and shamanic applications, but it is highly toxic and can be fatal even in small doses.

Magical Secrets

> *My virtuous Saint Cyprian, I beseech you in the name of your great virtue, do not forsake me as a martyr of insane love, as you did for the charming Elvira.*

This magic does not work from a woman to a man.

III

Enchantments of the black owl

Take an entirely black owl,[115] and upon the stroke of midnight, bury it alive in your backyard, and sow over it five grains of white corn in the shape of a triangle, in other words one in each corner and another in the middle [sic]. After the corn plants sprout, water them every day before sunrise, saying, at the same time, the following orison:

> *I (name), baptized by a priest of Christ, who died pierced on the cross to redeem us from the captivity in which the despots of the earth had us incarcerated, I swear over these five stems from which bread comes by the breath of God, and touched by the rays of the sun, that I will be faithful to (so and so), so that he does not stop loving me, nor take other loves as I exist, by the virtue of the black owl. P.N.A.M.*

When the stems, or ears of the corn, are matured, pluck them from the four corners and give the grains to one or more black hens with spines in their legs, making sure the cocks do not touch them, because it was by the crow of this animal that the disciple denied Christ. The stems from the corn plants, in the center of the triangle, must be dried in the chimney pot. Wrap them with some cloth which has sweat from whom you want to ensorcell and keep them, saying:

> *By God and by the Virgin I repent of all my sins. Amen.*

---

115 Here the original probably means the barn owl (*tytonidae*).

IV

Sorcery of the root of the willow

The root of the willow has one great virtue that few sorcerers know. This, along with other discoveries, where found at Montserrat, written on a parchment inside a bronze strongbox in the times of the Moors.

Cut, then, one root of willow and put it at night in a very dark place. You will start to see some vapors, like sulphur, which look like flames evaporating in the air. The person who wants to do evil to another should sprinkle some holy water over it, saying:

> *By the fire which warms the blood and by the cold which freezes it, as long as the will-o'-the-wisp of this root does not fade, (so and so) will not have a single moment of satisfaction.*

If the magic is for good, he must say the opposite, adding, with his hand over his heart:

> *The heart of (so and so) must glow with enthusiasm for me, like the sparks that are now coming from this blessed root.*

Note – This root lasts, generally, six months with these evaporations, that means, whilst it is still green. Because of that, it is good to be provident with another one, which receives the virtue of the dried one as soon as it finishes burning

V

Magic of the flower of the orange tree

When a girl has a great interest in marrying her boyfriend and he is accustomed to telling her to wait one year more, try to steal a handkerchief from him, with great care, so that he does not see it. Then, as soon as you go to church, soak the handkerchief in the baptismal font, and then ironing it, say these words, inhaling the fumes produced from the iron by the humidity:

> *Lustral water, you who possesses the virtue to make us Christians and opens for us the way to heaven, make (so and so) receive me as wife after a hundred suns and give to me so great trust as Joseph gave to the Virgin Mary. I deliver myself in his hands, ornamented with the flower with which I perfumed this handkerchief with which he cleans his lips wherein lies the consecrated host, which contains the Body, Blood, Souls, and Divinity of Our Lord Jesus Christ. Amen.*

With that done, you must perfume the handkerchief with the spirit of the flower of the orange tree and put it in the pocket, hidden.

VI

Magic of the seed kernel of the hawthorn

There is a wild shrub, full of spikes, belonging to the family of the pear tree which gives small fruits, very acrid to the taste. At the time of grafting, cut the thickest trunk, and after cutting it for the graft, put inside it a branch of the pear tree, fixing it well with sticky earth. After the branch takes well to the grafting, some branches will sprout which give pears at the end of two years. These pears have an excellent taste, but no other virtue.

In the seed kernel is where the secret lies. Take 24 of these kernels, and after grinding them in a mortar of copper or bronze, spray the head of the desired person with the resulting powder, and whilst this powder remains stuck to the skin, you can obtain from that person whatever you wish.

Orison – *I powder you by the grace of God, that as long as the hawthorn creates pears, you will not refuse my desires nor separate from me.*

Make the sign of the cross, adding:

God bless you, pear tree, who takes a thousand pains and generates loves; blessed be you under the sun of the morning.

VII

Magic of the navelwort

In the province of Mato Grosso in Brazil, there was a celebrated sorcerer, who was an indigenous negro, who died in 1884, and who performed amazing miracles for a long time,[116] such as the secret we will indicate to the readers.

Take a hand full of red navelwort and an equal portion of neverdie,[117] chew them up, and mix them in an infusion for 15 days. Put it in wine and give it to any individual of the other gender to drink. That person will do all that the person who gave the drink to them wants. Many Portuguese returned rich from that province, all thanks to the sorceries of this negro, who was named Piaga Ambongo. As soon as the person has drunk the first four doses of this liquid, you must put into the fifth and last two drops of blood from the left foot of a black dog, but one that has much friendship with the person who made the sorcery.

---

116 It is possible that the sorcerer mentioned here was inspired in Juca Rosa (1822–1889), a very important religious leader of African descent who lived in Rio de Janeiro, where he led a mysterious magical association with members coming from all levels of society. For many decades after his death, he was still remembered, and his name became a synonym for black sorcerer.
117 *"Erva de saião," Kalanchoe brasiliensis Cambess.*

Orison – *That the God of the Christians shelter me, that the Tupy[118] bless this leave, and that the pajé[119] soften this heart. S. R. Mother of mercy, etc.*

VII

Magic of the black donkey

In Shanghai, China, since ancient times, the following Portuguese sorcery is used, and having returned from there, the secret was made known:

When a lady flees from the temptations of a man who solicits her, he goes to a butcher who sells donkeys and buys the left testicle of a black donkey. Then, fry it, extract the fat, and mix with it the perfume of a thousand flowers. After that, grease the hair with that fat, and come close to the object of your love, in such a way that the smell of this preparation reaches her senses. It is affirmed that the woman begins, then, to fall in love with the man and does not rest until she gives herself to him.

Our informant says that it is not good to pass near donkeys that are in season, because they advance towards the individual, giving loud brays. We do not guarantee, however, the veracity of this magic, because it is not from Saint Cyprian.

---

118 *Tupi* being the name of an important indigenous group in Brazil, the reference here was probably to *Tupã*, a divine manifestation in the form of thunder which the Jesuits mistook for a god.
119 Shaman, witch-doctor.

IX

Recipe so that men be obliged to marry their lovers

Take 26 leaves of water cabbages[120] and, after cooking them in six deciliters of water, pour it into a white bottle, well corked, until it has some shreds in the bottom, and over the neck of this bottle pray the following orison:

> *Oh Saint Lucy, who heals the eyes, deliver me from the reefs, both night and day; oh Saint Lucy, be blessed, because blessed you are, in the heavens you rest.*

Here, take a *seven* from a deck of cards and put it over the bottle, saying:

> *In the name of the Father, of the Son, and of the Holy Spirit, I beseech thee, Lady, that as this card is safe, I have safe for all my life (so and so), whom I love with all my heart, and I ask you, Lady, to make him take me to the church, our mother, and receive me in front of Christ our Lord.*

Praying after that one crown to Our Lady, the woman can be sure that her lover will take her to the altar of God and will give to her happiness compatible with his possessions. It is necessary to keep the card under the bottle until the day of the marriage.

X

Sorcery of the stingray to bind loves

Every woman who wants to make a man love her greatly should buy a stingray when it has bloody evacuations, because it is the only fish who suffers this discomfort. This fish, then, cooked in a fish stew, with lots of annatto, saffron, and one drop of juice from the elderberry, with the juice

---

120 *Pistia stratiotes*, in the original *erva de Santa Luzia*, "herb of Saint Lucy."

of the tangerine, given to the man to eat makes him never want to part from the woman.

XI

Magic of the spurge-laurel[121] pulled away by a black dog

Saint Cyprian says, on page 23 of the *Inguerimanços*,[122] that every man who has the desire to attract a woman (noting that she must not be over 50 years old) should tie the tail of a black dog to one stem of wild spurge-laurel, and after it is pulled out, pass it over fire, take its bark, and make a belt to tie around the body, next to the skin. To speed up the sympathy of that woman, it is good to make a loop of the same skin [sic] and carry it on the right wrist, because if he presses the hand of the woman with this preparation, she begins to fall in love with him and grants him every kind of tenderness.

XII

Magic of the living lizard, dried in an oven

Take a living lizard, one with a blue back, put it into a new pan, and bake it in an oven. As soon as it is well dried, make a powder and put it into a sandal box.

For the woman or man who wishes to captivate the heart of any person, it is enough to put one small pinch of this powder in the wine or coffee of that person, and you will have them always at your command.

Jeronymo Cortez[123] says that this powder is also wonderful for extracting teeth without pain, rubbing the gums with it.

---

121 *Daphne lauréola.*
122 *Inguerimanços*, "sorceries." This is the name of the book mentioned in the story of Victor Siderol (see *The Origin of the Book* section). There are several mentions about a book written by Saint Cyprian inserted in the sorceries described here, but they all seem bogus.
123 Gerónimo Cortés (?–1615), mathematician, astrologer, and physician native to Valencia, Spain, who wrote *Book of Secrets*, a treatise on physiognomy and other related

XIII

Magic of the insole of the left shoe

For the husband to be faithful to his woman or lover, and have hate for the other women who have him bewildered, it is enough to take an insole from the left shoe, burn it in a strong flame with incense, rue, and oak acorn, without bark, and put the ashes of all that into a small bag and put it inside the mattress of the bed. If it can be done, it produces a great effect if introduced in any sewing of the clothes of the individual, as long it is above the knee. The woman will obtain a wonderful result, putting a small pinch of this sorcery over the top of the spine every Friday. This way, she has him bound for the rest of his life.

XIV

Magic of the melted wax

Whoever can obtain a portion of yellow wax from the candles lit beside coffins and melt it in fire made with cypress wood, while the deceased is not yet buried, obtains a great power to be loved by women. The man who possess this talisman makes a woman obey him in everything, and to do this, it is enough to light a wick with this wax, in a way that the lady of his thoughts sees this light.

This experiment must not be done on unlucky days, which are enumerated in the 2nd part of this *Great Book of Saint Cyprian*.

---

subjects and a Perpetual Lunar Calendar, very popular in Portugal.

XV

Magical force of the wheat bread

Every man who wants a lady to accept his courtship, when she gives to him little or no importance, should wait for confession, and on that day, at dinner, take some wheat bread which is not burnt in the oven and chew it with his thoughts on God the Creator and his soul on Jesus Christ Seer, saying:

> *By God I chew you, by God I bless you, with teeth I knead you, oh bread which is made of wheat. By the host so unleavened, I swear, my God, to amend myself always of my sins. For the good of your son, allow, Lord, that forever (so and so) feel love for me.*

After this hymn, you must call an uncastrated black cat to lick the bread and, afterwards, take care to put it into the pouch of the lady of his thoughts, and the result will be satisfactory.

The person who makes this responsory must not tell anyone because, as Saint Cyprian says, he will have great miseries in life and suffer from lack of bread for having publicly crushed that holy sustenance with libidinous ideas.

XVI

Sorcery of the faithful love

If a man has managed to unite his body with a woman, and he wants to be the exclusive enjoyer of her charms although she is a prostitute, he can do it without any need for payment; it is enough to give her physical enjoyment of his touch.[124]

On this occasion, he will say, with his eyes fixed on her eyes and caressing her:

---

124 The reference here is for the man to make the woman achieve orgasm.

> *Oh Saint Cyprian, friend of the unhappy boyfriends and father of black and white magic, by the true God, to whom you delivered the soul and the heart, I ask you to turn this woman toward me, in order that I be fortunate. A.M.G.P.*[125]

After that is done and after treating the woman kindly, and doing little kindnesses, that woman will not remove him from her mind and all other men will annoy her.

XVII

Infallible medicine to untie friendships

Do it in the following way:

Verbena, 2 grams – pomegranate seeds, 30 grams – root of the plant of a thousand men,[126] 20 grams – cress,[127] 150 grams – green banana peel, 100 grams.

Make a decoction with all these things and enough water, in a small, new clay pot, until it is reduced to a deciliter in volume. After this, put it in a frying pan of copper, melting into it:

Marrow of ram, 125 grams – pig's fat without salt, 50 grams – alcohol, 20 grams.

When this lard is ready, for eight days put a small portion in the food of the person you are annoying, saying:

> *For good or for evil, and with the help of God, whom I adore with all my heart, you will look for love in another place, far away from me, and whilst you do not abandon me, you will be damned by the power of the black jailer magic.*

---

125 We could not identify the meaning of these letters.
126 *Aristolochia gigantea.*
127 The reference here is to *Lepidium sativum,* although the original word "mestrunços" can indicate several different plants having in common a bad smell (from the Latin *nasturtium,* from the words *nasus,* nose, and *torquere,* twist, in reference to their smell). Source: Wikipedia.

At the end of the eight days, you must make an omelette, using the rest of the ointment and ram's meat as filling, and give it to a dog with a black sign on its head to eat. As soon as it finishes eating, hit it with a collarbone from the ram, burnt on both sides, until it whines three times. Release, then, the dog and throw the horn at him, saying these words: *That (so and so) flee from me forever with such quickness.*

XVIII

Recipe to help women get rid of men when they are bored of enduring them

When a lady is bored of enduring a man and wants to get rid of him without scandal, and also without risking his revenge, she need do no more than the following:

First, she must become slovenly with her body, not combing or washing her hair, nor taking the minimum carnal interest when he challenges her to vulgar acts. As soon as that is done, put 12 ant eggs, and two malagueta peppers inside a sea onion,[128] pierced, and put it into a clay pan, well calked, over the fire. The woman should go to bed and, as soon as the individual is sleeping, go to open the pan, and coming back to the bed pass the right arm over the chest of the man, saying these words with the thought:

> *In the name of the prince of hell, to whom I make testament of my soul, I conjure you, with sea onion, malagueta pepper, and eggs of ant, so that you put your countenance very far away from me, because you annoy me so much, as the cross annoys the angel of darkness.*

---

128 *Drimia maritime* (syn. *Urginea maritima, Urginea scilla, Scilla maritima*) has the common names sea squill, red squill, and sea onion.

XIX

Way to continue the magic

On the following night and for eleven more consecutive days, you must repeat this practice and put the powder of the malagueta pepper on the side of the bed where the man usually lays, which causes such affliction that it will make him become afraid of the house and abandon it.

IMPORTANT PREVENTION

Some men, suspicious, sometimes, of the itching they feel and of the suffocation produced by the fumes prepared above, use to put the woman on their side of the bed. In that case, the woman must be prepared, bathing every day their body with water of cassava[129] and male roquette,[130] which will prevent them from feeling the slightest discomfort.

Experiment, and you will see the beautiful result achieved.

XX

Recipe to not have children

Try to get a portion of corn chewed or bitten by a mule and then put it into a flask of glass with some hair of the same animal, cut from the tail, close to the body.

Afterwards, put over it the following:

Alcohol, 150 grams – powder of cypress apples, 26 grams – red holly flowers, 50 grams.

---

[129] Cassava (*Manihot esculenta*), also called manioc, yuca, balinghoy, mogo, mandioca, kamoteng kahoy, and manioc root, a woody shrub of the Euphorbiaceae (spurge family) native to South America,.

[130] *Eruca sativa* (syn. *E. vesicaria* subsp. *Sativa* (Miller) Thell., *Brassica eruca* L.) is an edible annual plant, commonly known as salad rocket, roquette, rucola, rugula, colewort, or arugula.

Close the flask tightly, and when the woman is determined to enter into sexual intercourse, she should open the flask and smell it three times, saying:

> *Oh cursed mule, which for wanting to kill the divine Redeemer, on the arrival at Bethlehem when he was born, you were condemned to never give fruit in your belly; let your saliva which is in this flask defend me from becoming a mother.*

To get the grains of corn chewed by the mule, grease its teeth with sebum in order that it will slide into the manger.

This preparation is easy and always gives an excellent result.

XXI

Way to operate miscarriages

As soon as in the first month the bloody tribute is missing, and the woman suspects she is pregnant, she must put her feet into very hot water, as much as she can endure, so that the miscarriage will take place when the monthly tribute should next come.

XXII

Sorcery of the sweet cake to do evil

This recipe is not well known; however, many people have done it with excellent results.

Take a cake of wheat flour and put it under your armpit, well tied and stuffed so it can take well the sweat, for seven days, and if you give it to any person to eat, you will get from her everything you wish: love, money, and even forgiveness for any crime.

But we do not, however, counsel the readers to do it, because as Saint Alberto the Lesser[131] says, after the person who ate the cake dies, she appears late at night to the one who gave it to her, and with such an insistence, that it can cause his death.

XXIII

Recipe to heat cold women

When a man is in love with a lady and she begins to dislike him, he must do as follows:

Root of cork oak,[132] 20 grams – seeds of wild salvia,[133] a fistful – hairs from the chest with their roots, 24 – peanut flour, 30 grams – Spanish fly (blister beetles),[134] 1 – hazelnuts, 4.

With all that ground and mixed well until it makes a ball, leave it in the open air for three nights, avoiding rain and dew. At the end of this time, open a hole in the straw of a mattress, saying:

> *By the wounds of Christ and by the love I devote to (so and so), I hide you cork oak, bound with saganha,[135] threads from the chest, peanut, Spanish fly, and the fruit of the hazel tree, by the virtue of Cyprian, so this woman binds herself to me by love and by flesh.*

After doing this, seldom does it happen that the woman does not start looking at the man with more heat and love.

---

131 The original says "Santo Alberto Mínimo"; however, we could not identify him. It is possible that the writer made a confusion with the name of Saint Albert Magnus, who was associated with occult knowledge.
132 *Quercus suber*.
133 *Salvia* is the largest genus of plants in the mint family, Lamiaceae, with approximately 700–900 species of shrubs, herbaceous perennials, and annuals. It is one of several genera commonly referred to as sage. Source: Wikipedia.
134 See note number 1 above, on Cantharidin.
135 *Saganha* and *saganho* are popular names for wild plants in Portugal.

This recipe is equally good to raise the enthusiasm of wives, who in the amorous dealings may receive their husbands with coldness.

XXIV

The power of the head of viper to do good and evil

Get one head of a viper and, after drying it, put it in a cane, an umbrella, or in a piece of horn and carry it with you.

So armed, you will achieve many things, good as well as evil.

As an example: Do you want an enterprise to fail? Say this: *Viper, to evil I call you.* Do you want it to go well? You must say: *Viper, to the good I claim your power.*

Do you want your enemy to ask you for mercy? You have the means to get it. It is enough to call the assistance of the viper and confide to it in a low voice: *Viper, command (so and so) to come here with humility.* And this person will appear, immediately after that, with soft words asking you for forgiveness. Is it necessary for you to gain a favor from someone you are not friendly with? Say these words: *Viper, through paths without gravel, send me (so and so) here to help me or condemn him to suffer from jealousy his entire life.*

To achieve good success, it is useful that everything is said with the mind on God and that no one else knows your secret, otherwise it loses all its magic.

XXV

Magic of the pregnant rabbit hanged in the ceiling

Take a young female rabbit which has not been covered by a male yet, and hang it, tied by the ears, in the ceiling of the house, for six hours, saying:

> *If you perhaps do not die, (so and so) will be mine by the power of Lucifer and all demons from hell.*

If during this time it doesn't die, it is because it is good for magic, and you should send it quickly to be covered by a rabbit that has some dark spot on its back.

After 36 hours, kill the female rabbit, opening it up while still warm; take from it the ovaries of generation and put them inside a wild duck egg by a hole made by the side of a path in a dark place which can be found by candlelight.

Wrap the egg well with silk paper, covered with Arabic gum, and put it under a hen which is brooding.

When the chicks hatch, that egg will become entirely a yellow color; you must quickly take it and put into a glass flask, closed with a cap made of cypress wood tied with wire.

The person who possesses this egg will achieve everything in his love. The man will dominate all the women who please him, and the woman all the men; however, the possessor of this talisman can never possess a virgin person.

It is necessary to take this egg with great care, because if it happens that it breaks, the person who made it will be very sorry for his indiscretion.

When some individual wishes a great evil to another, he can execute his revenge by sending him the egg. However, we do not counsel it, because the person who does it revenges himself, as his business, generally, will not progress.

XXVI

Way to know if an absent person is faithful

Make in the earth a pit two feet deep; put into it, as a dough, the following: 30 pounds of powder of sulfur, equal portion of iron filings iron, and a sufficient amount of water. Over this dough, put the portrait of the absent person wrapped in leather. If a portrait is lacking, a paper can be put on which the name of the person is written. This done, cover the pit with the same earth taken from it, saying:

Cyprian, by your magician's wisdom and by your saintly virtue, make me know if (so and so) is faithful to me.

After 15 hours, the earth will form a volcano and begin to expel from it fires and ashes. If the portrait of the person is respected by the fire, it is because she remains faithful; if it is attacked, it is because that person is also burnt by love.

If the portrait remains inside the pit, it is because the person is bound in strong ties of sympathy; if it is thrown at a short distance, it is because the person is trying to get free from their prison; if it is thrown far away, it is because the absent person, breaking all ties, leaves and comes to unite with the one calling him.

XXVII

Ingenious way to know the identity of those who wish us ill

On the occasion in which someone feels a great itch on the palm of the right hand, to know if someone wishes her ill or who is talking badly about him, he should rub the part which is itching four times in the shape of a cross, saying this orison on his knees:

> *By God, by the Virgin*
> *By everything which is holy,*
> *Let this spell be broken*
> *With stones of salt...*

Put a few stones of salt into the fire, and when they start to crack, carry on saying:

> *I do not know the reason*
> *Why there is someone living*
> *Who wishes me ill*[136*]

---

136 *   In this new edition of the book, we can correct this verse, which in the parchment where it is transcribed is obliterated, which gave occasion to it becoming incorrect in the other editions [sic].

Make the sign of the cross three times and put into the fire some berries of anilina encarnada.

The person who said ill about us and wishes us ill will appear in 24 hours with as many red spots on their face as berries of aniline we had burned in the fire; then we will know our enemy, so we can get away from him.

Secrets of Sorcery Taken from One Manuscript of Great Antiquity

[LM2]

In a curious document that experts believe comes from the earliest ages of the Moorish domination in Spain, many very curious magical formulae appear, which are supposed to have been known and employed by Saint Cyprian in his time as sorcerer. In the following, many of them are copied, that means, the ones which seem to belong to the wisdom of the great repentant magician.

To bind a man

The woman who wants to safeguard her husband or lover will take three *varas*[137] of white ribbon, will make with it seven knots, and will tie with the same a doll to represent the beloved man.

To undo the sorcery, it is enough to cut the knots, saying at the same time:

> *I unbind N. from the sorcery that the knots operated over him, and I destroy the sorcery that by its virtue was formed.*

---

137   *Vara*: a measure of about 1.10 meters.

Magic against love

If we want to stop loving someone unworthy of our love, take the following philtre: On Monday, when the Moon is waning, at midnight, as soon as the cock with his chant has put to flee the demons of the night, leave your home and go to the bank of a stream, a lake, or the shores of the sea; enter the water barefoot and pluck three flowers of circe,[138] saying each time: *Phoebw seneæente remesio amoris internos.* Return to your house before the cock crows and put the three flowers in a flask of good white vinegar, with three medium-sized spoons; you will place this flask in a window for thirteen nights, under the influence of the stars, and during this time, you will do an extremely rigorous fast and will abstain from taking fermented liquors or others; on the thirteenth day, you will put into the flask three spoons of honey collected in Autumn and will add a big vase of the water you had put into the flowers, and at noon, being fasting, you will take this philtre, pronouncing the magical words said before. Soon after that, you will look for the person you love and without looking or touching, you will argue with the person and you will cease loving him.

This philtre also has the virtue of freeing from obesity and of preventing apoplectic attacks.

To obtain favors from a woman

Take an ounce and a half of pearl sugar, and powder it in a new mortar on a Friday morning, saying as you powder it: *abraxas abracadabra*. Mix this sugar with half a quarter of good white wine; keep the mixture inside a dark pit or in a room covered in black for twenty days; each morning, take the bottle which should not be entirely full, and stir it strongly for one minute, saying: *abraxas*. At night, do the same, but for three minutes,

---

138 Although we could not identify clearly which plant is mentioned here, it may be *snowdrop (Galanthus)*, a small genus of about 20 species of bulbous herbaceous plants in the family Amaryllidaceae, subfamily Amaryllidoideae. This plant is often associated with the mythical *moly* from the *Odyssey*, the plant the god Hermes gave to Odysseus to protect him against Circe's charms.

and three times you will say: *abracadabra*. At the end of twenty and seven days, move the philtre to a bottle of common wine, adding six grains of white mustard, and then the philtre will be ready. After three days, invite the person to eat and give her the philtre to drink, which she will take thinking it is wine. If she takes even half of it, you can be sure she will give you unmistakable proof of her love.

To cure someone from drunkenness

Take the blood of an eel, and put three drops into a bottle of wine, saying in a loud voice, *Astarot*; then, add two more drops, saying, *Aésaib*; at last, two more drops, saying, *Bacuéé*. That makes the cabalistic number 3, 5, and 7, and you should then give this wine to the drunk to drink, and he will not get drunk for a month.

To hunt snakes

The snakes are destroyed with the cabalistic words OSY, OSA, OSY. As soon as they hear them being pronounced, they close one of their ears with the tip of their tails and put the other ear against the ground so they can't hear them, because they make them fall into stupor and immobility. When you know they are in this state, it is very easy to kill them.

Against philtres

If you are in love with someone because of some philtre, que tome a dos manos su mesma camisa que habrá llevado durante los ratos de sus amores métase por el cabezón e a manga derecha and soon you will be free from the sorcery.

Infallible medicine to know the person who causes suffering or has done all kinds of evil, in the food as in the drink

Fill half of a glass pitcher with spirit of wine, half a pound of turpentine, and three ounces of laurel leaves (to be blessed) made into powder. Mix all this together, and for three days, you will move it every time the twelve clangs sound, in the day as well as in the night. After that, you will have a bottle of holy water. The way to apply this medicine is as follows: First, the person who has the illness must have a complete trust in whoever applies the medicine and will answer the questions he asks with resolution and with faith in the person who wants to heal him. Second, the one who will apply the medicine will ask the following questions: Q. *If he has suspicions that someone took, or that he lost, used cloth and that after finding it used it again?* A. *Yes* or *no.* Q. *If he went to eat at some suspicious house?* A. *Yes* or *no.* Q. *If of the invited people does he know someone who has hatred for him?* A. *Yes* or *no.* Q. *If he wants to be healed of the illness he suffers and has faith in the medicine that he will be?* A. *Yes* or *no.* Then, the one who asked the questions will answer, *so be it,* and the sick, *Amen.* After that, both will drink the holy water. Soon after that, take the composition we mentioned in the beginning and both go to the house of the person who makes said person suffer and will throw it in front of the door at midnight and bless the door. Put fire in the spilled liquid, saying this orison: *Eternal God, have compassion for this unhappy one who is suffering, let the ills that oppress his heart leave, let this poisonous viper leave his body. Oh Great God, make it fall on the malignant soul who causes suffering, chastise the one who disturbs his rest. God, with you I hope, with you I wait. Amen.* Twenty minutes of silence will be kept, after which the orison will be repeated: The ones who assist this operation will answer, *Amen.* If perhaps the fire is extinguished, light it again immediately, and when you see that it burns well, everyone will leave.

The following morning by the first hour, visit the sick and ask the following questions: *Whether from midnight until one in the morning he felt anxiety.* If he did, ask if it lasted more than half an hour, and if he answers yes, it will be a sign that the author [of the illness] is someone from the house. The same operations will be executed again for three consecutive days, asking the same questions to the sick person, and if he performs the experiment the same or stronger, the one who makes him suffer or made the sorcery against him will be discovered. If there is a suspicion about two or more people, perform the operation in their respective houses. The sick must ignore the medicine, because he could be mistaken and make others be mistaken.

Secret to know the person who made evil or made someone suffer

This wonderful secret, approved by a multitude of experiments, made known the persons who had done sorcery to make their fellows suffer. The infinite cures that I operated through its virtue are the ones that oblige me to explain the method to do it.

You will look for a small piece of bread bitten by the person you suspect of having made the sorcery, and when you have it, take a lizard, go to a mountain, and make a hole where the lizard will be buried with the bitten bread and leave it for ten days, at the end of which you will unbury the lizard and see if it ate the bread. If it did not, it is a sign that that is not the person who made someone suffer. If it did eat it, take the lizard and kill it. Dry it to make powder, which will be given to the person who made the evil to eat with bread or something else, who will then weaken whilst the one who was suffering will heal and fatten. This operation should be done in a way that both the person who made the evil and the one who was made sick by it do not know anything about it, because if they do, it will not achieve a good result.

An infinity of cures are credited to this medicine, among them that of Agrippina, mother of Nero, who suffered from epilepsy; the medicine was given to her enemy Priscilla during a great feast, and after that, she was healed, whilst the other weakened despite being a robust Roman matron.

The Magical Mirror of Solomon

Here is the method to make and use the mirror of Solomon, son of David, who was gifted with great wisdom and was a great knower of occult Science according to the proceedings of the wise Cabalists.

The mirror is prepared for forty and eight days, beginning on one corresponding to the new Moon and ending when the full Moon comes. After this term, the work must be finished.

By means of this mirror, you will be able to see all secret things you want to know in the name of the Lord, but it is necessary, first, that during the period of preparation mentioned you do not commit any evil act or work even in thought, and besides, you will consecrate them to do acts of piety and mercy.

To construct the mirror of Solomon, take a plank of steel that is very well polished and shiny, and write on the four corners of its upper side the words *Jehova, Eloim, Mitraton, Adonay*. Following this, keep the plank of steel wrapped in a perfectly white, new, clean cloth. On the day of the nearest new Moon, and at the moment of the first hour of the night, you will go to the window of the room in which you are and will look to the sky until you find the Moon and will say with solemn devotion:

> *O rex æterne Deus! Creato ineffabilis qui cuncta ad hominis sanitatem mea gratia, e oculto judicio creasti, respice me (dirás o teu nome), indigníssimum servum tuum, et ad intentionem meam, et mittere mihi dignare angelum **Anael** in speculum istud, qui mandet, et inspiret et jubeat cum sociis suis, et subditis nostris ut in nomine tuo qui fuisti, es et eris potens, et jus, judicent mihi quæqunque ab illis exposcan.*

You will look for a new coal made from laurel wood. You will light it and sprinkle perfume over the burning coal three times, saying at the same time:

> *In hoc, per hoc et cum hoc, quod effundo ante conspectum tuum, Deus meus, trinus et unus, benedictus, et per excelsius, qui vides super Cherubim et Seraphim et venturus est judicare seculum per ignem.*

That being said the third time, blow over the mirror and pronounce the following invocation:

> *Veni, **Anael**, et tibi complaceat esse per sócios tuos mecum, in nomine patris potentissimi, in nomine spiritus Sancti amabilissimi.*
> *Veni, **Anael**, in nomine terribilis **Jehova** veni, **Anael**, invirtute inmortalis **Eloim**, veni **Anael**, in brachio omnipotentis **Mitraton**.*
> *Veni, **Anael**, in potentia sacratisimi **Adonay**; venid ad me (pronunciareis vosso nome), in speculo isto, et jubeas subditis tuis ut cum amoré, gaudio et pace ostendant mihi oculta in oculis méis. Amen.*

And then, raising your eyes to the sky, you will say:

> *Domine Deu omnipotens, cujus nutu omnia moventur, exaudi deprecationem meam et desiderium meum tibi complaceat respice, domine, speculum istud, et benedic illi ut Anael, unus et subditis fuisse sistad inillo cum sociis et satisfaciat mihi famulo tuo (direis vosso nome) que vivis et regnas benedictus et excelsus, in secula seculorum. Amen.*

With the invocations finished, cross yourself and also make the sign of the Cross over the mirror, which must be repeated every day for the forty and eight prefixed days. On the last day, the angel *Anael* will make himself visible in the form of a very beautiful boy who will salute you and command his companions to obey you. It must be observed that the forty and eight days are not always needed to obtain the magical mirror, because frequently at the end of fourteen days, the operation will be finished according to the degree of devotion and the firm desire of the operator. When the moment comes to see the angel, you can ask whatever you wish and must beseech him to appear to your sight on every occasion you call him, to grant you whatever you want. After that moment, you can see in the mirror all that you want to see, without the need to first say the above orisons, but you must perfume the mirror while reciting the following:

Orison

*Veni, **Anael** veni, tibi complaceat esse persocios tuos mecum, in nomine mecum, in nomine patris potentissimi, in nomine filii sapientissimi, in nomine spiritu sancti amabilissime.*

*Veni, **Anael**, in virtutu inmortalis **Eloim**.*
*Veni, **Anael**, in brachio omnipotentis **Mitraton***
*Veni, **Anael**, in potentia sacratissimi **Adonay**; veni ab me (direis vosso nome), in speculo isto, et jubeas subditis tuis, ut cum amoré, gaudio et pace ostendant mihi occulta in oculis méis. Amen, amen, amen.*

At this moment, he will appear to satisfy your desire.

Dismissal of Anael

Gratias tibi ago, Anael, quod veniste, et petitione meæ satisfeciste, abi in pace et placeat tibi redire quando te vocavero.

Make the sign of the Cross over the invoker and the mirror.

Magical Secrets

The secret of the black hen

Take a hen that has never laid eggs or been covered by a cock. Try to catch it in a way that it does not cry out, and for that, you must go to fetch it at eleven o'clock at night when it is asleep. Take it by the neck with enough pressure so it does not cackle and go to a crossroad in a deserted place. When the twelve clangs of midnight sound, you will draw in the earth a circle using a rod of cypress; put yourself inside it and divide the hen in two down the middle of the body, pronouncing these words three times: *Eloim, Essaim, frugativi et apellavi.*

After that, turn your face to the Orient; you will put yourself on your knees and say an orison. After formulating the Great Conjuration, the Unclean Spirit will appear dressed in a coat of scarlet embroidered with gold, a yellow jacket, and blue-green trousers. His head will look that of a dog with donkey's ears and will be adorned with two horns; his legs and feet will look like the hooves of a bull. He will ask you what it is that you want, and you will ask for everything you want, because he cannot deny you anything. This way, you can convert yourself into the richest person and, therefore, the happiest in the entire world.

It is advisable to warn that to do what was said, it is necessary to prepare yourself with the practice of acts of devotion and not have anything reproachable on your conscience. Such is the importance of this that, if you do not attend to this instead of commanding the malign spirit as you want, he will have sovereignty over you and you will have to submit to him.

The Secret Mirror of Solomon

[TDH]

It is very important that you know how to make the mirror that the wise Cabalists used following the great Solomon son of David, who was gifted with wisdom and possessed the knowledge of the occult sciences.

This mirror is made in forty and eight days beginning on a New Moon until the next Full Moon.

You will see in this mirror all the secret things that you wish if this is the will of the superior spirits.

During this period, you will not commit any evil action nor will you have any evil thoughts, and you will do works of charity and piety.

Take a shining and well-polished board of steel and write on the four extremes these names, "Jehavan," "Eloim," "Mitraton," and "Adonai," and wrap said board of steel in a very clean and new sheet, and when you see the new Moon and in the first hour after the sunset go to a window and, facing the sky and the Moon with devotion, say:

> Oh king eternal and universal! You who dominates over all things and is knower of all mysteries, deign to grant me the gift of the gaze that sees all and make the angel Azrael deign to appear in this mirror.

Have ready new coals made of wood, pieces of laurel wood, and when lighting them, throw perfume over it three times and say:

> *On this and by this mirror, I think and desire to be wise by the supreme will and by the mediation of the angel of light Azrael.*

Say this invocation three times, throwing the perfume each time, and after which, blow over the mirror and recite this orison:

> *Come, Azrael, and deign to become my companion in the name of the one who can do and see all, and be disposed towards me with infinite wisdom.*
> *Come, Azrael, by the most sacred name of Jalma; come by my name to this mirror and with love and joy and peace, and show me the things which remain secret to my eyes.*

After this invocation is recited, raise your eyes to the sky and say:

> *Oh, supreme spirit, who puts in concordant movement all things: listen to my vows; be pleasant to my desire! Ordain to Azrael to attend in this mirror and you will fill with satisfaction this, your servant, who blesses You who reigns exalted throughout the ages. Amen.*

When you have recited these invocations, put your left hand over the mirror and stretch out the right one into the infinite space. We will repeat this ceremony during the 48 days, by the end of which, or maybe before which, the angel Azrael will appear in the figure of a very beautiful boy. Then, you can ask whatever you want the magical mirror to show.

GREAT SECRETS OF SORCERY FROM THE MAGE ARTHAPHERNES

[LM3]

Arthaphernes, mage of profound wisdom, who the initiates honored with the title of *Lord of the High Secrets,* had Saint Cyprian as his disciple, as it is said, and from such a reputed master, the Saint learned the most powerful means of sorcery, which since ancient times have been used to cause good and evil, according to the desires and intentions that inspire whoever knows how to put them into practice in each case.

Despite the great antiquity of these sorceries, they are certainly not the most well-known today and do not get passed from person to person, maybe because whoever knows them and are assured of their results make better profit of these advantages by hiding the way of achieving them than by putting them at the disposal of everyone.

It will not be convenient to the reader to be more explicit in his conversations. Keep to yourself the ways of doing good and evil here spoken, without doubting that, first, your conscience and the conscience of every honorable man authorizes its use, and last, under the responsibility of your conscience falls the enterprise, and if the crime is discovered by the eyes of human justice, there is another: un-nameable divine justice, from which nothing can hide, and from which punishment no one who deserved it has escaped, and cannot escape for long, no matter how much they imagine they can.

I could be silent, it is certain, about that part of the sorceries of Arthaphernes which refer to the cause of harm, but I believe that it is a thousand times preferable that my readers know such means, because every evil loses much of its efficacy when its actions and origins are known, as they indicate exactly to how the medicine can be created.

That being said, I will begin treating about the means by which the evil passions are used to destroy a hated person.

Malefaction of the Wax Figurine

Take a piece of wax, soften it in hot water, shape from it a figurine, thinking of the person you want to bewitch whilst fabricating the image, and repeat these words many times:

> *N.N., in your image and likeness, I make this figurine in order that you become bound in a way that its body is your body, and it be the place of all your sensations.*

If you have hair or other things from the body of the bewitched, put it on the figurine, and you can search for clothes or inner clothes, used by him, and will make with them a cloth which looks like the aspect and form that the individual has.

The doll being done, one night, you will cover it with insults and curses, believing very firmly the idea that you have before you the same person in body and soul; at last, you will throw the figurine in the fire, and, if all this you do like I say, and putting in it all your faith and force of imagination, do not doubt that as the wax melts and is consumed, so will the person be consumed, suffering acute pains in the parts corresponding to the wounds of the figurine.

Another way of bewitching with the wax figurine

The figurine being prepared in the given way, you will pierce it with thorns in the places of the body where you want the person to suffer, and wrapping it with a piece of fabric, you will bury it at the entrance of the house of your enemy, or in the places where he surely passes by every day.

In a short time, the bewitched person will begin to feel unbearable maladies in all the designated parts, which soon will become dreadful sufferings. Nothing and no one who ignores the cause will be able to soothe his pains; but if someone suspects the origin of the malefaction, you are lost when the figurine is thrown in the fire, because at the same moment the bewitched will become free and the sorcery will fall in retrocession over you with such speed and violence.

You must know that in all these sorceries you run the risk of taking the place of the victim when some knowing person finds it out or if, by negligence, you do not know how to direct them correctly.

Malefaction of the toad

Instead of a figurine of wax, you can use a living toad, which you will wrap with hair and cloth from the designated person, and soon you will pierce it with an iron nail, burying it at any of the places where the bewitched frequently passes by.

All these things must be done while fixing your attention and firmest thought on the desire and trust that the person can experience, and will experience, all the things done to the figurine, toad, or any other object of malefaction, and that he will necessarily die as does the toad or as the wax melts.

Not everything is given in the preparation, which is undoubtedly a great help; it is necessary that the sorcerer knows how to put all his force of will in what he does when he bewitches in the mentioned ways.

Malefaction of the clay figurine

With clay, you can make some figurines which can be used to bewitch in the way I will explain:

You will mix the clay and will make an image, which you will wrap in a piece of cloth coming from the clothes that the individual wears. This being done, you will take the figurine to the place where the dead are kept in their sepulchral mansions and leave the figurine in one where you are able, saying as a supreme dismissal:

> Let the earth be propitious to you, let it provide you with a ready and final refuge, and soon afterwards let the mysterious bosom of death open for you.

If the malefaction is well done, the bewitched will unexpectedly die before the third day passes.

Way to counteract the malefactions

When you see someone who suffers extreme anguishes, especially at certain hours of the night, followed by visions, nightmares, and other night terrors, who experiences acute pains of unknown cause, who languishes and debilitates for periods of time, who feels stricken by invisible enemies, offer the opinion that she is bewitched and the first thing to look for is the malefaction.

Make attentive observation your guide, and it is certain that you will find out where the cause of all these perturbations lies: Search and seize it, and when it is in your power, deliver it to the bewitched so he can in turn throw it in the fire.

From this instant on, she will be free and very soon the news will come that this or that person died of mysterious or terrible sickness; that person, do not doubt, was the malefactor who received a just punishment.

Magical Secrets

Way to make impotent the most vigorous man

Look for the penis and testicles of a wolf recently dead, and with these remains in hand, you will put yourself close to the person you want to incapacitate. You will call him by name and, when he answers you, tie the penis with a white silk thread, saying: *tied you stay.*

From that instant on, the bewitched will be deprived of all his vigor, and he will not recover it until you destroy the sorcery, or when the ensorcelled person seizes it and destroys it, in which case you will be tied.

Another way of achieving the same

Prepare a figurine of wax and mark clearly on it the genital parts. With a thread tie tightly the penis and keep the figurine or, even better, bury it in a place where the ensorcelled passes by.

You will achieve a certain outcome, but you run the same danger if the place where it is buried is found.

Way of making a man and woman love one another

Make two figurines of wax: one to represent her and the other him. Put them united in a reciprocal embrace and then bury them at the entrance of either of their houses.

As well as this, take hair and blood from both, mixing them all together, and bury this at the entrance of the house where you have put the figurines. The man and woman will love each other hereafter with an inextinguishable ardor.

Another way

When a woman and a man ask you for a way of making eternal their reciprocal affection, advise them to both make in the arm one small wound from which some blood can be spilled, and the man will drink from the woman and the woman from the man. Nothing more is necessary so that afterwards they will look for each other moved by superhuman influence.

Way that a woman can obtain the love of a man

Taking advantage of the time of her menses, the woman will collect from her blood some drops to put into any drink which the man of her desires drinks. Repeat this three days if it is necessary, and she will see fulfilled her amorous aspirations.

Way to heal a wound at distance

When you have in your power the weapon with which someone was wounded and which conserves the stain of blood, you can heal her from any distance if it is curable.

Take the dagger, sword, etc., sink it in a solution of *prodigious salt* (cupric sulfate), and leave it there, keeping the liquid at a moderate temperature. Soon after you do this, the wounded will begin to feel better, the maladies will gradually disappear, and he will heal fast.

If instead of the *prodigious salt* you dissolve in the water irritating substances, the person will begin to suffer horribly.

Keep carefully this secret, because you already see what can happen if it falls into wicked hands.

Way to dominate a person

There always was and always will be people who exert resolute influence over all those who surround them. In many of them, this is a product of natural conditions, but in some, it is the result of knowing how to proceed in the most convenient way. This is the secret I will now teach you.

Magical Secrets

Every time you meet with someone you want to dominate, speak before she does, looking firmly in the eyes and keeping the gaze without yielding even for a moment whilst you think with firm intention that you will be the owner of the will of the person you have in front of you.

When you send her off, do not stand back and do not retire the gaze first. Always do this that I tell you; command whoever it is with energetic and brief words; never turn your back to whoever is looking at you, and gradually you will see that you take hold of everyone who surrounds you and that your desire is obeyed each time more blindly.

The Execution of the Experiments

[TDH]

When the person who is going to execute the experiment has all the necessary knowledge and the sufficient vocation and faith, he must prepare those instruments that will serve him in the operation, which he will perfume, invoking into them the magical virtues with the following orison:

> Oh, admirable Adonay, who reigns and abides in all that is created, being the sovereign arbiter of all the planetary system! I humbly beseech your protection in this supreme hour to adorn these instruments I am going to use with all the necessary virtues, in order to achieve the result I desire in the magical experiment I want to execute. Grant my plea, oh powerful Adonay! As I implore with the true faith you require from whoever solicits your help. I offer in exchange for your service all that I am and value, and even the blood of my veins, if you want it, putting it as a seal of our pact of eternal friendship.

The previous orison being said and all the instruments being ready, you can move to execute the many experiments indicated in the following:

EXPERIMENT OF FLIGHT

This experience must be executed, as it is said, in the planetary hours, after the twelve of night. Before starting the work, and once you have everything ready, you will say the following invocation:

> *Atha, Milech, Nigheliona, Assermaloch. Bassamoin, Eyes, Saramelachin, Baarel, Emod, Egen, Gemos. All of you, invisible spirits, who pass through the firmament and all of creation without stopping, I want to invoke in this hour in order that you adorn me, if you find me worthy enough, with your powerful wings so I can know the force and efficacy of this experiment. I also come to you, Joh, magnanimous Cados, Eloy, Zenath, and Adonay! I reverently beseech you to gift me with the necessary virtue in order to be able to perfect this work I want to execute and bring to a good conclusion.*

After saying these words, you will take the sword with the left hand, showing it successively to the four cardinal points, or the Orient, Occident, Middleday, and North, and will say each time:

> *The hour has arrived to finish this experiment, there is nothing to tie me to the earth; all that is needed is you, spirits invoked in this supreme instant, to adorn me with the impalpable and potent wings to navigate by your side, Jot, Jot, Jot, ordain to the spirits to fulfill my desire.*

Extend your hands to the air, close your eyes, concentrating all your spirit on the flight, and soon you will notice perfectly that you are executing it. During the travel, take care not to open your eyes, because if you forget this detail you will irremissibly fall from high, wherever you are, and surely it will be last moment of your life. When you want the experience to finish, you will say:

Cease my travel and rest my feet again in the same place from where I left.

At this moment, you will note that you are again on earth, and you can open the eyes without a care.

For this experiment, it is convenient to prepare a glass of wine, in which you will pour a cup of liquor and will drink from it three times, in the intervals between the invocations. If the concentration of the spirit is done with great strength of will, you will note wonderful things, but if you do not concentrate well, it will be difficult to come to a successful conclusion of the experiment.

ON THE EXPERIMENT OF INVISIBILITY

Having prepared all the instruments for this experiment, you will say with all your heart the following words:

> *Scaboles, Hebrion, Elde, Erimgit, Baboli, Cemitrien, Metinoboy, Sabaniteut, Heremobol, Cañe, Methe, Baluti, Catea, Timeguel, to you, exalted spirits, I directed myself so the dominion you exert over all creatures helps me in this work so that through your mediation I can be invisible.*

Next you will say:

> *I invoke you, conjure you, and call you, spirits of invisibility, so without delay you consecrate this experiment, with the aim that I can certainly be invisible without any fear. The second time, I conjure you by the power of Lucifer, your sovereign and Lord, and by the obedience that you own him, to grant me your help consecrating this experience as soon as possible. Fiat, Fiat, Fiat.*

That being said, take the sword with the left hand, and you will execute the same operation indicated in the last experiment.

You must do in the same way the procedure with the glass of wine, because it represents blood, and the liquor that you add to it represents the spirit, and it possesses great efficacy in all magical arts. The ceremonies being finished you must say:

> *Oh, invisible and untouchable spirits! I, the most insignificant of the mortals, supplicate to you for the last time to cover my body with the mysterious fluid, which you possess, so no human person can see me during the time that this test of invisibility lasts.*

ON THE EXPERIMENT OF LOVE

To make the experience of love or to get the love of someone, be it man or woman, you must do the following: You will choose the hours of Venus and the Moon, and will make a figurine from virgin wax, which you will apply to the person whom you wish to love you. Once the figurine is done, these words will be said:

> *Noga, Ies, Astropolim, Asmo, Cocav, Bermona, Tentator, and Soigator, I conjure all of you, ministers of love and pleasure, by the one who is your sovereign and lord, that you consecrate this wax as it should be, in order that it acquires the desired virtue, which will be obtained by the power of the very powerful Adonay, who lives and reigns forever and ever.*

After that, you will write on the part of the chest and the belly of the figurine with the feather of a goose and the ink of the pacts these words:

I wish that N.N., whom this figurine represents, cannot live nor rest but at my side and to love me eternally. These characters that I draw I want to have sufficient magical virtue that so and so cannot want anyone but me, and the he (or she) be loved by no one that is not me.

Next, you will pronounce the following orison:

Oh you, very powerful king Paymon, who reigns and dominates in the occidental part of the universe! Oh, you, Egim, very strong king from the frozen empire and whose coldness you send to the earth! Oh, you, Asmodeo, who dominates the middle day! Oh, you, Aymemon, very noble king, who reigns in the Orient, and whose kingdom must last until the end of the centuries. I invoke and beseech to grant to this figurine all the enchantments, sorceries, and sortileges, so I can through your mediation achieve that so and so cannot want anyone but me, achieving by your influence that it comes to my house.

This being done, you will put the image under the head of the bed, and after three days, you will see admirable things.

If this experiment is done with care, neither earth nor iron nor chains will stop the person to whom this intention is applied from coming to you, and you can get from him or her whatever you desire. You can also make the figurine from lead or metal, but you will always write with the goose feather and the magical ink of the pacts.

EXPERIMENT OF GRACE AND KINDNESS

This experiment is useful to please and make a person cherished by everybody in general, and it can be dedicated to someone you wish to be loved by in particular.

You will choose the hours of Venus or the Moon for being the most convenient to dedicate to the experiment of love; you will write on a virgin parchment with a feather of a goose, well perfumed, wetting it in the ink of the pacts with the following words:

> *I beseech you, Adonay, to deposit in this immaculate parchment the mysterious effluvium of grace and the penetration with which the powerful king Alpha and Omega, lord and sovereign of all sciences and arts, has gifted you, to graciously grant to the mortals who are worthy of your gifts. I, the most miserable of all, wait to be favored by you with the necessary grace to deserve the general esteem and, particularly, from so and so, whose caress I desire to possess since this moment, and that I be eternal as is the sovereign lord of the cabalistic sciences Alpha and Omega. So mote it be.*

Once the parchment is written, you will fold it with care four times and will put it inside a piece of cloth of scarlet silk, which you will fix with a new pin putting it over your left side, over your heart. If the operation is well done and you are worthy of the grace, not a long time will pass without your desire being achieved.

EXPERIMENT OF HATE AND DESTRUCTION

This experiment is used to cause harm to any person to whom it is dedicated; as such, you must reflect a lot before putting it into practice.

No one can ignore that the harm that is done causes great remorse to whoever creates it. The tranquility of spirit values much and always causes a great satisfaction which cannot be enjoyed by the ones who for futile reasons cause harm which is difficult to avoid. You must have in mind that the spirits won't always grant what is asked if the one who asks is not truly worthy, or asks something which is not just and reasonable, in which case your supplication is not attended to.

As this experiment is repeated in the section treating sortileges, it will be convenient that the operator has present the following cares:

I

The operator must be clean and purified. Clean and purified means to be worthy and initiated in the Art and to be perfumed and properly dressed.

II

He must have a just motive to cause the harm he proposes to create.

III

He must put all his imagination and will, without weakness or doubts, in the operation to be executed. This operation is the work of a will and of an energy which dominates absolutely the other person, a phenomenon known in modern science as "suggestion" and "magnetism" and in the Magical Arts as "enchantment" and "sorcery."

IV

Know that the harm which is caused is difficult or impossible to fix and that, because of this, you must think much before practicing it.

With the above indications made, we will explain the way to do the operation or experiment of hate and destruction. You will make an image, be it of virgin wax, clay, or other white paste, which you will dedicate to the person you want to damn or annoy. Once the image is made, you will sprinkle it with water from a well and powders of asafoetida and sulfur.

Next, you will write over it with the lancet of Art the following:

> *Ulisore, Dilapidatore, Teniatore, Soignatore, Devoratore, Consitore et Seductore.*

This being done:

> *You, infernal and harmful spirits, I conjure and command you to put your diverse qualities at my service to torment, try, devour, and make to be hated so and so, to whom this image is dedicated. It is my desire that by the figures by which your names were engraved, each one of you penetrates his body and, exercising your infernal arts, do not allow him to stop or have peace, sleep, or rest, tormenting him with nightmares and illusions in order that I be avenged of the evils and harms that by his cause I have suffered. And this for all the time that the image keeps your names engraved, which will be as long as my will or my desire wants it so.*

When you desire the malefaction to cease, take the figure, sprinkle it with clear water from the river, and say:

> *I conjure you again, oh infernal spirits! To render free now the body of so and so, whose image I have purified with clear water, and to attend my call to see me destroy it, and also the engraved names, which I do in this moment in order to cease completely the malefaction and torment of so and so.*

This being said, you will throw it in the fire that you will have prepared for this. It is necessary that, when you keep the figurine, you put it into a dark closet where no one can see it, because it would be dangerous to anyone who is not initiated to contemplate it.

Useful explanations about the experiments and invocations

We will not finish this section without making some necessary indications to the good result of the expressed experiments in the previous chapter, as much as for the ones that in the course of this book we will expose.

For the invocations of the celestial and aerial spirits, it is convenient to do them during clear and serene weather, and the terrestrial and infernal ones during turbulent weather and under a sky filled with clouds.

The nature of the spirits being varied, the form they present themselves in is also varied. So, the ones of an aerial nature present themselves in the form of air; the ones of aquatic nature, in the form of rain; the ones of fire, surrounded by flames; and the celestial ones, in a beautiful and luminous form.

Although it is assumed that the spirits can be found at any point of the universe when doing the invocation, it is not too much to know that their ordinary residence is in the Orient for the aerial spirits, the South for the aquatic, the North for the ones of cold nature, and the Sunset for the ones with a fiery temper.

The invocations must be done always toward the four cardinal points of the Universe, to have the necessary efficacy, as it is the safest way to get right the place where in which the spirits whose apparition is solicited reside.

Erotic Spell of Cyprian of Antioch

[ACM]

I know that everything has passed me by. Everything has changed in my soul; everything has changed in my person. My heart has grown bitter. I have grown pale. My flesh shudders; the hair of my head stands on end. I am all afire. I have lain down to rest, but I could not sleep; I have risen, but I found no relief. I have eaten and drunk in sighing and groaning. I have found no rest either in soul or in spirit for being overwhelmed by desire. My wisdom has deserted me; my strength has been sapped. All contrivance has been brought to naught. Yet I am Cyprian, the great magician, who was the friend of the dragon of the abyss. He called me his son, and I called him father. He placed his crown and his diadem on my head. I suckled milk at his right breast. He made my place at his right hand. He subjected to me every power of his. I ascended up to the Pleiades, and they glided by under me like a ship. I learned the whispers of the stars; I took possession of the treasuries of the winds. I mastered the whole of astronomy. But all this did me no good with a virgin named Justina. She made my powers and the powers of Satan like a sparrow in the hand of a child. I came to understand in the depth of my heart, the meditation of my soul, and the pondering of my mind that no one, whether angel or archangel or cherubim or seraphim or dominion or power or any incorporeal being or authority, would be able to prophesy to my heart the answer it desired nor fulfill my command, no one except the father of the aeons and his only begotten son, Jesus Christ, and the pure holy spirit. So I reproved my wrath, laid my anger aside, and allayed my rage with great humility. Then I got to my feet, turned my face to the west, stretched my right hand out to heaven, cleansed myself of the dirt on my feet, snorted, and directed these spells at heaven, to the tabernacle of the father within the seven veils. I cried out to the father of the aeons, the lord of every lordship, of every power and every throne, voicing the following spells: ERISI TONAI CHA RIM BALI O king, AUTOUL OBIA KAKI AMOU AMOU! Seize the spirit you have deposited! Yea, yea! I do not need him still, he who sent out to me today the great minister of blazing flame, Gabriel, he with the great power of fire, in that he fills his fiery face with the fire that devours every other fire, that fire which is your divinity, lord god, and in that he fills his vessel full of longing and desire and fills his fiery wings with the river of fire that fills O your divinity with power, that fire in which every soul shall bathe before they come into your presence. He comes in the rush of his power at your command, O father of the aeons, to go to N. daughter of N., and reveal himself to her in a great revelation, relentless, irresistible, fascinating, filling her heart, her soul, her spirit, and her mind with burning desire and hot longing, with perturbation and disturbance, filling her from the toenails of her feet to the hair of her head with desire and longing and lust, as her mind is distracted, her senses go numb, and her ears are ringing. She must not eat or drink, slumber or sleep, for her garments burn her body, the sky's lightning sets her afire, and the earth beneath her feet is ablaze. The father must have no mercy upon her; the son must show her no pity; the holy spirit must give no sleep to her eyes, for her remembrance of god and her fear of him flee away from her, and her thoughts, her intentions, and her mind turn to devilry, as she hangs upon desire, longing, and disturbance because of N. son of N., as a donkey hangs upon her jackass, bitch upon her mate, as she whinnies like a mare, brays like a camel, purrs like a lioness, and hisses like a crocodile, for she hangs upon desire and longing for N. son of N., as a drop of water hangs from the lip of a jar. When one looks at her, he shall faint for the burning summer heat.

Magical Secrets

Yea, I adjure you, O Gabriel: Go to N. daughter of N. Hang her by the hair of her head and by the lashes of her eyes. Bring her to him, 130 N. son of N., in longing and desire, and she remains in them forever. As you brought the good news of the father to the pure virgin Mary as a true and actual message, so may the good news become true and actual for me, as my spells are swiftly fulfilled by you. Do not be heedless as you were on the day on which the lord sent you to the land of Eden and you returned to him without any land, emptyhanded, but carry out for me personally, today, for me, N. son of N., this good news and announcement, that when she hears it she cannot resist, yea, yea, at once, at once! I adjure you, O Gabriel, by the salvation that comes from the consubstantial trinity. I adjure you, O Gabriel, by the tabernacle of the father and by those who are within it. I adjure you, O Gabriel, by the throne of the almighty and by he who sits upon it. I adjure you, O Gabriel, by the powers of the celestial beings and by the song and the praise of the powers of heaven. I adjure you, O Gabriel, by the word and the breath of the father, the breath that went out to the virgin Mary. You announced the good news of him to her, while he came to dwell inside of her, he who was both god and human, whom she bore, who ascended the cross and redeemed us. I adjure you, O Gabriel, by the holy suffering which Jesus Christ underwent for our sakes on the wood of the cross and by the breath which he delivered into the hands of his father, which was the words, "Eloei Eloei Elemos Abaktane." I adjure you, O Gabriel, by the tears that the father shed on the head of Jesus, his only begotten son, on the wood of the cross. I adjure you by your sword, by which you tore the veil of the temple. I adjure you by the seven calls which the father first made to Jesus, his son, on the lord's day, until he rose from the dead, and by the spiritual sacrifice, the holy mass, and the mysteries of Jesus Christ, which the holy celebrate, and by the judgment that the almighty will carry out upon the whole world in the valley of Josaphat, that you may not detain or discount, neither for a single moment nor blink of an eye, until you come forthwith to your sign of the zodiac which I shall set afire. Go to N. daughter of N., and put fire and longing and desire and disturbance and agitation into her heart for N. son of N. Bring her to him in a state of humility and subjection, while he beholds her strip naked all the time, as his desire mingles with hers, as he sleeps with her and she never satiates him. Take the shame fastness from her face and from her eyes. Let him be her lord; let him become her lord, as she becomes his servant. Let her constantly ask after him, every moment, all the time, at every hour, her and his whole life long. Let every person and every soul and every breath be abominable, foul, putrid, and hateful to her except N. son of N. If he goes away from her, let her mourn in groaning and crying in bitterness of heart. If he turns his back on her, let her fall to her knees and do him obeisance in fear and humility. If he speaks, let her be silent. If he is angry, let her make him calm by treating him truly lovingly, giving him her gold and silver, her garments and perfumes, her food and drink, her gifts and her adornment on every occasion, every season, all her days, her whole life long. She must always stay with him, in accordance with these spells, while every day she sees to her beauty and her attractiveness in her heart, in her mind, in her thoughts, in her intentions, and her eyes, in which she shall have a day that is harder than any other day with all its hours together with every day and every night, yea, yea, at once! If you do not carry out my wishes, O Gabriel, and fulfill my command, I shall always despise you, cut you off from me, anathematize you, revile you, and loathe you. The father must assign you no place in heaven; the son must give you no rank in heaven; the holy spirit must not encourage your hymns of praise. The queen of women, the virgin Mary, must never take you to herself, nor shall people call you "bringer of good news," until you fulfill all the spells that I have spoken in my prayer. You must not bring any evil upon me, and you must not touch me with any evil or any suffering, but with every joy and honor. I, for my part, bless the father almighty; I give praise to Jesus, the only begotten; I sing hymns to the holy spirit; Amen.

The offering takes place for him with mastic, alouth, storax, daily prayers as long as you like, while you fast daily, while you fast, are in a state of purity, and wear the proper garments. [139]

---

[139] In the places the text was corrupted or illegible, I edited it for a better reading.

A Ritual for Making Saint Cyprian your Patron

[EXU]

This procedure involves a nine-day dedication for installing the saint. Obtain an image of him, be it a figurine or picture. You should also have at your disposal red and black cord, two white candles and one black, together with Saint Cyprian oil that you must have prepared beforehand.

The working must be done at midnight every day, starting on a Friday at the waxing moon, ensuring that the full moon is overseeing the completion of the work.

You will use as a nightly prayer the following:

> Salvé!
> Most Holy Saint Cyprian
> I beseech you as my Patron
> May you work upon me and keep me steady
> May you lend me your powers
> As I take you as a teacher, tutor, and Tatá
> Bless my house and my life
> As you close up the minds and mouth of my enemies
> Give my eyes double vision
> As my adversaries will be doubly blind

Great one, Blessed one
Most Holy Saint Cyprian
I beseech you as my Patron
I beg and pray
Heed my call
Amen!

While the prayer is said, anoint a one-foot length of the cords (both red and black) with the oil and tie it to the effigy or picture with three knots. On the ninth night, you will make sure that the image is reflected in the full moon and, with prayers, bathe the image or picture in oil and red wine, adding the last strand of cord. Then place leaves of acacia and laurel between the cords.

Watch carefully during this period. If parts of cat, toad, snake, or bat come to you in some way, these need to be placed in pouches of black cloth and tied to the effigy or picture with black cord. These can also be added over time as the relationship matures.

This being done, Saint Cyprian is given water, bread, black beans, and red wine as you burn incense of frankincense and myrrh before him.

Saint Cyprian Oil

[EXU]

Olive oil
Wormwood (*Artemisia absinthium*)
Dog's Mercury (*Mercurialis perenni*)
Pennyroyal (*Mentha pulegium*)
A pinch of bone dust
A pinch of sulphur
A pinch of goat horn filings
A pinch of copper fillings
Pine or cedar resin

In addition, you need to remove the *Book of Revelation* from the Bible, draw the sigil above on each page, leave a black candle on it, and wait until it has burned down. You will then burn the pages and add them to the oil.

Once made, this oil should rest with the image for seven days with a seven-day candle prior to use.

How to honor, serve, and work with Saint Cyprian

A Magical Secret by Docteur Caeli D'Anto

Saint Cyprian is called upon to aid in any workings when someone is dealing directly with the dead. His statue is placed inside a cauldron filled with graveyard dirt and surrounded by the ashes of the dead. He is given seven gold coins, seven acorns, seven nails, a dagger, a skull of a black dog, and a purple candle which is lit on Fridays, the day to observe the dead.

He is also given a second cauldron filled with liquids for divination.

On his feast day, September 26, light for him seven candles after sunset and feed him with fruits.

A traditional prayer from the Kimbanda, translated with modifications, by the Docteur Caeli D'Anto

In the name of Cipriano and his seven candles
on behalf of his black dog
and his seven gold coins
In the name of Cipriano and his silver dagger
In the name of Cipriano and his holy mountain
in the name of the tree of the zephyrs and the great oak
I ask and shall be answered
by the seven churches of Rome
the seven lamps of Jerusalem
the seven golden candles of Egypt
I will come out a winner
Amen.

The offering shrine for Saint Cyprian of Docteur Caeli D'Anto. Photography by Docteur Caeli D'Anto.

www.ingramcontent.com/pod-product-compliance
Lightning Source LLC
Chambersburg PA
CBHW020628230426
43665CB00008B/84